EDUCATIONAL INTERVENTIONS

Advances in Learning and Behavioral Disabilities
Thomas E. Scruggs and Margo A. Mastropieri, Series *Editors*

Volume 1-2, 1982–1983
   edited by Kenneth D. Gadow and Irv Bialer

Volume 3-6, 1984–1990
   edited by Kenneth D. Gadow

Supplement 1, 1986
   edited by Kenneth D. Gadow and Alan Poling

Supplement 2, 1987
   edited by H. Lee Swanson

Volume 7-14, 1992–2000
   edited by Thomas E. Scruggs and Margo A. Mastropieri

EDUCATIONAL INTERVENTIONS

Edited by THOMAS E. SCRUGGS
MARGO A. MASTROPIERI
Graduate School of Education
George Mason University

JAI PRESS INC.
Stamford, Connecticut

CONTENTS

LIST OF CONTRIBUTORS

Frederick J. Brigham

Department of Curriculum,
    Instruction, and Special Education
University of Virginia

Cesare Cornoldi

Department of General Psychology
University of Padua

Steven R. Forness

Neuropsychiatric Institute
University of California, Los Angeles

Maureen Hoskyn

Graduate School of Education
University of California, Riverside

Kenneth A. Kavale

Department of Curriculum and
    Instruction
University of Iowa

Margo A. Mastropieri

Graduate School of Education
George Mason University

Maria Chiara Passolunghi

Faculty of Psychology
University of Trieste

Thomas E. Scruggs

Graduate School of Education
George Mason University

Vicky Spencer

Graduate School of Education
George Mason University

H. Lee Swanson

Graduate School of Education
University of California, Riverside

Elizabeth Talbott

College of Education
University of Illinois, Chicago

Margaret P. Weiss

Private Consultant
Durham, NC

INTERVENTION RESEARCH FOR STUDENTS WITH LEARNING DISABILITIES:
A COMPREHENSIVE META-ANALYSIS OF GROUP DESIGN STUDIES

H. Lee Swanson and Maureen Hoskyn

ABSTRACT

This chapter summarizes a comprehensive synthesis of intervention studies that include students with learning disabilities. Effect sizes for 180 intervention studies were analyzed across instructional domains (e.g., reading, mathematics), sample characteristics (e.g., age, intelligence), intervention parameters (e.g., number of instructional sessions, instructional components), methodological procedures (e.g., internal validity, treatment integrity, random assignment), and article characteristics (e.g., funding source, number of co-authors, frequency of citations). The overall mean effect size of instructional intervention was positive and of high magnitude. Effects were more positive for a Combined Model which includes components of direct and strategy instruction than competing models, and these effects were mag-

Advances in Learning and Behavioral Disabilities, Volume 14, pages 1-153.
ISBN: 0-7623-0561-4

nified when (a) samples were defined as meeting cut-off score criteria (standardized IQ score at or above 84 and reading scores below the 25th percentile) and (b) dependent measures included reading. Other important findings were (1) only studies that investigated the domains of reading comprehension, vocabulary, and creativity approached Cohen's .80 threshold, (2) studies which produced the highest effect sizes had no psychometric information on intelligence and reading or reported a minimal discrepancy between intelligence and reading, (3) interventions that included instructional components related to controlling task difficulty, small interactive groups, and directed responses and questioning of students were significant predictors of effect size, and (4) interventions that vary from the control condition in terms of setting, teacher, and number of instructional steps yield larger effect sizes than studies that fail to control for such variations. Although a number of methodological artifacts had a significant influence on treatment outcome, a weighted least square regression analysis indicated that 16% of the variance in estimates of effect size were related to treatment. The results are supportive of the pervasive influence of cognitive strategy and direct instruction models for remediating the academic difficulties for children with LD, but the results also suggest that a Combined Model (which includes the instructional components related to controlling task difficulty, small group instruction, and structured verbal interaction) is a viable heuristic for positively influencing treatment outcomes.

INTRODUCTION

The number of children classified as learning disabled has increased substantially over the last 20 years. For example, seven hundred eighty-three thousand (783,000) children were identified with learning disabilities in 1976, but by 1992-1993, the LD population exceeded 2.3 million. These children currently comprise almost 50% of all placements into special education (U.S. Office of Education, 1994). Although learning disabilities as a diagnostic entity is the largest single category of students receiving special education, questions such as "Which intervention is best suited for learning disabled students?" or more appropriately, "Which intervention works best for the type of learning problem experienced by the learning disabled student?" cannot be answered. A review of literature reveals there have been few systematic, quantitative (or qualitative) analyses of instructional approaches for students who are learning disabled (Lessen, Dudzinski, Karsh, & Van Acker, 1989). For example, Lessen et al. (1989) wrote one of the few comprehensive reviews of intervention research published on LD samples since 1973 (see Chalfant & Scheffelin, 1969; Hallahan & Cruickshank, 1973; Kass, 1970; for review of earlier studies). Further, Lessen et al. (1989) suggested that "academic intervention research is crucial so that systematic analysis of a student's performance...should dictate teaching procedures, methods, and materials" (p. 107). Unfortunately, we have no clear understanding of the intervention approaches that work with a particular type of learning disabled child as a consequence of gender, age, intelligence and/or level of achievement. This is unfortunate because policy issues (such as "where" or "how" educational intervention should occur) related to instruction for students with learning disabilities will not be resolved without a clear understanding of intervention research (Martin, 1988; also see Bateman, 1992; Graham & Harris, 1996; Scruggs & Mastropieri, 1993, for a review). Kameenui (1991) assessed progress in the learning disabilities field, stating, "although we have made progress in recognizing the complexity of learning disabilities as a psychological, historical, and theoretical construct, very little progress has been made in recognizing...important developments of intervention for students with learning disabilities" (p. 365).

Clearly, students with learning disabilities are a heterogenous sample, and no general treatment approach can be recommended for these students. However, in partial response to the above concerns, the purpose of this article is to synthesize some of the empirical evidence derived from educational interventions for students with learning disabilities. That is, without an attempt to sort and choose studies on the basis of method, treatment variants, respondents, and the like, very few conclusions can be drawn about intervention procedures that yield positive outcomes unique to students with learning disabilities. Recent narrative reviews of instructional research on learning disabilities, although of theoretical and practical import, have been limited by their reliance on a narrow sample of interventions, domains (e.g., perceptual processing, social skills) and/or techniques to analyze studies. Thus, the present review uses meta-analytic techniques to aggregate the research literature on intervention. Meta-analysis is a statistical reviewing technique that provides a quantitative summary of findings across an entire body of research (Cooper & Hedges; 1994; Hedges & Olkin, 1985). Of interest in this article is the meta-analysis of research on the effects of treatments that are based on the manipulation of instructional variables that are intended to induce educational change, whether in academic (e.g., reading, mathematics), cognitive (e.g, problem solving), or behavioral domains (e.g., social skills).

Historical Context

Prior to outlining the primary questions of this synthesis, a historical context is necessary. Part of the LD field's claim as a unique professional entity came with its focus on identifying and remediating specific psychological processing difficulties (e.g., see Wiederholt, 1974; for review). Several tests were used to identify specific processing disorders (e.g., The Frostig Developmental Test of Visual Perception, The Illinois Test of Psycholinguistic Abilities) and various programs that remediate these specific processing deficits were published (Cruickshank, Bentzen, Ratzeburg, & Tannhauser, 1961; Kirk, 1963; Strauss & Kephart, 1955). Popular intervention approaches during the 1960s and 1970s included visual-motor, auditory sequencing, visual perception, or cross-modality training exercises. The rationale for these interventions was that the remediation of a deficient underlying learning process bolsters children's performance in such domains as reading and math.

Several criticisms were directed at these particular interventions on theoretical grounds (e.g., see Hallahan & Cruickshank, 1973 for a review). In addition, a number of empirical investigations questioned the efficacy of these processing approaches (Wiederholt & Hammill, 1971). Criticism of process training for students with learning disabilities spread from perceptual to psycholinguistic processes (Newcomer & Hammill, 1975), with reviews generally indicating that process training did not generalize to improvements in academics (e.g., Arter & Jenkins, 1979). Because of these controversies, the intervention focus of the field shifted. Process training as a means for treating learning disabilities was deemphasized, and a focus was placed on the direct instruction of academic skills. As suggested by Myers and Hammill (1990) "learning disabilities needed an approach with a better base for its foundation…the principals of direct instruction satisfied this purpose" (p. 42).

By 1977, dissatisfaction with a processing orientation to remediation of learning disabilities, as well as the influence of federal regulations implemented under PL 94-142, led to diminished emphasis on treatment of "psychological processes" as part of remediating the academic problems of learning disabled children in the public schools. Although learning disabilities was assumed to be related to basic psychological processes, such as memory deficits, the focus of assessment and intervention was directed toward minimizing the "discrepancy" between general ability and poor academic achievement. Possibly because of the focus on the discrepancy between general ability and performance in a particular academic domain, many intervention programs during this time period for children with learning disabilities were not distinct from remedial education (Martin, 1988; Myers & Hammill, 1990). These remediation programs focused on basic skills in reading and mathematics via individualized programming, direct continuous measurement (e.g., precision teaching, Lindsley, 1964), and criterion-based instruction (Stephens, 1977), with the setting of interventions usually occurring in resource rooms (i.e., the LD student spends a majority of the day in a regular class and goes to the resource room to work on specific academic deficits; Wiederholt, Hammill, & Brown, 1978; see Mercer & Mercer, 1981, for a review).

The mid-1980s witnessed a shift from the more remedial-academic approach of teaching to instruction that included both cognitive and direct instruction. Instruction was geared towards providing students with information and the metacognitive skills necessary for academic success through the use of principles of self-reinforcement, especially self-management and self-talk (e.g., Deshler et al., 1984a, 1984b; Wong, 1986). Studies within this time period suggested that LD children have trouble accessing and mentally coordinating a number of cognitive activities. The research in this area may be summarized as follows. LD children experience difficulty with such self-regulating mechanisms as checking, planning, monitoring, testing, revising, and evaluating during an attempt to learn or solve problems (e.g., Bos & Anders, 1990; Palincsar & Brown, 1988; Wong & Jones, 1982). Thus, such children were viewed as performing poorly on a variety of tasks requiring the use of general control processes involved in solution strategies (e.g., see Wong, 1991, for a review).

Under some conditions, well-designed strategy training improved performance (e.g., Gelzheiser, 1984), while at other times some general cognitive constraints prevent the effective use of control processes (see Cooney & Swanson, 1987, for a review). However, when training of information-processing components includes instruction related to self-evaluation (e.g., predicting outcomes, organizing strategies, using various forms of trial and error), enhancing attributions (beliefs) related to effective strategy use (e.g., Borkowski et al., 1989; see Harris & Pressley, 1991; for a review), and certain subprocesses are relatively familiar or automatized (see Spear-Swerling & Sternberg, 1994), training attempts were generally successful (e.g., Borkowski et al., 1989). The implication from findings during the 80s and early 90s is that the previous research, which focused on low order processing deficits (e.g., attention, short-term memory), incorporated findings which suggest that LD children suffer from higher-order processing problems (i.e, processes that monitor the whole cognitive system, see Swanson & Alexander, 1997, for a review).

Parallel to the cognitive literature, the late 1980s and early 1990s also witnessed a resurgence of direct instruction intervention studies, primarily influenced by reading research, which suggested that a primary focus of intervention should be directed to phonological processes. The rationale was that because a large majority of children with learning disabilities suffer problems in reading, and reading underlies several academic and high order domains (e.g., comprehension, problem solving; see Stanovich, 1986; discussion of Matthew effects), some of these children's reading problems are exacerbated due to a lack of systematic instruction in processes related to phonological awareness (the ability to hear and manipulate sounds in words and understand the sound structure of language). This lower-order skill was viewed as a specific processing deficiency that underlies higher-order cognitive-problems. This view has given rise to several interventions which focus heavily on phonics instruction, and intense individual one-to-one tutoring to improve children's phonological awareness of word structures and sequences (e.g., Vellutino, Scanlon, Sipay, Small, Pratt, Chen, & Denkla, 1996).

Limitations of Previous Meta-Analysis of Intervention Research

Given both the theoretical and practical interest for synthesizing intervention research, the purpose of this article is to evaluate the empirical evidence derived from educational interventions for students with learning disabilities. There have been a few meta-analyses of research in the field of learning disabilities (e.g., Forness, Kavale, Blum, & Lloyd, 1997, for a review), but none to our knowledge have considered intervention research across a broad array of academic domains.

The only synthesis we are aware of which provides an overall estimate of treatment effectiveness is by Swanson, Carson, and Sachse-Lee (1996). They assembled a collection of published group design studies (78) between 1967 to 1993, which focused on youth 6-18 years of age, and reported from a total of 324 effect sizes a mean effect size of .85 for treatment versus control conditions. Using Cohen's (1988) threshold of .80 for a "large" effect, their meta-analysis suggests that various instructional approaches have a significant beneficial effect for children and adolescents with learning disabilities.

There were two important findings from this earlier synthesis. First, their results suggest that *not all* forms of intervention work equally well. In their synthesis, studies were classified into one of four instructional orientations: therapeutic (eclectic), remedial, direct instruction, and cognitive strategies. The authors based their classification treatments on the hypothesis of the primary study, as well as key words in the introduction, abstract, and title of each article related to the treatment of choice. Mean effect size scores were .59 for the eclectic approaches (approaches not directed specifically to academic skills), .91 for direct instruction, .68 for remedial instruction, and 1.07 for strategy instruction. Thus, a higher effect size emerged for direct and strategy instruction when compared to the other approaches.

Second, no particular academic or behavioral domain (e.g., reading, mathematics, spelling, language, social skills, memory, cognition) was resistant to change as a function of intervention. Although most of the research related to intervention was conducted in the reading domain (reading comprehension, word recognition), no significant differences in effect sizes were found across targeted domains (reading, social skills, mathematics, spelling). There were qualifications, however, to these findings. For example, sample sizes were smaller for the categories of language, memory, and cognition when compared to the categories of writing, mathematics, spelling, reading, and intelligence. Younger children were more likely than older children to participate in studies on word skills, general intellectual processing, and perceptual training. There was also a bias related to publication year. Those studies that primarily focused on general language skills were more likely to be reflected in earlier publications. Regardless, the authors concluded that effect sizes were statistically comparable across domains of study, and that no deficit area emerged that was not responsive to treatment effects.

There are several limitations to this earlier synthesis which the current synthesis addresses. First, the results on treatment approaches are equivocal. Most problematic in the earlier synthesis was an over-reliance on coding the intervention approaches by how the primary author labeled the experimental condition rather than coding the actual procedures and components of instruction reported by the authors. This is problematic for several reasons. The most obvious is that the distinction between various treatments may be more artificial than real. For example, the advantage of Cognitive Instruction over Direct Instruction may not reflect a contrast between interventions. This is because Direct Instruction uses some of the same instruction techniques as the cognitive models (or visa versa), that is, corrective feedback, active frequent participation of the learner, teaching skills in a cumulative manner, and providing a reinforcement system.

Second, the previous analyses did not analyze the relationship between domain categories (targeted behaviors) and treatment. Therefore, we do not know if the various intervention approaches have broad general effects or whether treatments are more effective in some domains than others. There was much speculation on this issue by the authors. For example, the syntheses suggested that effective procedures for reading comprehension were direct instruction (e.g., Darch & Kameenui, 1987), cognitive strategy instruction (e.g., Palincsar & Brown, 1984), summarization (e.g., Gajria & Salvia, 1992 simultaneous-successive processing (e.g., Brailsford, Snart, & Das, 1984), and attribution-cognitive training (e.g., Schunk & Rice, 1992), whereas word recognition skills and spelling were best influenced by phonetic/decoding training (e.g., Gettinger, Bryant, Fayne, 1982; Gittelman & Feingold, 1983). In addition, the authors noted that the effects of cognitive strategy instruction were most pronounced in the reading comprehension and writing domain, but also suggested such procedures may be effective in the communication-language domain (Olson et al., 1990). They also argued that "it appears that phonetically regular materials seem to have a special benefit to students experiencing word recognition and spelling difficulty, whereas other students seem to learn this quite well with standard materials. Thus, the domains of reading recognition and spelling may be better served by remedial than cognitive approaches" (p. 387). Although not investigated directly, Swanson et al. (1996) also suggested that several domains were influenced by various treatment effects, even though these domains were not the main focus of intervention. For example, although cognitive strategy instruction was seen as robust treatment for reading comprehension and writing performance, they argued that when instruction focuses on a general domain (e.g., writing, reading), measures of cognitive processing were directly influenced, such as metacognition about the domain (e.g., Englert et al., 1992). None of these assumptions, however, were tested in their synthesis.

Third, the authors failed to operationalize the term learning disabilities. Selection criteria for article inclusion were: (a) primary authors stated that learning disabled subjects were provided treatment and (b) subject description was given to the notion of discrepancy (children and adolescents with learning disabilities suffer a discrepancy between their actual achievement and their expected level of achievement based on IQ scores). Swanson et al. (1996) assumed that broadly defined samples provide greater external validity for intervention effectiveness, although the inclusion of such studies sacrificed precision in predicting performance outcomes. Unfortunately, the usefulness of discrepancy criteria as a means of separating LD children from those who are generally poor learners is equivocal (see Stanovich & Siegel, 1994, for a review). To remedy this situation, the authors of the synthesis needed to compare discrepancy definitions with other operational definitions on treatment outcome. For example, recent operational definitions for defining learning disabilities have abandoned the discrepancy notions and identify LD children by using a cut-off score on standardized reading (children usually perform academically below the 25th percentile; see Morrison & Siegel, 1991, for discussion) and intelligence tests (a score at or above 85 on a standardized intelligence measure; see Swanson 1991, for review).

Fourth, as an extension of the above criticism, no explicit attempts were made at matching the various treatments to variation in aptitude. Thus, the previous synthesis adds little information about whether aptitude x treatment outcomes emerge across studies. Although these interactions were possibly overlooked because of the meager psychometric and demographic data reported in the primary studies, the previous synthesis failed to investigate treatment effects related to sample description. Thus, we cannot determine if many of the strategies or interventions that appear helpful to broadly defined students with learning disabilities may be helpful to a narrowly defined group of learning disabled students as well. For example, intervention approaches that include: (a) having the teacher describe and model the use of a strategy, (b) providing ample opportunity for students to apply the strategy and to practice conditions (provide assistance and feedback when needed), (c) helping students develop a verbal repertoire about the use of strategies, (d) having students set goals for the strategy, and so on, may be more appropriate for higher IQ LD students than relatively low IQ students. Without investigating this possibility, however, the generality of the results is in question.

Fifth, the authors failed to partial out the methodological artifacts from the effect sizes and therefore comparisons between treatment approaches are suspect. In the earlier syntheses, sample procedures for each study were classified into (1) intact groups in classroom or school nonrandom assignment, (2) intact groups, but counterbalancing of subjects in treatments on variables of gender, IQ, and ethnicity (subject-to-subject matching procedures), and (3) whether groups were randomly assigned to treatment. The mean effect sizes for studies with LD controls across domain measures were 1.55, 1.41, and .77, for intact, subject matching, and random or stratified sampling, respectively. Thus, there was a clear bias in effect sizes as a function of sampling procedures. Other methodological artifacts should also have been considered. For example, in addition to random assignment, striking design problems to consider are (a) exposing control students to different training materials and (b) not checking to determine if participants completed the treatment as directed. Most critically, less than 2% of the studies reported in their synthesis provide any information related to treatment integrity (fidelity or the degree to which the intervention program was carried out on a session by session basis as planned). Treatment integrity assumes that each and every component or procedure of the intervention is carried out as intended and recommended. This is necessary in order to validate the different instructional approaches (also see Graham & Harris, 1993, for discussion of this issue).

Finally, several methodological problems with the previous analysis and others (e.g., see Weisz et al., 1995 for a review) relate to the statistical analysis of the data. Previous meta-analyses have used an unweighted least squares general linear (ULS) approach outlined by Smith et al. (1980). To use this approach several assumptions must be met: (a) comparisons (e.g., an ANOVA for the dependent variables for different methods such as direct instruction vs. strategy instruction) among different studies must be of approximate or equivalent sample size and (b) the variance of individual effect sizes must be comparable across observations. In meta-analysis, Hedges and Olkin (1985) have argued that the variance of an effect size (i.e., the reliability) is not interpretable because it reflects, in part, the sample size of the study on which the effect size is based.

Treatment Comparisons

Although the previous meta-analysis was limited, and many of its limitations will be addressed in the present synthesis, it did suggest that strategy instruction and direct instruction may be important methods for inducing change in the academic performance of children with learning disabilities. What we don't know from the literature, however, is whether the two models of instruction contribute independently to effect sizes. Thus, we will attempt to operationalize the two models and assess the contribution of each approach to treatment outcomes.[1]

Prior to operationalizing the two models, however, it is critical to emphasize the commonalities of the two instructional approaches. The models overlap in two ways. First, both models (in one form or another) assume that effective *methods* of instruction include (1) daily reviews, (2) statements of an instructional objective, (3) teacher presentation of new material, (4) guided practice, (5) independent practice, and (6) formative evaluations (see Rosenshine, 1995; Rosenshine, & Stevens, 1986; Slavin, Stevens, & Madden, 1988; for a review). Second, both direct instruction and strategy instruction follow a *sequence of events*, such as the following:

1. State the learning objectives and orient the students to what they will be learning and what performance will be expected of them.
2. Review the skills necessary to understand the concept.
3. Present the information, give examples, and demonstrate the concepts/ materials.
4. Pose questions (probes) to students and assess their level of understanding and correct misconceptions.
5. Provide group instruction and independent practice. Give students an opportunity to demonstrate new skills and learn the new information on their own.

6. Assess performance and provide feedback. Review the independent work and give a quiz. Give feedback for correct answers and reteach skills if answers are incorrect.
7. Provide distributed practice and review.

No doubt, the above sequence has some variations within a strategy or direct instruction model (e.g., Graham & Harris, 1996; Guthrie, VanMeter, McCann, & Wigfield, 1996). For example, Graham and Harris (1993) outline a sequence to teach writing from a strategy model that includes some of the above steps. First, the teacher helps the student develop the prerequisite skills, including knowledge of the criteria for good writing (*Review the skills necessary to understand the concept*). Second, the teacher and student examine and discuss current writing performance and the strategies used to accomplish specific assignments (*Assess performance and provide feedback; Pose questions/probes to students and assess their level of understanding and correct misconceptions*). Third, the teacher models how to use the strategy employing the appropriate self-instructions (*Present the information, give examples, and demonstrate the concepts*). The self-instructions usually include a combination of problem definition, planning, strategy use, self-evaluation, error correction, and self-reinforcement. Fourth, there is a mnemonic for remembering self-statements. Fifth, students and teachers use a strategy of self-instructions collaboratively. Sixth, students use a strategy independently (*Provide independent practice*).

There are several characteristics of this strategy model that are different from the above sequence of events. For example, in strategy instruction there is verbal interaction between the teacher and students in which the students are viewed as collaborators in setting goals, completing the task, and modifying the procedures (e.g, Palincsar & Brown, 1984). In addition, the teacher provides individual tailored feedback and models the appropriate response based upon feedback (see Rosenshine, 1995, for a review).

Components of direct instruction are reviewed by Engelmann and Carnine (1982), Kameenui, Jitendra, & Darch (1995), Rosenshine (1982), Slavin (1987), and Spector (1995), and follow closely the sequence listed above. Direct instruction methods fall roughly into two distinct categories. One might be called master teaching models (Rosenshine, 1982) because they are based on practices of the most effective teachers. The other category of direct instruction might be called systematic instruction which is generally modeled after Distar. In general, however, this approach includes specific instructional materials which are highly organized, and includes systematic methods of teaching and motivating students, managing a classroom, and assessing student progress. Direct instruction emphasizes, however, fast paced, well sequenced, highly focused lessons. The lessons are delivered usually in small groups to students who are given several opportunities to respond and receive feedback about accuracy and responses.

Thus, both approaches involve the active presentation of information, clear organization, step-by-step progression from subtopic to subtopic, use of many examples, demonstrations, and visual prompts. All emphasize conscious assessment of student understanding and altering the pace of instruction according to this information. That is, there is a focus on independent performance. Instruction is criterion-based rather than time-based. There is a mastery of a particular stage before moving on to the next stage.

An example of a program that compares the elements of both strategy and direct instruction is provided in a study by Lovett, Borden, DeLuca, Lacerenza, Benson, & Brackstone (1994). In this study, a highly structured and graduated sequence of steps is introduced with multiple opportunities for over learning all content and skills covered in a strategy and direct instruction reading program. Both instructional models include cumulative review routines, mass practice, and teaching all component skills to a defined mastery criterion. What varies between the models is that the strategy program focuses on process or global skills for a general approach to reading, whereas a direct instruction model focuses on word segmentation and "sound getting skills." Both programs involve steps, isolating component skills, and mastery. The contrast between the two models is that the strategy model focuses on teaching a few words to mastery, whereas the direct instruction model focuses on a level of subanalysis or segmentation (phonological awareness). For the strategy model, as students learn sound units there is discussion given to metacognitive issues, such as strategy implementation, strategy choice, and self-monitoring. The teacher explains why something is being used. A particular strategy is given for a particular word, how it should be applied, and how to check to see if the strategy is working. These strategies are practiced in a very structured, systematic matter with the training of words. There is usually a compare and contrast activity that explicitly trains the students on what they need to know to help them decode a new word. Thus, in their study the distinction between strategy programs and direct instruction programs is the "unit of information" that is emphasized. Direct instruction focuses on subskills (sound units, such as letter sounds, or linguistic units such as *mat-cat-hat*), whereas strategy instruction focuses on processes and rules of use.

In summary, the two models under investigation in this synthesis overlap on a number of instructional components. We assume, however, that each approach offers some independence in predicting treatment outcomes. Our assumptions are based on recent cognitive models of learning disabilities which suggest that children with learning disabilities suffer both metacognitive and phonological difficulties.

Current Synthesis

Given the historical context of intervention research and the limitations of previous meta-analyses, the purpose of the current research is to identify effective interventions for students with learning disabilities. This synthesis has three major purposes.

The first is that we test whether treatments that include components of strategy instruction (SI), direct instruction (DI), and/or both instructional models yield significant difference in effect size. The two models were operationally defined as the occurrence or nonoccurrence of specific instructional components (to be described in the methods section) reflected in the treatment description. In addition to the components that are common to both approaches, *Strategy instruction* was defined as statements in the treatment condition that indicate: (1) verbal modeling by the teachers (or researcher) of multiple steps or processes to solve a problem (e.g., writing and essay, comprehending text), (2) elaborate explanations (i.e., 2 or more statements by the teacher or researcher) or visual-prompts (e.g., refer to a flow chart and evaluate progress) to direct task performance, (3) reminders to use strategies or procedures (i.e., the student is cued to use taught strategies, tactics, or procedures), (4) multi-step or multi-process instructions (usually indicated by an acronym, e.g., PASS), (5) verbal dialogue (via questions between students or between students and teacher on when and where to use strategies), and (6) teacher provides only necessary assistance (i.e., individually tailored feedback).

Likewise, in addition to the components that are common to both approaches, direct instruction models were defined in the synthesis as follows: (1) teacher models a skill (e.g., the teacher says "the sound the letter **c** makes is /**k**/ as in **C-A-T**), (2) breaking down a task into small steps or skills or breaking the instruction down into simpler phases, (3) administering probes and feedback repeatedly, (4) providing set materials at a rapid pace, (5) teacher asking directed questions (e.g., what sound does this letter make) related to skills, (6) teacher presenting new (novel) materials (e.g., Corrective Reading Series) and/or providing a pictorial or diagram presentation, (7) allowing for independent practice and individually paced instruction, and (8) instructing in a small group.

One approach to testing the contributions of these instructional models to estimates of effect size is by a weighted regression modeling procedure (Hedges & Olkin, 1985). There are a number of configurations that can be tested in this regression modeling, but most fall around three configurations: independence, redundancy, and complementary. The first model tested is the independence model. That is, direct instruction and strategy instruction make independent contributions to effect size. Support for this model is found when both direct instruction and strategy instruction contribute significant variance to the overall effect size.

The second model is the redundance model. This model assumes that direct instruction and strategy instruction correlate with each other and thus duplicate each other in treatment outcomes. Thus, prediction accuracy of effect size estimates is increased by minimizing this duplication or redundancy. For instance, if strategy instruction is merely a subcomponent of direct instruction, then this measure will *not* improve the accuracy of predictions when entered in a regression model after direct instruction.

A final model considers whether direct instruction and strategy instruction together exceed the sum of the individual contributions of each model. In this complimentary model (we refer to this as a Combined Model), the two predictors (direct instruction and strategy instruction) are complimentary if they both have positive contributions to effect size, but correlate weakly with each other.

The second purpose of this synthesis is to test the assumption that higher intervention effects are more likely to emerge in some domains than others. One conceptual model that has some consensus in the field is that learning-disabled children are of normal intelligence, but suffer information processing difficulties (e.g., Borkowski et al., 1989; Deshler & Shumaker, 1988; Fletcher et al., 1994; Stanovich & Siegel, 1994; Swanson & Alexander, 1997). A popular assumption that has emerged in the last few years is that learning-disabled (LD) children have specific processing deficits that are localized to low-order processes, particularly phonological processing deficits (e.g., Stanovich & Siegel, 1994; Francis, Shaywitz, Stuebing, Shaywitz, & Fletcher, 1996; Siegel, 1992). Phonological processing is "the association between sounds with letters, that is, understanding of the grapheme-phoneme conversion rules and the exceptions to these rules" (Siegel, 1993, p. 38). This assumption finds some consensus in the field because reading problems are pervasive in LD populations, and there is a plethora of research which suggests phonological coding underlies most of these problems (see Stanovich & Siegel, 1994, for a review). Although this may be true, there has been no synthesis of intervention studies to determine if specific processes or skills related to reading are more resistant to change than other academic domains. Thus, the common assumption that processing deficits underlie the poor performance of learning disabled students, and therefore one would expect some resistance to change in specific domains (such as reading) as a function of treatment when compared to other domains (e.g., social skills), has not been tested.

The final purpose of the synthesis was to test whether variations in how the sample of students with learning disabilities is defined interact with treatment outcome. A critical question is whether studies that include samples with intelligence and reading scores at various levels yield different treatment outcomes than those studies in which such levels are not specified. Reading scores at or below the 25th percentile in reading recognition (see Siegel & Ryan, 1989, Stanovich & Siegel, 1994) and standardized intelligence performance at or above 85 have been considered as critical cut-off scores for defining learning disabilities (see Morrison & Siegel, 1991; Stanovich & Siegel, 1994, for discussion of this issue). The rise in the use of cut-off scores in the experimental literature has been in response to the poor discriminant validity of discrepancy scores in defining children with learning disabilities from generally poor achieving children (see Stanovich & Siegel, 1994, for a review). The treatment validity of such a cut-off score definition, however, has not been tested as a function of treatment outcomes. That is, we assume

that the face validity of a definition is enhanced if one can show that such a definition is significantly related to treatment outcomes.

METHODS

Data Collection

The PsycINFO, MEDline, and ERIC on-line data bases were systematically
scanned for studies from 1963 to 1997 which met the inclusion criteria described
below.[2] The computer search strategy used the following terms: "learning disabled (disabilities)," or "reading disabled (disabilities)," or "dyslexic," or "educationally handicapped," or "slow learners," paired with variations of "intervention"
or "treatment" or "training" or "remediation" or "instruction." This search yielded
approximately 2900 abstracts which included articles, technical reports, chapters,
and dissertations. We examined all the abstracts prior to study selection to elimi-
nate those studies that clearly did not meet the inclusion criteria (e.g., articles
were reviews or position papers).

Because the computer search procedures excluded unpublished studies and the
most recent literature, researchers (as identified by journal board affiliations with
the *Learning Disability Quarterly*, *Journal of Learning Disabilities*, and *Learning
Disabilities Research and Practice* and/or membership in the International Academy for Research in Learning Disabilities) were sent letters requesting copies of
unpublished and/or ongoing intervention studies. We also hand searched the following journals for articles that did not emerge from the computer search: *Journal
of Learning Disabilities*, *Journal of Educational Psychology*, *Learning Disability
Quarterly*, *Reading and Writing*, *Learning Disabilities Research and Practice*,
Exceptional Children, and the *Journal of Special Education*. In addition, every
state department and 200 directors of educational research were sent a letter
requesting technical reports on intervention studies for children and adolescents
with learning disabilities.

Data Evaluation

The pool of relevant literature was narrowed down to studies that utilized an experimental design in which children or adults with learning disabilities received treatment to enhance their academic, social, and/or
cognitive performance. This procedure narrowed the search to *913*
data-based articles (or reports) that appeared potentially acceptable for
inclusion in the quantitative review. After a review of these studies, each
data-based report was evaluated on *five* additional criteria for study inclusion. These criteria include:

1. The study includes at least one between instruction comparison condition (i.e., control condition) or within design control condition (e.g., repeated measures design, or baseline as in a time series analysis) that includes participants with LD. Thus, studies that included *only* a pretest and posttest *without* an instructional control condition of LD participants were excluded.

2. The study provides sufficient quantitative information to permit the calculation of effect sizes. Effect sizes were calculated from the means and standard deviations of the performance outcomes for the experimental and control conditions, or from tests of the significance of the differences in performance between instruction conditions (e.g., *t*- or *F*-tests, X^2, exact *p* values).

3. The recipients of the intervention were identified as children or adults with average intelligence, but with problems in a particular academic, social, and/or related behavior domain. The mean IQ score reported for the LD participant sample could occur on any standardized verbal or nonverbal intelligence test, or subtest. The cut-off score for inclusion in the synthesis was a reported mean IQ score of > 84 for group design studies and for individuals in single-subject design studies. Studies that reported no IQ score, but stated that the group IQ scores were in the average range were included in the analysis. If a study did not report or *state* that IQ was in the average range, the study was not included in the general analysis.

4. The treatment group received instruction, assistance, or therapy which is over and above what they would have received during the course of their typical classroom experience. That is, the study focuses on treatment, rather than merely a description of the child's current placement followed by an evaluation. The fine line between intervention and experimentation was drawn by requiring that the training or remediation had to have been dispensed over a minimum of *three* days.

5. The study has to be written in English.

Although design issues (no control condition) were the most frequent criteria for article exclusion, the inability to calculate effect sizes, lack of clarity about whether students with learning disabilities were included (e.g., IQ scores < 84 or average IQ was not stated), the inability to separate the performance of students with learning disabilities from other ability groups, no information on sample size, and/or faulty statistical applications (e.g., incorrect degrees of freedom) were also frequent reasons for article exclusion.

Coding and Interrater Agreement

The general categories of coding for each article include: (a) sample characteristics, (b) demographics, (c) quality of research methodology, (d) components and parameters of instruction, and (e) conditions of treatment. Interrater agreements across various items exceeded 80% in some areas (instructional components, key terms) and 95% in others (dependent measures, statistical information). Interrater agreement was also obtained on rejected articles. The Principal Investigator determined initial rejection of the article based on the reasons stated in the preceding sections. Four doctoral students served as independent raters on the coding of each report. Raters were trained in coding of each category. Coding training was conducted during the first several months of this project. During this time, code definitions with low interrater agreement were refined and raters were provided feedback for coding. Approximate time to code each article varied from two to three hours. Interrater agreement on the dependent measures was calculated by using the formula agreements divided by the number of agreements plus disagreements, multiplied by 100. Interrater agreements below 80% called for a redefinition of the particular code and the retraining of raters relevant to information in each report.

In the initial stages of the project, the interrater procedure involved randomly selecting approximately 25% of the completed coding sheets for review. Both the Kappa procedure and agreements divided by agreements plus disagreements procedure were used to determine interrater agreement. The criteria for interrater agreement were set at 80%. Feedback on disagreements was given directly to the graduate students with retraining occurring if reliability fell below the criterion level. Although this procedure was relatively time-consuming, interrater agreement steadily increased over the duration of the project and remained at a high level (> 90%). Sixty-nine qualified studies (25% of the total number of studies) were randomly selected for independent coding to determine the percentage of interrater agreement per study, per code. Interrater agreement as calculated by Agreements divided Agreements plus Disagreements resulted in a mean agreement of 87% across studies with a range of 77-96%.

Categorization of Dependent Measures

The general categorical domains of the dependent measures were coded into one of 17 general categories. The categories are as follows:

1. The *Cognitive* domain included measures of self-monitoring, speed of processing, problem solving processes, synthesis, cognitive style, problem solving strategies, strategy use, and metacognition.
2. The *Word Recognition* domain included all measures of real word recognition.
3. The *Reading Comprehension* domain included all measures related to silent or oral reading comprehension.
4. *Spelling* included all measures of word spelling.

5. The *Memory* domain included all measures of auditory and visual recall, free or serial recall, and/or retelling of information.
6. The *Mathematics* domain included all measures of computation accuracy and word-problem accuracy.
7. *Writing* included all measures of prose, quality ratings, and grammar.
8. *Vocabulary* included all measures of single word meaning.
9. The *Affective/Self-Concept* domain included all measures of attitude, attribution, and self concept.
10. The *Intelligence* domain included all standardized measures of intelligence (e.g., from WISC-R, Slosson Intelligence Test, the Kaufman Ability Scale for Children K-ABC, etc).
11. *General Reading* included all composite scores that did not separate word recognition and comprehension into separate scores.
12. *Word skills-Phonological/orthographic* included all component measures of word recognition, such as phonics, nonword (pseudo-word) recognition, and orthographic (e.g., recognizing correct word patterns) coding.
13. *General Achievement* included all global scores related to achievement subtests and overall classroom grades.
14. *Creativity* included all measures from the Torrance Test of Creativity, measures of convergent and divergent thinking, creative writing, or related creativity measures.
15. *Social skills* referred to all measures of social interaction (e.g., peer ratings) and behavior ratings.
16. The *Perceptual* domain included all dependent measures related to visual-motor skills (e.g., tracing), mazes, auditory and visual discrimination.
17. The *Language* domain included all measures of verbal communication, pragmatics, articulation, verbal expressive or receptive language, and speech.

Categorization of Treatment Variables

There were 45 instructional components that were coded as present or not present in the study (see Swanson et al., 1999, p. 337 for example of coding form). Based on a preliminary analysis of the frequency of representation of these components and the detail (or lack of detail) of information about the independent variables in the primary studies, two general models were identified: direct instruction and strategy instruction. These two models were operationally defined as the occurrence or nonoccurrence of specific instructional components reflected in the treatment description.

Those components (see Swanson et al., 1999, p. 337) most frequently reported that reflect *direct instruction* were as follows: (1) breaking down a task into small steps, (2) administering probes, (3) administering feedback repeatedly, (4) providing a pictorial or diagram presentation, (5) allowing for independent practice and individually paced instruction, (6) breaking the instruction down into simpler phases, (7) instructing in a small group, (8) teacher modeling skill or behavior, (9) providing set materials at a rapid pace, (10) providing individual child instruction, (11) teacher asking questions, and (12) teacher presenting the new (novel) materials. Any procedure that included a minimum of four of these codes was labeled a direct instruction.

A second instructional variable, which we term *strategy instruction*, included at least three of the following instructional components: (1) elaborate explanations (i.e., systematic explanations, elaborations, and/or plan to direct task performance), (2) modeling from teachers (verbal modeling, questioning, and demonstration from teachers), (3) reminders to use certain strategies or procedures (i.e., cued to use taught strategies, tactics, or procedures),[3] (4) step-by step prompts or multi-process instructions, (5) dialogue-teacher and student talk back and forth, (6) teacher asks questions, and (7) teacher provides only necessary assistance. Thus, the independent variables were dummy coded (1 = strategy and 0 = nonstrategy; 1 = direct instruction and 0 = nondirect instruction).

As a validity check on our classifications, we compared our classification of the treatment conditions with that of the primary author's general theoretical model and/or the label attached to the treatment condition. There was substantial overlap (approximately 70% of the studies) between those studies we classified as direct instruction and strategy instruction models with the primary authors' titles or description of the independent variables. For example, frequent terms provided by the author were: "strategy," "cognitive intervention," "monitoring," "metacognition," "self-instruction," and "cognitive-behavior modification" for the strategy model. Those that were classified as direct instruction by our criteria used such labels as: "directed instruction," "advanced organizers," "adapting materials," "corrective feedback," or "direct computation." Those approaches that were neither direct instruction nor strategy intervention used, for example, such labels as "perceptual processing," "multisensory instruction," "Neuro-sensori condition," "CAI condition," or "social skills training."

Based on comprehensive reviews that have identified instructional components which influence student outcomes (e.g., see Harris & Pressley, 1991; Rosenshine, 1995; Simmons & Kameenui, 1996; Vellutino & Scanlon, 1991), we reclustered (or reconfigured) from our coding sheets the 45 instructional codes into approximately 20 clusters of components. These components were dummy coded (i.e., clusters were coded as occurring or nonoccurring [coded as 1 and 0, respectively] within the treatment description). Based on several reviews that have identified salient factors in instructional outcomes (e.g., Adams, 1990; Becker & Carnine, 1980; Brophy & Good, 1986; Pressley & Harris, 1994; Resnick, 1987; Rosenshine, 1995; Rosenshine & Stevens, 1986; Slavin et al., 1988), we coded the occurrence or nonoccurrence of the following instructional components (note the word "teacher" and "child" is used below) but the terms may reflect "experimenter" and "adult," respectively:

1. *Sequencing.* Statements in the treatment description about breaking down the task, fading of prompts or cues, matching the difficulty level of the task to the student, sequencing short activities, and/or using step by step prompts.

2. *Drill-repetition and practice-review.* Statements in the treatment description related to mastery criteria, distributed review and practice, using redundant materials or text, repeated practice, sequenced reviews, daily feedback, and/or weekly reviews.

3. *Anticipatory or preparation responses.* Statements in the treatment description related to asking the child to look over material *prior* to instruction, directing the child to focus on material or concepts prior to instruction, providing information to prepare student for discussion, and/or stating the learning objective for the lesson prior to instruction.

4. *Structured verbal teacher-student interaction.* Statements in the treatment description about elaborate or redundant explanations, systematic prompting students to ask questions, teacher and student talking back and forth-dialogue, and/or teacher asks questions which are open ended or directed.

5. *Individualization + small group.* Statements in the treatment description about independent practice, and/or individual pacing, and/or individual instruction, and small group instruction.

6. *Novelty.* Statement in the treatment description about the use of diagrams or picture presentations, specialized films or videos, instruction via computers, specification that new curriculum was implemented, and/or emphasis on teacher presenting new material from the previous lesson.

7. *Strategy modeling + attribution training.* Statements in the treatment description about processing components or multi-steps related to modeling from the teacher, simplified demonstrations modeled by the teacher to solve a problem or complete a task successfully, teacher modeling, teacher providing reminders to use certain strategies, steps, and/or procedures, think-aloud models, and/or the teacher presenting the benefits of taught strategies.

8. *Probing-reinforcement.* Statements in the treatment description about intermittent or consistent use of probes, daily feedback, fading of prompts and cues, and/or overt administration of rewards and reinforcers.

9. *Nonteacher instruction.* Statements in the treatment description about homework, modeling from peers, parents providing instruction, and/or peers presenting or modeling instruction.

10. *Segmentation.* Statements in the treatment description about breaking down the targeted skill into smaller units, breaking into component parts, segmenting and/or synthesizing components parts.

11. *Advanced organizers.* Statements in the treatment description about directing children to look over material prior to instruction, children

directed to focus on particular information, providing prior information about task, and/or the teacher stating objectives of instruction prior to commencing.

12. *Directed response/questioning.* Treatment description related to dialectic or socratic teaching, the teacher directing students to ask questions, the teacher and student or students engaging in dialogue, and/or the teacher asks questions.

13. *One-to-one instruction.* Statements in the treatment description about activities related to independent practice, tutoring, instruction that is individually paced, and/or instruction that is individually tailored.

14. *Control difficulty or processing demands of task.* Treatment statements about short activities, level of difficulty controlled, teacher providing necessary assistance, teacher providing simplified demonstration, tasks sequenced from easy to difficult, and/or task analysis.

15. *Technology.* Statements in the treatment description about utilizing formal curriculum, new developed pictorial representations, uses specific material or computers, and/or uses media to facilitate presentation and feedback.

16. *Elaboration.* Statements in the treatment description about additional information or explanation provided about concepts, procedures or steps, and/or redundant text or repetition within text.

17. *Modeling from teacher of steps.* Statements or activities in the treatment description which involve modeling from teacher in terms of demonstration of processes and/or steps the students are to follow.

18. *Group instruction.* Statements in the treatment description about instruction in a small group, and/or verbal interaction occurring in a small group with students and/or teacher.

19. *Supplement to teacher involvement besides peers.* Statements in the treatment description about homework, parent helps reinforce instruction.

20. *Strategy cues.* Statements in the treatment description about reminders to use strategies or multi-steps, the teacher verbalizing of steps or procedures to solve problems, use of 'think aloud models', and/or teacher presenting the benefits of strategy use or procedures.

As the reader can tell, there is overlap in how the 45 codes were sorted into the 20 instructional components. Further, if only one of the appropriate codes emerges related to some of the components, then the study is given credit for that component (coded as 1). It is important to note, however, that our focus was not on the amount of information in the treatment (i.e., the saturation of information), but on whether the information available reflected qualitatively different information. The independence of instructional components will be addressed in the subsequent regression analyses.

These 20 components capture an array of intervention approaches. For example, the *Segmentation* component would be a characteristic of analytic and synthesis approaches (e.g., phonics instruction), whereas the *Anticipatory or preparation responses* component characterizes treatment approaches that activate prior knowledge or provide a precursor to the main instructional activity (e.g., Meichenbaum's (1977) cognitive-behavioral model). The component that reflects the *Control of difficulty or processing demands of task* addresses the variations in teacher support (e.g., teacher provides necessary assistance, tasks sequenced from easy to difficult, i.e., help is provided to the student that covaries with the learner's ability) of the student and are reflective of activities such as mediated scaffolding (e.g., Palincsar & Brown, 1984). Modeling from teacher an explicit set of steps and prompting the use of these steps are important activities that underlie strategy instruction (Rosenshine, 1995). The *Strategy cues* component reflects some of these activities with reminders to children to use multiple step procedures.

In short, we coded the occurrence or nonoccurrence of these particular codes within the treatment description. Although we will test the contribution of global models, such as direct instruction or strategy instruction, to treatment outcomes, it is at the component level that we think we will be able to identify effective treatment procedures.

Control Group Parameters

The control conditions were identified based upon the study's designation. However, in a few instances no designation was made within the study and therefore decisions about coding a condition as a control treatment were made based on the hypothesis of the study. If *no* hypothesis was given, the nonpreferred treatment, based on the review of literature in the primary study, was assigned to the control condition. The coding of the control condition focused on the degree of treatment overlap with the experimental conditions. We coded the control condition by the similarities with the experimental group in terms of teachers, setting, materials, dependent measures, exposure (e.g., length of time) to instruction, primary focus (e.g., reading, math, etc.), and method overlap (number of steps in treatment vs. control condition that overlap or are the same).

Effect Size Calculation

Cohen's *d* (Hedges & Olkin, 1985) was the primary index of effect size. Cohen's *d* is calculated as the difference between control and experimental treatment posttest mean scores (partialed for the influence of pretest scores if information is available), or control and treatment (repeated measures design), divided by the pooled standard deviation of posttest (average of control and experimental posttest standard deviations), or control and treatment (repeated measures design), (Cohen, 1988; Hedges & Olkin, 1985).

To provide a common standard deviation across various studies, the *pooled* (average) standard deviation was calculated from posttest performance. When posttest standard deviations could not be calculated (such as with repeated measures, covariance, and gain scores), adjustments were made in standard deviations. For example, a few studies present gain scores without pre- or post-test data. The standard deviations of gain scores for the experimental and control groups are often substantially smaller than the standard deviation of posttest scores (see Rosenthal, 1994, p. 241, for discussion). Effect sizes from achievement gains are typically inflated, and therefore standard deviations of gain scores are less than those of posttest scores to the degree that the pre-post correlations often exceed .50. Thus, consistent with Rosenthal's (1994; see p. 241) review, we calculated the effect size for gain as $S_p = S_g / \sqrt{/2(1-r)}$, where ($S_g$) reflects the standard deviation of gain scores and (S_p) as the standard deviation of the posttest scores. If the pre-post correlations are not reported, effect sizes from gain scores were transformed to a scale using the following multiplier: Corrected ES = (ES $_{gain}$) $\sqrt{/2(1-R)}$, where R is the pretest and posttest correlation. The pretest-posttest correlation was assumed to be .80 (see Glass, McGraw, & Smith, 1981, for discussion). Substituting .8 in the formula, a multiplier of .632 deflates the effect size estimates from the gain score data (see Glass et al., 1981, for discussion). This procedure puts all effect size scores on the same metric.

Similarly, in the studies that statistically adjusted posttest scores for one or more covariates, ES were calculated on both adjusted and unadjusted mean scores divided by the unadjusted pooled group's standard deviations. Hedges (1994a, 1994b) has suggested that when adjustments in the standard deviations are employed, the synthesis should report both the adjusted and unadjusted effect sizes. Thus, where the effect sizes are discrepant (> .05), we reported both adjusted and unadjusted effect sizes. When means or standard deviations are omitted in the studies that *do* meet the inclusion criteria, effect sizes were estimated from t, F, X^2, r, or exact p values.

Multiple Interventions

There were multiple interventions in some studies we coded. For these multiple treatment studies we utilized a composite score. Gleser and Olkin (1994) state that in multiple treatment studies, "the treatments may all be regarded as instances or aspects of a common treatment construct" (p. 351). In addition, they state "there is strong reason a priori to believe that a composite effect size of treatment obtained by combining the end point effect sizes would adequately summarize the effect of treatment" (p. 351). Thus, although we coded effect sizes for each individual treatment, we primarily relied on an overall composite of effect size to reflect the treatment construct of each study.

Unit of Analysis

Effect sizes were calculated on all dependent variables in each study with positive signs given to the effect size when the experimental condition was attributed to higher performance. Depending on the experimental design, both the control and experimental group included learning disabled students.

Effect sizes were averaged for each study or reported separately for each major dependent measure category (e.g., word recognition, cognitive processing, mathematics). For each dependent measure category, several effect sizes were often extracted from a single study. Multiple effect sizes extracted from a single study can be problematic because the methods of research integration normally assume that the effect sizes are independent. No doubt, ignoring such dependence and treating the within group effects as independent effect sizes increase a Type I error rate of the homogeneity of effect size test (test of variability and effect sizes) (Gleser & Olkin, 1994). On the other hand, disregarding the data has the opposite effect, increasing the likelihood of committing a Type II error (see Cooper, Nye, Charlton, Lindsay, & Greathouse, 1996, for a discussion of these issues). In this meta-analysis, the problem of stochastically dependent effect sizes was partially addressed by (a) calculating the number of independent samples per feature (e.g., moderatator variables) from each study and (b) by comparing treatment outcomes with differing units of analysis. These variations allowed for study features to be represented (indexed) without throwing away valuable data (see Gleser & Olkin, 1994).

In terms of independent samples, the studies coded included separate LD samples in the control and treatment condition which were administered the same battery of tests (dependent measures). The control group and treatment group were considered as two independent samples. If additional (different) subjects where in another treatment (i.e., treatment 2), this was also considered as a separate independent sample, and so on. Therefore, because studies vary in the number of independent samples, this information is presented in subsequent tables. It is important for the reader to realize, however, that there are multiple ways that independent samples could have been calculated: SES, age, gender, and so on. Further, high and low IQ scores were other possibilities. Thus, our analysis of independent samples is not as accurate as we would like. However, it was the case in the majority of studies that included subgroups (e.g., age levels, math vs. reading disability) were infrequent or were not a priori defined (i.e., the sample was divided in a post hoc fashion for analysis). Therefore, we kept our analysis of independent samples at only the most general level. The maximum number of independent samples calculated for a single study was eight (2 controls, 6 treatments) and the minimum was 1 (a repeated measure design that included the same sample in the control and treatment condition).

Because there is some debate about what constitutes an independent estimate of effect size, we also used a shifting unit of analysis (Cooper, 1989) to analyze main effects across studies. Two units of analysis were considered because multivariate effect size data posed at least three problems. First, effect sizes calculated for any one sample within a particular study are correlated and therefore it is difficult to treat them as independent (e.g., Gleser & Olkin, 1994). On occasion, however, a single treatment may have different effects on different outcomes (e.g., word recognition vs. math computation) and, therefore, it may be inappropriate to average effect sizes in these studies or to choose simply a single outcome measure. Second, there are several methodological variations across studies that influence effect size. Therefore, it cannot be assumed that a particular intervention program will have the same effect on an outcome variable when methodology varies. Finally, studies vary in terms of their outcome measures. Some studies may focus on word recognition, whereas others measure word recognition and reading comprehension, and some measure only reading comprehension. Thus, there must be some modification in a traditional multivariate linear model to analyze the units of outcome.

In our synthesis, the effect size for each dependent measure category was first coded as if it were an independent event. So if a study included word recognition and reading comprehension measures, then these two effect sizes were coded separately. We also coded the average effect size for each study. Thus, a study would contribute only one effect size proportionately to the sample size. To determine the stability of various moderator variables on intervention outcomes, we compared the outcomes as a function of the two units of analysis. We assumed that if a moderator variable is stable in terms of its influence on outcomes, then significant effects would occur for both units of analysis. Further, because a Chi-square was used to assess the significance of moderators on effect size, and such a procedure is sensitive to variations in sample size, the stability of the moderator must be evaluated across variations in sample size. However, Hedges and Olkin (1985; see pp. 1175-1183) report that simulations of the effect sizes in educational research are reasonably accurate across the number of dependent measures and the number of studies reflected in this synthesis.

Analysis

To determine whether a set of ds shared a common effect size (i.e., d was consistent across the studies), a homogeneity statistic Q, which approximates Chi-square distribution with $k - 1$ degrees of freedom, where k is the number of effect sizes, was computed (Hedges & Olkin, 1985). A homogeneity test (Hedges & Olkin, 1985) was performed using a Proc GLM computer program for the domain categories. When the homogeneity of the sample size was rejected (i.e., a significant Chi-square was obtained), further exploration of the finding was done through analysis of the study features. A significant Chi-square indicated that the study features significantly moderated the magnitude of effect sizes. When there were two or more levels of a study feature, a Scheffe post hoc comparison was performed to test for the significant differences between levels.

As suggested by Hedges and Olkins, outliers were removed from the analysis of main effects and interactions. Outliers were defined as effect sizes lying beyond the first gap of a least one standard deviation between adjacent effect-size values in a positive or negative direction (Bollen, 1989). There were nine studies excluded from the analysis. Four of the studies included cognitive treatments. There did not appear to be any other particular pattern among these studies that we could discern. For reports of nonsignificant effects unaccompanied by any statistic, we followed a conservative procedure of estimating effect size at 0.00.

For the general analysis of outcomes, two different procedures were used to estimate effect sizes. First, we analyzed main effects related to methodological, article characteristics, LD characteristics, and treatment variables. For each measure, an effect size, based on the previous formula was computed. Each effect size was then weighted by the reciprocal in the sampling variance. The dependent measure for the estimate of effect size was defined as est $= (d/(1/v))$, where v is the inverse of the sampling variance, $v = (N_{trt}+N_{crtl})/(N_{trt} \times N_{crtl}) + d^2/[2(N_{trt}+N_{crtl})]$. We conducted planned tests that focused on the area of primary interest related to the instructional approach (i.e., description of the sample in terms of reading and intelligence, age, gender, and methodological variables). For each of these variables, we tested a simple main effect.

Second, as a follow-up to main effects we used a regression analysis. We tested the robustness of the main effect using a general linear model procedure to control statistically for each of the other variables. We tested the important main effects and whether they should be qualified by two way interactions. In order to characterize the relationships between study characteristics and outcomes, weighted least square fixed effects regression models were fitted to the empirical values, following methods recommended by Harwell (1992) and described by Hedges and Olkin (1985, pp. 168-174; see also Hedges, 1994, pp. 295-298). In the case of effect size analysis, test model specifications do exist whenever the number of studies exceeds the number of predictors (see Hedges, 1994, for a review). These tests of model specifications are an important part of model building. Thus, we assumed that a regression model provides a useful framework for addressing some of the common problems in the meta-analysis [e.g., magnitude of effect sizes varies from study to study, variation in study methodology, diversity of treatment implementation, sampling error, etc. (Bryk & Raudenbush, 1992)].

RESULTS

Table 1 provides an overview (synopsis) of the various interventions and effect sizes based on Cohen's *d*. The table lists by *broad* instructional categories, the studies used in

Table 1. Synopsis of Studies Included in the Meta-analysis

CATEGORY	Effect Size[a]	N
ATTRIBUTION TRAINING		
This experiment investigated how verbalization of subtraction with regrouping operations influenced learning disabled Ss' self-efficacy and skillful performance and also explored how effort-attributional feedback affected these achievement behaviors. Ss in one treatment group verbalized aloud while solving problems. Ss in the second treatment group verbalized only during the first half of training. The control condition utilized no verbalizing (Schunk & Cox, 1986).	.49	90
Ss received attributional retraining through cognitive self-instructional methods and group-processing sessions which included controlled instruction and transition to direct instruction. One group was referred to as "Cool Catss are Stars" (Catss: Can do-Ability-Try Hard-Strategy-Success) while the second treatment group received "Stars" only (Stars: Stop-Think-Act-Review-Success). Subjects included math, reading, and written instruction (Morgan, 1991, Dissertation).	.36	81
BIBLIOTHERAPY		
This study focused on the use of Bibliotherapy, a method through which adolescents can observe parallel stresses at an affective distance and incorporate change without a direct threat to personal independence. Ss read literature relevant to the problems they often faced. One group added a weekly discussion group (Lenkowsky, Barowsky, Dayboch, Puccio, & Lenkowsky, 1987).	1.70	96
SIMULTANEOUS AND SUCCESSIVE PROCESSING		
Reading Comprehension and Information Processing Strategies, specifically successive & simultaneous synthesis and verbalization of the child during task performance (Brailsford, Snart, & Das, 1984).	.93	24
Intervention was based on whether the child with LD had difficulties with simultaneous or sequential processing. Tasks in the domain of interest (i.e., math, reading, self-concept) were developed to facilitate development of these cognitive processes (Balcerzak, 1986)	.44	40
Cognitive remediation of decoding deficit was attempted by following a theoretically based program. The theory identifies four major cognitive processes: Planning, Attention, Simultaneous, and Successive processing (PASS) (Das, Mishra, & Pool, 1995).	.34	51

(continued)

Table 1. (Continued)

CATEGORY	Effect Size[a]	N
INSTRUCTIONAL SEQUENCE		
Systematic math instruction using the concrete-semiconcrete-abstract teaching sequence was provided to students who were identified as having math disabilities. Data were collected via a one-minute assessment probe at the end of each lesson for two purposes. he first purpose was to validate that this teaching sequence was effective for skill acquisition and short term retention. The second purpose was to determine when during the instructional sequence the students would make the association between the concrete or semiconcrete lessons and the abstract probe presentation (Miller & Mercer, 1993).	1.80	9

[a]Effect sizes are not weighted by the reciprocal of the sampling variable nor have outliers been removed.

COMPUTER-ASSISTED INSTRUCTION (CAI)		
CAI-Math		
The effectiveness of two drill and practice methods, computer-assisted instruction and workbook, was compared using six learning disabled and six normal learning students. Both instructional methods provided highly structured drill and practice of multiplication facts, but differed on several important dimensions: immediacy of feedback, individually-tailored practice of problems, and mode of presentation (Foster, 1983, Dissertation).	4.21	12,6
The study focused on the use of computer-assisted practice in achieving higher math computation skills through a mixture of visual and auditory modes (Kunka, 1984, Dissertation).	.24	110
The purpose of the study was to compare the effect of two types of instructional software on the math achievement of EMH, LD, and EH resource room students. The study also investigated the relationship between math achievement and attitude toward CAI for Ss learning math using the two types of math software. (Whitman, 1986, Dissertation).	.13	72
The study utilized a single-subject design to investigate whether learning of multiplication tables via computer programs transfers to paper/pencil tasks. The baseline phase used flashcards, math games, and worksheets of math facts. The treatment phase used the computer program which included a multiplication table, *A Treasure Hunt of Facts, Meteor Multiplication,* and a voice synthesizer (Chiang, 1986[*]).	1.40	6
The study examined the efficacy of Teacher Net, an inexpensive computer networking system. The major question was the extent to which Teacher Net could reduce the time teachers spend monitoring, grading assignments, and ooking for error patterns. By automating these activities (at one-tenth the cost of a regular network), teachers would have a lot more time for direct teaching (Moore, Carnine, Stepnoski, & Woodward, 1987).	0.0	27

(continued)

Table 1.   (Continued)

CATEGORY	Effect Size[a]	N
CAI-Reading		
Reading & CAI at the secondary level. Attitudes toward reading and self-concept as impacted by CAI were investigated (Porinchack, 1984, Dissertation).	.43	51
In this study, computer-synthesized speech was incorporated into a reading program to improve word recognition abilities of students with learning disabilities (Farmer, Klein, & Bryson, 1992).	.10	14
This study investigated the effects of presenting words to be read on a computer screen that represented the right or left visual field (Van Strien, Stolk, & Zuiker, 1995)	1.85	20
This alternating treatments design utilized computer-assisted instruction to aid in silent reading comprehension skills (Harper, 1986, Dissertation[*]).	1.24	9
The efficacy of the computer-assisted training procedures with reading decoding were assessed in the training of children with three specific types of reading disability: oral reading, intermodal-associative, and sequential. The training involved an integration of current theoretical issues: application of the automaticity theory and a combination of the task-analytic and process-oriented models. It was hypothesized that improved performance in the trained skills would result in transfer of training to untrained reading subskills, as well as to reading in general (Fiedorowicz, 1986).	1.87	15
This study investigated the effectiveness of computer assisted articulatory-based and non-articulatory based phonological analysis training on the reading and spelling of children with learning disabilities (Wise, Ring, Sessions, & Olson, in press).	.80	45
The relative efficacy of computer programs with and without synthesized speech support on the word recognition of children with learning disabilities was investigated (Farmer, Klein, & Bryson, 1992).	.11	.14
This alternating treatments design compared computer-assisted instruction and teacher instruction in the area of reading comprehension. In both treatments, the S read a short story twice and answered a series of multiple choice questions (Van den Meiracker, 1987, Dissertation[*]).	.87	9
Reading disabled students were trained on the *Autoskill Component Reading Subskills Program* (with computer) according to procedures specifically developed for three reading disability subtypes: Oral Reading, Intermodal-Associative and Sequential (Fiedorowicz & Trites, 1987).	.44	91
A new computer program, *Hint and Hunt 1,* designed to increase decoding fluency in reading was evaluated with a sample of 20 LD students (Jones, Torgesen, & Sexton, 1987).	1.96	30
Segmented or whole-word speech feedback (provided through a computer) was investigated. Speech feedback was hypothesized to be better for children in the early stages of reading (phonological recoding) than for children who were proficient readers (Van Daal, & Reitsma (1990).	1.33	17

(continued)

Table 1.   (Continued)

CATEGORY	Effect Size[a]	N
This study presented an overview of a computer program directed toward the remediation of children's deficits in word recognition and phonological decoding. Ss read stories on the computer and were trained to request synthetic-speech feedback for difficult words. Groups received either whole-word feedback or segmented-word feedback (Olson & Wise, 1992).	.66	35, 149
This study determined the degree to which computer mediated presentations of text influence LD Ss' reading comprehension, and whether cognitive factors related to metacognition, attribution, and working memory influence treatment effects. Ss were assigned to one of four treatments conditions: control, paper (off-line), computer-no reread, and computer reread. Within each condition, traditional and cloze comprehension questions were presented at three levels of passage difficulty (Swanson & Trahan, 1992).	.46	120
This study examined the effects of computer-based reading and spelling practice on the development of reading and spelling skills. Ss practiced hard-to-read words under three conditions: reading from the computer screen, copying from the screen, and writing from memory after presentation on the screen. For all words, whole-word sound was available on call during practice. To assess learning effects, both a dictation and a read-aloud task were administered in which nonpracticed control words were also presented. During training, the computer kept record of several aspects of the pupils' learning behavior (Van Daal & Van der Liej, 1992).	1.39	28
The study investigated the connection between reading comprehension and decoding skills by using a computer-based text-to-speech system. The Ss read the text on the computer screen. When a difficult word was encountered, the S could target the word for the computer to provide speech feedback (Lundberg & Olofsson, 1993).	.44	33
Disabled readers and normal beginning readers were compared on requesting help in the form of speech feedback during computer-based word reading. It was also examined whether it was best to give feedback on all words or to allow the disabled readers to choose. Normal beginning readers and reading-age matched pupils with reading problems engaged in reading practice with speech feedback on call for both difficult and easy words. A set of both difficult and easy sums was completed as a control task. Another group of reading-disabled pupils who were also matched on reading level practiced the reading of words with unsolicited speech feedback (Van Daal & Reitsma, 1993).	.09	46
Two CAI modes of instruction were compared. In the first condition, students read passages from a science textbook using a basic computer version (i.e. text, graphics, outline). In the second condition, the students read with the aid of speech synthesis, an online glossary, links between questions and text, highlighting of main ideas (MacArthur & Haynes, 1995).	.52	10

(*continued*)

Table 1. (Continued)

CATEGORY	Effect Size[a]	N
CAI-Reasoning Skills		
This study evaluated the role of instructional design in the field test and revision process for CAI in drawing conclusions and critiquing syllogistic arguments: Reasoning Skills (Collins & Carnine, 1988).	1.48	26
CAI-Spelling		
The study investigated the use of computer-assisted instruction and feedback in attaining higher spelling skills (Kitterman, 1984, Dissertation[*]).	.53	5
The study compared computer-assisted instruction and paper/pencil instruction as the means of delivering independent spelling practice in classes for learning disabled students. Both groups utilized identical content and similar activities, but differed in instructional design features (MacArthur, Haynes, Malouf, Harris, & Owings, 1990).	.63	44
The *SelfSpell* programs used in this study, provide a multi-media environment for dyslexic children which uses synthesized speech to augment the written text. The *SelfSpell* treatment condition was compared with the *SpellMaster* in the control condition (Fawcett, Nicolson, & Morris, 1993).	.97	12
The purpose of this study was to determine the efficacy of three motoric conditions (writing, tracing, and computer keyboarding) on the spelling performance of third- and fourth-grade students without learning disabilities and with learning disabilities. This study applied empirically-based procedures for teaching spelling, examined student performance over time, and incorporated student interviews concerning their preference for motoric condition (Vaughn, Schumm, & Gordon, 1993).	.66	48
Two experimental studies examined the effects of different types of phonemic segmentation training on phonemic segmentation, reading and spelling. Ss who were weak in phonemic segmentation were trained with the use of diagrams and alphabet letters, alphabet letters only, or with no visual support at all. The study incorporated computer-assisted instruction (Kerstolt, Van Bon, & Schreuder, 1994).	.31	48,49
The purpose of this study was to investigate the impact of integrated proofreading strategy training, combining the use of a computer-based spelling checker and student strategies, on the proofreading performance of high-school aged students with learning disabilities (McNaughton, Hughes, & Ofiesh, 1997[*]).	1.78	3
CAI Writing		
Study participants generated text (story writing)and error monitoring and correction at microcomputers both alone and as members of dyads (Hine, Goldman, & Cosden, 1990).	.92	11

(*continued*)

Table 1.   (Continued)

CATEGORY	Effect Size[a]	N
COMPREHENSION MONITORING STRATEGIES		
Error Correction		
Two procedures for correcting oral reading errors during training in word-attack strategies in a naturalistic setting were examined (Meyer, 1982).	.62	58
An alternating treatments design was used to investigate the relative effectiveness of two error-correction procedures: word supply and phonic analysis on oral reading performance (Rose, McEntire, & Dowdy, 1982[*]).	1.49	5
Study participants generated text (story writing)and error monitoring and correction at microcomputers both alone and as members of dyads (Hine, Goldman, & Cosden, 1990).	.92	11
Students were encouraged either to make active student responses during error correction, or in the case of the control, they made no overt response. Effects of intervention on the acquisition and maintenance of geography facts was nvestigated (Barbetta & Heward, 1993[*]).	.65	3
Self-questioning strategies		
The study looked at the effects of Cognitive Monitoring, Creative Problem Solving, and a combination of the two instructional programs on reading disabled third graders' oral comprehension (Manning, 1984).	1.08	100
Reading Comprehension: Cooperative Skills Training in reading with the strategies of self-questioning and paraphrasing, and in writing with the strategies in sentences and error monitoring. Cooperative Skills Training included four parts: Orientation to types of goal structures, Activation, Skill training, and Pre-strategy training (Beals, 1985, Dissertation[*]).	1.50	28
Ss were trained in one of four techniques while reading comprehension passages. The techniques were: read-reread, self-questioning and underlining, self-questioning only, and underlining only. LD children were matched on reading age with regular class children (Chan & Cole, 1986).	.97	72
The purpose of this study was to investigate the effects of using a questioning strategy with LD Ss to increase discussion participation and to increase reading comprehension (Dixon, 1984, Dissertation).	.58	60
The study investigated the use of dialogical thinking-reading lessons in which the S was engaged in reasoning and reflective thinking in order to decide what to believe about a central issue related to a story. Ss were asked to consider the evidence for two hypothesized explanatory conclusions regarding an important question (Commeyras, 1992).	1.34	14

(continued)

Table 1.   (Continued)

CATEGORY	Effect Size[a]	N
This study investigated the hypothesis that insufficient metacomprehension is one possible cause underlying learning disabled adolescents' comprehension problems, and that training them to monitor their understanding of important textual elements fosters metacomprehension and improves their comprehension performance. Half of the Ss received a 5-step self-questioning training in which they learned to monitor their understanding of important textual units. The other half of the Ss received no training, but had the same materials as the experimental group (Wong & Jones, 1982).	.56	120
The study examined the effectiveness of two methods of teaching an efficient questioning strategy to Ss with learning disabilities. The study compared cognitive modeling alone in the use of constraint-seeking questions, and cognitive modeling and verbalization in the use of constraint-seeking questions, involving explicit and consistent instruction and feedback (Simmonds, 1990).	.27	60
This study addressed the effectiveness of teacher acquisition and implementation of two methods for improving the comprehension skills of LD Ss: Instruction in teaching specific questioning strategies (Question - Answer - Response QARS) and selected traditional methods of reading comprehension instruction (Simmonds, 1992).	1.54	447
This study describes and evaluates an instructional program designed to help students with learning disabilities learn about the concept of theme, identify theme in stories and apply themes to real life (Williams, Brown, Silverstein, & deCani, 1994).	1.36	69
This study compared the effects of vocabulary instruction on reading comprehension. Students were instructed either in determining meanings of words in context, or received vocabulary definitions (Pany & Jenkins, 1978).	3.11	6

CONSULTATIVE SERVICES

CATEGORY	Effect Size[a]	N
Tested the role of a child advocate and coordinator of services for LD children. Two treatment groups and one untreated control group were incorporated into the study. One of the treatment groups used the child advocate while the other was a school-informed group, but no advocacy services given (Pihl, Parkes, Drake & Vrana, 1980).	1.14	90
The effects of a collaboration consultative model on the reading recovery of primary grade children with learning disabilities was investigated (Larson & Gerber, 1987[*]).	1.74	5
This study compared the achievement of LD Ss in reading and written language across four conditions: one period of resource room instruction per day, two periods of resource room instruction per day, consultative services combined with in-class instruction, and consultative services to classroom teachers (Schulte, Osborne, & McKinney, 1991).	.46	67

(continued)

Table 1. (Continued)

CATEGORY	Effect Size[a]	N
This study describes the use of a consultation-collaboration model of intervention in which a psychologist and a teacher worked jointly to establish a remedial reading program for five special needs children placed in a regular primary school class (Cochrane & Ballard, 1986*).	1.37	5

COUNSELLING

Adlerian

| The inclusion of group counseling was expected to facilitate the treatment of children involved in prescriptive remedial programs, specifically a significant increase in vocabulary and comprehension skills was anticipated. The therapeutic style was primarily Adlerian (McCollum & Anderson, 1974). | .29 | 48 |

Biofeedback

| This study examined the effects of biofeedback-induced relaxation training on attention to task, impulsivity, and locus of control (Omizo & Williams, 1982). | .56 | 32 |
| Ss were provided with long-term, symptom duration, sensorimotor rhythm biofeedback training for the remediation of learning disabilities. (Tansey, 1985*). | .80 | 8 |

Career counselling

| The study investigated the effects of a counseling program designed to promote career maturity among youth with LD and other youth at risk of dropping out of school. Activities focused on self-awareness and an exploration of career options. Discussion, teacher modeling and cognitive processing/thinking aloud were utilized in the treatment (Hutchinson, Freeman, Downey, & Kilbreath, 1992). | .58 | 16 |

Rational Emotive (Reality) Therapy

| The purpose of this study was to determine the effects of Rational-Emotive Education (REE) counseling group sessions on LD Ss' self-concept and locus of control orientation. Ss met twice weekly in a peer-group situation for 12 consecutive weeks. Among other topics, Ss discussed problem-solving issues and skills, rational coping strategies, and how to give support, empathy and encouragement to others in the group (Omizo, Cubberly, & Omizo, 1985). | .77 | 54 |
| The authors investigated the effects of a rational-emotive education (REE) program on LD adolescents' self-concept and locus of control (Omizo, Lo, & Williams, 1986). | .82 | 50 |

Relaxation Therapy

| Children participated either in a relaxation training session (listening to 30 minute audio-tapes) or in a social skills group to reduce acting out behavior (Amerikaner & Summerlin, 1982). | .44 | 46 |
| This study compared two treatment groups: Self-instruction (Meichembaum, 1977) and relaxation training (Jacobson, 1938*), and a no-treatment control group. Treatment groups were given 10 half-hour sessions over four weeks and were assessed before and after the treatment on cognitive tasks requiring deliberation (Zieffle & Romney, 1985). | .56 | 30 |

(continued)

Table 1.   (Continued)

CATEGORY	Effect Size[a]	N
CREATIVITY TRAINING		
The Purdue Creative Thinking Program was used to stimulate the LD experimental group's divergent thinking abilities (Jaben, Treffinger, Whelan, Hudson, Stainback & Stainback, 1982).	1.38[3]	49
The Purdue Creative Thinking Program included two 45-minute sessions per week using a set of 28 audio tapes and printed materials designed to stimulate divergent thinking, figural and verbal fluency, flexibility, and originality. Separate studies in different journals: (Jaben, 1983, 1985, 1986, 1987).	1.50 .39 .40 .58	49 52 98 50
This study examined whether intermediate-grade LD students could generalize creativity training to increase competency on a spontaneous writing task. Seven intact classrooms were used to analyze differences between groups on initial creative productive-thinking level. Experimental Ss engaged in brainstorming activities where each child was free to share ideas which were recorded and posted for observation (Fortner, 1986).	.37	51
CURRICULUM BASED MEASUREMENT—PROGRAMMING		
The study examined the effectiveness of innovative curriculum-based measurement (CBM) classwide decision-making structures within general education mathematics instruction, with and without recommendations for how to incorporate CBM feedback into instructional planning (Fuchs, Fuchs, Hamlett, Phillips, & Bentz, 1994).	.48	120
DIAGNOSTIC PRESCRIPTIVE		
This study compared two treatment groups with a no-treatment control group. One treatment group included intense remediation of deficits through tutoring while in the second treatment group, teachers were instructed to teach to the Ss' strengths (Warner, 1973, Dissertation)	.59[2]	30
Use of ability measures to predict the most appropriate method or sequence of mathematics instruction for learning disabled junior high school students (Glaman, 1974, Dissertation).	.23	33
This study examined the effects of psycholinguistic training on improving psycholinguistic skills. Training activities focused on 12 psycholinguistic areas and Ss received training in their deficit areas (Sowell, Parker, Poplin, & Larsen, 1979).	.25	63
The purpose of this study was to compare the effects of: (1) Remediation of hypothesized component deficits given prior to remediation of known academic deficiencies and (2) Remediation of known academic deficiencies alone (Wade, 1979, Dissertation).	.22	76
Ten planned comparisons of pretest and posttest scores on the Slosson Oral Reading Test support the position that LD students regress in their reading skills when they experience extended breaks in their educational programs during the summer months. This study looked at a five-week summer program during either the first or last half of the summer and if that can prevent reading regression (Cornelius & Semmel, 1982).	.61	60

(continued)

Table 1.   (Continued)

CATEGORY	Effect Size[a]	N
Ss received instruction based on an individualized remediation technique utilizing the deficits of the neuropsychological testing. The treatment included a more-lively teacher presence, organized and structured sessions, frequent change of activities, success-oriented activities, and individualized and concrete instructional materials (DeBoskey, 1982, Dissertation).	1.06	23
Ss with major levels of retardation in reading were divided into two subgroups for intervention purposes. During the first phase of treatment one group received diagnostic-prescriptive remediation (control), and the other a direct instruction program (Distar Reading II, a phonetically weighted program), both delivered for equal amounts of time each day by the same teacher (Branwhite, 1983).	2.33	14
Three intervention programs were constructed for Ss with deficits in the areas of auditory closure and visual sequential memory. The first was designed to alleviate the specific disabilities in the areas of deficit. The second was based on a more general approach to language development. The third group (control) undertook a simple number program (Naylor & Pumfrey, 1983).	2.13	60
The purpose of the study was to compare the effects of remediation of hypothesized component deficits given prior to remediation of known academic deficiencies, and remediation of known academic deficiencies alone. A corollary purpose was to study the immediate effect, if any, of the component deficit remediation on the criterion measure (Wade & Kass, 1987).	.42	76

DIRECT INSTRUCTION

Attention

	Effect Size	N
This study investigated improving attending behaviors and incorporated two treatment groups and a no-treatment control group. The first treatment group received training in attending behaviors by a direct instruction method. The second group was exposed to modeling of the attending behaviors but received no other formal training (Argulewicz, 1982).	.95	72

Math

	Effect Size	N
This study examined the influence of a modeling technique on the acquisition of long division computational skills by eight adolescents with learning disabilities (Rivera, & Deutsch Smith, 1988[*]).	1.66	8
This study examined the comparative effectiveness of direct instruction alone and direct instruction combined with supplemental homework assignments on the acquisition of basic mathematics skills among elementary school-aged students with learning disabilities (Rosenberg, 1989[*]).	1.31	6,4
Direct Instruction Math and its components (strategy teaching and sequencing problems) in isolation to determine which was the most effective for teaching LD Ss to identify the correct algorithm for solving addition and subtraction word problems (Wilson, 1989, Dissertation).	.68	62

(continued)

Table 1.   (Continued)

CATEGORY	Effect Size[a]	N
The effects of token reinforcement, cognitive behavior modification and direct instruction on LD Ss' math skills were compared. Math skills were measured by 2-minute classroom timings of basic addition and subtraction problems (Ross & Braden, 1991).	.26	94

Reading

CATEGORY	Effect Size	N
This study compared the effectiveness of three instructional strategies which varied in the amount of direct instruction provided on reading comprehension. Specifically, the study measured recall of word meanings and recall of facts from a story (Pany & Jenkins, 1978).	5.32	6
During the first phase of treatment one group received diagnostic-prescriptive remediation (control), and the other a direct instruction program (Distar Reading II, a phonetically weighted program), both delivered for equal amounts of time each day by the same teacher (Branwhite, 1983).	2.32	14
A comparison was made of the efficacy of metacomprehension (self-monitoring) plus direct instruction, direct instruction alone, and a control training condition in finding the main idea (Graves, 1986).	3.13	24
Two approaches were used in teaching elementary LD students three critical reading skills (ability to detect faulty generalization, ability to detect false causality, ability to detect invalid testimonial). The experimental group utilized direct instruction and the control group used discussion and a workbook. The study had three major purposes: to evaluate whether a systematic direct instruction approach, found successful with nonhandicapped students, would be effective with LD students; to assess the relative effectiveness of two approaches to teaching critical reading; and to examine the effects of each instructional approach on several dependent measures to identify any differential effects of instruction (Darch & Kameenui, 1987).	1.22	25
Ss with reading difficulties were selected for this study. Three intervention conditions were utilized which included: psycho-motor, self-esteem enhancement, and Direct Instruction (Somerville & Leach, 1988).	1.24	40
The efficacy of instructional variables were examined comparing a progressive time-delay and trial-and-error strategy in teaching sight word acquisition. Observational learning versus direct instruction was also assessed by having children observe each other being taught different words (McCurdy, Cundari, & Lentz, 1990[*]).	1.77	2
Children with reading disabilities were assigned to one of two word identification training programs or to a study skills control. One treatment remediated deficient phonological analysis and blending skills and provided direct instruction of letter-sound mappings. The other program taught children how to acquire, use, and monitor four metacognitive decoding strategies (Lovett, & Steinbach, in press).	.77	122

(continued)

Table 1. (Continued)

CATEGORY	Effect Size[a]	N
Science		
The purpose of this study was to compare the effectiveness of two instructional approaches on mildly handicapped and nonhandicapped Ss' science achievement. Ss were assigned at random to one of two conditions: direct instruction or discovery teaching. The content of the lessons remained constant across conditions and focused on such concepts as displacement, flotation, variable, controlled experimentation, and scientific prediction (Bay, Staver, Bryan, & Hale, 1992).	2.41	68
Vocabulary		
This study examined the efficacy of direct instruction corrective reading program which focused on vocabulary, sentence memory, logical reasoning, following directions and common information (Lloyd, Cullinan, Heins, & Epstein, 1980).	.84	23
GOALSETTING		
This study focused on a training program designed to teach LD junior high school Ss to set realistic achievement goals, to expend effort to reach the goals, and to accept personal responsibility for achievement outcomes (Tollefson, Tracy, Johnsen, Farmer, & Buenning, 1984).	.30	61
The experiment tested the hypothesis that participation in goal setting enhances self-efficacy and skills. Included in the study were three groups: Self-set goals, Assigned goals, and No goals (Schunk, 1985).	1.14	30
The study examined the impact of a goal-attainment intervention related to the completion of project-type assignments. The study included seven steps: task evaluation, options generation, goal specification, plan identification, plan expansion, demands consideration, and self-monitoring (Lenz, Ehren, & Smiley, 1991[*]).	1.69	6
This study was conducted to determine if a planning and writing strategy would improve the essay writing of Ss with LD. Four Ss were taught a strategy designed to facilitate the setting of product and process goals, generation and organization of notes, continued planning during writing, and evaluation of goal attainment. A multiple-probe across subjects design was used (Graham, MacArthur, Schwartz, & Page-Voth, 1992[*]).	1.66	4
This study extended previous research on components of effective strategy instruction operationalized in an approach referred to as self-regulated strategy development (SRSD). Comparisons were made among LD Ss on composition and self-efficacy in four conditions: SRSD, SRSD without goal setting and self-monitoring, direct teaching, and practice control (Sawyer, Graham, & Harris, 1992).	1.78	43
HEMISPHERIC STIMULATION		
Hemispheric stimulation of left hemisphere is attained by presenting target words to the right hand of the child as the child reads. Treatment begins at letter level and progresses to word level. Treatment varies according to whether one is P-dyslexic or L-dyslexic (Bakker, Bouma, & Gardien, 1990).	2.26	56

(continued)

Table 1.   (Continued)

CATEGORY	Effect Size[a]	N

LANGUAGE STRATEGIES

Oral Language

Paradigmatic Language Training: The effect that training paradigmatic language structures has upon the reading process was investigated with LD children. The effects of intelligence, special training, and training over time were analyzed in a pretest-posttest control group design (Cartelli, 1978). — 2.25 — 46

Ss in this study either received training in word recognition and decoding skills, oral and written language, or classroom survival skills (Lovett, Ransby, & Barron, 1988). — .41 — 112

Ss in this study either received training in word recognition and decoding skills, oral and written language, or classroom survival skills (Lovett, Ransby, Hardwick, Johns, & Donaldson, 1989). — .39 — 178

Outcomes of mini-lessons in adverbial phrases was compared with results of mini-lessons on possessives for students in the intermediate grades (Dowis & Schloss, 1992[*]) — 1.58 — 4

Language Experience (reading)

Individual classes were divided into three groups, an experimental group which focused on Language Experience, and two control groups (based on reading level) termed action and double action. On a daily basis, each group alternated between working with the aide & worksheets, and working with the investigator and interactive instructional activities. Ss were graded on spelling, capitalization, punctuation & English usage, and were encouraged to correct errors. Syllabication and phonics were used with vocabulary words (Lerner, 1978 Dissertation). — .11 — 60

Phoneme Awareness

This study examined the effects of psycholinguistic training (Minskoff, Wiseman, & Minskoff, 1972[*]) on improving psycholinguistic skills. Training activities focused on 12 psycholinguistic areas and Ss received training in their deficit areas (Sowell, Parker, Poplin, & Larsen, 1979). — .25 — 63

The study analyzed the effect on literal reading comprehension of providing instruction in the application of psycholinguistic strategies used intuitively in apprehending meaning in discourse. A multiple-choice cloze procedure was used to implement the investigation (Vivion, 1985, Dissertation[*]). — 1.42 — 6

The study examined the possibility that phonemic discrimination training could improve the phonemic segmentation ability of children with reading disabilities (Hurford, 1990). — .40 — 48

(continued)

Table 1.   (Continued)

CATEGORY	Effect Size[a]	N
Students with severe learning disabilities who received the Auditory Discrimination in Depth Program (Lindamood & Lindamood, 1975[*]) on an intensive basis, in addition to a comprehensive remedial program, were matched for Verbal IQ, chronological age, reading, spelling, and phonological awareness abilities with 10 other students with severe learning disabilities who also received the comprehensive remedial program but not the Lindamood program component. Progress in reading, spelling, phonological awareness, use of phonetic principles in spelling of real and nonwords, and phonetic reading of nonwords were documented in December and May (Kennedy & Backman, 1993).	.35	20
This study is one component of a five year program of research aimed at generating knowledge about the effectiveness of different approaches to the prevention and remediation of reading difficulties among children in the emergent stages of reading acquisition. Children with learning disabilities were assigned to one of two instructional groups: phonological awareness training (Auditory Discrimination in Depth Program, Lindamood & Lindamood, 1975[*]) or implicit phonological awareness training plus phonics instruction embedded within real word reading and spelling activities (Torgesen, Wagner, Rashotte, Alexander, & Conway, 1997).	.27	31

Phonics

The purpose of this research was to investigate rule learning in reading disabled and normal children when required to abstract phonetic rules independently and when required to use phonetic rules after instruction (Fletcher & Prior, 1990).	.51	20

Vocabulary

Three experiments were conducted to assess the effects of vocabulary instruction on word knowledge and reading comprehension. Treatments varied in the amount of direct instruction (Pany, Jenkins, Schreck, 1982).	5.32	12, 6, 10
The study examined the effects of prior knowledge on the reading comprehension performance of Ss with learning disabilities. Instruction in nformation and vocabulary concepts was provided to junior high school Ss who lacked prior knowledge required. Reading Comprehension performance on three types of reading passages was also examined: textually explicit textually implicit, and scriptually implicit (Snider, 1989).	1.58	26

MEMORY STRATEGIES

The objective of this study was to utilize a mnemonic device to teach ten letter cluster sound associations to 17 reading disabled subjects. Direct Instruction was incorporated into the intervention (Smith, 1989, Dissertation).	.74	34

(*continued*)

Table 1.   (Continued)

CATEGORY	Effect Size[a]	N
Three classrooms of junior high school students with learning disabilities were taught U.S. history content over an 8 week period, in which mnemonic and non-mnemonic materials were alternated (Scruggs & Mastropieri, 1989).	1.01	26
Three classrooms of adolescent students with learning disabilities were taught U.S. history content alternatively using mnemonic and nonmnemonic materials to improve recall of chapter information (Scruggs & Mastropieri, 1989).	.99	20
The study investigated the effectiveness of predictable and unpredictable trial sequences during small-group instruction in three experiments in teaching word and abbreviation identification to Ss with learning disabilities. The same Ss were used in each experiment (Ault, Wolery, Gast, Doyle, & Martin, 1990[*]).	1.82	5,4,4
A count-by technique was taught to a fourth-grade student with learning disabilities. The procedure involved learning to translate a multiplication problem into a count-by problem as a way of quickly determining answers for difficult to master multiplication tables (McIntyre, Test, Cooke, & Beattie, 1991[*])	1.78	1
The use of mnemonics to learn and remember information holds promise for students with learning and memory problems. Keyword mnemonics were used in two of three instructional procedures taught to Ss with mild handicaps in this study. Ss were required to learn and remember definitions of previously unfamiliar science terms. Systematic teaching, an imposed keyword method and an induced keyword method were compared (King-Sears, Mercer, & Sindelar, 1992).	1.80	37
This study evaluated the effectiveness of classroom mnemonic instruction of science content (Scruggs & Mastropieri, 1992).	1.12[2]	20
This investigation was intended to determine the effects of metamemory training on both metamemory knowledge and related memory performance, as well as its effects on other metacognitive and cognitive domains. The first experiment focused on metamemory training while the second experiment focused on a metamemory training group, a metacognitive reading group, and a control group (Lucangeli, Galderisi, & Cornoldi, 1995).	.64	166
The purpose of the study was to evaluate the effects of instructing Ss to use a mnemonic strategy to identify and remember pairs or small groups of information (Bulgren, Hock, Schumaker, & Deshler, 1995[*])	1.77	12
This study investigated whether LD adolescents would transfer the use of four study rules from instructed materials (pictures) to a prose recall task. Two groups of LD Ss received extensive direct instruction that was informed, varied, explicit, extended, and included problem isomorph recognition training (Gelzheiser, 1984).	.54	80

(continued)

Table 1.   (Continued)

CATEGORY	Effect Size[a]	N
MULTI-SENSORY APPROACH		
Word Recognition: A whole-word approach that used a multi-sensory technique for developing reading skills, including the Fernald Method of tracing letters and a Total Body Movement Learning Game (Waterman, 1974, Dissertation).	.96	34
Sight words and letter sounds were taught, tested and reviewed. V.A.K.T. (Visual, Auditory, Kinesthetic, Tactile) procedures were used and compared with an equated visual-auditory procedure (Bryant, 1979, Dissertation).	.39	42
This study examined the effectiveness of the Tomatis Program (plus direct instruction in comparison to direct instruction only control on the general academic achievement of children with learning disabilities (Kershner, Cummings, Clarke, Hadfield, & Kershner, 1990).	.32	26
Multisensory instructional approaches have been used in teaching handicapped children for many years, but have never been adequately validated. Using a multiple-baseline design and direct measurement of words read and spelled as the dependent variable, this study evaluated the effects of the kinesthetic-tactile component in VAKT (Visual, Auditory, Kinesthetic, Tactile) instruction (Thorpe, Lampe, Nash, & Chiang, 1981[*]).	1.22	3
NEUROLOGICAL IMPRESS METHOD (NIM)		
The Neurological Impress Method (NIM) was used to teach reading skills by having the pupil and the teacher read aloud in unison. The study examined if the use of NIM would increase comprehension and word-recognition abilities among LD Ss, and if the NIM method would work less effectively with Ss who have auditory rather than visual or unidentified Lds (Lorenz & Vockell, 1979).	.27	54
PEER MEDIATION (PM)		
PM-Behavior		
A single-subject design to help a 14-year old LD student overcome extreme use of obscenities. Peers in the math class participated by refraining from laughter and from responding to the S's obscenities (Salend & Meddaugh, 1985[*]).	1.80	1
The study used a multiple baseline design and evaluated the effects of four fifth-grade LD students tutoring one third-grade and three second-grade LD students on word-recognition skills (Chiang, Thorpe, & Darch, 1980[*]).	1.77	8
This study examined the feasibility of an instructional management program for learning disabled, incarcerated youths. It compared peer tutors and learning disabilities teachers as implementers of a computational mathematics program for incarcerated, learning disabled juvenile delinquents (Kane & Alley, 1980).	.26	38

(continued)

Table 1.   (Continued)

CATEGORY	Effect Size[a]	N
The study evaluated the effectiveness of social skills training and cross-age tutoring for improving academic skills (specifically spelling) and social communication behaviors. The treatment groups included: social skills training and tutoring, social skills training only, and a no treatment control group (Trapani & Gettinger, 1989).	.17	20
The authors investigated the combined effects of direct instruction and precision teaching by peer tutors in a high school driver education curriculum (Bell, Young, Salzberg, & West, 1991[*]).	1.48	1
The study focused on classwide peer tutoring involving instructional procedures (provision of frequent, immediate feedback) that are known to be successful for children with Attention Deficit Hyperactivity Disorder (ADHD) (DuPaul & Henningson, 1993[*]).	1.46	1

PM-Math

The impact of grouping, learning handicap, locus of control and self-esteem on students' performance on a math problem-solving program was assessed. Students worked alone in one group and worked in dyads in the treatment group taking turns at the computer (Cosden & English, 1987).	2.58	12

PM-Reading

The study used a multiple baseline design and evaluated the effects of four fifth-grade LD students tutoring one third-grade and three second-grade LD students on word-recognition skills (Chiang, Thorpe, & Darch, 1980[*]).	1.77	8
This study investigated the efficacy of an intervention that involved parents as reading tutors at home during the summer (Duvall, Delquadri, Elliott, & Hall, 1992[*]).	1.16	3
The study examined the effects of using repeated-reading and sustained-reading methods as classwide peer-mediated learning activities while manipulating and testing the effect of the level of text difficulty. Special education resource room teachers were assigned randomly to three conditions: peer-mediated repeated reading, peer-mediated sustained reading, or control (Mathes & Fuchs, 1993).	.61	6
The purpose of this study was to investigate the effect of two treatments: (a) reciprocal teaching in combination with cross-age tutoring and (b) reciprocal teaching in combination with cooperative grouping on the acquisition of reading comprehension strategies among middle school aged ESL students with learning disabilities (Klingner, & Vaughn 1996).	.33	26

PM-Writing

Interactive dialogues between teacher and student (individual condition) or between student and student (dyad condition) were used to teach revision skills in writing. The study focused on instructing adolescents with LDs in the writing process and utilized interactive dialogues to promote understanding and inculcation of revision skills (Wong, Butler, Ficzere, Kuperis, Corden, & Zelmer, 1994).	.84	2

(continued)

Table 1. (Continued)

CATEGORY	Effect Size[a]	N
The present study examined the effects of an intervention that attempted to improve students' expository writing abilities through an instructional emphasis on teacher and student dialogues about expository writing strategies, text structure processes, and self-regulated learning (Englert, Raphael, Anderson, Anthony, & Stevens 1991).	.39	183
Two students with learning disabilities participated in a peer mediated procedure to increase acquisition and generalization of written capitalization rules (Campbell, Brady, & Linehan, 1991[*]).	1.58	2
PM-General		
The study evaluated the effectiveness of social skills training and cross-age tutoring for improving academic skills (specifically spelling) and social communication behaviors. The treatment groups included: social skills training and tutoring, social skills training only, and a no treatmen control group (Ruhl, Hughes, & Gajar, 1990).	.63[2]	30

PERCEPTUAL-MOTOR STRATEGIES

CATEGORY	Effect Size[a]	N
This study investigated Kephart's perceptual-motor training procedures on the reading performance of poor readers, including chalkboard exercises, ocular pursuit exercises, and sensory-motor exercises in balance, laterality, & directionality (Sullivan, 1972).	.34	82
This study focused on the degree to which different programs of supplementary instruction affect the acquisition of early formal reading competence in children who have been identified as being at risk of reading failure. Four groups were studied with matched individuals: supplemental perceptual training, remedial reading, placebo play activities, no-treatment control group (Belmont & Birch, 1974).	.85	58
An individualized program with an occupational therapist form the core of the intervention. Treatment goals concern equalization and integration of tactile proprioceptive and vestibular system (Carte, Morrison, Sublett, Uemura, & Setrakian, 1984)	.48	66
This study evaluated a procedure using positive reinforcement in the remediation of severe perceptual-motor disorders in the handwriting of two LD boys (Study 1) and of another two LD boys (Study 2), having high frequency errors of orientation & sequence in copying words, "mirror writing" or "reversals" (Lahey, Busemeyer, O'Hara & Beggs, 1977[*]).	1.39	2,2
This study compared the effect of sensory integration therapy, perceptual-motor training and no treatment on the performance of children with LD and sensory integrative dysfunction (Humphries, Wright, Snider, & McDougall, 1992).	.64	103
The purpose of this study was to test the hypothesis that children with LD and certain identifiable types of sensory integrative dysfunction who receive remedial activity, specifically for the integrative dysfunction would show greater gains in academic scores than would LD Ss and the same degree and type of sensory integrative dysfunction who received the equivalent amount, in time, of academic work instead of remedial activity (Ayres, 1972).	.63	84

(continued)

Table 1.   (Continued)

CATEGORY	Effect Size[a]	N
HANDWRITING		
Handwriting/Spelling		
A reversal design with multiple-baseline features was used to assess the efficacy of self-instruction, self-correction, and a combination of the two on an LD boy's handwriting performance (Kosiewicz, Hallahan, Lloyd, & Graves, 1982[*]).	1.70	1
This study focused on handwriting. A card showing seven self-instructional questions designed to prompt Ss to think about important aspects of handwriting was provided to two LD elementary students in a multiple baseline design. Daily assessments were made regarding letter formation, letter proximity to the line, letter height, and word spacing (Blandford & Lloyd, 1987[*]).	1.66	2
This study investigated an intervention designed to improve spelling achievement of children with LD. Emphasis was on unit size, distributed practice, and training for transfer (Gettinger, Bryant, & Fayne, 1982).	.90	39
The effects of mechanical interference, rate of production, and contentless production signals to write more on the quantity and quality of fourth- and sixth-grade LD Ss' compositions were examined (Graham, 1990).	1.02	23
PHARMACOLOGY		
The relative effectiveness of the motivational system on hyperactivity and academic performance in math and reading was evaluated as an alternative to drug control of hyperactive children (Ayllon, Layman, & Kandel, 1975[*]).	1.64	3
A double-blind 12-week trial of piracetum (2-pyrrolidone acetamide) versus placebo was undertaken to determine whether the drug treatment would selectively improve the verbal learning of dyslexic boys (Rudel & Helfgott, 1984).	.15	59
Piracetam, a drug thought to enhance learning and memory consolidation, was given in a 3300 mg daily dose to half of a group of 55 dyslexic boys aged 8 to 13 years, in a 12-week, double-blind, placebo controlled study (Chase, Schmitt, Russell, & Tallal, 1984).	.30	54
A double blind, parallel experiment was conducted to determine the effects of Piracetram on reading speed and accuracy among elementary aged boys with reading disabilities (Wilsher, Atkins, & Manfield, 1985).	.25	46
REINFORCEMENT PROCEDURES		
Two types of learning environments were compared, an intensive behavior engineered resource-room program with the regular classroom, for LD Ss who were observed as spending low percentages of time on-task (O'Connor, Stuck, & Wyne, 1979).	1.84	108

(continued)

Table 1.   (Continued)

CATEGORY	Effect Size[a]	N
The purpose of this study was to investigate, through an applied behavior analysis model, the interrelationships of three reading variables: correct oral reading rates, error oral reading rates, and percentage of comprehension. The intervention package included a combination of instructional and reinforcement procedures (Roberts & Smith, 1980[*]).	.94	8
This study examined the relative efficacy of self- and externally imposed schedules of reinforcement on improving oral reading fluency (Billingsley, 1977[*]).	.81	8
In this study, the operant technique of errorless discrimination training of digraphs was investigated (Schimek, 1983[*]).	1.62	1
Aimed toward non-self-controlled problem children: Two treatment groups, cognitive-behavioral, *behavioral* and an attention-control group. Individual therapist contact focusing on psychoeducational, play, and interpersonal tasks and situations, including self-instruction, modeling and contingencies for the cognitive-behavioral group & modeling and contingencies in the behavioral group (Kendall & Braswell, 1982).	.42	54
Oral Reading: Beginning reading was taught to four LD Ss using a Direct Instruction program, *Distar*. The teacher systematically varied the rate of instructional presentation (rapid v. slow pace) and frequency of praising (praise v. no praise) (Darch & Gersten, 1985).	1.51	4
An interdependent group-managed response-cost system mediated by fee tokens was employed to decrease the inappropriate verbalizations of two groups of students with learning disabilities (Salend & Lamb, 1986[*])	1.80	6
The effects of using a daily report card system on inappropriate verbalizations were examined using a combination ABAB and changing criterion design (Burkwist, Mabee, & McLaughlin, 1987[*]).	1.02	1
Ss were taught planning, organizing and writing paragraphs by using four steps. Modeling, interactive guided practice and independent practice were also used along with verbal reinforcement and tokens (Boyer, 1991, Dissertation[*]).	1.68	3
The effects of token reinforcement, cognitive behavior modification and direct instruction on LD Ss' math skills were compared. Math skills were measured by 2-minute classroom timings of basic addition and subtraction problems (Ross & Braden, 1991).	.26	94
This investigation was intended to evaluate the effects of teacher enthusiasm as an alterable variable on the academic and behavioral performance of Ss with LD. Ss with LD in two junior high school special education classrooms were given instruction in science over a two-week period with levels of teacher enthusiasm manipulated in a crossover design (Brigham, Scruggs, & Mastropieri, 1992).	3.51	16

(*continued*)

Table 1.   (Continued)

CATEGORY	Effect Size[a]	N
The efficacy of a dependent group evaluation system was examined in a class of students with disabilities using a reversal design. The group evaluation system involved giving each group member evaluation forms; having each group member rate the group's behavior during a specified time period; selectin randomly a group member whose rating represented the group's rating; comparing the selected group member's rating to the teacher's rating; and delivering reinforcement to all members of the group based on the group's behavior and the selected individual's accuracy in rating their behavior (Salend, Reeder, Katz, & Russell, 1992[*]).	1.76	9
The relative effectiveness of the motivational system on hyperactivity and academic performance in math and reading was evaluated as an alternative to drug control of hyperactive children (Ayllon, Layman, & Kandel, 1975[*]).	1.37	3

SELF-MONITORING

CATEGORY	Effect Size	N
The effects of self-monitoring of attention (on/off task behavior) on handwriting and math achievement was investigated for a 7 year old boy with learning disabilities and attention problems (Hallahan, Lloyd, Kosiewicz, Kauffman, & Graves, 1979[*]).	1.67	1
The effects of self-monitoring on attention to task during small-group instruction were investigated. Three LD Ss with severe attentional problems were taught to self-monitor their on-task behavior while participating in oral reading tasks. A reversal design demonstrated marked increases in attention to task for all three Ss (Hallahan, Marshall, & Lloyd, 1981[*]).	1.50	3
Two experiments investigated the effects of self-recording, tokens and contingent free time on the reading comprehension of elementary school aged children with learning disabilities (Swanson, 1981[*]).	1.34	3,5
This study investigated the effectiveness of self-monitoring procedures on increasing on-task behavior among adolescents with learning disabilities (Prater, Joy, Chilman, Temple, & Miller, 1991[*]).	1.29	4
This study investigated the effects of self-graphing on improving the reactivity of self-monitoring procedures for two students with learning disabilities (DiGangi, Maag, & Rutherford, 1991[*]).	1.30	2
Self monitoring of attention was compared with self-monitoring of productivity on on-task behavior and rate of academic response for children with attention difficulties (Harris, 1986[*]).	1.32	4
Students were taught to use self-monitoring and self-recording for on-task performance (Blick & Test, 1987[*]).	1.33	12

(continued)

Table 1.   (Continued)

CATEGORY	Effect Size[a]	N
This study extended previous research on components of effective strategy instruction operationalized in an approach referred to as self-regulated strategy development (SRSD). Comparisons were made among LD Ss on composition and self-efficacy in four conditions: SRSD, SRSD without goal setting and self-monitoring, direct teaching, and practice control (Sawyer, Graham, & Harris, 1992).	1.78	43
The study compared the effects of two types of self-monitoring on attention and academic performance. LD Ss were taught a spelling study procedure (SSP), followed by instruction in self-monitoring of performance (SMP) and self-monitoring of attention (SMA) (Reid & Harris, 1993)	.48	28
The effectiveness of two self-monitoring interventions on the attentional and academic performance of Ss with learning disabilities was compared in two separate experiments. The first experiment investigated if attention and performance monitoring had differential effects on the spelling study behaviors of four students. The second experiment used the same design and procedures with self-monitoring applied to story writing (Harris, Graham, Reid, McEdlroy, & Hamby, 1994[*]).	1.54	4,4
The skills used in this study included behavior contracting, self-recording, self-monitoring, and self-reinforcement. Self-instructional materials in reading, writing, and math were used as the curriculum, and the dependent variables in the study were the number of lessons completed per student per day in the three academic areas (Seabaugh & Schumaker, 1994[*]).	1.29	11
The effects of self-monitoring alone, and in combination with external contingent reward, on sight word acquisition were compared across two groups of learning disabled students (Lalli & Shapiro, 1990[*]).	1.77	8
In this study, three forms of self-monitoring (attention, productivity, and accuracy) were investigated (Maag, Reid, & DiGangi, 1993[*]).	1.28	6
In this study, the first experiment was designed to test the effects of self-instructional procedures on the academic performance of children with learning disabilities (Swanson & Scarpati, 1985[*]).	1.51	3
The effects of overt, semi-overt, and covery self-instructional procedures on reading comprehension was examined in this study (Weidler, 1986[*]).	1.03	4
SOCIAL SKILLS TRAINING		
The purpose of this study was to measure the impact of resource interventions upon the level of peer acceptance and self-concept (Sheare, 1978).	.75	82
The efficacy of training adolescents with learning disabilities in social and problem-solving skills was evaluated by conducting a group skill-training program which emphasized giving positive and negative feedback, accepting negative feedback, resisting peer pressure, negotiation and problem solving in social situations (Hazel, Schumaker, Sherman, & Sheldon, 1982[*]).	1.67	7

(continued)

Table 1.   (Continued)

CATEGORY	Effect Size[a]	N
The study used a post-test only control group design to test the relationship between a nonverbal-oriented social acceptance training method and social ratings. The goal was to sensitize the Ss' to appropriate use of nonverbal behaviors (Straub & Roberts, 1983[*]).	.83	33
Social skills training was based on a Human development program (16 weeks). Discussion was a primary focus of the intervention. Media was used to support concepts introduced in discussion (e.g. video). (Wanat, 1983).	.34	30
Behavioral instruction procedures designed to teach the skills involved in completing employment application materials were evaluated using a multiple baseline design (Mathews & Fawcett, 1984[*]).	1.68	3
The effects of training procedures in the area of social skills were evaluated in this study. The study focused on positive styles of interaction in the workplace, specifically explaining a problem to a supervisor, providing constructive criticism, accepting criticism, accepting a compliment, accepting an instruction, and providing a compliment (Whang, Fawcett & Mathews, 1984[*]).	1.52	2
The study evaluated the effectiveness of social skills training and cross-age tutoring for improving academic skills (specifically spelling) and social communication behaviors. The treatment groups included: social skills training and tutoring, social skills training only, and a no treatment control group (Ruhl, Hughes, & Gajar, 1990).	$.64^2$	30
Public Law 101-467, the Individuals with Disabilities Education Act of 1990, specifies that students with disabilities, especially secondary-level students, should have an opportunity to participate in IEP conferences. This study investigated the effectiveness of strategy instruction designed to foster Ss' active participation in IEP conferences. High school students and their parents participated in either strategy instruction or an orientation lecture/discussion (Van Reusen & Bos, 1994).	.59	21

STRATEGY INSTRUCTION (SI)

SI- Behavior

The impact of alternative thinking on overt behavior of learning impaired second and third graders was examined. Measures of alternative problem solutions, classroom behavior, and reading proficiency were obtained before and after subjects participated in a therapeutic tutoring program. Some Ss received formal training in interpersonal problem solving as well as tutoring while others received only tutoring (Helper, Farber, & Feldgaier, 1982).	.28	86
Special education resource teachers trained impulsive learning disabled children to use Verbal Self-Instruction (VSI) to decrease the children's impulsivity. Ss were identified as impulsive by the Matching Familiar Figures Test and ratings by regular classroom teachers (Graybill, Jamison, & Swerdlik, 1984).	.56	16

(continued)

Table 1.   (Continued)

CATEGORY	Effect Size[a]	N
Verbal self instruction procedures were used to modify impulsivity in boys with learning disabilities. (Nelson, 1985).	.62	18
This study compared two treatment groups: Self-instruction (Meichembaum, 1977) and relaxation training (Jacobson, 1938[*]), and a no-treatment control group. Treatment groups were given 10 half-hour sessions over four weeks and were assessed before and after the treatment on cognitive tasks requiring deliberation (Zieffle & Romney, 1985).	.56	30
This study focused on enhancing Ss' roles as control agents for overall strategic functioning in the classroom. The goal was to increase the ability of Ss to generate new strategies or adapt previously learned task-specific strategies for meeting varying demands of the regular classroom. The SUCCESS Strategy (Ellis, 1985[*]) was highlighted (Ellis, Deshler, & Schumaker, 1989).	1.48	13

SI-General Problem Solving

LD students trained to use planful strategic behavior in the game-instruction situation. Three strategies were taught: Main ideation, Subordinate ideation, and Sequencing (Olsen, Wong, & Marx, 1983).	1.47	30
The study used a Strategies Intervention Model which focused on Ss being taught *how* to learn instead of mastering specific content material. Ss learned a problem-solving strategy for word identification, paraphrasing to improve recall of main ideas, and sentence construction skills (Losh, 1991, Dissertation).	.20	64

SI-Handwriting

This study examined the effect of allowing a student to choose among two handwriting strategies in comparison to teacher determined choices of strategies on the handwriting performance on a paragraph-copying task. The first strategy emphasized review of typical handwriting rules (such as punctuation, staying on the line, and correct proportioning of letters) prior to copying the paragraph. The second strategy emphasized circling quality work on the paper immediately following the copying task (Kosiewicz, Hallahan, & Lloyd, 1981[*]).	1.69	1

SI-Health

This study investigated the effectiveness of an explicit strategy as a means of linking facts, concepts, and problem solving in an unfamiliar domain of learning. Ss were learning disabled and were taught health facts and concepts, which they then applied to problem-solving exercises presented through computer-simulation games (Hollingsworth & Woodward, 1993).	.67	37

SI-Math

Instruction focused on strategies for solving word problems. Ss were trained in computational selection which included strategies for identifying when to use addition and subtraction. Ss were also trained in five problem-solving steps (Fantasia, 1982, Dissertation[*]).	1.19	6

(continued)

Table 1.   (Continued)

CATEGORY	Effect Size[a]	N
Two experiments were designed to test the effects of self-instructional procedures on the academic performance of educationally handicapped children. Experiment 1 focused on Reading/Spelling; Experiment 2 focused on Math (Swanson & Scarpati, 1985[*]).	1.41	2, 1
This study investigated the effect of an eight-step cognitive strategy on verbal math problem solving performance of six LD students. The cognitive strategy was designed to enable students to read, understand, carry out, and check verbal math problems that are encountered in the general math curriculum at the secondary level. During treatment, Ss received strategy acquisition training, strategy application practice and testing. The eight steps included reading the problem aloud, then paraphrasing it, visualizing by graphically displaying it, stating the problem, hypothesizing how many steps to the problem, estimating the answer, calculating it and self checking (Montague & Bos, 1986[*]).	1.62	6
This investigation was conducted to test the effectiveness of strategy teaching and sequencing practice problems in teaching LD Ss to identify the correct algorithm for solving addition and subtraction word problems (Wilson & Sindelar, 1991).	.68	62
Participants were taught a strategy for comprehending math problems and devising an appropriate solution. Ss learned to apply the strategy first to addition word problems, then to subtraction word problems (Case, Harris, & Graham, 1992[*]).	1.12	4
The study examined the effects of cognitive and metacognitive strategy instruction on the mathematical problem solving of six middle school Ss with learning disabilities. The cognitive strategy was combined with direct instruction (Montague, 1992[*]).	1.34	6
The study investigated the effects of a two-phase cognitive strategy on algebra problem solving of adolescents with LD. The strategy was designed to enable students to represent and solve three types of word problems. The study used a modified multiple baseline with 11 replications as well as a two-group design. Conditions of the multiple-baseline design included baseline, instruction to master, transfer, and maintenance (Hutchinson, 1993[*])	3.97	20
The effects of cognitive strategy instruction on mathematical problem-solving performance was examined. The study included three treatment conditions and two cycles of treatment: Direct Instruction in cognitive strategies, Metacognitive activities for solving mathematical word problems, and a combination of cognitive and metacognitive strategy instruction (Montague, Applegate, & Marquard, 1993).	.35	96
The effects of tape-recorded cues on the mathematics performance of students with learning disabilities were investigated. The conditions included: SIT -Ss received Self-Instruction Training; Ss observed SIT, but did not partake (Wood, Rosenberg, & Carran, 1993[*]).	1.39	1
In this study, the efficacy of using manipulatives in teaching elementary aged student with learning disabilities to identify the correct operation to use when solving math problems was investigated (Marsh & Cooke, 1996)	1.82	3

(continued)

Table 1. (Continued)

CATEGORY	Effect Size[a]	N
SI-Reading		
This study investigated the hypothesis that insufficient metacomprehension is one possible cause underlying learning disabled adolescents' comprehension problems, and that training them to monitor their understanding of important textual elements fosters metacomprehension and improves their comprehension performance. Half of the Ss received a 5-step self-questioning training in which they learned to monitor their understanding of important textual units. The other half of the Ss received no training, but had the same materials as the experimental group (Wong & Jones, 1982).	.56	120
A comparison was made of the efficacy of metacomprehension plus direct instruction, direct instruction alone, and a control training condition in finding the main idea (Graves, 1986).	3.13	24
This study reported two interrelated, exploratory training studies to promote word knowledge and textual comprehension through elaboration in poor readers compared with their controls (Leong, Simmons, & Izatt-Gambell, 1990).	1.04	30,41
The participants in the study were taught to use a self-questioning strategy for the identification of main ideas. They were randomly assigned to either a standard instruction or a generalization induction condition. In the latter, informed training and self-instructional training techniques were employed to promote generalization of strategy use. The study aimed to examine the effects of strategy generalization instruction on the comprehension performance of students with reading disabilities (Chan, 1991).	.81	60
The study investigated the use of dialogical thinking-reading lessons in which the S was engaged in reasoning and reflective thinking in order to decide what to believe about a central issue related to a story. Ss were asked to consider the evidence for two hypothesized explanatory conclusions regarding an important question (Commeyras, 1992).	1.34	14
The study utilized a comprehension procedure that makes visible to students their prior knowledge about a topic and the structures in expository text. The procedure used reciprocal-like teaching formats for the design of group interactions during instruction, as well as semantic mapping to make text structures apparent to students (Englert & Mariage, 1991).	1.32	28
The study used a Strategies Intervention Model which focused on Ss being taught *how* to learn instead of mastering specific content material. Ss learned a problem-solving strategy for word identification, paraphrasing to improve recall of main ideas, and sentence construction skills (Losh, 1991, Dissertation).	.20	64
This author investigated using self-instruction to aid readers in looking for clues in reading (Reilly, 1991, Dissertation).	.32	39
The Interactive Teaching Project tested an instructional model designed to facilitate text comprehension and content learning for LD Ss. Semantic Mapping and Charting of concepts were compared (Bos & Anders, 1992).	.70	73

(continued)

Table 1. (Continued)

CATEGORY	Effect Size[a]	N
This study examined the effectiveness of a summarization strategy for increasing reading comprehension of Ss with LD. Direct Instruction was used (Gajria & Salvia, 1992).	4.46	30
This study addressed the effectiveness of teacher acquisition and implementation of two methods for improving the comprehension skills of LD Ss: Instruction in teaching specific questioning strategies (Question - Answer - Response QARS) and selected traditional methods of reading comprehension instruction (Simmonds, 1992).	1.54	447
This study investigates an instructional program designed to help students with learning disabilities learn about the concept of theme, identify themes in stories, and apply themes to real life (Williams, Brown, Silverstein, & deCani, 1994).	.94	30
This study investigated the effectiveness of an interactive vocabulary instructional strategy, semantic feature analysis, on the content area text comprehension of adolescents with learning disabilities (Bos, Anders, Filip, & Jaffe, 1989)	1.63	50
In this study, the effects of a story mapping procedure on reading comprehension was investigated among intermediate level students with learning disabilities (Idol & Croll, 1987[*]).	1.63	4
Five 8-10-year-old children with dysphonetic and dyseidetic dyslexia were given instruction in reading comprehension using a story grammar strategy in which story instruction was differentially designed to match the simultaneous or sequential mental processing strengths of each dyslexia subtype (Newby, Caldwell, & Recht, 1989[*]).	1.21	5
The purpose of this study was to determine whether adolescent students with learning disabilities could effectively be taught a reading comprehension strategy within a main-streamed educational environment. The strategy emphasized steps to identify key information in content-area text, depict how that information is related or organized and apply that information (Scanlon, Deshler, & Schumaker, 1996).	.80	17
This study examined the unique and combined contributions of instruction in goal setting and self-instructions on the acquisition, maintenance, and generalization of a reading comprehension strategy by fourth through sixth grade students with learning disabilities (Johnson, Graham, & Harris, 1997)	47	.59
The efficacy of a package of cognitive self-control procedures for decreasing the attention deficits and increasing academic productivity among twelve year old students with learning disabilities was investigated (Brown, & Alford, 1984).	.65	20
Writing		
The purpose of this study was to determine the effect of teaching LD adolescents an error-monitoring learning strategy with spelling, capitalization, punctuation and appearance errors. The COPS (Capitalization, Overall appearance, Punctuation, Spelling) was used (Schumaker, Deshler, Alley, Warner, Clark & Nolan, 1982[*]).	1.50	9

(continued)

Table 1. (Continued)

CATEGORY	Effect Size[a]	N
The single subject experiment explored the effect of providing an additional oral prompt to "write as many words and ideas as you can about a picture" on the amount of writing produced during a writing activity (Kraetsch, 1981[*]).	1.58	1
Writing: Cooperative Skills Training in reading with the strategies of self-questioning and paraphrasing, and in writing with the strategies in sentences and error monitoring. Cooperative Skills Training included four parts: Orientation to types of goal structures, Activation, Skill training, and Pre-strategy training (Beals, 1985, Dissertation[*]).	1.50	28
Ss taught the three stages of writing (five steps of prewriting, then drafting, revision). Ss wrote about topics in which they could express an opinion. Two revision strategies were taught: COPS (Capitalization, Overall appearance, Punctuation, Spelling) and Evaluative and Directive Phrases (Reynolds, 1986, Dissertation).	.52	54
This study focused on handwriting. A card showing seven self-instructional questions designed to prompt Ss to think about important aspects of handwriting was provided to two LD elementary students in a multiple baseline design. Daily assessments were made regarding letter formation, letter proximity to the line, letter height, and word spacing (Blandford & Lloyd, 1987[*]).	1.66	2
Self-instructional strategy was the focus of this study with Ss exhibiting composition deficiencies. Incremental effects of explicit self-regulation procedures were examined in terms of writing performance measures (Graham & Harris, 1989).	.40	33
The effects of mechanical interference, rate of production, and contentless production signals to write more on the quantity and quality of fourth- and sixth-grade LD Ss' compositions were examined (Graham, 1990).	1.19	23
The study investigated the impact of a reciprocal peer editing strategy on students' knowledge about writing and revising, their actual revising activity, and the quality of their writing. Ss learned to work in pairs to help each other improve their compositions. The process approach to writing instruction was used with word processing to support the writing process (MacArthur, Schwartz, & Graham, 1991).	.59	29
This study was conducted to determine if a planning and writing strategy would improve the essay writing of Ss with LD. Four Ss were taught a strategy designed to facilitate the setting of product and process goals, generation and organization of notes, continued planning during writing, and evaluation of goal attainment. A multiple-probe across subjects design was used (Graham, MacArthur, Schwartz, & Page-Voth, 1992[*]).	1.66	4
The study examined the effects of a socially mediated instructional program, Cognitive Strategy Instruction in Writing (CSIW). The program emphasized talk about the writing process, strategies, and text structures and incorporated the four features of strategy instruction (Englert, Raphael, & Anderson, 1992).	1.26	63

(continued)

Table 1. (Continued)

CATEGORY	Effect Size[a]	N
This study investigated the effectiveness of a metacognitive strategy, the *PLEASE* strategy, for teaching Ss with LD to write paragraphs. (P- *Pick* a topic, audience, format; L - *List* information regarding the topic to used in the organizational planning; E - *Evaluate* how to best organize information; A - *Activate* the paragraph with a topic sentence; S - *Supply* supporting sentences; E - *End* with a concluding sentence and evaluate (check work) (Welch, 1992).	2.11	18
The study investigated the effectiveness of an instructional intervention which was designed to teach students with LD to write a sequential expository paragraph (i.e. a set of directions) through strategy instruction and the use of a set of structured writing frameworks (Cole, 1993, Dissertation[*]).	1.78	12
The study examined the effectiveness of embedding strategy instruction in the context of a process approach to writing in inclusive classrooms. Through a series of extended mini-lessons during writers' workshop, both Ss with and without LDs were taught a previously validated writing strategy and procedures for regulating the strategy and the writing process (Danoff, Harris, & Graham, 1993[*]).	1.57	6
This study investigated the effects of procedural and substantive facilitation-specifically, instruction in character development-on the quality and length of narratives written by 9 junior high school students with learning disabilities. A multiple baseline design across triads was used to determine the effects of treatment (Montague & Leavell, 1994[*]).	.96	9
Instruction in how to dictate plans for writing persuasive essays was compared with instruction in how to make handwritten plans. Of interest was the effects of intervention on time for advanced planning, number of propositions in students plans, transformations, composing rate, and coherence, and quality of essays (De La Paz, 1995).	1.57	42
The study examined the effects of a self-management procedure designed to teach Ss with learning and behavior problems to improve the completeness (inclusion of identified story elements) and quality (organization and coherence) of their story compositions. The procedure was based on two strategies: teaching the students to plan stories composed in a narrative style, and teaching them to monitor the inclusion of elements from the plan with a check-off system (Martin & Manno, 1995[*]).	1.34	3
Students were taught how to use a prestructured web to assist them in planning narrative writing. Of interest was the effects of intervention on planning time and quality of writing for children in the intermediate grades (Zipprich, 1995[*]).	1.33	13
The purpose of the study was to determine whether a self-control strategy training procedure was effective in improving the quality of compositions generated by adolescents with learning disabilities (Harris & Graham, 1985[*]).	1.44	2
This study investigated the effects of teaching a metacognitive text structure strategy upon the paragraph writing skills of eighth-grade students with learning disabilities. The technique, called Statement-Pie (Hanau, 1974[*]), teaches students to understand the relationship of supporting details to a main idea (Wallace & Bott, 1989[*]).	1.45	4

(continued)

Table 1. (Continued)

CATEGORY	Effect Size[a]	N
Adolescent students with learning disabilities were taught how to plan, write, and revise opinion essays using interactive dialogue and compared to a no-treatment control (Wong, Butler, Ficzere & Kuperis, 1996).	1.90	38
The efficacy of the self-regulated strategy development model of writing nstruction as an approach to planning persuasive essays before and during composing was investigated (De La Paz, 1997).	1.76	2

STUDY SKILLS TRAINING

CATEGORY	Effect Size	N
Ss were given eight 20-minute sessions of training in test-taking skills particular to the Stanford Achievement Test. Eight scripted lessons for each grade were provided in a direct instruction format. Specific test-taking strategies were taught for each reading subtest in the SAT (Scruggs & Tolfa 1985).	.56	16
Experimental Ss received training in how to take the Math and Reading Subtests on the Stanford Achievement Test (SAT). Training included deductive reasoning strategies, checking their work, monitoring their place on the answer sheet and more. The treatment was compared with a no-treatment control group (Scruggs, Mastropieri, & Tolfa-Viet, 1986).	.33	85
The purpose of this study was to design and evaluate the effects of teaching a comprehensive test-taking strategy to adolescents with LD. The strategy, which comprised a carefully sequenced set of cognitive and overt behaviors designed for the test-taking task, was taught to six secondary Ss using a seven-stage instructional methodology including description, modeling, verbal rehearsal, initial practice, advanced practice, posttesting and generalization. A multiple-probe across-subjects design was used to assess the Ss acquisition of the strategy (Hughes & Schumaker, 1991[*]).	1.83	6
The study investigated a test-taking strategy which included writing mnemonic symbols (Letter Mnemonic Strategy and Paired Associates Strategy) and incorporated self-instruction and goal-setting for learning the strategy (Kim, 1992 Dissertation).	1.26	8
The effects of explicit and implicit training of test taking skills was examined for fourth grade Ss classified as LD. Both the Explicit and the Implicit Groups received four hours of scripted training exercises involving worksheet activities and completion of simulated tests (Maron, 1993, Dissertation).	.49	13

VISUAL DISPLAY

Graphic Organizers

CATEGORY	Effect Size	N
The study examined the relative effectiveness of two approaches to teaching LD Ss literal comprehension during content area instruction in social studies and science. One approach utilized an advanced organizer as a visual spatial display and was compared to a method in which Ss were presented content via text. Both groups were provided with study strategies (Darch & Carnine, 1986[*]).	1.43	24

(*continued*)

Table 1.   (Continued)

CATEGORY	Effect Size[a]	N
This study examined the relative effectiveness of visual spatial displays to enhance comprehension of important information during science instruction with adolescent LD Ss. The treatment group utilized a graphic organizer as a visual spatial display and was compared to a method in which Ss were presented content via text (Darch & Eaves, 1986).	1.26	22
Two direction-setting activities designed to increase high-school LD students' comprehension of important concepts during content area instruction were compared. One group was taught with prereading activities based on a basal approach to teaching comprehension. The major focus was on developing student interest and motivation, highlighting the relevance of the passage to the students' past experience, and offering a general introductory discussion. The second group received instruction using an advanced organizer in the form of a text outline designed to help Ss process information from the text (Darch & Gersten, 1986).	1.13	24
Graphic Organizers were examined as a means for increased acquisition and recall on science content (Griffin, Simmons, & Kameenui, 1991).	.41	28
Semantic Mapping		
The Semantic Mapping technique, with three different types of semantic maps, was compared with the verbal readiness approach for reading comprehension (Sinatra, Stahl-Gemake & Berg, 1984).	.22	27
The focus of instruction was on semantic mapping to aid in memorization of information read (Carter, 1985, Dissertation).	.55	8
Reading Comprehension: Semantic Feature Analysis (SFA) used with a content area vocabulary and reading comprehension instructional strategy. The control group used a vocabulary look-up approach (Bos, Anders, Filip & Jaffe, 1985).	1.63	50
This study examined the potential of a specific strategy, text structure recognition and use, for increasing LD high school students' recall of expository prose (Smith & Friend, 1986).	2.52	54
Semantic Mapping to aide in memorization and reading comprehension of information read. "Thinking aloud protocols" were used to identify cognitive processes during prose recall (Swanson, Kozleski, & Stegink, 1987[*]).	.92	2
The study evaluated the effectiveness of Concept Diagrams and a related Concept Teaching Routine. Ss were evaluated relative to performance on Tests of Concept Acquisition, regular classroom tests, and notetaking before and after implementation of the Concept Teaching Routine (Bulgren, Schumaker, & Deshler, 1988).	.63[2]	64
This study compared the effectiveness of three interactive vocabulary strategies. The three interactive strategies were: semantic mapping, semantic feature analysis, and semantic/syntactic feature analysis. The control group received definition instruction (Bos & Anders, 1990).	.66	61

(continued)

Table 1.   (Continued)

CATEGORY	Effect Size[a]	N
The Interactive Teaching Project tested an instructional model designed to facilitate text comprehension and content learning for LD Ss. Semantic Mapping and Charting of concepts were compared (Bos & Anders, 1992).	.89	73

Visual Imagery

This study was designed to examine the extent to which Ss with reading disabilities would benefit from instruction in the use of a visual-imagery strategy for word recognition and reading comprehension relative to younger average readers with comparable word-recognition skills (Chan, Cole, & Morris, 1990).	.37	78

WORD DISCRIMINATION STRATEGIES

Phoneme discrimination

   1. *Spelling*

The investigation of this study looked at the degree to which varying the number of spelling words taught relates to the percentage of words spelled correctly by learning disabled children. Ss were divided into three treatment groups that differed only in the number of phonemically irregular spelling words taught (three, four, or five per day) across three days of instruction (Bryant, Drabin, & Gettinger, 1981).	.84	64
The study investigated the effects of instructing Ss in a strategy for spelling new words by using spelling patterns from known words. This method was contrasted with Ss who learned to read and spell sight word vocabulary (Englert, Hiebert, & Stewart, 1985).	.77	22
The study utilized the Simultaneous Oral Spelling (SOS) method. The study had two purposes. The first was to evaluate both the short- and long-term effectiveness of the SOS procedure for a group of children with long-standing unremediated reading disability. The second was to investigate the validity of the dysphonetic/dyseidetic (Chinese/Phonecian) classification among a group of disabled readers in terms of differential effects of the remedial procedure (Prior, Frye, & Fletcher, 1987).	1.24	27
Blending and spelling training were compared in this experiment to determine which intervention would improve the decoding skills of two first-grade boys with learning disabilities who were in the phonetic cue stage of reading. Additionally, the two boys received pre-and posttest administrations of a phonemic segmentation task (DiVeta & Speece, 1990[*]).	.59	2

   2. *Reading*

The study focused on the use of an intensive phonetic teaching program for reading remediation over four months in comparison with non-specific academic tutoring (Gittelman & Feingold, 1983).	.50	56

(continued)

Table 1.   (Continued)

CATEGORY	Effect Size[a]	N
The study was designed to increase an adult male's oral reading performance. A direct instruction approach was used to teach lacking phonics skills (Idol-Maestas, 1981[*]).	.67	1
Two experiments using pseudo-words as stimuli were reported, showing that poor readers from third grade were inferior to good readers in the utilization of intraword redundancy (Experiment 1) and that poor readers' performance with redundant stimuli can be increased when the stimuli are grouped into syllables (Experiment 2). A reading intervention program was then presented in which the children were taught how to segment words into syllables (Scheerer-Neumann, 1981).	1.23	30
Ss in this study either received training in word recognition and decoding skills, oral and written language, or classroom survival skills (Lovett, Ransby, & Barron, 1988).\	.41	112
College students diagnosed as learning disabled were studied to determine whether they would make more progress in a summer program if taught by an adaptation of the Orton-Gillingham phonics approach (Guyer & Sabatino, 1989).	0	30
Ss in this study either received training in word recognition and decoding skills, oral and written language, or classroom survival skills (Lovett, Ransby, Hardwick, Johns, & Donaldson, 1989).	.39	178
The objective of this study was to utilize a mnemonic device to teach ten letter cluster sound associations to 17 reading disabled subjects. Direct Instruction was incorporated into the intervention (Smith, 1989, Dissertation).	.74	34
The study included two experiments. Experiment 1 examined disabled and nondisabled readers' ability to discriminate between combinations of two-syllable, phoneme pairs with varying intersyllable intervals. Experiment 2 Ss were those who performed poorly in Experiment 1. They were trained on phonemic stimuli which became increasingly complex (Hurford & Sanders, 1990).	.40[2]	52,32
The study included two word recognition and spelling training programs and a problem-solving & study skills training program. One word-training program taught orthographically regular words by whole word methods alone; the other trained constituent grapheme-phoneme correspondences. The word-training groups made significant gains in word recognition accuracy and speed and in spelling (Lovett, Warren-Chaplin, Ransby, & Borden, 1990).	.76	54
Children identified in kindergarten as being at risk for reading disability were taught in grades one and two using one of two strategies for word recognition, a structured phonics code-emphasis approach or an approach emphasizing use of context (Brown, & Felton, 1990).	.50	48
Ss in this study included delinquents in two detention facilities. The treatment group received remedial reading instruction using an Orton Gillianham approach (Simpson, Swanson, & Kunkel, 1992).	.54	63

(continued)

Table 1. (Continued)

CATEGORY	Effect Size[a]	N
This study compared two forms of word identification training to promote transfer of learning by children with dyslexia. One program trained phonological analysis and blending skills and provided direct instruction of letter-sound correspondences. The other trained the acquisition, use and monitoring of four metacognitive decoding strategies (Lovett, Borden, DeLuca, Lacerenza, Benson, & Brackstone, 1994).	.56	62

Whole word discrimination

 1. *Spelling*

The study investigated the effects of instructing Ss in a strategy for spelling new words by using spelling patterns from known words. This method was contrasted with Ss who learned to read and spell sight word vocabulary (Englert, Hiebert, & Stewart, 1985).	.77	22

 2. *Reading*

Word Recognition: A whole-word approach that used a multi-sensory technique for developing reading skills, including the Fernald Method of tracing letters and a Total Body Movement Learning Game (Waterman, 1974, Dissertation).	.95	34
The Oralographic Reading Program (Kobler & Kobler, 1979[*]) was compared with the progress of disabled learners in current special reading programs. The components of the program included printed lessons sheets and sound disks or tapes, used with a Talking Typewriter, printed extended reading selections and record keeping materials (Ratekin, 1979).	.88	89
Written reproduction technique to increase word recognition. Student looks at target word on a computer and copies the word using pencil and paper (Berninger, Lester, Sohlberg, & Mateer, 1991).	1.19	28
The study evaluated the effect of applying a mastery learning model to sight word instruction for LD elementary school children. Ss were taught 30 sight words in nine lessons which incorporated mastery learning strategies, and a comparison group with methods that are typically used in the teaching of sight words (Bryant, Fayne, & Gettinger, 1982).	1.59	48
The study included two word recognition and spelling training programs and a problem-solving & study skills training program. One word-training program taught orthographically regular words by whole word methods alone; the other trained constituent grapheme-phoneme correspondences. The word-training groups made significant gains in word recognition accuracy and speed and in spelling (Lovett, Warren-Chaplin, Ransby, & Borden, 1990).	.76	54
The effect of varying rates of practice on learning sight words was compared among students in the intermediate grades (Cuvo, Ashley, Marso, & Zhang, 1995[*]).	1.81	5

(continued)

Table 1.   (Continued)

CATEGORY	Effect Size[a]	N
Oral reading practice		
Oral Reading: Two oral-reading previewing procedures were investigated. *Silent* reading previous to reading aloud and *listening* to the teacher read the passage aloud previous to reading aloud (Rose & Sherry, 1984[*]).	1.72	5
The relative efficacy of three error-correction techniques on the oral reading of adolescent students with learning disabilities was investigated. The three procedures were: drill, word-supply, and phonic-drill (Rosenberg, 1986[*])	1.05	3
The relative efficacy of three error-correction techniques on the oral reading of adolescent students with learning disabilities was investigated. The three procedures were: drill, word-supply, and phonic-drill (Rosenberg, 1986[*])	1.05	3
This study examined the effects on reading fluency of two interventions involving rereading of passages (Weinstein & Cooke, 1992[*]).	1.75	3
The study used the instructional hierarchy to compare the effects of three instructional interventions (listening passage preview, subject passage preview, and taped words) on subjects' oral reading performance on word lists and passages (Daly & Martens, 1993[*]).	1.00	4

Notes: Effect sizes reported are the absolute average effect size using LD comparison groups for each study. ES for maintenance conditions are not included in the average effect size. Studies were categorized according to the *primary* focus of intervention. Some studies are reported under more than one category if they addressed more than one type of intervention in the study.

[*]These studies are single-subject designs. The complete references are found on pages 133-136 in H. L. Swanson & C. Sachse-Lee (2000). A meta-analysis of single-subject-design intervention research for students with LD. *Journal of Learning Disabilities, 33,* 114-136.

[1]Due to missing data, maintenance data was used in the calculation of the effect size.

[2]Non-LD control group outcomes were used to calculate effect sizes.

[3]Effect size was calculated using adjusted means.

the meta-analysis (with outliers removed) and the instructional domains they cover. The right-hand column of Table 1 reports an overall mean treatment effect size found in each study and the sample size. The dependent measures (e.g., achievement measures) which were different than the focus of the study are *not* reported in this table (Instead see Appendix D, Swanson et al., 1999). As is evident in Table 1, some studies and some academic or cognitive domains are represented in more than one category of treatment. Effect sizes, averaged within studies as a function of the 17 general categories of *dependent* measures (to be discussed), are provided in Appendix D of Swanson et al. (1999).

Prototype Study

Table 2 provides a summary of the most frequent (or average) characteristics of studies. The table is divided into characteristics related to articles, instruction,

Table 2. Characteristics of Group Design
Studies in Synthesis (outliers removed)

Group Design	Total (n = 180)*	
	M	SD
Effect Size (Cohen d)	.56	.67
Effect Size-absolute	.79	.52
Article Characteristics		
Year of Pub	1987	5.41
Number—Authors	1.32	1.23
Number—Citations	1.80	3.37
Number—Citations (%)	57% not cited	
Author Gender (%)	41% male	
Funding Source (%)		
No Funding Cited	64%	
U. S. Dept of Educ	12%	
NICHD	4%	
State/Province	4%	
Other	10%	
Publication Outlets (%)		
Dissertation	13%	
Journal of Learning Disabilities	16%	
Learning Disability Quarterly	13%	
Learning Disabilities Research & Practice	7%	
Exceptional Children	7%	
Journal of Special Education	4%	
Journal of Educational Psychology	4%	
Other	36%	
Most Frequent Affiliation		
1. Columbia University University of Arizona University of Houston University of Maryland Michigan State University	15% (each contributed 3% or more)	
2. Purdue Simon Frasier University of Southern California University of Miami Arizona State University University of Toronto (Children's Sick Hospital)	14% (each contributed between 1.5 and 3%)	

(continued)

Table 2.   (Continued)

Group Design	Total (n = 180)[*]	
	M	SD
Instructional Parameters		
Time of Instruction	M	SD
Number Instruction Sessions	22.47	29.71
Length of Session (Min)	35.72	21.72
Number—Sessions per Week	3.58	1.58
Setting of Intervention (%)		
No Information	56%	
Self-Contained (other)	18%	
Resource Room	23%	
Regular Class	2%	
Primary Focus of Intervention (%)		
Reading	54%	
Math	10%	
Written Language	11%	
Language	2%	
Information Processing Abilities	6%	
Behavior	1%	
Problem Solving	1%	
Perceptual	1%	
Other	14%	
Sample Parameters (%)		
Most frequent reason for participant exclusion from study [*](Those who reported reasons n = 30)		
[*]Other than normal intelligence	20%	
*No reading problems	10%	
*No reading or math problems	3%	
*Achievement consistent with general ability	10%	
*Other	57%	
Of those not reporting reasons for study exclusion	85% (n = 153)	

(continued)

Table 2. (Continued)

Group Design	Total (n = 180)[*]		
	M	SD	
Geographic location of sample (%)			
No Information	30%		
Midwest	12%		
Southeast	8%		
Non-U.S.	20%		
Educational History (%)			
No Information	50%		
Resource Room	28%		
Other	22%		
Sample Size	27.06	40.15	–
Number of Males	15.54	10.42	(84)[a]
Number of Females	6.66	8.33	(88)
Ethnicity Reported			
Asian American	4.71	6.01	(7)
African American	7.42	7.97	(25)
Anglo	11.67	8.45	(36)
Hispanic	9.36	10.11	(11)
Native American	1.0	-	(2)
Other	2.46	2.07	(2)
Chronological Age	11.16	3.22	
Grade Range (%)			
Elementary	54%		
Secondary	18%		
Mixed	28%		
SES (%)			
No information	40%		
Middle Income	30%		
Mixed	30%		
Psychometric Standardized			
Intelligence	93.51	16.85	(104)
Reading	71.44	26.65	(82)
Math	75.36	25.38	(12)
Methodology Parameters			
Internal Validity[b]			
Rating Scale (ABBR.)			
(4-12 high to low intv)	7.32	1.95	
Complete Scale (10-30)	22.16	2.64	
Variation of CTRL from Treatment (%)			
% Similarity of overlap			
Same Teacher	24%		
Same Materials	27.8%		
Same Setting	34.5%		
Same Instruction Focus	61.9%		

(continued)

Table 2. (Continued)

Group Design	Total (n = 180)[*]	
	M	SD
Group Design (%)		
% Studies Pre-Post Control Group Design	70%	
Measure of Treatment Integrity	18%	
Sampling Procedure (%)		
Intact Sample-No Random Assign. of Treatment	35%	
Intact Sample & Random Assign. of Treatment	42%	
Other (or no information)	23%	
Type of Design (%)		
A. Pretest-Posttest Control Group Design	70%	
B. Posttest only Design W/Random Assign	10%	
C. Factorial Variations of pretest-posttest control group design (e.g., repeated measures design)	18%	
D. Other	2%	
Number of Experiments Reported for Article (%)		
One Experiment	95%	
Two Experiments	4%	
Three Experiments	1%	
Type of Hypothesis (%)		
Directional	34%	
Null	15%	
Nonstated	51%	
Dependent Measures for Treatment Effects	M	SD
Mean Number-Exp. Measures	3.53	4.30
Mean Number Reliability Info.	1.73	1.51

(continued)

Table 2. (Continued)

Group Design	Total (n = 180)[*]	
	M	SD
Number Standardized Measure	2.57	5.73
Freq. Reporting Social Validity Info (%)	20%	

Notes: Some percentages for categorizing comparisons are less than 100% because item examples from 1% to 5% were not listed

[a] ( ) = Number of studies that report information. If left blank, the number of studies reporting information is > 80%.

NIF = No information; TRT = Treatment; CTRL = Control Group; ( ) = % of studies reporting information

sample, and methodology. With outliers removed (N = 9), the analyses yielded 180 group design studies which included 1,537 effect sizes comparing LD students in the experimental condition with LD students in the control condition. The unweighted mean effect size across the 180 studies was .56 (SD = .67) and the absolute value was .79 (SD = .52).[4]

Some of the important characteristics of the studies reported in Table 2 can be summarized as follows. A prototypical intervention study includes 22.47 minutes (SD = 29.71) of daily instruction, 3.58 times a week (SD = 1.58), over 35.72 (SD = 21.72) sessions. The mean sample size for the study is 27.06 (SD = 40.15). The mean treatment age is 11.16 with a standard deviation of 3.22. The most frequent sampling and treatment assignment procedures use (a) participants from an intact sample (a nonrandomly selected sample) with no random assignment to treatment conditions (35%), or (b) an intact sample with random assignment to treatment and control conditions (42% of studies). Approximately 30% of the studies do not indicate the geographic region from which the sample is drawn. For the number of articles reporting the geographic region where the sample was drawn, 20% of the studies include non-U.S. samples of children (e.g., Canada) and 12% of the samples are drawn from the Midwest.

Although the majority of studies had samples identified as LD, studies varied tremendously on the criteria and detail for participant selection. In terms of reporting group mean scores on psychometric information, only 104 studies (64%) reported group mean scores for intelligence, 84 studies (50%) reported group mean scores on achievement scores in reading, and 22 studies (12%) reported group mean scores in mathematics. Beyond IQ, reading, and mathematic scores, psychometric information on other characteristics of the sample was infrequently reported (< 3% of the studies). In terms of those studies that reported scores, 83.7% of the studies that reported IQ scores used the WISC-R as the measure of intelligence, and 20% of the studies that reported achievement scores used the Wide Range Achievement Test as the measure of reading achievement. The mean reported treatment IQ for the LD sample was 93.51 (SD = 16.51, range of 85 to 115). Of those studies reporting standardized reading scores (42%), the mean reported standard score was 71.44 (SD = 25.38).

The average year of publication for studies was 1987 (SD = 5.41), with publication dates ranging from 1972 to 1997. The most frequent year of publication was 1992 (12% of the studies). The most frequent publication outlets were the *Journal of Learning Disabilities* (16%), *Learning Disabilities Research and Practice* (7%), *Learning Disability Quarterly* (13%), and *Exceptional Children* (7%). Thirteen percent of the studies in the synthesis analysis were drawn from dissertations.

Approximately 57% of published articles are not cited in the scientific literature. Approximately 64% of the studies do not report a funding source. Approximately 12% of the studies were funded by the U.S. Department of Education. Approximately 90% of the studies have authors affiliated with institutions of higher education. A typical group design study includes only one experiment (95%).

In terms of subject description, of the studies that report some criteria for subjects identified as LD, more than 50% mention the concept of a discrepancy between achievement and IQ, and differences in IQ and achievement scores, and/ or that LD children were presently placed in a special education class (e.g., pull out classroom). Approximately 56% of the studies do not report the setting in which treatment occurred and 23% report that interventions occurred in resource rooms. Approximately 60% of the studies do not report the time of day that intervention occurred. Based on our coding criteria, approximately 60% of the studies do not report enough detail for replication. Less than half the studies (42.8%) make recommendations for teachers, students, or instruction. Approximately 57% of the studies fail to report the degree or accuracy to which treatment was implemented (referred to as treatment integrity or fidelity).

The internal validity of each study was rated on the following items: (1) subject mortality, (2) Hawthorne effects and selection bias, comparable exposure between treatment and/or controls, (3) materials, (4) instruction time, and (5) teacher, (6) procedural validity checks, (7) practice effects on the dependent measure, (8) floor and ceiling effects, (9) interrater reliability, (10) regression to the mean ruled out as an alternative explanation of findings and, (11) homogeneity of variance between groups. For each of the 11 items, a score of 1 reflects internal validity control, 2 reflects no validity control and 3 reflects no validity information. The mean rating for the 11 items and an abbreviated rating for items 1 to 4 are shown in Table 2.

As shown in Table 2, most studies on the abbreviated internal validity form (items 1 to 4) yield moderate internal validity ratings (rating score around 7, a score of 4 reflects high internal validity). In terms of reporting reliability of

Table 3. Weighted Mean Effect Sizes for Group Design Studies as a Function of Dependent Measure Category

LD Treatment vs. LD Control	N	K	Effect Size d Unweighted*	Effect Size d Weighted[a]	95% Confidence Interval for Weighted Effects Lower	Upper	Standard Error	Homogeneity (Q)
1. Cognitive Processing	41	115	.87 (.64)	.54	.48	.61	.03	311.67**
1a. Metacognitive	9	27	.98	.80	.66	.94	.07	83.91**
1b. Attribution	7	17	.79	.62	.44	.79	.08	31.99*
1c. Other Processes	25	71	.65	.46	.38	.53	.03	176.07**
2. Word Recognition	54	159	.71 (.56)	.57	.52	.62	.02	431.45**
2a. Standardized	23	79	.79	.62	.54	.69	.04	205.61**
2b. Experimental	35	80	.72	.53	.48	.60	.03	223.073**
3. Reading Comprehension	58	176	.82 (.60)	.72	.68	.77	.02	565.95**
3a. Standardized	16	38	.45	.45	.36	.54	.05	33.87
3b. Experimental	44	138	.84	.81	.75	.86	.02	489.54**
4. Spelling	24	54	.54 (.53)	.44	.37	.52	.04	100.44**
4a. Standardized	8	20	.61	.45	.34	.57	.06	34.45
4b. Experimental	18	34	.48	.44	.33	.54	.05	65.94**
5. Memory/Recall	12	33	.81 (.46)	.56	.43	.70	.06	42.72
6. Mathematics	28	71	.58 (.45)	.40	.33	.46	.04	128.28**
6a. Standardized	9	22	.41	.33	.23	.46	.05	25.72
6b. Experimental	21	49	.59	.42	.34	.51	.04	101.43***

(continued)

Table 3. Weighted Mean Effect Sizes for Group Design Studies as a Function of Dependent Measure Category

LD Treatment vs. LD Control	N	K	Effect Size d Unweighted*	Effect Size d Weighted[a]	95% Confidence Interval for Weighted Effects		Standard d Error	Homogeneity (Q)
7. Writing	19	67	.84 (.60)	.63	.54	.72	.05	157.45**
7a. Standardized	3	7	.37	.36	.14	.58	.11	5.01
7b. Experimental	16	60	.80	.68	.59	.78	.04	145.27**
8. Vocabulary	11	20	.79 (.44)	.78	.66	.89	.05	38.58**
9. Attitude/Self-Concept	25	86	.68 (.69)	.39	.33	.45	.03	210.65**
10. Intelligence	9	32	.58 (.59)	.41	.30	.52	.06	54.37**
11. General Reading	15	31	.60 (.50)	.52	.41	.65	.06	55.15*
12. Phonics/orthographic Skills	29	175	.70 (.36)	.64	.60	.69	.02	453.70**
12a. Standardized phonics	8	60	.72	.67	.62	.73	.03	275.87**
12b. Experimental phonics	21	78	.76	.60	.52	.67	.04	175.22**
13. Global Achievement (grades, total achievement)	10	21	.91 (.76)	.45	.31	.58	.07	56.64**
14. Creativity	3	11	.84 (.49)	.70	.52	.87	.09	33.61**
15. Social Skills	13	36	.46 (.22)	.41	.30	.51	.05	28.46
16. Perceptual Processes	10	37	.74 (.65)	.26	.17	.35	.04	46.64
17. Language	9	52	.54 (.48)	.36	.28	.44	.04	75.53*

Notes: * $p < .01$. ** $p < .001$
( ) = standard deviation

68

dependent measures, on an average, studies provide reliability information on about 1 of 3 dependent measures.

Materials for the experimental conditions were commercial (33% of the studies), novel (i.e., materials developed by the researcher, 54% of the studies), or a combination of commercial and novel (9% of the studies), or were not classifiable (4 of the studies). The most frequent commercial materials ($N = 54$) were related to direct instruction (e.g., Corrective Reading, Distar, SRA,; 8%), Houghton Mifflin series (4%), Orton-Gillingham approach (4%), and Lindamood-Bell (4%). For those studies that primarily utilized commercial materials in the experimental treatment, 25 of the 54 studies (46%) did not report the materials used (or used no commercial materials) in the control condition. In terms of student activities during treatment, thirty of the studies had participants monitor or evaluate (via recording, counting, charting, checking, graphing, and/or verbalizing) their academic behavior.

Domains of Instruction

Prior to the analysis of effect sizes, it was necessary to separate the effect sizes into categories of dependent measures. The seventeen (17) categories discussed earlier reflect a broad array of treatment domains (e.g., reading, writing, etc). Appendix D in Swanson et al. (1999) provides the mean d effect sizes for each study, as a function of seventeen categorical domains.

Table 3 provides the weighted means and standard deviations of effect sizes (absolute value of d) as a function of the dependent measures across studies. Typically, no intervention study yielded a negative effect size. Some negative effect sizes emerged on the social skill measures (consistent with the expected direction of change for these interventions) and therefore d was converted to an absolute value. If the number of dependent measures (K) within a category exceeded 50, we attempted to subgroup the categories by standardized (normed referenced measures) and experimental (researcher developed) measures. This was not possible for all categories, however, because of the infrequent use of standardized measures. For example, the cognitive processing category was divided into metacognitive, attribution, and "other" because few standardized measures were reported in the primary studies.

There are two findings of primary interest in Table 3. First, the most frequent dependent measures reflected across the various studies are measures of reading. These studies include measures of word recognition, word skills, reading comprehension and general reading. Also frequently represented are measures of cognitive processing. Categories of dependent measures infrequently represented are measures of intelligence, vocabulary, global achievement (grades), creativity, language processing, and memory.

Second, the magnitude of the estimates of effect size related to treatment impact vary considerably across categorical domains. Table 3 shows the

unweighted and weighted mean Cohen's *d* effect sizes for the general categories and subcategories. Based on the weighted effect sizes reported in Table 3,
effect sizes to be considered marginal according to Cohen's criteria (effect
sizes below .45) occurred in the domains of spelling, mathematics, attitude,
intelligence, social skills, perceptual processes and language processes. Those
areas which approached Cohen's (1988) threshold of .80 for a "large effect"
are reading comprehension (.72), vocabulary (.78), and creativity (.70). When
the categories are divided into subcategories, the high effect sizes related to
reading comprehension emerged on experimental ($M = .84$) measures when
compared to standardized measures ($M = .45$). The subcategory related to
metacognition also yielded an effect size (.80) that met Cohen's criteria.

The relationship between the year of publication and the type of dependent
measure was analyzed to determine if some domains have been researched
more recently. The point biserial correlations between the domain of the
dependent measures (scored dichotomously as 1 and 0, e.g., word recognition
measure = 1 and other measures = 0) and year of publication were all weak in
magnitude, all $rs < .20$. The two coefficients of the highest magnitude indicate
that the year of publication and nonstandardized word skill measures were positively related, ($r = .17$, $p < .05$), whereas a decrease in the use of standardized
real word recognition measures has emerged over the years ($r = -.19$, $p < .01$).

Overall, the striking feature of the categories of dependent measures (data
reported in Table 3) is the strong skew toward high effect sizes across all academic domains when unweighted effect sizes are considered. It appears that most
experimental treatments have a bias for positive effects, as well as small sample
sizes, and therefore, it seems implausible we have presented a valid picture of the
efficacy of interventions for students with learning disabilities. Further, these
effect sizes are difficult to interpret because comparisons are not really between a
treatment and a nontreatment condition, but rather reflect a treatment of interest to
the researcher (typically the experimental treatment) and "treatment as usual"
which includes typical classroom instruction (see Lipsey & Wilson, 1993, for further discussion of this issue). Because the homogeneity tests were significant
across the majority of dependent measures, the subsequent analysis requires inter-
pretations beyond the mean level of effects. The subsequent analyses will attempt
to identify some variables that mediate the effect sizes.

Main Effects

Table 4 provides a comparison of weighted and unweighted effect sizes as a
function of study variations in methodology, article characteristics, setting, sample characteristics and general instructional models. The weighted mean effect
size estimate is the primary measure used to compare studies across the various
contrasts. To assess the stability of the results, two units of analysis were considered. One unit calculates effect size estimates for each dependent measure as if all

Table 4. Effect Size Estimates as a Function of Unit of Analysis, Methodological, Instructional, and Sampling Variables (outliers removed)

	Sample Size	K	Mean	SD	Weighted Mean	Ind. Sample	X²
All Studies	33,845	1207	.66	.59	.54	362	–
	4,871	180	.79	.52	.61		
I. Methodology							
Number of Treatment Sessions							
3 to 10	8,103	353	.66	.57	.51	–	
	1,750	72	.77	.53	.71	138	
11 to 30	7,137	330	.72	.63	.62	–	
	1,462	64	.85	.53	.78	126	
> 31	16,885	507	.62	.57	.57	–	15.72**
	1,411	41	.74	.50	.66	88	3.32[a]
Treatment Integrity (Procedural Validity)							
Reported	18,714	722	.62	.58	.47		
	2,209	67	.81	.51	.74		
Not Reported	12,635	411	.72	.60	.59	132	37.29**
	2,330	103	.82	.55	.69	104	.60
Internal Validity Rating (Includes 5 variables)[b]							
Low	24,668	927	.67	.60	.56	274	
	3,629	135	.83	.55	.74		
High	6,681	206	.63	.54	.48		8.81**
	913	35	.74	.74	.62	66	2.97

(continued)

71

Table 4. (Continued)

All Studies	Sample Size	K	Mean	SD	Weighted Mean	Ind. Sample	X^2
Total Sample Size							
1. < 25	8,643	588	.77	.63	.63		
	1,672	116	.88	.55	.78	232	
2. > 24 and < 50	15,366	508	.55	.55	.48		
	1,624	52	.64	.47	.55	102	
3. > 49 and < 100	5,167	85	.56	.41	.50		
	409	6	.49	.14	.47	12	
4. > 99	4,566	28	.60	.50	.79		94.49**
	1,165	6	.80	.43	1.12	16	49.68**
							(4>1>2=3)
Variation of Teacher (Researcher) in the Admin. of Treatment							
1. Different Teacher-CTRL & Exp	6,254	218	.60	.42	.64		
	1,447	41	.66	.35	.76	80	
2. Same Teacher-CTRL & Exp	12,927	506	.64	.57	.49		
	1,487	70	.77	.47	.62	136	
3. Cannot Determine (no info)	14,561	483	.71	.67	.55		38.92**
	1,936	69	.90	.63	.75	132	6.03*
							(1=3>2)[b]

(continued)

Table 4. (Continued)

All Studies	Sample Size	K	Mean	SD	Weighted Mean	Ind. Sample	X^2
Variation of Setting between CTRL and TRT							
1. CTRL & TRT Occur in different classroom/setting/school	11,786	413	.69	.63	.58	110	
	1,505	60	.82	.53	.69		
2. CTRL & TRT occur in same classroom	8,849	368	.61	.56	.50	64	
	775	39	.70	.45	.59		
3. No Information	13,107	426	.67	.57	.60	188	22.08**
	2,509	81	.82	.54	.71		(3=1;
							3>2,2=1)
							6.31*
							(3=1>2)
Variation of Materials							
Same materials used (booklets commercial materials)	5,079	240	.70	.55	.74	78	
	880	44	.81	.50	.67		
Different materials used	24,165	835	.64	.60	.52	224	
	3,283	112	.84	.56	.73		
No information	4,498	132	.70	.59	.63	58	28.85**
	708	24	.65	.33	.62		2.34

(continued)

73

Table 4. (Continued)

All Studies	Sample Size	K	Mean	SD	Weighted Mean	Ind. Sample	X^2
Domain (Instructional) Focus of Control Group							
1. Same Domain as TRT	16,248	680	.69	.61	.60		
	2,862	108	.82	.33	.74		
2. Different Domain	14,209	410	.58	.54	.47		
	1,439	48	.74	.51	.64		
3. Cannot Determine	3,284	117	.74	.63	.53	–	44.93**
	659	24	.78	.42	.69		3.77
Standardized Testing Included in Pre & Posttest							
1. No	9,058	387	.86	.65	.75		
	2,883	86	.92	.52	.87	166	
2. Yes	20,249	714	.55	.53	.45		208.38**
	1,991	79	.69	.50	.57	190	30.37**
Variation of control from treatment in the number of instructional components and/or steps							
High overlap (> 4 sequences, steps)	10,823	405	.56	.54	.45		
	1,767	67	.71	.51	.58	134	
Low overlap (< 5)	22,919	802	.71	.61	.59		31.06**
	3,104	113	.85	.53	.78	228	12.75**

(continued)

74

Table 4. (Continued)

All Studies	Sample Size	K	Mean	SD	Weighted Mean	Ind. Sample	X^2
Type of Treatment Assignment							
1. No random assignment	7,703	354	.72	.66	.52		
	1,317	61	.67	.53	.67	100	
2. Random assignment	17,965	611	.58	.51	.51		
	2,215	69	.69	.43	.69	138	
3. No information	5,851	242	.78	.63	.66		46.22**
	1,338	50	.77	.59	.77	112	2.73
Methods composite variable (Max. score 14)							
1. < 7	16,620	631	.77	.64	.59		
	3,399	126	.83	.55	.74	244	
2. > 6 & < 11	15,483	528	.55	.51	.50		157.57**
	1,358	51	.72	.45	.62	108	11.33**
3. > 10	1,639	48	.37	.43	.35		(1 > 2 > 3)
	113	3	.46	.11	.41	10	

(continued)

Table 4. (Continued)

All Studies	Sample Size	K	Mean	SD	Weighted Mean	Ind. Sample	X^2
II. Publication Characteristics							
Funding (stated)							
No	16,658	641	.68	.63	.58		
	2,945	117	.84	.57	.75	220	3.20
Yes	15,468	549	.64	.55	.55		
	1,678	60	.70	.41	.65	134	3.71
Publication Outlet							
Journal	31,013	1,065	.68	.60	.59		
	4,416	155	.83	.54	.76	308	
Dissertation/Technical Report	2,729	142	.52	.48	.34		36.45**
	454	25	.57	.32	.42	54	21.59**
III. Setting of Treatment							
Reported Information							
Setting Reported	8,430	397	.77	.64	.62		
	1,956	78	.87	.57	.79	162	
Setting Not Reported	20,613	711	.59	.55	.53		15.12**
	2,915	102	.74	.48	.66	200	7.09*

(continued)

76

Table 4. (Continued)

All Studies	Sample Size	K	Mean	SD	Weighted Mean	Ind. Sample	X^2
Type of Classroom							
1. Self-contained	2,789	161	.72	.57	.57		
	590	33	.84	.57	.69	80	
2. Resource room	4,638	203	.86	.69	.80		
	1,213	41	.90	.59	.89	72	
3. No information	20,613	711	.59	.55	.49		153.59**[a]
	2,032	86[a]	.76	.50	.64	160	16.93**[a]
4. Regular class	1,002	33	.48	.51	.35		(2>1=3=4)
	151	4	.78	.50	.66	8	
IV. Sample Characteristics							
Discrepancy							
Reported > 1 year	7,769	347	.55	.49	.51		
	1,355	29	.76	.43	.74	62	
No information or < 1 year	21,252	759	.70	.63	.59		9.58**
	3,356	136	.82	.55	.72	164	.02

(continued)

Table 4. (Continued)

All Studies	Sample Size	K	Mean	SD	Weighted Mean	Ind. Sample	X^2
Amount of reported psychometric information on sample							
1. No information on intelligence & reading	15,460	517	.75	.66	.62		
	2,560	73	.83	.50	.82	144	
2. Intelligence	6,776	295	.61	.58	.48		
	1,111	55	.80	.58	.62	112	
3. Intelligence & reading	6,290	245	.60	.54	.52		
	849	39	.76	.54	.63	74	
4. Intelligence & reading & mathematics	5,215	150	.53	.41	.46		$X^2 = 58.19^{**}$
	349	13	.66	.28	.60	32	$X^2 = 13.50^{**}$
							(1 > 2 = 3 = 4)
Age							
1. Young (< 12)	15,080	543	.56	.55	.52		
	1,077	51	.79	.63	.72	96	
2. Adolescent (> 11 & 17)	5,421	250	.60	.68	.52		
	770	40	.84	.57	.64	92	
3. Adult (> 16)	713	49	.72	.67	.51		
	155	9	.76	.41	.61	18	
4. Multi-age (Elem-Secondary)	6,847	257	.88	.67	.71		68.77^{**}
	2,867	80	.78	.48	.75	162	3.53

(continued)

Table 4. (Continued)

All Studies	Sample Size	K	Mean	SD	Weighted Mean	Ind. Sample	X²
Gender Ratio in Sample							
1. Low male ratio (< 70%)	780	330	.58	.51	.48		
	645	31	.65	.42	.66	70	
2. High male ratio (> 69%)	7,559	303	.64	.61	.52		
	1,034	48	.69	.54	.65	86	
3. Cannot calculate ratio	18,374	574	.71	.62	.59		31.10**
	3,072	96	.80	.55	.74	196	3.43
Intelligence							
1. > 84 & < 92	4,703	159	.69	.69	.66		
	1,464	69	.77	.57	.63	154	
2. No information	17,490	597	.72	.66	.59		
	2,822	86	.82	.50	.77	166	
3. > 91	11,549	451	.56	.51	.45		71.84**
	584	25	.79	.48	.66	50	7.43*
							(2>3=1)

(continued)

Table 4. (Continued)

All Studies	Sample Size	K	Mean	SD	Weighted Mean	Ind. Sample	X^2
Reading Severity							
1. < 85	7,776	261	.66	.52	.55		
	771	35	.86	.52	.71	70	
2. > 84 & < 91	979	51	.47	.46	.43		
	127	9	.57	.39	.51	10	
3. No score	22,571	800	.69	.62	.57		
	3,629	122	.80	.54	.73	254	
4. > 90	2,415	95	.53	.57	.38		35.96**
	293	14	.69	.44	.55	22	6.36*
							(1=3>2=4)
Independent Variables (General models)							
Strategy Instruction							
Strategy Instruction	11,889	423	.76	.60	.66*		
	2,489	83	.86	.51	.84	194	
Non Strategy Instruction	21,854	784	.60	.58	.52		35.57**
	2,382	97	.74	.53	.67	168	9.59**

(continued)

Table 4. (Continued)

All Studies	Sample Size	K	Mean	SD	Weighted Mean	Ind. Sample	X^2
Direct Instruction							
Direct Instruction	11,950	519	.68	.58	.60		
	2,725	102	.82	.53	.82	198	
Non Direct Instruction	21,792	688	.64	.60	.54		8.05**
	2,145	78	.76	.52	.66	164	7.92**

Notes: [a]Chronological partialed out
* $p < .05$; ** $p < .01$
K = number of dependent measures
Top row—unit of analysis calculated across all studies and dependent measures
Bottom row—unit of analysis averaged within each study
Ind. = Number of Independent Samples
[b]Read as 1 and 3 ("Different teacher" and "cannot determine") are statistically comparable but both are significantly larger in effect sizes than 2 (same teacher)
CTRL = Control Condition
EXP—Experimental Conditon
The variation between setting not reported (N = 102) and no information for the type of classrooms (N = 86) is because some studies failed to report age.
[c]Age and methodology composite scores are partialed out in the analysis.

81

the measures were independent of each other. The second averages the effect sizes across dependent variables within each study (i.e., each study contributes only 1 effect size to the analysis).

As shown in Table 4, the number of independent samples was also computed (see previous discussion, also see Cooper et al., 1996, for the complete rationale). When the number of independent samples exceeds $2 \times K$ (the number of studies), then the studies included more than one experimental treatment. When the number of independent samples is lower than $2 \times K$, then there was reliance on using the same participants in multiple treatments. In cases of repeated measures, effect sizes were recalculated using the aforementioned formula which takes into consideration the correlation between the control and treatment condition. A Chi-square based on the WLS analysis is presented for all independent measures for both types of units of analysis. When the degrees of freedom were greater than 1, a Scheffe test was used to make comparisons between the estimates of the mean effect size.

Methodology

The methodological characteristics of each study were first analyzed, because several of these measures were used to compute a methodological composite score. The methodological composite score (to be discussed) was used to qualify treatment outcomes (effect sizes).

As shown in Table 4, studies that include from 11 to 30 sessions yield higher effect sizes than those that include between 3 and 10 sessions. No significant differences in effect sizes were found between studies that lasted over 31 sessions and those that lasted between 3 and 10 sessions. However, when the unit of analysis includes averaging effect size estimates within studies, no significant differences emerge in effect size as a function of the number of sessions. Those studies which report treatment integrity (i.e., the degree to which independent variable is carried out as designed) yield lower effect sizes than those that report treatment integrity, but the differences in effect size were not significant when effect sizes were averaged within studies.

Because internal validity was moderately weak across the majority of the studies (see Table 2), we categorized studies into high and low internal validity on the variables of setting, different materials, comparability of teachers across conditions, reporting of reliability, procedural validity, and random assignment (scores ranged from 6 to 18, with a score of 6 reflecting high internal validity). As shown in Table 4, studies with high internal (scores < 10) validity yield lower effect sizes than studies of low internal validity. However, when effect sizes are averaged within each study there is no significant difference in estimates of effect size in studies with high and low internal validity.

One variable of interest was whether the studies which randomly assign treatments to subjects yield higher effect size than those that do not. As shown, when the type of treatment assignment was classified into (a) nonrandom assignment, (b) random assignment, or (c) those studies that reported ambiguous information or no information about how groups were assigned to treatment, differences in estimates of effect size emerged. When the unit of analysis was averaged within study, however, there were no significant differences in effect sizes related to how treatments were randomly assigned. Those studies that included standardized testing as part of the pre- and posttest measures had significantly lower effect sizes when compared to studies that relied on experimental measures (.92 vs. .69).

Those studies that had a high degree of overlap between the control group and the treatment group in terms of the number and types of instructional components yield significantly lower effect sizes than those studies with minimal overlap (.71 vs. .85). As expected, those studies that report lower effect sizes include larger samples sizes than those that include small samples. A Scheffe test showed that studies that had a total sample of less than 25 yielded higher effect sizes than those with samples below 100. However, 6 studies which had sample sizes that totaled greater than 100 yielded an effect size of 1.12.

Because some methodological variables were clearly related to the magnitude of effect sizes, it was necessary to create a methodological composite score related to internal validity and methodological sophistication for the subsequent comparisons. Studies that included: (1) instructional sessions greater than 10 (selection of this variable was based on the assumption that the intensity of instruction-as reflected by the number of session- yields more reliable and stable outcomes than shorter intervention sessions), (2) random assignment to treatment, (3) measures of treatment integrity, (4) utilization of standardized tests, (5) internal validity scores on the abbreviated scale of 5 (number reflects highest possible ratings on items on the variables related to the comparability of setting, materials, and teachers across conditions and the reporting of procedural validity), and (6) high control and treatment condition overlap in terms of steps and procedures (at least 3 steps and/or procedures overlap), were assigned a score. The amount of psychometric data reported was also included in the methodological composite score [if additional psychometric information beyond an IQ score was reported (e.g., reading scores) the study was weighted positively]. For each of the seven variables weighted positively and negatively, a score of 2 or 0 was assigned for each variable, respectively. For each study, the weighted score varied from 14 to 0, with 14 reflecting methodologically superior studies.

Based on the methodological composite score, studies were divided into three classifications, high (score greater than 10), medium (score between 6 and 11), and low methodological sophistication (score less than 6). As shown in Table 4, studies that achieved higher methodological sophistication had significantly lower effect size estimates than those studies weak in methodological sophistication. Regardless of whether the unit of analysis was averaged within studies or each dependent measure was considered as a separate effect size, significant differences in effect size estimates occurred between studies as a function of ratings on the methodological composite score. A Scheffe test indicated that higher effect sizes occurred for those studies with low methodological composite scores followed by those studies which received medium ratings. The lowest effect size occurred for those studies with higher methodological sophistication. This methodological composite score was used in the subsequent analysis to qualify the outcomes related to effect size estimates. The mean methodological composite score across studies was 7.25 ($SD = 2.92$).

A comparison was made between the 17 dependent measure categories (also referred to as domains) with the methodological composite score partialed from the analysis. The average effect size per study as a function of domain was the unit of analysis. Significant differences in effect size were found between categories, X^2 (16, $N = 377$) = 45.71, $p < .001$. The weighted least square (WLS) mean effect sizes, with the influence of the methodological composite score partialed out, that approximated Cohen's threshold were reading comprehension (.81), vocabulary (.73), and creativity (.78). Those WLS means of moderate magnitude (> .60 and < .70) were the categories of cognitive processing (.69), word recognition (.65), memory (.66), writing (.65), intelligence (.61), attitude-self concept (.60), phonics/orthographic skills (.60), and global achievement (.64). Those categories of relatively weak (< .55) magnitude were spelling (.51), mathematics (.45), general reading (.46), social skills (.47), perceptual processes (.53), and language processes (.50). A Scheffe test indicated that significant differences ($p < .05$) emerged between studies that included measures of effect size near Cohen's threshold and those of weak magnitude (< .55). No significant differences emerged between those categories of dependent measures of moderate magnitude when compared to those measures near Cohen's threshold and those of weak magnitude. These results qualify the weighted means reported in Table 3 by partialing out the influence of artifacts related to methodological sophistication.

Article Characteristics

Table 4 shows the mean outcomes on effect size as a function of the characteristics of studies in terms of funding and the type of publication. No significant differences emerged in the magnitude of effect size for studies that reported a funding source and those that did not. Those studies that were published in dissertations had significantly lower sizes than those published in journals.

Setting of Intervention

Studies were sorted by those that reported the setting in which treatment occurred and those that did not. As shown in Table 4, those studies that do not report the setting ($N = 102$) in which the intervention occurred yield lower effect sizes than those that do report the setting. Setting information was further divided into those studies that reported that treatment occurred in a self-contained classroom, resource room, regular classroom, or failed to report the type of classroom setting where the treatment occurred. As shown in Table 4, the number of studies reporting no information ($N = 102$) was reduced ($N = 86$) in the comparisons between the type of classrooms because 16 of these studies failed to report a mean age score (instead age or grade ranges were provided) for the sample. As shown, however, only 4 studies, with a total sample size of 151 participants, provided information on effect sizes related to the regular classroom. As shown in Table 4, significant differences related to setting occurred whether the unit of analysis was averaged within study or each dependent measure was considered as a separate independent event. As shown, larger effect sizes occurred in resource rooms when compared to other settings.

Sample Characteristics

Several effect size differences emerged related to information on sample characteristics. The general pattern was that studies which fail to report psychometric information on participants with LD yield significantly higher effect sizes than those studies that report psychometric information. For example, studies were categorized by the amount of psychometric information reported. Four categories were developed for comparisons (no information, standardized intelligence test scores, standardized intelligence scores + standardized reading test scores, and standardized intelligence test scores + reading scores + mathematics scores). As shown in Table 4, a significant Chi-square emerged for both units of analysis. The Scheffe test indicated that those studies which provided no psychometric information on the LD sample produced larger effect sizes than those studies that report intelligence, reading, and/or mathematics scores. No significant differences were found between those studies that reported intelligence scores and those that reported standardized intelligence scores and reading and/or math scores.

Given that psychometric information is related to effect size, the sample characteristics were further categorized by the reported range in intelligence scores and the range of reading scores. Three categories for comparison were created for intelligence: those studies that reported mean standard scores between 85 and 92, those that reported mean standardized intelligence scores greater than 92, and those that did not report standardized information. If studies provide multiple IQ scores (verbal, performance, nonverbal, etc.), these scores were averaged within studies. As shown in Table 4, the highest effect sizes occur when no information is presented.

The next category considered in our sample analysis was reading severity. If multiple standardized reading measures were provided in the study, reading scores were averaged across word recognition and reading comprehension. Four categories were created for comparisons: scores below 85, scores above 84 and less than 91, scores greater than 90, and no standardized scores reported. Significant Chi-squares emerged between the four categories of reading for the two types of unit of analysis. When examining the differences using the WLS method, high effect sizes emerge when no IQ and Reading scores are reported when compared to the other conditions. However, when methodology was partialed out in the analysis, effect sizes for studies which report scores below 85 were comparable to those studies that reported no scores. The lowest effect sizes occurred between studies that reported reading scores between 84 and less than 91 and those studies that reported scores above 90.

Because the discrepancy between intelligence and achievement scores was a frequent way of defining samples, we categorized studies that "stated" the sample has a discrepancy between potential or IQ and achievement (or some specific academic domain) vs. those that did not. Although we placed no restrictions on the type of discrepancy reported, the study must use the term discrepancy and state that the participants were at least one year behind in some achievement domain. As shown in Table 4, the influence of the discrepancy variable is only significant when the unit of analysis was not averaged within studies. Higher effect sizes occurred when no discrepancy information is presented when compared to those studies that report discrepancy information. However, no significant differences were found in effect sizes when averaged within studies.

Sample characteristics that fail to emerge as significant when considering the main effects were the age and gender of the participants. When we examined the age differences using the WLS method and effect sizes were averaged within studies, we found larger mean effect sizes in studies that included both elementary and secondary age children ($n = 80$, mean $= .75$) than for studies treating adults ($n = 9$, mean $= .61$), adolescents (12 years of age and older; $N = 40$; mean $= .64$), and children 11 years of age and younger ($n = 51$, mean $= .72$), but the differences were not significant, $p > .05$.

As shown in Table 4, few studies provided information that allowed us to investigate the effects of gender on treatment outcome. Thus, we calculated the median ratio of those studies that reported the number of males and females in each study. We computed a gender ratio (number of males/total in the sample) and divided the studies by the median ratio (.70) across the 180 studies. Those studies that report males and females samples but include greater than 69% males in the sample were compared to those studies that report less than 70% males in the sample. These two categories were compared with those studies in which the gender ratio of the sample could not be computed. As shown in Table 4, only 31 studies were considered to have a low-male ratio. When examining the effect sizes differences using the WLS method, larger effect sizes occurred for those studies in which we could not calculate the gender ratio. However, the results indicated that no main effects emerged related to gender ratio when the unit of analysis included effect sizes averaged within studies.

Type of Intervention

The final analysis of main effects considered the type of intervention. Studies that reflected the components of strategy instruction discussed earlier were assigned a 1 (dummy coded) and those studies that included instructional components below the threshold (less than three of the components) were assigned a 0. The same dummy coding procedures were used to classify those studies that utilized direct instruction (studies that included at least four of the possible eight components were coded as 1 and those studies that included less than four of the possible eight components were dummy coded as 0) and nondirect instruction methods. Prior to our analysis, however, it was necessary to partial the influence of methodology from the WLS analysis. This variable was then used to partial estimates of effect size related to the two treatments.

As shown in Table 4, studies that include strategy instruction produce larger effect sizes than those studies that do not. This occurs whether the unit of analysis is averaged within studies or each dependent measure is considered as an independent effect size. In addition, the magnitude of the effect size is maintained even when the effects of the methodology composite score are partialed from the main effects. The least square mean effect size, weighted by the reciprocal of the sampling variance, is .84 vs. .67 for strategy vs. nonstrategy studies, respectively. Also provided in Table 4 are the effect sizes related to direct instruction and nondirect instruction. Similar to the strategy instruction models, the direct instruction model is more powerful than the nondirect instruction model. Least square mean effect size, partialing the influence of methodology, yields an effect size of .82 for direct instruction studies and .66 for studies that do not use direct instruction.

In summary, regardless of the unit of analysis, studies that include components related to strategy instruction or direct instruction yield larger effect sizes than studies that use nonstrategy and nondirect instruction models. Both models appear to yield the same approximate magnitude in effect size estimates, and therefore, the independent contribution of each model will be investigated in the subsequent analysis.

Intervention Models and Outcomes: A Three-Tier Analysis

The previous analysis of main effects does not allow for a qualification of treatment outcomes. For example, we are uncertain if strategy and direct instruction models are independent models. To isolate the locus of treatment effects on outcome measures, a three tier structure was used to investigate the various instructional approaches (also see Wiesz, Weiss, Han, Granger, & Morton, 1995, discussion of a similar approach). The unit of analysis was the aggregated (averaged) effect size of each study.

For the first tier, as in the previous analysis on treatment main effects, we determined if studies that were classified strategy models contributed independent

Table 5. Hierarchical Regression Model with
Weighted Least Squares for Effect Size Estimates

	df^a	χ^2	$\underline{R}^2$	Increment in R^2
Forced Entry				
1. Methodology	158^b	309.27^{**}	.07	–
Chronological Age				
1. *Forced Entry*				
Methodology				
Chronological Age				
Direct Instruction	157	304.04^{**}	.08	–
2. Strategy Instruction	156	298.70^{**}	.10	.02
1. *Forced Entry*				
Methodology				
Chronological Age				
Strategy Instruction	157	301.58^{**}	.09	–
2. Direct Instruction	–	ns	–	–

Notes: $^{**}p < .01.$ $^*p < .05$
^{a}df is K-P
^{b}df includes a total of 160 studies because 20 studies
included only ranges in age or grade and not means.

variance to estimates of effect size when compared to studies that included direct instruction models. It could be argued, based on the comparable magnitude of effect sizes (.84 strategy instruction and .82 direct instruction) that these two intervention approaches overlap with a number of studies, and therefore the two approaches are not independent of each other. To determine the independence of these two models, phi coefficients were calculated on the two dummy variables. The phi coefficient showed a weak but significant correlation, $r = .179, p < .05$. To further address the independence issue, however, a weighted least squares (WLS) hierarchical regression model assessed whether the general instructional models contributed independent variance to estimates of effect size.

As shown in Table 5, methodology composite score and age were forced to enter the equation first followed by the alternating order of direct instruction and strategy instruction. As shown in Table 5, strategy instruction was the only

Table 6. Four General Conditions as a Function of Effect Size Estimates

Instructional Components	Direct Instr. Alone (DI)			Strategy Instr. Alone (SI)			Direct+Strategy Inst. (DI + SI)			Non-Direct & Nonstrategy Instr. Non DI & SI			χ^2 [a]
	N	M	SD	N	M	SD	N	M	SD	N	M	SD	
Total Model	47	.79	.51	28	.78	.47	55	.85	.54	43	.69	.53	21.77**
Weighted least square mean with method & age partialed out		.68			.72			.84			.62		12.79**[b]

Notes: $p < .05$, ** $p < .01$, *** $p < .001$

[a] χ^2 Assesses whether weighted $\underline{d}$ is significantly different.

Means for each commponent are unweighted

[b] Scheffe ($p < .05$) indicated DI+SI>SI=DI; SI>Non DI & SI; DI=NonDI & SI

instructional approach that contributed independent variance to effect size esti-mates. When direct instruction was entered after strategy instruction (also forced first in entry were the methodological composite score and chronological age), no significant variance emerged in predicting effect size. In contrast, when strategy instruction followed direct instruction, strategy instruction contributed significant variance (2% of the variance) to effect size estimates. Thus, support is found that the general model of strategy instruction contributes significant variance to effect size estimates that is independent of direct instruction. However, it is important to note that not all studies reported mean age scores (they reported grade ranges rather than ages) and therefore were excluded from the analysis. In addition, some studies could be classified as both direct and strategy instruction and therefore there is a partial overlap in variance that predicts effect size. More importantly, a contribution of 2% of the variance to effect sizes would not be considered mean-ingful in practical terms. Thus, a further refinement of our analysis of the contri-bution of treatment to effect size estimates was necessary.

Those studies that overlapped in components between direct and strategy instruction were separated for analysis. Studies that qualified as direct instruction and strategy instruction based on the type of instructional components reported in the treatment conditions were considered as a separate model (referred to as the Combined Model). Thus, four general interventions models were compared. The four general models are direct instruction alone (direct instruction components, but no strategy components), strategy instruction alone (strategy components, but no direct instruction components), direct instruction coupled with strategy instruction (*Combined Model* which includes both strategy and direct instruction components), and those studies that do not include any of the components of direct instruction or strategy instruction (referred to as the *NonSI & NonDI Model*).

The mean effect sizes and standard deviations for the four models of this first tier of analysis are shown in Table 6. As shown, the four models were compared by partialing out the influence of the methodological composite score. A Scheffe test indicated that the Combined Model [combination of direct (DI) and strategy instruction (SI)] yielded significantly higher effect sizes (all $ps < .05$) than the other models (SI & DI > DI Alone = SI Alone = NonDI & NonSI).

The next tier refines the four models into instructional components because it is unclear how many of the components in the NonDI & NonSI model were compa-rable to the *Combined Model*. Thus, tier two analysis included a fine grain description of the components of instruction that underlie the four models. The importance of this tier is to determine whether the instructional components of the four models are qualitatively different. Such a determination would establish the discriminant validity of the four general models. Chi-squares (df = 3) were com-puted across the four instructional approaches on the twenty instructional compo-nents discussed earlier in the methods section.

Table 7. Four General Treatment Conditions as a Function of the Percent of Instructional Components and Effect Size Estimates (Total N = 180)

Instructional Components	Direct Instr. Alone			Strategy Instr. Alone			Direct + Strategy Inst.			Non-Direct & Nonstrategy Instr.			$X^{2 a}$
	%	M	SD	%	M	SD	%	M	SD	%	M	SD	
1. Sequencing (e.g., process or task analysis to goal, shaping)	91	.79	.52	64	.95	.52	87	.86	.56	25	.78	.54	68.50***
2. Drill-Repetition-Practice-Feedback	48	.85	.55	53	.89	.29	47	.89	.64	20	.74	.59	14.91**
3. Orienting to Process or Task (e.g., preparatory to task, Meichenbaum)	40	.91	.56	42	.92	.37	30	.97	.68	6	1.27	.78	18.75***
4. Question/Answer Sequence (e.g. structured verbal interaction, socratic)	6	.40	.25	42	.92	.47	21	.81	.43	11	.58	.23	18.90***
5. Individual + Group Instruction	97	.81	.51	57	.84	.42	98	.86	.54	88	.71	.56	19.13***
6. Novelty (pictorial presentation, flow chart, related visual presentation, mapping, new material or curriculum)	87	.80	.80	82	.96	.47	80	.84	.48	39	.67	.53	37.79***
7. Attributions/Benefits to Instruction (e.g., this approach works when .., this will help you...)	2	.72	–	57	.82	.42	92	.82	.54	4	.29	.10	136.22***
8. Systematic Probing (CBM, daily testing)	38	.77	.49	14	1.46	.63	40	.78	.40	11	.72	.59	17.29**
9. Peer Modeling/Mediation (e.g., peer tutoring)	4	.69	.18	10	3.62	.31	10	.62	.34	2	.72	–	4.51
10. Segmentation (e.g., sounds divided into units then synthesized)	74	.76	.49	42	.79	.37	82	.81	.49	13	.82	.66	62.04**
11. Advanced organizer (overview of task)	40	.91	.56	42	.92	.37	30	.97	.68	6	1.27	.78	18.75***
12. Directed response/questioning (child directed to summarize, asked what's the thing to do	6	.40	.25	32	.87	.53	18	.69	.33	11	.58	.23	10.60*

(continued)

Table 7. (Continued)

Instructional Components	Direct Instr. Alone			Strategy Instr. Alone			Direct + Strategy Inst.			Non-Direct & Nonstrategy Instr.			χ^2 [a]
	%	M	SD	%	M	SD	%	M	SD	%	M	SD	
13. One-to-one Instruction	89	.81	.51	42	.97	.59	87	.85	.56	48	.57	.53	43.14***
14. Control Task Difficulty (adapting material to reading level)	55	.88	.55	67	.90	.52	36	.92	.55	13	.78	.59	30.40***
15. Technology (computer mediated, high structured materials)	57	.87	.51	53	.83	.54	60	.75	.41	34	.64	.65	11.38*
16. Elaboration (additional information, examples, rely on context)	–	–	–	16	1.09	.13	5	1.12	.60	–	–	–	8.84*
17. Teacher Models Directly (models problem solving, steps, correct sounds)	21	.66	.51	67	.92	.50	70	.83	.59	18	.49	42	48.64***
18. Small interactive groups (reciprocal, directive, therapy groups)	36	.85	.51	71	.94	.50	72	.89	.51	62	.72	.56	16.46**
19. Mediators other than peer or teacher (homework, parents)	4	1.10	.18	–	–	–	–	–	–	2	1.94	–	3.36
20. Strategy Cuing (reminders to use strategies or tactics)	–	–	–	39	.73	.28	43	.87	.56	0	–	–	51.001***

Notes: *
**
***

The twenty components are listed in Table 7 as a function of the four instructional models. Reported in Table 7 are the percentage of studies (%) in each model that include each instructional component. Also included is the unweighted mean Cohen's *d* for each study that includes the component. A Chi-square analysis (df = 3) of the frequency of components reflected in each study was computed for each of the 20 components between the four models. To facilitate the visual analysis of the Table 7, when the Chi-squares were significant, the highest percentiles were underlined that separated one model from another. If more that one percentile score is underlined across the rows, differences were not found between those treatments, but those treatments were significantly higher than the remaining treatments.

There are three important findings reported in Table 7. First, we are able to identify the components that make up the NonDI & NonSI Model. This condition reflects an emphasis on individual and/or small group instruction. No other components characterized this condition (the remaining components are less than 50%). Second, based on the number of significant Chi-squares (18 of 20), there is discriminant validity among the treatments. As shown in Table 7, significant effects emerged on all components as a function of the four models except for peer modeling (see #9) and nonteacher mediation (#19).

Finally, some components are unique to the Combined Model. Because of the classification procedures, it was expected the Combined Model (SI + DI) would reflect more components than either of the remaining three models. However, it was not clear which components overlapped and which components were most characteristic (no overlap) of the competing models. As shown in Table 7, a high representation (> 70%) of components that occurs for the Combined Model includes the following instructional components: 1, 5, 6, 7, 10, 13, 17, and 18 (refer to Table 7 to attach labels to the numbers), when compared to DI Alone (components > 70% were 1, 5, 6, 10, 13), SI Alone (6, 18) and NonSI & DI (component 5) models. As shown in Table 7, Components 4, 7, 17, 18, and 20 were more frequent in the Combined Model than the DI Alone Model. The DI alone model was more frequent in its representation of component 14 (control of task difficulty) than the Combined Model.

Significant differences in component representation occurred between the Combined Model and SI Alone Model (i.e., components 1, 5, 7, 8, 10, and 13 were more frequently represented in the Combined Model). Components 4, 12, 14, and 16 were more frequent in the SI Alone Model than the Combined Model.

In sum, the previous analyses suggest that the instructional models vary in the components represented in treatment. The Combined Model appears distinct from the other approaches because of its inclusion of attributions (#7), teacher modeling of problem solving steps (#17), and emphasis on small interactive groups (#18, see Table 7). Problematic to the analysis in Table 7 is whether the estimates of effect size for each of instructional components vary as a function of the four general models. To address this issue, differences among effects sizes for each

Table 8. Weighted Least Square Means for Instructional Components as a Function of the Four General Interventions ($N = 180$)

	1 Direct Instr. Alone	2 Strategy Instr. Alone	3 Direct Instr. & Strategy	4 No Direct Instr. and No Strategy Instr	N	Difference[b]	X^{2a}
1. Sequencing (e.g., process or task analysis to goal, shaping)	.72	.76	.89	.65	119	$3>2=1=4^b$	8.03[*]
2. Drill-Repetition-Practice-Feedback	.66	.83	.96	.68	72	$3=2>1=4$	11.13[**]
3. Orienting to Process or Task (e.g., preparatory to task, Meichenbaum)	.93	.81	.83	1.20	50	–	2.93
4. Question/Answer Sequence (e.g., structured verbal interaction, socratic)	.57	.74	.72	.45	31	–	3.41
5. Individual + Group Instruction	.69	.80	.86	.63	156	$2\&3>1\&4$	12.76[**]
6. Novelty (pictorial presentation, flow chart, related visual presentation, mapping, new material or curriculum)	.78	.69	.91	.60	117	$3>1=2,2=4$	5.19[**]
7. Attributions/Benefits to Instruction (e.g., this approach works when ..., this will help you...)	.69	1.19	.87	.30	76	$2>3>1>4$	11.44[*]
8. Systematic Probing (CBM, daily testing)	.65	1.23	.67	.69	48	–	5.82

(continued)

94

Table 8. (Continued)

	1 Direct Instr. Alone	2 Strategy Instr. Alone	3 Direct Instr. & Strategy	4 No Direct Instr. and No Strategy Instr	N	Difference[b]	X^{2a}
9. Peer Modeling/Mediation (e.g., peer tutoring)	.90	.59	.49	.74	11	–	1.79
10. Segmentation (e.g., sounds divided into units then synthesized)	.68	.62	.85	.55	97	3>1=2=3	9.46**
11. Advanced organizer (overview of task)	.92	.81	.83	1.20	50	–	2.93
12. Directed response/questioning (child directed to summarize, asked what's the thing to do when ...)	.51	.64	.62	.45	26	–	1.41
13. One-to-one Instruction	.68	.69	.86	.49	122	3>1=2>4	19.16**
14. Control Task Difficulty (adapting material to reading level)	.80	.73	1.07	.66	70	3>1=2,2=4	13.42**
15. Technology (computer mediated, high structured materials)	.77	.61	.88	.53	89	3>2,3=1,2>4	13.92**
16. Elaboration (additional information, examples, rely on context)	1.09	1.09	1.03	–	5	–	.001

(continued)

Table 8. (Continued)

	1 Direct Instr. Alone	2 Strategy Instr. Alone	3 Direct Instr. & Strategy	4 No Direct Instr. and No Strategy Instr	N	Difference[b]	χ^{2a}
17. Teacher Models Directly (models problem solving, steps, correct sounds)	.52	.76	.89	.44	75	3>2>1=4	21.55**
18. Small interactive groups (reciprocal, directive, therapy groups)	.80	.79	.93	.65	103	3>1=2>4	12.56**
19. Mediators other than peer or teacher (homework, parents)	1.06	–	–	2.03	2	–	2.08
20. Strategy Cuing (reminders to use strategies or tactics)	–	.69	.74	–	34	–	.11

Notes: * $p < .05$; ** $p < .01$
[a]χ^2 partialed for methodological composite score,
[b]post-hoc Scheffe

component as a function of the four instructional models were computed, via WLS analysis. As shown in Table 8, the magnitude of the effect sizes as a function of each component varied across the four general models. As shown, when the effect sizes were weighted by the reciprocal of the sampling variance and the methodological composite score is partialed from the analysis, the significant estimates of effect size in favor of the Combined Model are isolated to the components of sequencing, drill-repetition-practice, novelty, segmentation, one-to-one instruction, control of task difficulty, technology, teacher modeling of strategies, and small interactive groups.

It was also of interest in this second tier of analysis to determine whether the treatment approaches and instructional components varied in their emphasis in studies over the 30 year period. The correlation between the overall unweighted effect size ($M = .79$, $SD = 52$) averaged across studies and year of publication ($M = 1987$, $SD = 5.41$) was not significant, r (178) $= .05$, $p > .45$. In addition, none of the point biserial correlation coefficients between year of publication and the 20 instructional components were of sufficient magnitude (all $rs < .16$) to be of interest. The point biserial correlation between year of publication and direct instruction (coded as 1 was for direct instruction and 0 for studies not including direct instruction) was not significant, r (178) $= .09$, $p > .20$. A significant positive point biserial correlation (although moderate) emerged between year of publication and strategy instruction (coded as 1 for the occurrence of strategy instruction and 0 for nonstrategy instruction), r (178) $= .23$, $p < .01$. The emergence of strategy models has increased positively over the years.

A third tier of analysis attempted to determine which of the 20 components, either in isolation or in combination with other components, best predicted effect sizes. Those components that made up the Combined Model that yielded the highest effect sizes when compared to the competing models included: sequencing, novelty, segmentation, one-to-one instruction, teacher modeling, and small interactive groups (components 1, 5, 6, 7, 10, 13, 17, and 18 shown in Table 8). However, it is clear from Table 8 that several components yield effect sizes above .80 threshold (16 of 20), suggesting that the instructional components may not be independent. In addition, we have not identified the instructional components most important in predicting effect size, as well as those components that when combined, account for most of the variance in treatment outcomes.

Three approaches in a WLS regression analysis were used to isolate the instructional components that play a significant role in predicting effect size. These approaches were used to control partially for preselection bias (control for order) of the instructional components and our capitalization on chance in the WLS regression analysis. To determine the relationship between the 20 instructional components and effect size estimates, weighted least square fixed effects regression models were fitted to the empirical values, following methods recommended by Harwell (1992) and described by Hedges and Olkin (1985, pp. 168-174; see also Hedges, 1994b, pp. 295-298). Because mean age was not reported in 20 studies and the grade ranges were 3-7, we assigned an age of 10.6 so as not to delete those studies from the analyses. Further, based on the previous analysis, age was not a significant predictor of effect size, and therefore the assignment of a constant score for missing values was appropriate. Our goal was to identify those components that when combined and/or in isolation contribute important variance to the prediction of effect size.

First, we used a stepwise selection procedure in which the order of entry is determined via a mathematical maximization procedure. That is, after the methodological composite score and age are entered, the component with the largest correlation to effect size enters followed with the second component with the largest semi-partial coefficient correlation, etc. The results indicated that methodological composite score and age contributed approximately 6% of the variance in predicting effect size, $R^2 = .058$, $X^2 (2,N = 180) = 20.81$, $p < .001$. The first instructional component to enter the regression model was control of task difficulty, increment in $R^2 = .056$, $X^2 (3,N = 180) = 40.80$, $p < .001$, followed by small interactive groups with an increment in $R^2 = .049$, $X^2 (4,N = 180) = 58.49$, $p < .001$, followed by directed response/questioning; increment in $R^2 = .022$, $X^2 (5,N = 180) = 66.22$, $p < .001$. The complete model was significant, $R^2 = .18$, $X^2 (174,N = 180) = 290.34$, $p < .001$. Thus, three components (control of task difficulty, small interactive groups, and directed response/questioning) contributed approximately 12% of the variance in predicting effect sizes estimates. No other components entered significantly into the model.

Second, we identified those components that when combined yield the highest adjusted R^2 in predicting effect size estimates. The squared multiple correlation, adjusted for the number of explanatory variables, was used to quantify the predictive power of the given model. The SAS regression program (SAS Institute, 1989) was used to conduct the statistical analysis using the "best model" option. The adjusted R square procedure was used to find the model with the highest R^2 within the ranges of effect sizes. The adjusted R^2 was .04 when the methodological composite score and age was used to predict effect sizes across studies. The adjusted R^2 was improved to .20 when methodological composite score and age included sequencing (#1; see Tables 7 & 8), drill-repetition and practice (#2), segmentation (#10), directed response/questioning (#12), control of task difficulty (#14), technology (#15), small interactive groups (#18), mediation other than peer or teachers (#19), and strategy cuing (#20). Thus, nine instructional components (sequencing, drill-repetition and practice, segmentation, directed response/questioning, control of task difficulty, technology, small interactive groups, mediation other than peer or teachers, and strategy cuing) contribute 16% of the variance in predicting effect size estimates.

The final analysis attempted to identify those components that in isolation (i.e., when the contributions of the remaining components are partialed out) contribute

Table 9.   Weighted Least Square Regression on Effect Size Estimates to Determine Independent Influence of Isolated Instructional Components

	χ^2 [a]	β	SE
I. Methodology	13.80***	−.03	.01
Age	.21	−.005	.02
II. Instructional Components			
1. Sequencing	3.39*	.17	.12
2. Drill-Repetition-Practice Feedback	1.83	.08	.08
3. Orienting to process or task	.01	.02	.09
4. Question/Answer Sequence	.36	.24	.52
5. Individual + Group Instruction	3.43*	.23	.16
6. Novelty	.12	.02	.10
7. Attributions/Benefits to Instruction	2.14	.12	.11
8. Systematic Probing	.27	−.03	.08
9. Peer Modeling/Mediation	.93	−.11	.15
10. Segmentation	3.44*	−.15	.10
11. Advanced Organizers	.01	.001	.01
12. Directed Response/Questioning	1.14	−.43	.52
13. One-to-one Instruction	5.00**	−.17	.10
14. Control Task Difficulty	6.65**	.16	.08
15. Technology	.20	.02	.09
16. Elaboration	.02	−.004	.47
17. Teacher Models Problem Solving	.12	−.02	.09
18. Small Interactive Groups	2.74	.11	.09
19. Mediators other than peer or teacher	1.59	.36	.37
20. Strategy cuing	3.48*	−.16	.11
R^2	.25		
N	179		
df	158		
Q_E	267.30**		

Notes: R^2 for methods & age is .06
  *p < .10, **p < .05, ***p < .01
  [a]Type III Sum of Squares

to effect sizes when all variables are entered into the equation simultaneously. Based on the question we proposed, a Type III sum of squares (which corresponds to Yates' weighted squares of means analysis) was used. A Type III sum of squares is used because the calculation adjusts for the effects of other variables. The Type III sum of squares partials the influence of variables on a single variable, that is, the results when the variable is entered last in the equation.

Table 9 shows the independent contribution of the instructional components, as well as the methodological composite score on effect size estimates as a function of the total studies. As shown, the results indicate that when all dependent measures were averaged within studies, the component that positively predicted effect size estimates at the .05 alpha level was Controlling task difficulty. The isolated component that was significantly (alpha = .05) related to lower effect sizes (negative beta weight) included one-to-one instruction. The interpretation of negative beta weights (as well as positive) when dummy variables are used in a partial regression coefficient (β) must be done carefully (see Cohen & Cohen, 1983, pp. 193-198 for discussion). For example, one-to-one instruction is not compared to non one-to-one instruction, but rather to all other studies. The βs are recorded in Table 9, "but in the context of nominal scale coding they are not particularly useful (Cohen & Cohen, 1983, p. 194). Thus, the X^2 test is of singular importance in our analysis. The important findings are that only two components significantly contribute to effect size estimates. Only one of these components (control of task difficulty) overlaps with the stepwise regression model and the regression model that specifies the maximum number of components that yield the highest R-square.

Specificity of Treatment Effects

An important question is whether the four general treatments have broad effects across all domains or are specific to an academic domain. This is a difficult question to answer from the previous analysis because in some cases, outcomes measures are highly similar to treatment activities (see Weisz et al., 1995, for discussion of this issue), and therefore confound conclusions that can be drawn about the independent effects of treatment. For example, when one treats an LD child's poor word recognition with phonics instruction, the most valid test of the LD child's ability to read is a test of real word recognition and not performance on pseudowords or phonics measures. Another is when one treats a child's poor writing with metacognitive training, the ability to write a coherent essay rather than metacognition, is probably the most valid test of training. Thus, isolating the specific effects of treatment requires control of confounds related to the dependency between domain (category of dependent measures) and independent variable (treatment). A WLS regression has been suggested as one approach to handle a wide variety of these multivariate statistical problems (Gleser & Olkin, 1994), and therefore was utilized in this analysis. Thus, the overlapping variance related to various treatments (global vs. specific), correlations between treatment and outcomes measures, and the correlation between multiple outcome measures, were partialed out in the subsequent analysis.

To address the issue of whether treatment influences broad or specific domains of dependent measures, contrast variables were created between broad and specific outcome domains as well as the four general instructional models (Combined strategy and direct instruction, direct instruction alone, strategy instruction alone, and nonstrategy plus nondirect instruction).

Four domain contrast variables were created. [The coding of contrast variables follows the regression model outlined by Cohen and Cohen (1983, see pp. 196-217).] The first general contrast variable separated the seventeen dependent measure categories (See Table 3) into *high language domains* (this includes the domains of word recognition, reading comprehension, cognitive processing, memory, writing, vocabulary, general reading, word skills, language) vs. other (referred to as *less or low language domains*, that is, the remaining seven categories shown in Table 3). The appropriate dependent measures were coded 1 vs. −1, respectively. The second contrast variable compared on the general domain of *reading* (this included the domain categories of word recognition, reading comprehension, general reading and word skills) with nonreading measures (all other domains). The reading contrast variable was coded 1 vs. −1, respectively.

Thus, the first contrast variable reflects a broad domain of instructional behaviors and the second isolates the general area of reading. Because reading is the most thoroughly investigated domain, we refined our comparison to more specific areas of reading. A third contrast variable was created within the domain of reading which compared real word recognition and reading comprehension. This variable was coded +1 reading comprehension, −1 word recognition, and 0 for the other domains. (Note: For this trichotomy: 1, −1, 0, the 0 coded groups are omitted in the β coefficients of the regression model. We will follow-up potential interactions that emerge in the regression modeling, however, by only describing properties of the 1 and −1 coded group).

A fourth contrast variable focused on the skills or processes that underlie the transfer measures (e.g., real word recognition and reading comprehension). The word skill and cognitive process categories of dependent measures were contrasted because it was assumed they underlie transfer to reading words, comprehension, writing, etc. We created a variable to compare the word skill domain and the cognitive process domain. Thus, the fourth variable assessed *skill* (i.e., word skills, category related to phonics, orthographic) and process (category related to cognitive processes). These domains were coded 1 and −1, respectively. A code of 0 was assigned to the other domain categories.

Three contrast variables were created related to instruction. The first contrast variable compared the combined, SI alone, and DI alone models with the NonSI and NonDI model (coded 1, 1, 1 vs. −3, respectively). We termed the SI and DI

Table 10. Weighted Least Square Analysis of Effect Size
Estimated on Treatment Domain and Treatment Approach to
Determine Target Domain × Treatment Interactions[a]

Predictors	X^2 (df = 1)	β	SE^b
1. Method Composite	21.59***	−.03	.009
Setting			
2. State Setting	.21	.02	.09
3. Type of Setting	.26	−.01	.05
4. Unit of Instruction	2.81	.07	.06
Instructional Domains			
5. *Language* vs. Nonlanguage	1.41	.03	.03
6. *Reading* vs. Nonreading	.07	−.006	.03
7. Comprehension vs. Word (*Word*)	8.15**	.09	.04
8. *Skill* vs. Process	.02	−.009	.08
Type of Instruction			
9. Undifferentiated vs. other (*General*)	.58	−.0093	.01
10. Bottom-up vs. top-down (*Orientation*)	5.33*	.090	.05
11. Strategy + DI (*Combined*) vs. SI & DI in Isolation	10.17**	.07	.03
Sample Characteristics			
12. Age	6.70*	−.02	.01
13. Gender Ratio	.00	.00	.04
14. Discrepancy	2.91	.08	.07
15. Intelligence	.001	−.001	.03
16. Reading Severeity	1.47	−.03	.04
Interactions			
17. Lang * General	1.40	.01	.01
18. Lang * Orient	1.03	−.04	.06
19. Lang * Combined	1.86	−.03	.03
20. Read * General	3.06	−.01	.03
21. Read * Orient	.83	.03	.05
22. Read * Combined	6.83**	.03	.03
23. Word * General	4.12*	.03	.02
24. Word * Orient	7.95**	−.13	.06
25. Word * Combined	2.47	.04	.04
26. Skill * General	.05	.005	.03
27. Skill * Orient	.02	.01	.11
28. Skill * Combined	.27	.02	.07
df			
X^2	306		
r^2	660.24**		
	.14		

Notes: [a]Type III sum of squares (partials influence of all variables).

[b]Standard errors are approximations because the Proc GLM program does not correct by factors of $\sqrt{MS_e}$ a procedure suggested by Hedges and Olkin (1985) where MS_E is the error or residual mean square of regression.

alone models and the Combined Model contrast as an *undifferentiated* model. Thus, the three generally effective models (undifferentiated models) were compared with a model that primarily includes one-to-one and small group instruction (nonstrategy & nondirect instruction). The second contrast variable directly compares a bottom-up approach (direct instruction-alone) to a top down (strategy instruction-alone) approach. The DI-alone and SI-alone Models were coded +1 and −1, respectively. The Combined Model and weak overlap model (the NonDI & NonSI model) were coded 0 (these are irrelevant models and therefore are omitted in the regression analysis). The third contrast compared the *Combined Model* with direct and strategy instruction in isolation (coded 3 for the Combined Model, and −1 for the SI Alone Model, −1 for the DI Alone Model, and −1 for NonDI & NonSI, respectively).

In general, we sought to determine if the contrasts related to instructional domains (language vs. other; reading vs. other; recognition vs. comprehension; and skills vs. processes) and to instruction interacted with each other. Because comparisons were made between categories or domains of dependent measures, we changed the unit of analysis from the averaging of all effect sizes within studies to one effect size, to averaging effect sizes within each study as a function of the category of the dependent measure. Because the coding scheme did not necessarily yield independent effect sizes within studies, it was necessary to partial the effects of all the variables, via a Type III sum of squares. The methodological composite score, setting, and sample variables were also entered into the equation to partial out their influence on potential interactions.

For the main effects (See Table 10), the important findings were: (1) the significant positive beta weight reflects higher mean effect sizes for reading comprehension when compared to word recognition measures, (2) bottom-up instruction (direct instruction) yields higher mean effect sizes than top down instruction (strategy instruction), and (3) the Combined Model yields higher mean effect sizes than the competing models. The significant negative beta weights indicate: (1) studies of low methodological sophistication yield higher effect sizes than those with higher methodological composite scores, and (2) younger children had higher effect size scores than older children. As shown in Table 10, three significant treatment x domain interactions (read x combined; word x general approach; and word x orientation) emerged, and therefore qualify the main effects.

Table 11 provides a follow-up of these interactions by reporting the weighted least square mean effect sizes. Mean scores are also provided for the variables coded as 0. However, it is important for the reader to remember that the variables coded 0 are not important to interpreting the significant interactions. As shown in Table 11, the interaction related to reading x intervention model (read × combined) reflects higher effect sizes on reading measures (this included the categories of word recognition, reading comprehension, general reading, and word skills) when compared to nonreading measures for the Combined Instructional

Table 11. Follow-up to Instruction × Domain Interactions

Reading Instruction[a] Read × Combined Instruction	Sample Size	K	Mean	SD	Weighted Mean	Number of Ind. Sample	Scheffe
I Reading Domain							
1. Nonstrategy or nondirect instr.	1,615	51	.67	.49	.67	92	
2. Combined strategy & direct instr.	1,344	34	.84	.67	.98	78	
3. Strategy or direct instr. in isolation	2,116	71	.74	.50	.59	164	
II Non Reading Domain							
4. No strategy instruction or direct instr.	2,368	76	.60	.61	.58	122	
5. Combined strategy & direct instr.	1,235	62	.74	.56	.65	148	
6. Strategy or direct instr. in isolation	2,004	83	.76	.54	.63	204	$(2>1=5=6=3=4)$
Word × General Interaction[b]							
I Word Recognition							
1. General (combinations of SI or DI)	1,280	50	.71	.59	.58	108	
2. Nonstrategy & nondirect instruction	862	28	.57	.48	.63	48	
II Non Reading (coded as 0)							
3. General	3,530	149	.76	.52	.63	354	
4. Nonstrategy/direct instruction	2,378	77	.64	.61	.60	120	

(continued)

Table 11. (Continued)

Reading Instruction[a] Read × Combined Instruction	Sample Size	K	Mean	SD	Weighted Mean	Number of Ind. Sample	Scheffe
III Reading Comprehension							
5. General	1,889	51	.82	.60	.82	130	
6. Nonstrategy/nondirect instruction	737	22	.68	.54	.66	44	(5>6=1=2)
Word × Orientation Interaction[c]							
I Word Recognition							
1. Direct instruction—alone	589	27	.76	.52	.67	50	
2. Combined + other approaches (0)	127	41	.58	.55	.62	82	
3. Strategy instruction—alone	426	10	.75	.67	.36	34	
II Non reading behavior (coded as 0)							
4. Direct instruction—alone	1,093	54	.80	.59	.65	104	
5. Combined + other approaches	3,606	39	.68	.56	.62	278	
6. Strategy instruction—alone	1,209	33	.74	.44	.54	102	

(continued)

105

Table 11. (Continued)

Reading Instruction[a] Read × Combined Instruction	Sample Size	K	Mean	SD	Weighted Mean	Number of Ind. Sample	Scheffe
III Reading Comprehension							
7. Direct instruction—alone	379	16	.64	.45	.56	28	
8. Combined + other approaches (0)	1,824	43	.85	.67	.86	100	
9. Strategy instruction—alone	423	14	.71	.43	.68	40	(1=9>7>3)

Note: [a]The question addressed is:
Does it matter if combinations of both direct or strategy instructions are compared with each model in isolation?
Answer: Yes, but only in the domain of reading.
Reading Domain includes measures of word recognition, word skill, and reading comprehension
[b]Question: Does undifferentiated instruction (general combinations of direct and strategy models) produce larger effect sizes when compared to the competing model?
Answer: Yes, but only for reading comprehension.
[c]Question: Does direct instruction-alone yield higher effect size estimates than strategy instruction-alone?
Answer: Yes, but only on word recognition measures. The reverse effect emerges for strategy instruction on reading comprehension measures

Model. No significant differences ($ps > .05$) were found between various instructional models on the nonreading measures.

Table 11 also shows the interaction related to various combinations of strategy and direct instruction models (labeled as general or undifferentiated SI and DI models) vs. a model that includes minimal components related to strategy instruction and direct instruction (NonSI and NonDI model). As shown in Table 11, high effect sizes emerged on reading comprehension measures for undifferentiated (general) models when compared to word recognition measures. No differences emerged between reading measures for the NonDI and NonSI model.

Table 11 also shows the weighted means related to the reading skill x orientation (top-down vs. bottom-up; i.e., SI Alone vs. DI Alone) interaction. As shown, the results indicated that strategy-instruction alone models yield lower effect sizes on word recognition measures than direct instruction-alone models (the nonreading measures and the combination and NonDI and NonSI model were ignored in the analysis). In contrast, the direct instruction-alone model yields smaller effect sizes on reading comprehension measures than the strategy instruction-alone model.

In summary, the results support the notion that treatment specificity emerges between reading and nonreading domains, as well as within the reading domain. The *Combined Model* (direct instruction + strategy instruction) has its most pronounced effect on measures of reading. The SI Alone model yields substantially lower effect sizes on word recognition when compared to DI-alone model, whereas SI-alone model yields larger effect sizes on comprehension measures than the DI-alone model. The comparisons of outcome measures show no significant difference in effect size between treatments at a global level (high language vs. low language demand measures) or at a skill or process level (word skill vs. the cognitive process category).

Domain and Treatment Outcomes as a Function of Aptitude

Intelligence and Reading Severity

Standardized measures of intelligence (primarily a Full Scale IQ score on the Wechsler Intelligence Scale for Children) and reading (primarily word recognition) were the most frequent means of identifying the learning disability sample. The independent results of the intelligence and reading severity variable on outcomes for the two primary interventions (direct instruction, strategy instruction) were provided in Table 4. Effect size estimates, averaged within each of the 180 studies, were next analyzed to determine whether combinations of intellectual and reading level influenced treatment outcomes. This analysis was done because standardized scores at or below the 25th percentile in reading recognition (see Siegel & Ryan, 1989; Stanovich & Siegel, 1994) along with standardized intelligence scores above 84 are considered reasonable cut-off scores towards operationalizing the term learning disabilities (See Morrison & Siegel, 1991, for discussion of this issue). Four levels of reading severity (no information, < 85, > 84 and < 91, > 90) and three levels of intellectual performance [no information, low-average (< 90), average (> 91)] were analyzed, via a WLS with the methodological composite score partialed from the analysis. Direct instruction and strategy instruction were analyzed separately because some cell sizes for intelligence and reading were too small (< 5 studies) for the complete analysis. Studies that did not report mean ages of the sample ($N = 20$) were excluded from the analysis.

A 2 (direct vs. nondirect) × 3 (Intelligence: high vs. low vs. no information) × 4 (reported reading severity: < 85, > 84 and < 92, > 91 and no information) WLS (analogue to an ANOVA and ANCOVA) which partials the influence of methodology and chronological age, was computed. When methodology and age were partialed from the analysis, significant effects were isolated to the severity of reading x intelligence interaction, $X^2(6, N = 160) = 13.95$, $p < .05$ and the partialing influence of the methods composite score, $X^2(1, N = 160) = 14.12$, $p < .001$. No other effects were significant. The WLS means, when partialed for age and methodology for the intelligence categories of no formation, high scores, low scores were .89, .61, and .64 for studies that include no reading scores, .58, .72, and .74 for studies that report standardized reading scores below 85, .31, .55, and .90, for studies that report scores between 85 and 90, and .62, .68, and .18 for studies that report scores above 89, respectively. Thus, no aptitude x treatment interaction emerges when the results are partialed for the influence of the methodology composite score and age.

A 2 (strategy vs. nonstrategy) × 3 (Intelligence: high vs. low vs. no information) × 4 (reported reading severity: < 85, > 84 and < 92; > 91 and no information) WLS (which partials the influence of methodology and chronological age), was again computed of effect size estimates. When methodology and age were partialed from the analysis, a significant effect occured for severity of reading × intelligence, $X^2(6, N = 160) = 14.08$, $p < .05$, and the partialing influence of methods, $X^2(1, N = 160) = 14.72$, $p < .001$. Thus, the results are similar to those of direct instruction.

In sum, across direct instruction and strategy instruction studies, we found that the magnitude of effect sizes interacted with intelligence and reading severity level. Three findings emerged related to this interaction. First, studies which produced the highest effect sizes had (a) no psychometric information on intelligence or reading *or* (b) report a minimal discrepancy between intelligence and reading [low-average intelligence scores (< 91) and comparable reading scores (between > 84 and 91)] when compared to other conditions. Second, studies which yield the lowest effect sizes reported (a) reading scores that were slightly higher than intelligence scores (i.e., reading scores are above a standard score of 90 and intelligence scores are in the standard score range of 84 to 90), or (b) reported reading scores between 84 and 90 with no information on intelligence. Finally, the results suggest a pattern related to reading for studies that report intelligence scores below 90. Effect sizes were significantly higher when reading scores were in the 84 to 90 range when compared to the severe (< 85) and average range (> 90). Thus, when intelligence scores approximate reading scores (i.e., both intelligence and reading scores are comparable and are in the 84 to 90 range), effect sizes are higher when compared to the other conditions.

The Influence of Operational Definitions on Domain and Treatment Outcome

There are two problems with the previous analyses on the influence of intelligence and reading severity. First, we did not take into consideration the issue of domain generality and domain specificity. As shown in our previous analysis, some combinations of treatment (Combined DI & SI model) interact with treatment domain (reading vs. nonreading domains) and, therefore, aptitude × treatment interactions emerge when domain is taken into consideration. Second, the combinations of intelligence and reading scores are not placed within a context of operational definitions of LD. For example, there has been debate on whether intelligence has any influence on outcome measures when groups are primarily deficient in reading (see Stanovich & Siegel, 1994, for discussion of this issue). Thus, in the next analysis we compared various configurations of IQ and reading scores that have application to the definitional issues of learning disabilities.

We assume that the face validity of a definition is enhanced if one can show that such a definition is significantly related to treatment outcomes. To this end, we created three contrast variables related to the definition of learning disabilities. The first contrast variable compares studies that report psychometric information (report reading and/or intelligence scores) versus those studies that fail to report psychometric information. We defined this contrast variable as those studies which reported psychometric *criteria* (report psychometric scores) versus those studies which reported no psychometric information (i.e., no reported psychometric criteria). Studies were coded as 1 and −1, respectively. Thus, the first contrast compares those studies which report psychometric information (reading and/or intelligence scores; 57% of the studies) to those that fail to report any psychometric information (43%).

For the second contrast variable, studies were coded as meeting cut-off criteria (20% of the studies) and those that met other criteria (coded as +1 and −1, respectively). A cut-off score in reading at or below the 25th percentile (i.e., the 25th percentile is a standard score of 90) and intelligence scores at or above 84 is considered one possible operational definition of learning disabilities (see Morrison & Siegel, 1991, Stanovich & Siegel, 1994). A final contrast variable compared discrepancy defined samples in which IQ is above 90 (IQ scores > 90 and reading scores < 91, this represents 13.5% of the studies) and discrepancy defined samples in which intelligence is below 90 (intelligence and reading < 91; 17 % of the studies). The discrepancy between IQ and reading was a difference score > 12. We were unable to make adequate comparisons between nondiscrepancy defined

Table 12. WLS Regression Analysis of Aptitude
Interactions Related to Domain and Instruction

Predictors	$\chi^{2\,a}$	B	$\chi^{2\,b}$	B
1. Methods Composite	26.71***	−.02	14.77***	−.02
Main Effects				
Instructional Domain				
2. *Language* vs. Nonlanguage	9.58***	.06	2.83	.06
3. *Reading* vs. Nonreading	1.98	.02	.60	−.02
4. Comprehension vs. *Word* Recog	2.69	.03	5.16**	−.08
5. *Skill* vs. Process	10.67***	−.11	.94	−.06
Type of Instruction				
6. *General* (undifferentiated) vs. other	27.74***	.07	8.40***	.07
7. Bottom-up (DI) vs. top-down (SI) *orientation*	1.92	.03	5.74**	.08
8. SI plus DI (*Combined*) vs. SI and DI in Isolation	15.68***	.05	9.61***	.07
Sample				
9. Age	.70	−.004	2.29	−.013
10. Report Psychometric *Criteria* vs. No Criteria	.96	−.01	1.68	.03
11. Report *Cutoff* scores vs. No Information	1.13	−.02	.90	−.04
12. *Discrepancy*-High IQ vs. Discrepancy-Low IQ	.01	.0001	.00	.005
Interactions-Domain				
13. Lang * Criteria	12.63***	−.04	7.83***	−.05
14. Read * Criteria	.58	.01	5.97**	.05
15. Word * Criteria	.82	−.01	9.19***	−.09
16. Skill * Criteria	25.25***	.14	2.17	.07
17. Lang * Cutoff	2.0 4	.02	.13	.01
18. Read * Cutoff	4.96*	−.03	.19	−.01
19. Word * Cutoff	.76	.02	.50	−.02
20. Skill * Cutoff	6.73**	−.09	1.98	−.09
21. Lang * Disc	.06	.009	.38	.04
22. Read * Disc	.002	.001	.007	−.004
23. Word * Disc	5.29**	−.081	.75	−.05
24. Skill * Disc	4.91*	.12	1.06	.10
Interactions-Instruction				
25. General * Criteria	1.29	−.007	.14	−.004
26. Orient * Criteria	26.02***	−.13	12.06***	−.16
27. Combined * Criteria	9.77***	−.04	10.10***	−.68
28. General * Cutoff	7.56***	.04	2.93	.04
29. Orient * Cutoff	11.49***	.10	6.83**	.13
30. Combined * Cutoff	2.08	.02	4.29*	.05
31. General * Disc	10.69***	−.08	3.33	−.08
32. Orient * Disc	1.16	.04	.36	.03
33. Combined * Disc	1.53	−.02	.05	−.009

(continued)

Table 12. WLS Regression Analysis of Aptitude
Interactions Related to Domain and Instruction

Predictors	$\chi^{2\ a}$	B	$\chi^{2\ b}$	B
DF	1140		310	
N	1173		343	
χ^2	2510.63[*]		709.81[*]	
R^2	.17		.16	
Mean ES	.54		.61	

Notes: [a]Unit of analysis considers all dependent measures as independent
[b]Unit of analysis averaged within domains (e.g., mathematics measures) for each study
Underline indicates significant results for both units of analysis.
[*]$p < .05$. [**]$p < .01$. [***]$p < .001$

groups because many of these children were excluded from the analysis (i.e., the majority of studies include school identified LD samples and, therefore, most of the studies include samples placed in special education related to some form of discrepancy criteria). Coding of the studies was +1 for high IQ discrepancy defined samples, −1 for low IQ discrepancy defined samples, and 0 for the remaining samples.

To test the robustness of potential interactions related to the sample definition, two units of analysis were used in a WLS analysis. One unit considers every effect size in a study as independent and the other averages effect sizes within the 17 domains (see Table 3) for each study. The results are presented in Table 12. Because setting and gender were not significant predictors in the previous analysis, they were removed from the analysis so they would not take variance from the primary variables of interest.

As shown in Table 12, several significant interactions emerged. However, when effect sizes were based on averages within studies for each domain, only the language × reported criteria, orientation of instruction × reported criteria, combined instruction × reported criteria, and combined instruction × cut-off score interactions remained significant. Table 13 provides the weighted least square means for the various interactions when the unit of analysis is averaged within domain and study. Also provided are the mean IQ and reading scores across studies. To facilitate interpretation, the high and low score of the weighted least square mean is underlined.

The important patterns of the definition × domain interactions were that high effect sizes emerge in the areas of language and reading when compared to other

Table 13. Main Interactions Related to Domain and Instruction as a Function of LD Definition—Group Design

Domain as a Function of Reported and Nonreported Psychometric Information

	Sample Size	K	Mean	SD	Weighted Mean	Intelligence			Reading		
						M	SD	K	M	SD	K
I. Language × Criteria											
High Language Demands											
1. Criteria	4,112	162	.69	.51	.61[a]	97.53	6.67	145	82.83	10.81	90
2. No Criteria	3,899	110	.83	.61	.57	–	–	–	–	–	–
Low Language Demands											
3. Criteria	1,305	52	.62	.56	.71	97.01	8.20	45	84.16	11.63	21
4. No Criteria	1,249	52	.65	.57	.50	–	–	–	–	–	–
II. Reading* Criteria											
Reading											
1. Criteria	2,427	97	.74	.55	.65[b]	97.00	6.67	87	83.57	10.64	55
2. No Criteria	2,643	59	.94	.70	.56	–	–	–	–	–	–
NonReading											
3. Criteria	3,102	118	.62	.48	.70	97.74	1.04	104	82.57	11.29	55
4. No Criteria	2,505	103	.79	.62	.61	–	–	–	–	–	–

(continued)

Table 13. (Continued)

Domain as a Function of Reported and Nonreported Psychometric Information

	Sample Size	K	Mean	SD	Weighted Mean	Intelligence			Reading		
						M	SD	K	M	SD	K
*III. Word * Criteria*											
Reading Comprehension											
1. Criteria	1,044	46	.74	.61	.64[c]	96.26	6.83	39	86.29	10.28	27
2. No Criteria	1,582	27	.82	.55	.90	–	–	–	–	–	–
Other (Score as 0)											
3. Criteria	3,122	117	.65	.49	.59	97.55	7.05	104	82.30	9.80	52
4. No Criteria	2,786	109	.79	.60	.60	–	–	–	–	–	–
Word Recognition											
5. Criteria	1,363	52	.67	.52	.62	98.00	7.16	48	81.33	12.83	32
6. No Criteria	780	26	.64	.66	.46	–		–	–	–	–
I. Orientation × Criteria											
Strategy Instruction—Alone											
1. Criteria	672	22	.80	.47	.73[d]	95.57	5.43	22	75.04	10.11	16
2. No Criteria	1,385	35	.69	.49	.48	–	–	–	–	–	–
Other											
3. Criteria	3,296	127	.65	.55	.59	98.32	6.00	111	84.37	8.36	62
4. No Criteria	3,261	96	.75	.62	.68	–	–	–	–	–	–

(continued)

113

Table 13. (Continued)

Domain as a Function of Reported and Nonreported Psychometric Information

	Sample Size	K	Mean	SD	Weighted Mean	Intelligence M	Intelligence SD	Intelligence K	Reading M	Reading SD	Reading K
Direct Instruction—Alone											
5. Criteria	1,560	66	.67	.47	.60	96.35	8.95	58	84.53	13.86	33
6. No Criteria	501	31	.93	.65	.73	-	-	-	-	-	-
II. Combination × Criteria											
Combined SI & DI											
1. Criteria	1,221	61	.73	.55	.62[e]	97.27	6.25	56	84.89	8.47	20
2. No Criteria	1,358	35	.86	.67	.95	-	-	-	-	-	-
Other											
3. Criteria	2,075	66	.58	.54	.56	99.38	5.59	55	84.13	8.40	42
4. No Criteria	1,903	61	.68	.61	.57	-	-	-	-	-	-
Strategy or Direct Instruction-Alone											
5. Criteria	2,233	88	.70	.47	.62	96.13	8.11	80	81.44	13.42	49
6. No Criteria	1,887	66	.81	.58	.58	-	-	-	-	-	-
III. Orientation x Cut-off Scores											
Strategy Instruction - Alone											
1. Cut-off Score	544	15	.61	.31	.67[f]	93.50	3.11	15	73.94	9.36	15
2. No Cut-off	1,514	42	.78	.52	.52	100.00	6.88	7	92.0	-	1

(continued)

Table 13. (Continued)

Domain as a Function of Reported and Nonreported Psychometric Information

	Sample Size	K	Mean	SD	Weighted Mean	Intelligence		K	Reading		K
						M	SD		M	SD	
Other (Coded as 0)											
3. Cut-off Score	1,073	37	.67	.50	.67	97.79	4.15	37	80.51	5.70	37
4. No Cut-off Score	5,484	186	.70	.60	.63	98.58	6.75	74	90.09	8.47	25
Direct Instruction											
5. Cut-off Score	535	23	.76	.46	.77	92.42	4.99	23	77.85	8.18	23
6. No Cut-off Score	1,527	74	.75	.57	.59	98.93	10.6	35	99.88	11.96	10
IV. Combination × Cut-off Scores											
Combined SI & DI											
1. Cut-off	367	14	.90	.61	.81^g	97.84	5.93	14	82.58	5.93	14
2. No Cut-off	2,212	82	.75	.60	.72	97.08	6.41	42	90.28	11.47	6
Non DI & SI											
3. Cut-off	706	23	.52	.37	.58	97.75	2.71	23	79.25	5.30	23
4. No Cut-off	3,271	104	.65	.60	.57	100.56	6.77	32	90.04	7.70	19

(continued)

115

Table 13. (Continued)

Domain as a Function of Reported and Nonreported Psychometric Information

	Sample Size				Weighted Mean	Intelligence			Reading		
		K	Mean	SD	Mean	M	SD	K	M	SD	K
Strategy or Direct Instruction-Alone											
5. Cut-off	1,079	38	.70	.41	.70	92.85	4.31	38	76.31	8.76	38
6. No Cut-off	3,041	116	.76	.55	.59	99.11	9.54	42	99.17	11.60	11

Notes: Criteria = Study reports psychometric scores
No Criteria = Study does not report psychometric scores
[a]Total K possible for 17 domains averaged within studies is 376
[a]Scheffe 3>2&4;3=1;3>4
[b]Scheffe 1>2;1=3&4;2=4
[c]Scheffe 2>1=5=6
[d]Scheffe 1=6>5>2
[e]Scheffe 2>1=5=6=3=4
[f]Scheffe 5>2; 1>2,3=4=5; 5>6
[g]Scheffe 1>5>3; 2>4=6
All weighted means are partialed by the methodological composite score and age

domains for studies which fail to report psychometric information on the sample. Important findings related to the instruction interactions were:

1. Direct instruction-alone yields higher effect sizes than strategy instruction-alone when no psychometric information is reported. Strategy instruction-alone is significantly lower when no psychometric information is reported than when it is reported, whereas direct instruction yields approximately the same magnitude in effect sizes under both reported and nonreported psychometric conditions. Strategy instruction is comparable to direct instruction conditions when psychometric scores are reported.
2. The Combined Model yields substantially higher effect sizes than competing models (SI Alone, DI Alone, NonSI, & NonDI) when no psychometric information is reported. No significant differences emerged in effect size between instructional models for those studies that report psychometric information.
3. When cut-off scores (IQ > 84 and reading < 90) are computed, higher effect sizes emerge from the Combined Model (SI + DI) when compared to competing models (SI Alone, DI Alone, NonSI & NonDI).

GENERAL DISCUSSION

This article summarizes group design intervention research conducted in the last 30 years for students with learning disabilities. The current findings, combined with an earlier meta-analysis (Swanson et al., 1996), provide evidence that educational intervention for students with learning disabilities produces positive effects of respectable magnitude. We will address five major findings on the current synthesis.

1. The magnitude of change related to treatment is greater in some academic domains than others. The instructional areas we know most about in terms of treatment are in the domains of reading (e.g., word recognition, reading comprehension). The least researched domains are in the areas of intelligence, creativity (e.g., divergent and convergent thinking), and language. Based on Cohen's criteria of .80 as a substantive finding, only studies in the domains of reading comprehension, vocabulary, and creativity approached a threshold for a large effect when the confounds related to methodology were partialed from the analysis. The magnitude was .81 for reading comprehension, .73 for vocabulary, and .78 for creativity. Studies that produced effect sizes in the moderate range (>.60 and <.70) were in the domains of cognitive processing (.69, e.g., metacognition, attribution, problem solving), word recognition (.65, real word recognition), memory (.66), writing (.66), intelligence (.61, performance on standardized tests), attitude-self concept (.60, e.g., attitude scales), phonics/orthographic skills (.60, e.g., word skills such as reading pseudowords or recognizing correct spellings), and global achievement (.64, e.g., teacher grades, class ranking).

Those categories of dependent measures in which effect sizes were relatively moderate (< .55) across intervention studies were spelling (.51), mathematics (.45), general reading (.46, these include measures in which word recognition and comprehension cannot be separated or are confounded on standardized tests), social skills (.47, e.g., behavior ratings), perceptual processes (.53, e.g., visual-motor, handwriting), and language processes (.50, e.g., listening comprehension).

2. Not all treatments are equally effective. Before we isolate effective treatments, it is important to preface our conclusions with three observations. First, we assume that effective treatments (those that yield high effect sizes relative to the control condition) which reflect diverse theoretical perspectives share some commonalities related to instructional components, tactics, and/or procedures. Our task was to identify those instructional and methodological ingredients that contitute an effective intervention for students with learning disabilities. Thus, we did not rely on the label of the independent variable provided by the authors to characterize treatments. Instead, we coded the methods and instructional components that made-up the treatments. Therefore, based upon the occurrence or nonoccurrence of component information, studies were sorted into four general instructional models [Combined Model (Combined Strategy & Direct Instruction), Strategy Instruction Alone, Direct Instruction Alone, and NonDI and NonSI model, i.e., treatments that primarily include small group and individual instruction] were analyzed.

Second, variations in methodology have a profound impact on treatment outcomes. As shown in Table 4, if studies include control and treatment conditions that differ in (a) teachers, (b) setting, and/or (c) instructional loads (the steps and procedures of treatment conditions have minimal overlap with the control condition), and if studies fail to report psychometric data on the students with learning disabilities, then these studies yield high effect sizes no matter what the treatment. Thus, we attempted to partial out the artifacts across studies prior to making judgements on potentially effective treatments.

Finally, what we know about treatment is biased by the publication of positive outcomes. The issue we confronted continually in our analysis is whether we could clearly differentiate instructional treatments that supersede others given that the literature is biased toward publishing positive outcomes. This is a formidable task for individuals who conduct a meta-analysis because what is commonly concluded from disseminated manuscripts on instruction is that everything works. This conclusion, affectionately called the "The Dodo verdict" (i.e., "everybody has won and all must have a prize"; see Parloff, 1984; Weisz et al., 1995), emanates from the landmark meta-analysis of Smith, Glass, and Miller (1980). In this synthesis, they found that therapy "is beneficial… consistently so and in may ways.. different types of psychotherapy (verbal or behavioral, psychodynamic, client-centered, or systematic desensitization) do not produce different types or degrees of benefit… It is clearly possible that all psychotherapies are equally effective…" (pp. 184, 186).

Our results suggest that this picture is quite different in the area of learning disabilities. We find, generally, that when both published and nonpublished literatures (dissertations) are considered, a *Combined* Direct Instruction and Strategy Instruction Model is an effective procedure for remediating learning disabilities when compared to other instructional models. The important instructional components that make up this treatment are: attentions to sequencing, drill-repetition-practice, segmenting information into parts or units for later synthesis, controlling of task difficulty through prompts and cues, making use of technology, the teacher systematically modeling problem solving steps, and making use of small interactive groups. We also found that regardless of the general model of instruction, only a few instructional components increase the predictive power of treatment effectiveness beyond what can be predicted by variations in methodology and age. These instructional components, the majority of which are reflected in the *Combined Model* were:

1. *Sequencing* (breaking down the task, fading of prompts or cues, sequencing short activities, step by step prompts).

2. *Drill-repetition* and *practice-review* (daily testing of skills; e.g., statements in the treatment description related to mastery criteria, distributed review and practice, using redundant materials or text, repeated practice, sequenced review, daily feedback, and/or weekly review).

3. *Segmentation* (breaking down targeted skill into smaller units and then synthesizing the parts into a whole, for example, statements in the experimental condition included breaking down the task into short activities or step by step sequences, breaking down targeted skill into smaller units, breaking the text or problem into component parts, segmenting and then synthesizing components parts).

4. *Directed Questioning and Responses* (the teacher verbally asking "process-related" and/or "content related" questions of students, for example, treatment may include dialectic questioning, students are directed by teacher to ask questions, teacher and student engage in dialogue, the teacher asks questions).

5. *Control difficulty or processing demands of a task* (task sequenced from easy to difficult and only necessary hints and probes are provided the child, for example, statements in treatment reflect short activities with the level of difficulty controlled, the teacher provides necessary assistance, the teacher provides simplified demonstration, the task is sequenced from easy to difficult, discussion is given to a task analysis).

6. *Technology* (e.g., use of a computer, structured text, flow charts to facilitate presentation; utilization of a structured curriculum, emphasis on pictorial representations, uses of specific or structured material, use of media to facilitate presentation and feedback).

7. *Modeling of problem solving steps by teacher* (teacher provides demonstration of processes or steps to solve problem or how to do a task, e.g., writing, comprehension, decoding words).

8. *Group Instruction* (instruction occurs in a small group; students and/or teacher interact within the group).

9. *A supplement to teacher and peer involvement* (may include homework, parent or others assist instruction).

10. *Strategy cues* (reminders to use strategies or multi-steps, the teacher verbalizes problem solving or procedures to solve, instruction makes use of "think-aloud" models, teacher presents benefits of strategy use or procedures).

We used a three-tier procedure to arrive at the above conclusions. In the first tier of our analysis we focused on two general (although not mutually exclusive) instructional models the literature considers as having a positive influence on treatment outcomes. We considered one approach (direct instruction) a bottom-up model and the other (strategy instruction) a top-down model. No doubt, there has been some lively debate over the years in the literature as to whether instruction should be top-down, via emphasizing the knowledge base, heuristics and explicit strategies, or a bottom-up emphasis which entails hierarchical instruction at the skill level (e.g., Adams, 1990; Palincsar & Brown, 1984; Vellutino & Scanlon, 1991). We considered both approaches viable for students with learning disabilities, and, therefore, we first considered in our analysis these two approaches as competing models.

Three findings emerged from this first tier of analysis: (1) Strategy instruction produces larger effect sizes than those studies that do not use such procedures, (2) Direct instruction models yield higher effect sizes than the nondirect instruction models, and (3) When strategy instruction and direct instruction presentation orders are varied in a regression model, strategy instruction bolsters outcomes (i.e., improves the R^2 of the effect size estimate) independent of the contribution of direct instruction. Thus, the two models operate independent of each other.

Given that the two models were weakly correlated ($r = .17$), the results provide support for an independence model (i.e., both models make independent contributions to effect size). However, we found that only 1% of the variance for direct instruction and 2% of the variance for strategy instruction was related to estimates of effect size after the methodological composite score was entered in the analysis. Thus, the results of the first tier of analysis yield results of equivocal practical importance.

For the second tier of our analysis we divided the two general models into four models [*Combined* Direct Instruction and Strategy Instruction *(Combined* DI &

SI), SI alone, DI alone, and NonSI & NonDI]. We found that the *Combined* Direct Instruction and Strategy Instruction Model yields higher effect sizes than the three competing general models. We also addressed the issue of whether the four models were actually reflective of distinct treatments (discriminant validity) by analyzing the instructional composition of each approach. Significant differences were found between the models in terms of the frequency of instructional components, as well as to components significantly related to the magnitude of effect sizes. Three components of the Combined DI & SI Model were distinct from the other models in predicting effect size. Those components were related to attributions about strategy use, teacher modeling of problem solving steps, and instruction occurring in the context of small interactive groups.

For the third tier of analysis, we ignored the four general models and attempted to isolate those components of instruction that predicted effect size. Those components that optimally predicted effect size estimates across all categories of dependent measures were sequencing, drill-repetition-practice, controlling task difficulty, segmentation of information, technology, small interactive groups, augmentation of teacher instruction (e.g., homework), directed questioning/responding, and strategy cuing. The important findings were that only nine of the 20 components significantly contributed to effect size estimates.

3. *Some treatment effects are specific to the academic problems.* Based on the previous discussion, the Combined Direct Instruction and Strategy Instruction model [a model that includes the components of sequencing, drill-repetition-practice, segmentation, directed response/questioning, control of task difficulty, technology, small interactive groups, supplements to teacher instruction (e.g., homework), and strategy cuing] is a solid research-based approach towards the effective instruction of students with learning disabilities. As with any heuristic, however, the model reflects a general approach to remediation, and therefore needs modification, refinement, and/or elaboration when applied to isolated academic domains. Thus, there are instances in which various combinations of strategy and direct instruction models (and by implication the instructional components that make up these models) interact with domains of instruction. Before summarizing the findings related to treatment × domain interactions, three comments are necessary.

First, we reconfigured the treatment domains in our regression analysis by collapsing the 17 general categories (e.g., Table 3) into four general contrast variables. These contrast variables reflect a progression from general treatment domains to specific domains. This reconfiguration was done to control for obvious confounds (correlations) related to treatment and domain. That is, a common problem in synthesizing treatment research is that the independent variables (e.g., strategy training or phonics instruction) and dependent measures (e.g., metacognition or phonological awareness) are sometimes correlated. This occurs because the treatments use activities, probes, and/or materials etc. in daily instruction that overlap considerably with the dependent measures. Thus, to partially control for this confound, we clustered the dependent measures into four general contrast variables. The first contrast variable compared high language domains (such as reading, writing, spelling) with areas that "make fewer demands on language" or reflect fewer specialized language skills (e.g., mathematics draws on visual-spatial processing skills, as well as language skills). The second contrast variable compared reading measures and nonreading measures. Reading is clearly the most research area in learning disabilities and, therefore, the outcomes of studies that include reading measures were compared to all other domains. The third contrast variable focused on the important transfer measures of reading-real words and reading comprehension. That is, the purpose of reading intervention for students with learning disabilities is to increase their ability to read words and understand text. A final contrast variable focused on comparing low order skills (the category of dependent measures related to word skills) with high order processes (the category of dependent measures related to cognitive processing).

Second, the four general treatments (Combined SI & DI, DI Alone, SI Alone, NonDI & NonSI) were also reconfigured into various combinations. One contrast compares an undifferentiated model of strategy or direct instruction (a treatment with high overlapping and minimal overlapping instructional components) with a model void of the majority of SI and DI components (referred to as the NonDI & NonSI model). This latter model primarily reflects the components of one-to-one and small group instruction. The second contrast variable compares a bottom-up model (direct instruction model-only) with top-down instructional model (strategy instruction only). This contrast considers the issue of whether instruction in a domain is best predicted by a bottom-up or top-down model. The final contrast variable compares the Combined Strategy instruction and Direct Instruction Model with all other models.

Finally, we did not investigate potential three-way interactions between domain × treatment and related variables (aptitude, setting of instruction). This was because of the limited number of studies that could actually fill the various cell sizes in the analysis. Instead we partialed from the analysis setting and aptitude variables to better isolate treatment × domain interactions.

The important findings related to the WLS regression analysis of main and two way interactions for domain and treatment were as follows:

1. The Combined Model is more effective on reading related (e.g., word recognition and comprehension) measures than nonreading (e.g., mathematics, social skills) related measures.
2. Bottom-up instruction (direct instruction alone) yields higher effect sizes than top down (strategy instruction alone) models on word recognition, but not reading comprehension measures.
3. Classifications of dependent measures into very broad domains of tasks highly embedded in language (such as reading, writing, spelling) or less

embedded in language domains (such as in the areas of social skills, mathematics, attitude) or subskill or process domains of transfer measures (e.g., phonics and metacognition may underlie word recognition and reading comprehension, respectively) were not sensitive to the influence of the treatment model combinations.

Taken together, the results support the notion that a certain level of treatment specificity emerges across academic domains. The comparison of outcome measures showed that the effectiveness of the Combined Model is most pronounced on reading-related domains. The results indicate that the advantages of bottom-up instruction when compared to other models emerge primarily on word recognition measures.

Why is this latter finding important? The conception of reading, as a bottom up process, is firmly rooted in intervention for LD readers (e.g., see Gittelman & Feingold, 1983; Lovett et al., 1990). Researchers from a bottom-up model reason that accurate word recognition is a necessary condition for comprehension, and therefore emphasize oral word recognition and decoding in reading instruction. Instruction in processing begins with letter features, which give rise to letter identification, which in turn lead to word recognition. Once readers recognize words, they translate that into some sort of code, and derive meaning in much the same manner as when listening to spoken language (see Byrne, Freebody, & Gates, 1992, for a review). Although several instructional approaches emphasize bottom-up processes in which meaning is constructed from the sum of letters, words, and sentences on a page, skilled reading has been also viewed an interactive process between low and high-order processing components (Adams, 1990). Thus, sharp divisions exist about the most effective method of teaching reading (see Palincsar & Brown, 1984; Chall, 1967; Vellutino & Scanlon, 1991, for a review). Not surprisingly, divergent conceptions of the reading process have yielded a difference of opinions in how best to meet the needs of readers with learning disabilities. For example, in contrast to the bottom-up model, other models of reading assume that meaning construction proceeds from the reader's knowledge base rather than from the page up (see Dole, Duffy, Roehler, & Pearson, 1991, for a review). In this top-down approach, reading success is dependent on the reader's cognitive and language abilities, including familiarity with the topic of discourse, perspective, and knowledge of syntax (e.g., Baker & Brown, 1984; Palincsar & Brown, 1984; Paris, Cross, & Lipson, 1984; see Pressley et al., 1990; Wong, 1991, for review). These instructional approaches focus on (a) understanding the gist of topics, (b) summarizing information to differentiate important from unimportant ideas, and (c) deciding whether a question must be answered with their prior knowledge alone or with a combination of prior knowledge and text information.

Given the different theoretical orientations of these approaches, the superiority of the Combined Model over others in the reading domain is an important finding.

The results are consistent with the notion that lower-order and higher-order skills interact in order to gather meaning from text. Clearly, comprehension of text cannot occur without some critical threshold of word recognition skills. Learning disabled readers vary in these skills. What was unclear from the literature, however, is how treatments that focus on high or low order skills vary in outcomes. It appears that the bottom-up model is only pronounced at the word recognition level.

4. How the LD sample is defined influences outcome. There are two common assumptions related to sample characteristics and intervention we addressed. The first assumption is that the sample characteristics are irrelevant to the effect of treatment approaches. Support for this assumption emerges when treatment effects are independent of the characteristics of the sample. This assumption is derived from behavioral treatments that focus on the functional relationships between contingencies in the classroom context and the intensity and reliability of treatment delivery. Such procedures place secondary importance on sample description.

Our results suggest that variables related to gender and age were independent of treatment effects. Thus, no matter what the gender ratio for instruction or the age of the sample, the main effects of treatment across these variables are comparable. We found in our regression modeling that younger children yield higher effect sizes when setting, methodological, and aptitude variables were partialed from the analysis. However, all age levels produced high effect sizes suggesting that instructional procedures are effective across a broad age spectrum.

No support for the above assumption (treatment effects are independent of the characteristics of the sample), is found, however, when the aptitude variables of intelligence and reading severity were considered. The important results related to the IQ × Reading Severity interaction are:

1. Studies which produced the highest effect sizes had no psychometric information on intelligence or reading or reported the smallest discrepancy between intelligence and reading (intelligence scores between 84 and 91 and reading scores between 84 and 91) when compared to other studies reporting higher IQ (intelligence scores > 91) and reading scores between 84 and 91.

2. Studies which yielded the lowest effect sizes reported reading scores that were higher than intelligence scores (i.e., reading scores are above a standard score of 90 and intelligence scores are in the standard score range of 84 to 90) or reported reading scores between 84 and 90 with no information on intelligence.

Taken together, these studies suggest there are some sample characteristic variables that relate to treatment outcome. Perhaps the most important findings related to treatment outcomes are that the sorting of studies into operational definitions and nonoperational definitions did influence treatment outcomes. Reading scores at or below the 25th percentile in reading recognition (see Stanovich & Siegel, 1994; Siegel & Ryan, 1989) and standardized intelligence performance above 84 have been considered as critical cut-off scores for defining learning disabilities. The treatment validity of such a cut-off score definition, however, has not been tested as a function of treatment outcomes. The results support the notion that cut-off scores moderate treatment outcomes. The Combined Model yields higher effect sizes when cut-off scores can be computed when compared to studies in which cut-off scores cannot be computed.

5. *Methodological Variations have a Significant Impact on Treatment Outcome.* The mean effect size values generated by our current analysis suggest that the previous estimates of magnitude were inflated (Swanson et al., 1996). Our previous meta-analysis reported a .91 effect size for direct instruction and 1.07 for strategy instruction, whereas the current analysis reports .82 for direct instruction and .84 for strategy instruction. This is because the previous meta-analysis (a) used unweighted least squares to estimate effect size estimates, and/or (b) failed to partial out the influence of variations in methodology, and therefore generated mean effect values at a higher range.

The results of the current synthesis show that there are a number of other key variables related to methodology which influence treatment outcome. Although we took care to calculate the effect size for those studies that made comparisons between conditions from those that used repeated measures, there were a number of effects related to methodology that influenced outcomes. Before we indicate those variables, those methodological variables that in isolation did not seem to have an influence on treatment outcomes are considered.

One variable that did not significantly influence effect size was the number (or intensity) of instructional sessions. Although shorter instructional sessions were seen to have a trend toward larger effect sizes, those studies that included more sessions (greater than 31 sessions) were not significantly different in effect size from studies that included shorter sessions. Another variable that did not seem to be critical was the variation in materials (commercial or experimentally developed) between the control and experimental condition. Specifically, although there was a trend that different materials between conditions yield slightly higher effect sizes, there were no significant differences in effect size between these conditions. Another methodological variable that did not appear to be important is the "focus" of the control condition. We reasoned that control conditions that focus on the very same domain as a treatment condition would yield smaller effect sizes than those control conditions that focus on a completely different domain (i.e., mathematics vs. reading). We found a trend that the same domain as treatment had a slightly higher effect sizes when compared to the other conditions. However, this comparison was not significant.

Surprisingly, the variables related to treatment integrity and our internal validity rating scale did not separate the studies in terms of the magnitude of effect size. These two variables, however, were included in our methodological composite score. Although not significant in isolation, another methodological variable added to the composite score was the type of treatment assignment (random vs. nonrandom). Although there was a slight trend found that those studies providing no information on how treatments were assigned to subjects yielded larger effect sizes, these conditions did not vary from studies using a random assignment of treatment and those using no random assignment of treatment. Again this methodological variable was used in the composite score and its added effect had an influence on treatment outcomes.

The results clearly show that outcomes are influenced by variations in some methodological variables. Those isolated methodological variables that yield significant effects on the magnitude of effect size estimates are summarized as follows:

1. Those studies that used a different teacher between control and experimental groups yield significantly larger effect sizes than those studies that use the same teacher.
2. Those studies in which control and treatments occur in a different setting (i.e., classroom and school) yield significantly higher effect sizes than those in the same classroom setting.
3. Those studies that rely on experimental measures yield significantly higher effect sizes than those studies that rely on standardized measures.
4. Those studies published in dissertations yield significantly lower effect sizes than those published in journals.
5. Those studies that have a low overlap in terms of the number of instructional components between control and experimental conditions yield significantly higher effect sizes than those studies that have a high overlap in terms of instructional components (sequences, steps, methods, and procedures).
6. Those studies that do not report the setting in which the intervention occurred yield significantly lower effect sizes than those that do report the setting.
7. Those studies in which treatment was administered in the resource room yield significantly higher effect sizes when compared to other settings. No significant differences emerged between studies that take place in a self-contained, regular classroom, or report no information on the setting.

A pessimistic conclusion from the above observations is that almost any intervention that varies from the control condition in terms of setting, teacher, and number of instructional steps (and the results are published in journals) yield larger effect sizes than studies that fail to control for such variations. Thus, poor methodology must be taken into consideration when interpreting treatment effects. For example, of the 4 studies that included treatments in the regular classroom, two involved administering the experimental condition in one school and the control condition in another school. Thus, different teachers and setting confounded any meaningful interpretation of treatment effects.

We think probably the most serious threat to interpreting treatment effects are situations where intervention studies "stack the treatment condition" with more steps and procedures than the control condition. This artifact alone guarantees that the experiential condition will unequivocally yield higher effect sizes than studies with minimal overlap across all designs and domains.

In sum, we found substantial support for the assumption that artifacts related to methodology have a profound influence on treatment outcomes. However, we also found that when we partialed out the weighted composite score related to methodology, significant effects related to the type of treatment emerged.

Qualifications

Before we discuss the implications of our findings, we would like to qualify any conclusions we might make. First, very few state departments of education or research organizations provided us technical reports. Therefore, we cannot generalize our findings beyond articles and dissertations. Although data were readily available across categories of children placed in special education in unpublished reports or state-department documents, no state department or research organization provided treatment data (i.e., means and standard deviations) that focused primarily on learning disabled students.

Second, the synthesis is biased toward identified samples. Because of this bias, we also implemented a computer search of articles that emerged for the combined terms "high risk" and "treatment" or "intervention" or "instruction." We conducted a hand search of the top five journals over a 30 year period (see Table 2) to locate intervention studies that include samples of children considered at risk for learning disabilities. These studies of "nonidentified" learning disabled students were included in our synthesis if IQ's were reported to be at or above 84 (or reported that subjects were in the average range based on standardized scores) and a standardized achievement score was reported (or stated) to be at or below the 25th percentile. Thirty-four studies were located. Eighteen studies were included in the synthesis and 16 were eliminated because of methodological flaws (e.g., inability to calculate effect sizes) and limited sample information.

Third, we did not direct our analysis of state or district policies on how LD samples are defined. The only variable we used to capture the influence of policy on the sampling procedures was whether studies stated that participants exhibited a discrepancy between potential (usually reflective of an IQ test) and achievement (usually reflected by scores on some standardized achievement measures). This variable was dummy coded (studies mention discrepancy or related term plus state that students are one or more years behind vs. other studies). According to Mercer, Jordan, Allsopp, and Mercer (1996), most states (34 states) attempt to operationalize learning disabilities by reporting a discrepancy between intelligence and achievement. Consistent with this finding, the most frequent basis for selecting LD subjects (> 70% of the studies, however, only 16% of the studies stated subjects were at least a year behind in achievement) stated by the primary authors was that the participants exhibit a discrepancy between academic performance and intellectual performance. However, we found this variable problematic because most studies report discrepancies across all sorts of achievement domains. Unfortunately, we did *not* test whether broadly defined samples versus narrowly defined discrepancy defined samples provide greater external validity for intervention effectiveness (although the data is available to us). We did find, however, those studies that included reading measures yielded higher effect sizes for studies that reported a year or more behind in achievement versus those that reported a year or less.

Thus, we sorted studies by a priori sample characteristics. Based on the literature, we imposed our own definitions of learning disabilities for comparisons between studies rather than relying on Federal, state, or particular school district definitions. Although there should have been greater homogeneity in our sample selection in terms of matching subject characteristics to the specific treatments (e.g., LD children exhibit clear deficits in reading as opposed to mathematics performance when placed in a reading intervention program), we assume those learning difficulties in the present studies bear a logical relationship to the target intervention.

Fourth, it is important to note that many of the studies published prior to 1980 did not meet the methodological criteria for inclusion in our analysis. No doubt, methodological factors that we examined in the articles and dissertations may create a bias in what we analyzed. On the other hand, it is worth mentioning that we used a number of sensitivity analyses (e.g., weighted regression analyses of methodological variables, investigated the relationships between measures and year of publication) to analyze variables that best predicted overall treatment effects. If effect sizes were related to the unreliability of measurement, range restrictions, or incomplete information and so forth, these were taken into account when explaining treatment effects.

Finally, our synthesis indicated that the majority of studies published on intervention for students with learning disabilities are poorly designed, have poor internal validity, fail to indicate if the LD sample is in the normal range of intelligence, and/or fail to provide usable information. Of the approximately 900 studies that were reviewed that actually reported data, less than a fourth of those studies met the criteria for inclusion in our synthesis. Thus, approximately *seventy-five percent* of the studies that report intervention outcomes for students with learning disabilities have flawed designs (e.g., no control condition). In addition, of those studies that were included in the synthesis, less than 5% actually would be considered credible studies on the methodological criteria (i.e., high weighting on the methodological composite score, see Table 4) we have outlined. These criteria are cumulative scores related to internal validity, treatment integrity, adequacy of description of the control condition, the breadth of sample description, adequacy of treatment sessions and sampling procedures, and the use of reliable dependent measures. This is not meant to be a pessimistic conclusion on the state of intervention research in learning disabilities, but only to provide direction for future publications and funding needs for children with learning disabilities.

Given these caveats, we will now address some the implications of our synthesis. The outline for discussion includes (a) methodological issues, (b) theory and intervention research, and (c) policy issues related to instruction.

METHODOLOGICAL ISSUES

As indicated previously, there is a clear relationship across studies between methodological procedures and effect size. Methodological variables significantly predict effect sizes across all intervention domains. There are many caveats in the various studies in terms of internal validity. The most serious threats to interpreting LD group design research were clearly related to (a) classroom by treatment confounding and (b) the unit of analysis (i.e., nonindependence for treatments administered in groups). The majority of group design studies in our synthesis suffer from a classroom by treatment confound. This occurs when the treatment is implemented in one classroom and the control occurs in another. Although some interesting information can be derived, it is extremely difficult from this design to assess the impact of learning. To overcome this issue the study must treat each classroom as an experimental unit in which the classroom mean scores replace the individual scores. In addition, in most of the studies analyzed, treatment procedures were implemented in small groups. Thus, student scores are not independent because they are due to the events unique to small group sessions. For example, during a small group presentation some student's behavior might be disruptive and have an effect upon the others in the small group. Given that the disruption can negatively impact the score, those scores cannot be considered independent. Unfortunately, few if any studies reported mean scores of instructional units.

THEORY AND INTERVENTION RESEARCH

The findings of this synthesis pose two conceptual problems for the field of learning disabilities. The first problem relates to the common assumption that specific lower-order processing deficits (e.g., problems in word recognition, word skills, spelling) are the major contributors to academic problems in LD students. The second relates to the assumption that learning disabilities is not due to poor instruction, but reflects information processing constraints primarily in the area of language. Both of these assumptions would predict that some domain areas are not easily amendable to intervention. Thus, we expected the magnitude of effect sizes to be < .20 in areas related to language, such as reading. Related to these issues, however, the LD participants in these intervention studies exhibited no deficit that would suggest that one process is more resistant to treatment than another. Because low order processing deficits have been primarily tied to the reading domain, we would expect extremely low effect sizes in reading (of .10 to .20 magnitude) when compared to other domains. This finding did not emerge in the present synthesis. Interestingly, all domains of reading (comprehension, word recognition, word skills) showed moderate effect sizes. The lowest effect size occurs in the domain of mathematics (.45) and when reading comprehension and word recognition were confounded (.44).

How does one reconcile these outcomes of intervention research with current models of learning disabilities which suggest that academic problems are related to specific processing deficits? We suggest that the results of this synthesis are consistent with most information processing models of individual differences (e.g., Kail & Bisanz, 1993). These models suggest that elementary processes are best understood in the context of their combination with other operations. Although it is important to identify elementary processes that underlie LD readers' performance, such an approach may not be sufficient in explaining how cognitive processes are organized and work in unison to remediate academic deficits.

There are three possible explanations that can be garnered to explain the lack of "specificity" (i.e., performance in one domain is more resistant to change than another domain) in intervention effects. The first means of reconciling the conceptual problem of "specificity" is to suggest that academic difficulties reflect "bootstrapping effects" (see Stanovich, 1986, p. 364, for discussion of this concept). For example, in the area of reading, Stanovich (1986) stated, "Many things that facilitate further growth in reading...general knowledge, vocabulary...are developed by reading itself" (p. 364). Thus, due to the mutual facilitation between reading and cognitive processing, such interrelationships would be expected to increase with skill improvement. The implicit assumption, however, is that deficits in lower order skills underlie such bootstrapping effects, and that the majority of domains investigated reflect secondary problems.

On the other hand, one may argue that because of specific processing deficits, LD students engage in compensatory processing to gain information across a wide array of domain areas. Strategy and direct instruction facilitates such compensatory processing. That is, a weakness at one level of processing (e.g., the phonological level) is compensated for by a greater reliance on skills that are intact at other levels (Stanovich, 1980) and a combined strategy and direct instruction model facilitates such compensation. The most common example of this hypothesis is applied to word recognition. For example, because of LD readers' poor phonological coding ability, such children's word recognition is augmented by visual, semantic, nonverbal, and contextual clues (e.g., Stanovich, 1980). Support for a compensatory hypothesis can be tested several ways (also see Walczyk, 1993, for compensatory model predictions). Most directly, the relative differences across domains can be compared. Again, we find no indirect evidence across the intervention studies *within* the language domain which suggests that greater gains occur in one domain when compared to another.

The second explanation suggests that no one process in isolation dominates others. Although several studies indicate deficiencies in LD readers are related to phonological processes (e.g., Stanovich & Siegel, 1994), additional studies indicate problems in orthographic (e.g., McBride-Chang, Manis, Seidenberg, Custodio, & Doi, 1993), semantic (e.g., Zecker & Zinner, 1987; Waterman & Lewandowski, 1993), metacognitive (e.g., Wong, 1987), and working memory processes (e.g., Siegel & Ryan, 1989; Swanson, 1992).

The third means of reconciling the specificity issue is to suggest that higher order cognitive processing problems can exist in LD children, *independently* of their specific problems in low-order processes, such as phonological coding. Thus, LD children may be viewed as having difficulty accessing higher-level information and/or lower-order skills (phonological codes), or switching between the two levels of processing. Several studies have characterized LD children as having difficulties in executive processing that relate to checking, planning, testing, and evaluating their performance (e.g., see Wong, 1991; Swanson, 1993; for a review). Difficulties in coordinating multiple pieces of information have been applied to LD children in various information processing models (e.g., see Pressley's, 1991, good information processor model) and strategy intervention programs (e.g., see Wong, 1991, for a review).

Regardless of these explanations, some would argue that our inability to find areas which show *a resistance to change in some domains* (low effect sizes related to other domains), especially in the area of reading, undermines the concept of specificity. We would argue, however, that in the context of intervention, a focus on isolated skills or processes (e.g., word skills, metacognition) may not be an appropriate focus. Processing components seldom act independently of other processes when engaged in a meaningful cognitive activity (such as the domains reflected in the current synthesis). Our synthesis identified some instructional components that together influence performance across a broad array of domains. We also suggest that what appears to moderate outcomes are levels of severity related to intelligence and reading and not necessarily isolated processes. Clearly, performance at complex levels (writing prose, inferring the meaning of text) cannot occur without some critical threshold of skills. However, based on our findings related to the Combined Model, effective instruction is neither a bottom-up nor top-down approach in isolation. Lower-order and higher-order skills interact in order to influence treatment outcomes.

Policy Issues Related to Intervention Research

Four implications of the present syntheses related to policy and the funding of intervention research are considered. These relate to Funding Practices, Publication, Definitional/Classification Issues, Reading, and Special Education Placement. We will attempt to generalize, as well as qualify, from our synthesis findings related to each of these issues.

Funding and Publication

The results indicated several of the methodologically sound studies cite no funding source. We also found a slight trend that some funding sources are isolated to some academic domains. Another interesting finding is that a large number of studies that we rejected from our synthesis, because we could not calculate effect size (and other sorts of methodological variables that contaminated our interpretation), cite a funding source. We also found that a large number of these studies that were rejected were published in major special education journals. Thus, indirectly, there may be a relationship between studies we considered credible and funding/publication variables. An interesting finding to us was that few intervention studies build upon each other (as indicated by the citations, frequency of similar authors, institutional affiliation of studies) within articles or by independent researchers (as indicated by the *Social Science Index*). A further vexing situation is that minimal information is available on the fidelity (treatment integrity) and/or degree to which intervention studies carry out their treatment approach.

One of many possible solutions to some of the above problems is to increase the *veracity* of the studies that show positive outcomes. Few studies provide measures of treatment integrity and even fewer intervention studies do follow-up or independent replications of their findings. Perhaps the lack of follow-up studies and independent replication is a "policy and/or researcher consensus problem". Intervention researchers are leery about their work being replicated, the same way teachers don't like the idea of somebody verifying their claims that reading program "X" worked with student A, but not student B. A common defense when outcomes differ from what is in the mainstream is that the replication was done poorly and the particular version of the intervention created by the investigators did not represent well the intervention as studied previously. Sometimes this defense is appropriate, but at other times replication failure should be taken seriously (see Pressley & Harris, 1994; whole issue for a review of these issues). A change in the consensus of opinion about independent replication appears appropriate.

Definitional Issues and Intervention Outcomes

An important issue to consider when evaluating intervention research is the validity of how LD groups are defined and what role these definitions play in predicting treatment outcomes. In our synthesis we found that the detail to which a sample is defined (i.e., how much psychometric information is provided, and whether cut-off scores can be calculated) interacts with combinations of strategy and direct instructions approaches in predicting treatment *outcomes*.

Our synthesis clearly indicated that one of the most frequent identifiers of children with learning disabilities provided by the primary authors, across all studies, is that some "sort of" discrepancy exists between the targeted sample's current grade placement and/or IQ and their current achievement. Perhaps the implicit assumption for the inclusion of discrepancy groups is that children who experience reading, writing, math and/or other difficulties, unaccompanied by a low IQ, are distinct in processing from the general "run of the mill" poor, garden variety, slow, or mildly retarded learners. Yet, the validity of this assumption has been seriously questioned. That is, when compared to nondiscrepancy defined poor achievers, learning disabled defined groups are more similar in processing difficulties than different (e.g., Stanovich & Siegel, 1994; however see Fuchs, Fuchs, & Mather, in press). Our synthesis only partially addressed the issue of whether discrepancy defined groups responded differently than groups who had achievement scores that were in the same range as their IQ scores.

We found that those studies that include samples with IQ's in the 85-90 range and reading scores in the 85 to 90 range yield higher effect sizes in treatment outcomes than studies that include samples with IQ's in the 90+ range and reading scores in the 85 to 90 range. We say partially addressed, because our sorting of studies into different definitional categories may not reflect variables that underlie how subjects were selected for intervention in the first place. For example, we relied on standard reading scores as a means of sorting studies for analysis, but some of the studies included groups with a broad array of academic difficulties of which reading was only one of the problems.

Reading Instruction Issues

Reading is clearly the most investigated domain in our synthesis. We also found that several intervention studies in the last 10 years have placed an emphasis on word recognition and word skills, primarily because of the high incidence of deficits related to phonological awareness in LD samples. There have been consistent cases made that phonological awareness skills are a primary deficit in children with learning disabilities particularly in the area of reading (Foorman, Francis, Fletcher, & Lynn, 1996; Stanovich & Siegel, 1994). As stated in the introduction, however, there has been some debate about whether the emphasis of intervention in word reading should be directed at the whole word level, and/or at the analytic level (isolated sounds), and/or at the synthesis level (sound units).

Our synthesis clearly shows that direct instruction (i.e., which usually includes phonics instruction) influences word recognition. However, the issue of whether instruction should occur at the word or unit level is equivocal. To illustrate, several individual studies will be briefly reviewed. For example, Vellutino et al. (1996) suggested that after 15 weeks of 30 minute, daily one-to-one tutoring emphasizing phonological awareness, the alphabetic principal and sight word vocabulary and comprehension strategies were successful in remediating at-risk readers. However, when we analyzed this particular study we were unable to calculate effect sizes for at-risk LD readers (See Tables of the original article). That is, the one-to-one intensive tutoring when compared to two other conditions (traditional remedial programs in the schools) did not yield any effect sizes that were computable from the information presented. We could compute from the tables combined effect sizes on high and low readers among the three conditions of which two were variations of the school approach of tutoring and classroom remediation when compared to the experimental treatment of intensive one-to-one instruction. The effect sizes were less than .10. In another study, Torgesen, Wagner, Rashotte, Alexander, and Conway (1997) suggested gains for reading disabled students (approximately 10 years old) who received one-to-one tutoring and synthetic and analytic phonics with a skilled clinician for 2 hours daily over 8 weeks. However, when we calculated effect sizes for real word recognition measures, the magnitude of change was .19 (Word Identification subtest of the Woodcock Reading Mastery Test) when compared to the control conditions. In a study by Kennedy and Backman (1993) participants were instructed using a Lindamood Program which emphasized identification of speech sounds and orthographic symbols. The Lindamood Program was a supplement to regular private school LD instruction which includes phonics. Control subjects also received private instruction which included phonics. With only 10 subjects in each condition, the effect size on the Slosson Oral Reading Test was .14 and the Gray Oral Reading Test was .28. As in other studies, high effect sizes were found for the processes directly related to instruction (phonics), but meager effect sizes were found related to real word recognition.

Lovett et al. (1994) yield effect sizes between the strategy instruction and phonics instruction combination (the Benchmark Program, $N = 20$) of $-.24$ (in favor of the control condition) for word recognition on the Wide Range Achievement Test (WRAT) and $-.67$ (in favor of the control condition) on the Woodcock Reading Mastery Test (WRMT) word recognition subtest compared to the control condition which included *no* reading instruction. When the phonics-direct instruction-alone condition was compared to the control condition the effect size was .60 on the WRAT and $-.12$ (in favor of the control) on the WRMT. Approximately 20 participants were in the three conditions with participant ranging in age from 8 to 13 years. Thus, the control condition which included no reading instruction yielded higher effect sizes than the combined conditions (phonics + strategy instruction), and the direct instruction+phonics conditions were superior on one measure (WRAT), but inferior on a parallel measure (WRMT). These findings are difficult to interpret, especially because different materials and age variations confound the results.

Brown and Felton (1990) argue they had significant trends in their data supporting a structured phonics approach (using the Lippincott Basic Reading Program, 1991) over literature based instruction or whole word instruction for first graders at risk for reading deficits due to poor phonological processing. Although we calculated the effect size after two years of instruction to be .52 on the word identification test of the WRMT (in favor of the phonics condition), it is important to realize that two different school settings were used for comparisons (which means by inference that at least two different teachers were used). As we have indicated in our results section, whenever different settings or teachers are used when comparing treatment to controls, effect sizes are highly inflated.

A study that overcomes some of these artifacts (which unfortunately we were made aware of too late to include in our synthesis) is reported by Foorman, Francis, Winikates, Mehta, Schatshneider, and Fletcher (1997). They compared three interventions (synthetic phonics-Orton Gillingham Approach, analytic phonics-focus on onsets and rimes, and sight word programs) in second and third graders identified with reading disabilities for 60 minutes a day for 1 school year. For word reading (an experimental measure of words selected from first and second grade cumulative vocabulary lists in which half the words include predictable patterns and half unpredictable or exceptional spelling patterns), no significant differences emerged between treatment conditions (see Table 8, p. 270). The estimated effect sizes varied from 0 to .18 for the various comparisons.

In sum, the research does not seem to suggest unequivocally that phonics instruction is sufficient condition for transfer to real words. There have been other reviews that suggest phonological awareness is an important, but not necessarily a sufficient, condition for learning to read (Adams, 1990; Vellutino & Scanlon, 1991, for a review).

Full Inclusion

We narrowly define full inclusion in the context of our syntheses as students with learning disabilities who receive full-time education (with or without treatment) in a general (regular) education classroom. The settings of intervention and the effect sizes that emerge in these settings were directly coded in our analysis. The results were as follows (see Table 4). Those studies that do not report the setting ($N = 102$) in which the intervention occurred yield lower effect sizes than those that do report the setting. Setting information was further divided into those that report treatment occurring in the self-contained classroom, the resource room, regular classroom, and where no information is provided about the type of classroom setting in which the treatment occurred. Larger effect sizes occurred in resource rooms when compared to other settings. As shown, however, only 4 studies, with a total sample size of 151 participants, provided information on effect sizes related to the regular classroom. Of these 4 studies, two were confounded by using different schools to represent treatment and control conditions.

Overall, our results show that interventions that took place in the pull-out classroom yielded larger effect sizes than other settings. Of course, this conclusion calls for a qualification about how many intervention studies actually reported where treatment occurred. The more substantive issue, however, is whether teachers in the regular classroom can effectively accommodate such children. We have *no data* on this issue in our synthesis. There was not enough information in the articles to code whether treatment was better carried out by the regular classroom teacher than the special education teacher. In addition, generalizations on treatment outcomes as a function of setting in our synthesis data are constrained by the lack of direct contrasts between Special vs. Regular Education settings *within* a study. Further, the research question "Which setting parameters of an instructional environment best maximizes potential and productivity (however defined) in a general setting?" is not directly addressed in our synthesis.

A conservative interpretation of our intervention studies supports a full continuum of services (high effect sizes were found in both placements). This is a generous interpretation on two accounts: (1) the trend in the data support pull-out programs, and (2) there are few studies on intervention that occur in the regular classroom setting. Unless it can be shown that all children with LD don't benefit from pull-out programs (our synthesis suggests they do) when compared to integrated classrooms, special education placements should be left in place.

Summary

Our synthesis has characterized intervention research within the field of learning disabilities over the last 30 years. We identified studies that yield high effect sizes and those that are methodologically sound. In spite of the limitations in subject descriptions, we were also able to identify some aptitude variables (intellectual range and severity of reading deficiency) that played an important role in predicting treatment outcomes. One aptitude variable, whether groups met IQ and reading cut-off score criteria, influenced treatment outcomes. We also provide information on the controversial issue of reading and conclude that direct instruction does make a significant contribution to treatment outcome for real word, but a combined direct and strategy instruction better contribute to reading comprehension than competing models.

AUTHOR NOTE

1.   This chapter is part of a 1997 final report submitted to the U.S. Department Of Education. The report was supported by a U.S. Department of Education Grant (H023E40014), the Chesapeake Institute, and Peloy Endowment Funds awarded to the first author. The views of this report, and thus this chapter, do not necessarily reflect the U.S. Office of Education or the Chesapeake Institute. A significantly shorten version of this chapter appears in Swanson and Hoskyn (1998). This chapter was the very first piece written about our synthesis project. This chapter was originally sent to the *Review of*

Educational Research, but the editor required us to reduce the manuscript from its current length to 35 pages. Thus, the full length of the article is reflected in this chapter. The complete report of the meta-analysis project submitted to the U.S. Department Of Education that includes a comprehensive analysis of both group and single subject designs as well as instructional and policy implications is published in Swanson, Hoskyn, and Lee (1999).

NOTES

1. In the literature, the term "strategy" has been used in reference to particular learning skills, such as rehearsal, imaging, and outlining, to more general types of self-management activities such as planning and comprehension monitoring, and to complex plans that combine several techniques (see Borkowski & Turner, 1990; Levin, 1986; Pressley & Ghatala, 1990 for review). In this report we assume that strategies are made-up of two or more goal oriented tactics and sequential methods. A tactic is a single processing technique, such as self-monitoring, elaboration, or organization. Strategies depend on prerequisite learning of certain core skills and subskills. For example, organizing and monitoring information in a text is a strategy that requires the subskills representing word recognition, vocabulary, and spelling. However, the strategies are directed toward higher-order thinking such as problem solving, comprehending (e.g., reading comprehension, and composing (writing prose), and rule-learning (such as algorithms for word problems). In the present context, strategy instruction is assumed to direct students to focus on higher order skills, such as metacognition, self-monitoring, rule learning, and/or awareness of task parameters to direct their problem solving, memory, and/or "information handling" behavior. Strategy instruction is distinguished from other approaches because of instructions directing students to access information from long-term memory about strategies (e.g., procedural knowledge).

As a point of contrast, we tested whether a direct instruction model provided a better account of the variance in treatment outcomes than strategy instruction. That is, in contrast to strategy instruction, effective instruction for students with learning disabilities may be best captured in studies which identify their orientation as a skills approach (drill-repetition, and/or instruction focusing on low order skills such as phonological coding which in turn are reflected in such domains word recognition and spelling). In this case, studies that yield the high effect sizes may be isolated to specific skill domains, such as word recognition. Of course it is possible that neither approach in isolation, but rather both in combination predict effect sizes. To test these competing hypotheses, the instructional components of the various experimental interventions were coded into those that reflect cognitive strategies, those that reflect the remediation of specific skills, and those that do not focus on particular academic domains.

2. Three constructs were important in our synthesis: learning disabilities, treatment, and outcome. First, although we took a nonjudgmental stance on the quality of the definition of learning disabilities reflected in intervention studies (e.g., operational vs. a school district definition vs. Federal Register definition), we held to a general parameter that such students must have at least normal intelligence (standardized intelligence scores at or above 85) or the study states *explicitly* that participants are in the normal range of intelligence. The study must also state that the participants perform poorly (as indicated by teachers and/or psychometric tests) in at least one academic (e.g., reading) and/or behavioral domain (social skills). We coded the variations of definitions reflected in the data base (discrepancy vs. cut-off scores; school identified vs. research identified; specific academic difficulty vs. multiple academic difficulties) to investigate the relationship between the definitional parameters related to learning disabilities and actual treatment outcomes.

3. We coded whether children charted their behavior or evaluated their behavior in some fashion (e.g., children were directed to ask themselves a question about how they were doing). We considered this to be an observable (codeable) form of self-monitoring. This information overlapped with the verbal dialogue code, and therefore was not separated in the analysis.

Second, the term *treatment* or *intervention* was defined as the direct manipulation (assigned at will by the experimenter; see Campbell & Stanley, 1963, p. 200) by the researcher of psychological (e.g., metacognitive awareness), medical (e.g., drug) and/or educational (e.g., teaching, instruction, materials) variables for the purposes of assessing learning (a) efficiency (e.g., rate, time), (b) accuracy (e.g., percent correct), and/or (c) understanding (e.g., amount of verbal elaboration on a concept). In general, treatment was administered in the context of school as an extension of the regular classroom, special education classroom and/or clinical services. This extension varied from three instructional sessions to several continuous instructional sessions over months or years. Because of the vastness of the topic, however, additional boundaries were necessary in our analysis. The intervention literature that focuses on administrative decisions and *does not* reflect a manipulation of treatment conditions (e.g., educational placement - resource room) falls outside the boundaries. Educational research based on intervention which occurs as an extension of the educational placement of children, adolescents, and adults with LD within various educational (e.g., classroom or college) placements is included. Moreover, attention is directed to only those instructional interventions that include students with learning disabilities. Excluded from the analysis, however, are interventions in which the effects of intervention on students with learning disabilities cannot be directly analyzed or partialed out in the analysis. Also, within the area of educational intervention, it was necessary to place parameters on the level or scope of intervention. At one end of a rough continuum, we distinguished between treatment techniques that include separable elements, but that do not, by themselves, reflect a freestanding treatment (e.g., teacher presents advance organizers). At the other end of this continuum, are broad approaches that reflect policies and organizational arrangements (e.g., consulting teacher model which provides help to a LD student in a regular classroom). We excluded those treatments that were at the top of the continuum. Although there are some gray areas in our selection, we have found it possible to identify instructional programs that are added to the typical instructional routine.

Finally, treatment outcomes included six general categories of information. These categories were: (1) article or technical report identification (authors, affiliation, funding sources, citations), (2) design and methodological characteristics (e.g., sampling procedure, single vs. group design, reliability and validity of measures, internal and external validity; treatment integrity), (3) sampling characteristics (e.g., psychometric information, chronological age, gender, ethnicity, sample size, type of definition, marker variables), (4) parameters of intervention (e.g., domain, setting, materials, duration and length of session), (5) components of intervention (e.g., group vs. individual instruction, number and description of steps in intervention, level of student response to instruction, maintenance and transfer), and (6) effect size (e.g., magnitude of treatment effects).

4.   Four recently published studies were identified as meeting inclusion criteria prior to the submission of this article. Thus, because other studies may have been inadvertently left out of our synthesis (as well as the fact that published studies are biased), we calculated the number of studies necessary (i.e., studies that report null results) that would threaten our overall conclusions (i.e., the File Drawer Problem). We calculated the tolerance levels for null results (see Hunter and Schmidt; 1990; Table 22.2, p. 511 for the number of null results as a function of the number of studies). In the present synthesis, the mean effect size was .61. Effect sizes were converted to r (i.e., $r = d/[\text{square root}(d^2 + 4)$ and then to mean Z values $[Z = 1.15 \log(1+r/1-r)$; mean Z was .31]) to utilize a formula reported in Hunter and Schmidt (1990, p. 510). The number of studies required to indicate an inclusion bias for this synthesis is 971 $(X = 180/2.706)[180(.31)^2 - 2.706]$. Thus, 971 group design studies meeting the synthesis criteria and reporting null results would have to been *not* retrieved before one can conclude our selection of studies reflects a sampling bias.

REFERENCES

[**Note**: References with an asterisk indicate those studies included in the meta-analysis]
Adams, M.J. (1990). *Beginning to read.* Cambridge, MA: MIT Press.

*Amerikaner, M., & Summerlin, M.L. (1982). Group counseling with learning disabled children: Effects of social skills and relaxation training on self-concept and classroom behavior. *Journal of Learning Disabilities, 15*(6), 340-343.

*Argulewicz, E.N. (1982). Effects of an instructional program designed to improve attending behaviors of learning disabled students. *Journal of Learning Disabilities, 15*(1), 23-27.

Arter, J.A., & Jenkins, J.R. (1979). Differential diagnosis-prescriptive teaching: A critical appraisal. *Review of Education Research, 49,* 517-555.

*Ayres, A.J. (1972). Improving academic scores through sensory integration. *Journal of Learning Disabilities, 5*(6), 338-343.

Baker, L., & Brown, A.L. (1984). Metacognitive skills of reading. In D.L. Forrest-Pressley, G.E., MacKinnon, & T.G. Waller (Eds.). *Metacognition, cognition, and human performance* (Vol. 1, pp. 155-205). San Diego, CA: Academic Press.

*Bakker, D.J., Bouma, A., & Gardien, C.J. (1990). Hemisphere-specific treatment of dyslexia subtypes: A field experiment. *Journal of Learning Disabilities, 23*(7), 433-438.

*Balcerzak, J.P. (1986). The effects of an aptitude treatment interaction approach with intermediate aged learning disabled students based on emphasizing the individual's strength in simultaneous or sequential processing in the areas of mathematics, reading and self-concept. (Doctoral dissertation, State University of New York, 1985). *Dissertation Abstracts International, 47*(3-A), 630.

Bateman, B. (1992). Learning disabilities: The changing landscape. *Journal of Learning Disabilities, 25,* 29-39.

*Bay, M., Staver, J.R., Bryan, T., & Hale, J.B. (1992). Science instruction for the mildly handicapped: Direct instruction versus discovery teaching. *Journal of Research in Science Teaching, 29*(6), 555-570.

Becker, W., & Carnine, D. (1980). Direct instruction: An effective approach for educational intervention with the disadvantaged and low performers. In B. Lahey & A. Kazdin (Eds.), *Advances in child clinical psychology* New York: Plenum.

*Belmont, I., & Birch, H.G. (1974). The effect of supplemental intervention on children with low reading-readiness scores. *The Journal of Special Education, 8*(1), 81-89.

*Berninger, V.W., Lester, K., Sohlberg, M.M., & Mateer, C. (1991). Interventions based on the multiple connections model of reading for developmental dyslexia and acquired deep dyslexia. *Archives of Clinical Neuropsychology, 6*(4), 375-391.

Bollen, K.A. (1989). *Structural equations with latent variables.* New York: Wiley-Interscience.

Borkowski, J.G., Estrada, M.T., Milstead, M., & Hale, C.A. (1989). General problem-solving skills: Relations between metacognition and strategic processing. *Learning Disability Quarterly, 12,* 57-70.

Borkowski, J.G., & Turner, L.A. (1990). Transsituational characteristics of metacognition. In W. Schneider & F.E. Weinert (Eds.), *Interactions among aptitudes, strategies, and knowledge in cognitive performance* (pp. 159-176). New York: Springer-Verlag.

*Bos, C.S., & Anders, P.L. (1990). Effects of interactive vocabulary instruction on the vocabulary learning and reading comprehension of junior-high learning disabled students. *Learning Disability Quarterly, 13*(1), 31-42.

*Bos, C.S., & Anders, P.L. (1992). Using interactive teaching and learning strategies to promote text comprehension and content learning for students with learning disabilities. *International Journal of Disability, Development and Education, 39*(3), 225-238.

*Bos, C.S., Anders, P.L., Filip, D., & Jaffe, L.E. (1985). Semantic feature analysis and long-term learning. *National Reading Conference Yearbook, 34,* 42-47.

*Bos, C.S., Anders, P.L., Filip, D., & Jaffe, L.E. (1989). The effects of an interactive instructional strategy for enhancing reading comprehension and content area learning for students with learning disabilities. *Journal of Learning Disabilities, 22,* 384-390.

*Brailsford, A., Snart, F., & Das, J.P. (1984). Strategy training and reading comprehension. *Journal of Learning Disabilities, 17*(5), 287-293.

*Branwhite, A.B. (1983). Boosting reading skills by direct instruction. *British Journal of Educational Psychology, 53*(3), 291-298.

*Brigham, F.J., Scruggs, T.E., & Mastropieri, M.A. (1992). Teacher enthusiasm in learning disabilities classrooms: Effects on learning and behavior. *Learning Disabilities Research & Practice, 7*(1), 68-73.

Brophy, J., & Good, T. (1986). Teacher-effects results. In M. C. Wittrock (Ed.), *Handbook of research on teaching* (3rd ed.). New York: Macmillan.

*Brown, I.S., & Felton, R.C. (1990). Effects of instruction on beginning reading skills in children at risk for reading disability. *Reading and Writing: An Interdisciplinary Journal, 2*, 223-241.

*Brown, R.T., & Alford, N. (1984). Ameliorating attentional deficits and concomitant academic deficiencies in learning disabled children through cognitive training. *Journal of Learning Disabilities, 17*, 20-26.

*Bryant, N.D., Drabin, I.R., & Gettinger, M. (1981). Effects of varying unit size on spelling achievement in learning disabled children. *Journal of Learning Disabilities, 14*(4), 200-203.

*Bryant, N.D., Fayne, H.R., & Gettinger, M. (1982). Applying the mastery learning model to sight word instruction for disabled readers. *Journal of Experimental Education, 50*(3), 116-121.

*Bryant, S.T. (1979). Relative effectiveness of visual-auditory versus visual-auditory-kinesthetic-tactile procedures for teaching sight words and letter sounds to young, disabled readers. (Doctoral dissertation, Columbia University, 1979). *Dissertation Abstracts International, 40*(5-A), 2588-2589.

Bryk, A.S., & Raudenbush, S.W. (1992). *Hierarchical linear models: Applications and data analysis methods.* Newberry Park, CA: Sage.

*Bulgren, J., Schumaker, J.B., & Deshler, D.D. (1988). Effectiveness of a concept teaching routine in enhancing the performance of LD students in secondary-level mainstream classes. *Learning Disability Quarterly, 11*(1), 3-17.

Byrne, B., Freebody, P., & Gates, A. (1992). Longitudinal data on relations of word-reading strategies to comprehension, reading time, and phonemic awareness. *Reading Research Quarterly, 27*, 140-151.

*Carte, E., Morrison, D., Sublett, J., Uemura, A., & Setrakian, W. (1984). Sensory integration therapy: A trial of a specific neurodevelopmental therapy for the remediation of learning disabilities. *Developmental and Behavioral Pediatrics, 5*(4), 189-194.

*Cartelli, L.M. (1978). Paradigmatic language training for learning disabled children. *Journal of Learning Disabilities, 11*(5), 54-59.

*Carter, B.G. (1985). For the learning disabled: Semantic mapping or SQ3R? (Doctoral dissertation, University of Nevada-Reno, 1984). *Dissertation Abstracts International, 46*(3-A), 674.

Chalfant, J.C., & Scheffelin, M.A. (1969). *Central processing dysfunctions in children: A review of research, phase three of a three phase project. NINDS Monograph.* Bethesda, MD: U.S. Department of Health, Education, and Welfare.

Chall, J. (1967). *Learning to read: The great debate.* New York: McGraw-Hill.

*Chan, L.K.S. (1991). Promoting strategy generalization through self-instructional training in students with reading disabilities. *Journal of Learning Disabilities, 24*(7), 427-433.

*Chan, L.K.S., & Cole, P.G. (1986). The effects of comprehension monitoring training on the reading competence of learning disabled and regular class students. *Remedial and Special Education, 7*(4), 33-40.

*Chan, L.K.S., Cole, P. G., & Morris, J.N. (1990). Effects of instruction in the use of a visual-imagery strategy on the reading-comprehension competence of disabled and average readers. *Learning Disability Quarterly, 13*(1), 2-11.

*Chase, C.H., Schmitt, R.L., Russell, G., & Tallal, P. (1984). A new chemotherapeutic investigation: Piracetam effects on dyslexia. *Annals of Dyslexia, 34*, 29-48.

Cohen, J. (1988). *Statistical power analysis for the behavioral sciences* (2nd ed.) New York: Academic Press.

Cohen, J., & Cohen, P. (1983). *Applied mulitple regression/correlation analysis for the behavioral sciences*. Hillsdale, NJ: Lawrence Erlbaum.

*Collins, M., & Carnine, D. (1988). Evaluating the field test revision process by comparing two versions of a reasoning skills CAI Program. *Journal of Learning Disabilities, 21*(6), 375-379.

*Commeyras, M. (1992). Dialogical-thinking reading lessons: Promoting critical thinking among "learning-disabled" students. (Doctoral dissertation, University of Illinois, 1991). *Dissertation Abstracts International, 52*(7-A), 2480-2481.

Cooney, J., & Swanson, H.L. (1987). Overview of research on learning disabled children's memory development. In H. L. Swanson (Ed.), *Memory and learning disabilities* (pp. 2-40). Greenwich, CT: JAI Press.

Cooper, H., & Hedges, L.V. (1994). *Handbook of research synthesis*. New York: Russell Sage Foundation.

Cooper, H., Nye, B., Charlton, K., Lindsey, J., & Greathouse, S. (1996). The effects of summer vacation on acheivement scores: A narrative and meta-analysis review. *Review of Educational Research, 66*, 227-268.

*Cornelius, P.L., & Semmel, M.I. (1982). Effects of summer instruction on reading achievement regression of learning disabled students. *Journal of Learning Disabilities, 15*(7), 409-413.

*Cosden, M.A., & English, J.P. (1987). The effects of grouping, self esteem, and locus of control on microcomputer performance and help seeking by mildly handicapped students. *Journal of Educational Computing Research, 3*(4), 443-459.

*Darch, C., & Eaves, R.C. (1986). Visual displays to increase comprehension of high school learning-disabled students. *The Journal of Special Education, 20*(3), 309-318.

*Darch, C., & Gersten, R. (1986). Direction-setting activities in reading comprehension: A comparison of two approaches. *Learning Disability Quarterly, 9*(3), 235-243.

*Darch, C., & Kameenui, E.J. (1987). Teaching LD students critical reading skills: A systematic replication. *Learning Disability Quarterly, 10*(2), 82-90.

*Das, J.P., Mishra, R.K., & Pool, J.E. (1995). An experiment on cognitive remediation of word-reading difficulty. *Journal of Learning Disabilities, 28*(2), 66-79.

*DeBoskey, D.S. (1982). An investigation of the remediation of learning disabilities based on brain-related tasks as measured by the Halstead-Reitan Neuropsychological test battery. (Doctoral dissertation, The University of Tennessee, 1982). *Dissertation Abstracts International, 43*(6-B), 2032.

*DeLaPaz, S. (1995). *An analysis of the effects of dictation and planning instruction on the writing of students with learning disabilities*. Unpublished doctoral dissertation University of Maryland,

*DeLaPaz, S. (in press). Strategy instruction in planning: Teaching students with learning and writing disabilities to compose persuasive and expository essays. *Learning Disability Quarterly*.

*Deno, S.L., & Chiang, B. (1979). An experimental analysis of the nature of reversal errors in children with severe learning disabilities. *Learning Disability Quarterly, 2*, 40-50.

Deshler, D.D., & Schumaker, J.B. (1988). An instructional model for teaching students how to learn. In J. Graden, J. Zins, & M. Curtis (Eds.). *Alternative educational delivery systems: Enhancing instructional options for all students* (pp. 391-411). Washington, DC: National Association of School Psychologists.

Deshler, D.D., Schumaker, J.B., & Lenz, B.K. (1984a). Academic and cognitive interventions for LD adolescents: Part I. *Journal of Learning Disabilities, 17*, 108-117.

Deshler, D.D., Schumaker, J.B., Lenz, B.K., & Ellis, E. (1984b). Academic and cognitive interventions for LD adolescents: Part II. *Journal of Learning Disabilities, 17*, 170-187.

*Dixon, M.E. (1984). Questioning strategy instruction participation and reading comprehension of learning disabled students. (Doctoral dissertation The University of Arizona, 1983). *Dissertation Abstracts International, 44*(11-A), 3349.

Dole, J.A., Duffy, G.G., Roehler, L.R., & Pearson, P.D. (1991). Moving from the old to the new: Research on reading comprehension instruction. *Review of Educational Research, 61*(2), 239-264.

*Ellis, E.S., Deshler, D.D., & Schumaker, J.B. (1989). Teaching adolescents with learning disabilities to generate and use task-specific strategies. *Journal of Learning Disabilities, 22*(2), 108-130.

Engelmann, S., & Carnine, D.W. (1982). *Theory of instruction: Principles and applications*. New York: Irvington.

*Englert, C.S., Hiebert, E.H., & Stewart, S.R. (1985). Spelling unfamiliar words by an analogy strategy. *The Journal of Special Education, 19*(3), 291-306.

*Englert, C.S., & Mariage, T.V. (1991). Making students partners in the comprehension process: Organizing the reading "Posse". *Learning Disability Quarterly, 14*(2), 123-138.

*Englert, C.S., Raphael, T.E., & Anderson, L.M. (1992). Socially mediated instruction: Improving students' knowledge about talk and writing. *The Elementary School Journal, 92*(4), 411-449.

*Englert, C.S., Raphael, T.E., Anderson, L.M., Anthony, H.M., & Stevens, D.D. (1991). Making strategies and self talk visible: Writing instruction in regular and special education classrooms. *American Educational Research Journal, 28*(2), 337-372.

*Farmer, M.E., Klein, R., & Bryson, S.E. (1992). Computer-assisted reading: Effects of whole word feedback on fluency and comprehension in readers with severe disabilities. *Remedial and Special Education, 13*, 50-60.

*Fawcett, A.J., Nicolson, R.I., & Morris, S. (1993). Computer-based spelling remediation for dyslexic children. *Journal of Computer Assisted Learning, 9*(3), 171-183.

*Fiedorowicz, C.A.M. (1986). Training of component reading skills. *Annals of Dyslexia, 36*, 318-334.

*Fiedorowicz, C.A.M., & Trites, R.L. (1987). *An evaluation of the effectiveness of computer-assisted component reading subskills training*. Ontario: Queen's Printer.

*Fletcher, C.M., & Prior, M.R. (1990). The rule learning behavior of reading disabled and normal children as a function of task characteristics and instruction. *Journal of Experimental Child Psychology, 50*(1), 39-58.

Fletcher, J., Shaywitz, S.E., Shankweiler, D.P., Katz, L., Liberman, I., Stuebing, K., Francis, D., Fowler, A., & Shaywitz, B.A. (1994). Cognitive profiles of reading disability: Comparisons of discrepancy and low achievement definitions. *Journal of Educational Psychology, 86*, 6-23.

Foorman, B.R., Francis, D.J., Fletcher, J.M., & Lynn, A. (1996). Relation of phonological and orthographic processing to early reading: Comparing two approaches to regression-based, reading-level-match design. *Journal of Educational Psychology, 88*, 639-652.

Foorman, B.R., Francis, D.J., Winikates, D., Mehta, P., Schatschneider, C., & Fletcher, J.M. (1997). Early interventions for children with reading disabilities. *Scientific Studies of Reading, 1*(3), 255-276.

Forness, S.R., Kavale, K.A., Blum, I.M., & Lloyd, J.W. (1997). Mega-analysis of meta-analyses: What works in special education and related services. *Teaching Exceptional Children, 29*(6), 4-9.

*Fortner, V.L. (1986). Generalization of creative productive-thinking training to LD students' written expression. *Learning Disability Quarterly, 9*(4), 274-284.

*Foster, K. (1983). The influence of computer-assisted instruction and workbook of the learning of multiplication facts by learning disabled and normal students. (Doctoral dissertation, Florida State University, 1983). *Dissertation Abstracts International, 42*(9-A). 3953.

Francis, D.J., Shaywitz, S.E., Stuebing, K.K., Shaywitz, B.A., & Fletcher, J.M. (1996). Developmental lag versus deficit models of reading disability: A longitudinal, individual growth curves analysis. *Journal of Educational Psychology, 88*, 3-17.

*Fuchs, L. S., Fuchs, D., Hamlett, C.L., Phillips, N.B., & Bentz, J. (1994). Classwide curriculum-based measurement: Helping general educators meet the challenge of student diversity. *Exceptional Children, 60*(6), 518-537.

*Gajria, M., & Salvia, J. (1992). The effects of summarization instruction on text comprehension of students with learning disabilities. *Exceptional Children, 58*(6), 508-516.

*Gelzheiser, L.M. (1984). Generalization from categorical memory tasks to prose by learning disabled adolescents. *Journal of Educational Psychology, 76*(6), 1128-1138.

*Gettinger, M., Bryant, N.D., & Fayne, H.R. (1982). Designing spelling instruction for learning disabled children: An emphasis on unit size, distributed practice, and training for transfer. *The Journal of Special Education, 16*(4), 439-448.

*Gittelman, R., & Feingold, I. (1983). Children with reading disorders-I. Efficacy of reading remediation. *Journal of Child Psychology and Psychiatry, 24*(2), 167-191.

*Glaman, G.M.V. (1975). Use of ability measures to predict the most appropriate method or sequence of mathematics instruction for learning disabled junior high students. (Doctoral dissertation, University of Minnesota, 1974). *Dissertation Abstracts International, 35*(11-A), 7154.

Glass, G.V., McGraw, B., & Smith, M.L. (1981). *Meta-analysis in social research*. Beverly Hills, CA: Sage.

Gleser, L.J., & Olkin, I. (1994). Stochastically dependent effect sizes. In H. Cooper & L. V. Hedges (Eds.), *The handbook of research synthesis* (pp. 339-355). New York: Russell Sage. Foundation.

*Graham, S. (1990). The role of production factors in learning disabled students' compositions. *Journal of Educational Psychology, 82*(4), 781-791.

*Graham, S., & Harris, K.R. (1989). Components analysis of cognitive strategy instruction: Effects on learning disabled students' compositions and self-efficacy. *Journal of Educational Psychology, 81*(3), 353-361.

Graham, S., & Harris, K.R. (1993). Cognitive strategy instruction: Methodological issues and guidelines in conducting research. In S. Vaughn & C. Bos (Eds.), *Research issues in learning disabilities* (pp. 146-158). New York: Springer-Verlag.

Graham, S., & Harris, K.R. (1996). Self-regulation and strategy instruction for students who find writing and learning challenging. In C.M. Levy & S. Ransdell (Eds.), *The science of writing: Theories, methods, individual differences, and applications* (pp. 347-360). Mahwah, NJ: Lawrence Erlbaum Associates.

*Graves, A.W. (1986). Effects of direct instruction and metacomprehension training on finding main ideas. *Learning Disabilities Research, 1*(2), 90-100.

*Graybill, D., Jamison, M., & Swerdlik, M.E. (1984). Remediation of impulsivity in learning disabled children by special education resource teachers using verbal self-instruction. *Psychology in the Schools, 21*(2), 252-254.

*Griffin, C.C., Simmons, D.C., & Kameeenui, E.J. (1991). Investigating the effectiveness of graphic organizer instruction on the comprehension and recall of science content by students with learning disabilities. *Reading, Writing, and Learning Disabilities, 7*(4), 355-376.

Guthrie, J.T., VanMeter, P., McCann, A.D., & Wigfield, A. (1996). Growth of literacy engagement: Changes in motivations and strategies. *Reading Research Quarterly, 31*(3), 306-332.

*Guyer, B.P., & Sabatino, D. (1989). The effectiveness of a multisensory alphabetic phonetic approach with college students who are learning disabled. *Journal of Learning Disabilities, 22(7)*, 430-434.

Guyer, B.P., & Sabatino, D. (1989). The effectiveness of a multisensory alphabetic phonetic approach with college students who are learning disabled. *Journal of Learning Disabilities, 22(7)*, 430-434.

Hallahan, D.P., & Cruickshank, W.M. (1973). *Psychoeducational foundations of learning disabilities*. Englewood Cliffs, NJ: Prentice-Hall.

Harris, K.R., & Pressley, M. (1991). The nature of cognitive strategy instruction: Interactive strategy construction. *Exceptional Children, 57*, 392-404.

Harwell, M.R. (1992). Summarizing monte carol results in methodological research. *Journal of Educational Statisitics, 17*, 297-313.

Hedges, L.V. (1994a). Statistical considerations. In H. Cooper & L.V. Hedges (Eds.), *The handbook of research synthesis* (pp. 29-38). New York: Russell Sage Foundation.

Hedges, L.V. (1994b). Fixed effects models. In H. Cooper & L.V. Hedges (Eds.), *The handbook of research synthesis* (pp. 285-299). New York: Russell Sage Foundation.

Hedges, L.V., & Olkin, I. (1985). *Statistical methods for meta-analysis.* San Diego, CA: Academic Press.

*Helper, M.M., Farber, E.D., & Feldgaier, S. (1982). Alternative thinking and classroom behavior of learning impaired children. *Psychological Reports, 50*(2), 415-420.

*Hine, M.S., Goldman, S.R., & Cosden, M.A. (1990). Error monitoring by learning handicapped students engaged in collaborative microcomputer-based writing. *The Journal of Special Education, 23*(4), 407-422.

*Hollingsworth, M., & Woodward, J. (1993). Integrated learning: Explicit strategies and their role in problem-solving instruction for students with learning disabilities. *Exceptional Children, 59*(5), 444-455.

*Howell, R., Sidorenko, E., & Jurica, J. (1987). The effects of computer use on the acquisition of multiplication facts by a student with learning disabilities. *Journal of Learning Disabilities, 20,* 336-341.

*Humphries, T.W., Wright, M., Snider, L., & McDougall, B. (1992). A comparison of the effectiveness of sensory integrative therapy and perceptual-motor training in treating children with learning disabilities. *Developmental and Behavioral Pediatrics, 13*(1), 31-40.

Hunter, J.E., & Schmidt, F.L. (1990). *Methods of meta-analysis: Correcting error and bias in research findings.* Newbury Park, CA: Sage.

*Hurford, D.P. (1990). Training phonemic segmentation ability with a phonemic discrimination intervention in second- and third-grade children with reading disabilities. *Journal of Learning Disabilities, 23,* 564-569.

*Hurford, D.P., & Sanders, R.E. (1990). Assessment and remediation of a phonemic discrimination deficit in reading disabled second and fourth graders. *Journal of Experimental Child Psychology, 50*(3), 396-415.

*Hutchinson, N.L., Freeman, J.G., Downey, K.H., & Kilbreath, L. (1992). Development and evaluation of an instructional module to promote career maturity for youth with learning disabilities. *Canadian Journal of Counselling, 26*(4), 290-299.

*Jaben, T.H. (1983). The effects of creativity training on learning disabled student's creative written expression. *Journal of Learning Disabilities, 16*(5), 264-265.

*Jaben, T.H. (1985). Effect of instruction for creativity on learning disabled students' drawings. *Perceptual and Motor Skills, 61*(n3, pt1), 895-898.

*Jaben, T.H. (1986). Impact of instruction on behavior disordered and learning disabled students' creative behavior. *Psychology in the Schools, 23*(4), 401-405.

*Jaben, T.H. (1987). Effects of training on learning disabled students' creative written expression. *Psychological Reports, 60*(1), 23-26.

*Jaben, T.H., Treffinger, D.J., Whelan, R.J., Hudson, F.G., Stainback, S.B., & Stainback, W. (1982). Impact of instruction on learning disabled students' creative thinking. *Psychology in the Schools, 19*(3), 371-373.

*Johnson, L., Graham, S., & Harris, K.R. (in press). *The Effects of Goal Setting and Self-Instructions on Learning a Reading Comprehension Strategy: A Study with Students with Learning Disabilities.*

*Jones, K.M., Torgesen, J.K., & Sexton, M.A. (1987). Using computer guided practice to increase decoding fluency in learning disabled children: A study using the Hint and Hunt I Program. *Journal of Learning Disabilities, 20*(2) 122-128.

Kail, R., & Bisanz, J. (1993). The information processing perspective on cognitive development in childhood and adolescence. In R. Sternberg & C.A. Berg (Eds.), *Intellectual development* (Vol. 1, pp. 229-260). New York: Cambridge University Press.

Kameenui, E.J. (1991). Toward a scientific pedagogy of learning disabilities: A sameness in the message. *Journal of Learning Disabilities, 24,* 364-372.

Kameenui, E.J., Jitendra, A.K., & Darch, C.B. (1995). Direct instruction reading as contronym and eononime. *Reading & Writing Quarterly: Overcoming Learning Difficulties, 11*(1), 3-17.

*Kane, B.J., & Alley, G.R. (1980). Tutored, instructional management program in computational mathematics for program in incarcerated learning disabled juvenile delinquents. *Journal of Learning Disabilities, 13*(3), 148-151.

Kass, C.E. (1970). *Final report: Advanced institute for leadership personnel in learning disabilities.* Tucson: Department of Health, Education, and Welfare, University of Arizona.

*Kendall, P.C., & Braswell, L. (1982). Cognitive-behavioral self-control therapy for children: A components analysis. *Journal of Consulting and Clinical Psychology, 50*(5), 672-689.

*Kennedy, K.M., & Backman, J. (1993). Effectiveness of the Lindamood Auditory Discrimination in Depth Program with students with learning disabilities. *Learning Disabilities Research & Practice, 8*(4), 253-259.

*Kershner, J.R., Cummings, R.L., Clarke, K.A., Hadfield, A.J., & Kershner, B.A. (1990). Two-year evaluation of the tomatis listening training program with learning disabled children. *Learning Disability Quarterly, 13,* 43-53.

*Kerstholt, M.T., Van Bon, W.H.J., & Schreuder, R. (1994). Training in phonemic segmentation: The effects of visual support. *Reading and Writing: An Interdisciplinary Journal, 6*(4), 361-385.

*Kim, Y.O. (1992). The effect of teaching a test-taking strategy to high school students with learning disabilities. (Doctoral dissertation, West Virginia University, 1991). *Dissertation Abstracts International, 53*(1-A), 121.

*King-Sears, M.E., Mercer, C.D., & Sindelar, P.T. (1992). Toward independence with keyword mnemonics: A strategy for science vocabulary instruction. *Remedial and Special Education, 13*(3), 22-33.

Kirk, S.A. (1963). Behavioral diagnosis and remediation of learning disabilities. *Proc. Conf. Explor. Probs. Perpet. Handicapped Child, 1,* 1-23.

*Klingner, J.K., & Vaughn, S. (1996). Reciprocal teaching of reading comprehension strategies for students with learning disabilities who use English as a second language. *Elementary School Journal, 96,* 275-293.

*Kunka, A.S.K. (1984). A modality-instruction interaction study of elementary learning disabled students using two types of electronic learning aids for math instruction. (Doctoral dissertation, University of Pittsburg, 1983). *Dissertation Abstracts International, 45*(2-A), 387.

Leinhardt, G., & Greeno, J.G. (1986). The cognitive skill of teaching. *Journal of Educational Psychology, 78*(2), 75-95.

*Lenkowsky, R.S., Barwosky, E.I., Dayboch, M., Puccio, L., & Lenkowsky, B.E. (1987). Effects of bibliotherapy on the self-concept of learning disabled, emotionally handicapped adolescents in a classroom setting. *Psychological Reports, 61*(2) 483-488.

*Leong, C.K., Simmons, D.R., & Izatt-Gambell, M.A. (1990). The effect of systematic training in elaboration on word meaning and prose comprehension in poor readers. *Annals of Dyslexia, 40,* 192-215.

*Lerner, C.H. (1978). The comparative effectiveness of a language experience approach and a basal-type approach to remedial reading instruction for severely disabled readers in a senior high school. (Doctoral Dissertation, Temple University 1978). *Dissertation Abstracts International, 39*(2-A), 779-780.

Lessen, E., Dudzinski, M., Karsh, K., & Van Acker, R. (1989). A survey of ten years of academic intervention research with learning disabled students: Implications for research and practice. *Learning Disabilities Focus, 4,* 106-122.

Levin, J.R. (1986). Four cognitive principles of learning strategy instruction. *Educational psychologist, 21,* 3-17.

Lindsley, O.R. (1964). Direct measurement and prosthesis of retarded behavior. *Journal of Education, 147,* 62-81.

Lipsey, M.W., & Wilson, D.B. (1993). The efficacy of psychological, educational, and behavioral treatment: Confirmation from meta-analysis. *American Psychologist, 48*(12), 1181-1209.

*Lloyd, J., Cullinan, D., Heins, E.D., & Epstein, M.H. (1980). Direct instruction: Effects on oral and written language comprehension. *Learning Disability Quarterly, 3*(4), 70-76.

*Lorenz, L., & Vockell, E. (1979). Using the neurological impress method with learning disabled readers. *Journal of Learning Disabilities, 12*(6), 420-422.

*Losh, M.A. (1991). The effect of the strategies intervention model on the academic achievement of junior high learning-disabled students. (Doctoral dissertation, University of Nebraska, 1991). *Dissertation Abstracts International, 52*(3-A), 880.

*Lovett, M.W., Borden, S.L., DeLuca, T., Lacerenza, L., Benson, N.J., & Brackstone, D. (1994). Treating the core deficits of developmental dyslexia: Evidence of transfer of learning after phonologically- and strategy-based reading training programs. *Developmental Psychology, 30*(6), 805-822.

*Lovett, M.W., Ransby, M.J., & Barron, R.W. (1988). Treatment, subtype, and word type effects on dyslexic children's response to remediation. *Brain and Language, 34*(2), 328-349.

*Lovett, M.W., Ransby, M.J., Hardwick, N., Johns, M.S., & Donaldson, S.A. (1989). Can dyslexia be treated? Treatment-specific and generalized treatment effects in dyslexic children's response to remediation. *Brain and Language, 37*(1), 90-121.

*Lovett, M.W., & Steinbach, K.A. (in press). The effectiveness of remedial programs for reading disabled children of different ages: Is there decreased benefit for older children? *Learning Disability Quarterly.*

*Lovett, M.W., Warren-Chaplin, P.M., Ransby, M.J., & Borden, S.L. (1990). Training the word recognition skills of reading disabled children: treatment and transfer effects. *Journal of Educational Psychology, 82*(4), 769-780.

*Lovitt, T., Rudsit, J., Jenkins, J., Pious, C., & Benedetti, D. (1986). Adapting science materials for regular and learning disabled seventh graders. *Remedial and Special Education, 7,* 31-39.

*Lucangeli, D., Galderisi, D., & Cornoldi, C. (1995). Specific and general transfer effects following metamemory training. *Learning Disabilities Research & Practice, 10*(1), 11-21.

*Lundberg, I., & Olofsson, A. (1993). Can computer speech support reading comprehension? *Computers in Human Behavior, 9*(2-3), 283-293.

*MacArthur, C.A., & Haynes, J.B. (1995). Student assistant for learning from text (SALT): A hypermedia reading aid. *Journal of Learning Disabilities, 28*(3), 150-159.

*MacArthur, C.A., Haynes, J.A., Malouf, D.B., Harris, K., & Owings, M. (1990). Computer assisted instruction with learning disabled students: Achievement, engagement, and other factors that influence achievement. *Journal of Educational Computing Research, 6*(3), 311-328.

*MacArthur, C.A., Schwartz, S.S., & Graham, S. (1991). Effects of a reciprocal peer revision strategy in special education classrooms. *Learning Disabilities Research, 6*(4), 201-210.

*Manning, B.H. (1984). Problem-solving instruction as an oral comprehension aid for reading disabled third graders. *Journal of Learning Disabilities, 17*(8), 457-461.

*Maron, L.R. (1993). A comparison study of the effects of explicit versus implicit training of test-taking skills for learning-disabled fourth-grade students. (Doctoral dissertation, The University of Wisconsin-Madison, 1992). *Dissertation Abstracts International, 53*(9-B), 4613.

*Marsh, L.G., & Cooke, N.L. (1996). The effects of using manipulatives in teaching math problem solving to students with learning disabilities. *Learning Disabilities Research & Practice, 11,* 58-65.

Martin, E. (1988). Response to: Intervention research in learning disabilities. In S. Vaughn & C. Bos (Eds.), *Research in learning disabilities* (pp. 173-184). San Diego, CA: Little, Brown, and Company.

*Mathes, P.G., & Fuchs, L.S. (1993). Peer-mediated reading instruction in special education resource rooms. *Learning Disabilities Research & Practice, 8*(4), 233-243.

McBride-Chang, C., Manis, F.R., Seidenberg, M.S., Custodio, R., & Doi, L.M. (1993). Print exposure as a predictor of word reading and reading comprehension in disabled and nondisabled readers. *Journal of Educational Psychology, 85,* 230-238.

McCollum, P.S., & Anderson, R.P. (1974). Group counseling with reading disabled children. *Journal of Counseling Psychology, 21*(2), 150-155.

Meichenbaum, D. (1977). *Cognitive behavior modification.* New York: Plenum.

Mercer, C.D., Jordan, L., Allsopp, D.H., & Mercer, A.R. (1996). Learning disabilities definitions and criteria used by stated education departments. *Learning Disability Quarterly, 19,* 217-232.

Mercer, C.D., & Mercer, A.R. (1981). *Teaching students with learning problems.* Columbus, OH: Charles E. Merrill Publishing Co.

*Meyer, L.A. (1982). The relative effects of word-analysis and word-supply correction procedures with poor readers during word-attack training. *Reading Research Quarterly, 17*(4), 544-555.

*Miller, S.P., & Mercer, C.D. (1993). Using data to learn about concrete-semiconcrete-abstract instruction for students with math disabilities. *Learning Disabilities Research & Practice, 8*(2), 89-96.

*Montague, M., Applegate, B., & Marquard, K. (1993). Cognitive strategy instruction and mathematical problem-solving performance of students with learning disabilities. *Learning Disabilities Research & Practice, 8*(4), 223-232.

*Moore, L., Carnine, D., Stepnoski, M., & Woodward, J. (1987). Research on the efficiency of low-cost networking. *Learning Disability Quarterly, 20*(9), 574-576.

*Morgan, A.V. (1991). A study of the effects of attribution retraining and cognitive self-instruction upon the academic and attentional skills, and cognitive-behavioral trends of elementary-age children served in self-contained learning disabilities programs. (Doctoral dissertation, The College of William and Mary, 1990). *Dissertation Abstracts International, 51*(8-B), 4035.

Morrison, S.R., & Siegel, L.S. (1991). Learning disabilities: A critical review of definitional and assessment issues. In J.E. Obrzut & G.W. Hynd (Eds.), *Neurological foundations of learning disabilities* (pp. 7997). San Diego, CA: Academic Press.

Myers, P., & Hammill, D.D. (1990). *Learning disabilities: Basic concepts, argument practices, and instructional strategies.* Austin, TX: Pro-Ed.

*Naylor, J.G., & Pumfrey, P.D. (1983). The alleviation of psycholinguistic deficits and some effects on the reading attainments of poor readers: A sequel. *Journal of Research in Reading, 6*(2), 129-153.

*Nelson, S.L. (1985). Modifying impulsivity in learning disabled boys on matching, maze, and WISC-R performance scales. (Doctoral dissertation, University of Southern California, 1984). *Dissertation Abstracts International, 45*(7-B), 2316-2317.

Newcomer, P.L., & Hammill, D.D. (1975). ITPA and academic achievement. *Teacher, 28,* 731-741.

*O'Connor, P.D., Stuck, G.B., & Wyne, M.D. (1979). Effects of a short-term intervention resource-room program on task orientation and achievement. *The Journal of Special Education, 13*(4), 375-385.

*Olofsson, A. (1992). Synthetic speech and computer aided reading for reading disabled children. *Reading & Writing, 4*(2), 165-178.

*Olsen, J.L., Wong, B.Y.L., & Marx, R.W. (1983). Linguistic and metacognitive aspects of normally achieving and learning disabled children's communication process. *Learning Disability Quarterly, 6*(3), 289-304.

Olson, R.K., Wise, B., Conners, F., & Rack, J.P. (1990). Organization, heritability, and remediation of component word recognition and language skills in disabled readers. In T.H. Carr & B.A. Levy (Eds.), *Reading and its development: Component skills approaches* (pp. 261-322). San Diego, CA: Academic Press.

*Olson, R.K., & Wise, B.W. (1992). Reading on the computer with orthographic and speech feedback. *Reading and Writing: An Interdisciplinary Journal, 4*(2), 107-144.

*Omizo, M.M., Cubberly, W.E., & Omizo, S.A. (1985). The effects of rational-emotive education groups on self-concept and locus of control among learning disabled children. *Exceptional Child, 32*(1), 13-19.

*Omizo, M.M., Lo, F.G., & Williams, R.E. (1986). Rational-emotive education, self-concept, and locus of control among learning-disabled students. *Journal of Humanistic Education, 25*(2), 58-69.

*Omizo, M.M., & Williams, R.E. (1982). Biofeedback-induced relaxation training as an alternative for the elementary school learning-disabled child. *Biofeedback and Self-Regulation, 7*(2), 139-148.

Palincsar, A.S., & Brown, A.L. (1984). Reciprocal teaching of comprehension--fostering and comprehension monitoring activities. *Cognition and Instruction, 1,* 117-175.

Palincsar, A.S., & Brown, A.L. (1988). Teaching and practicing thinking skills to promote comprehension in the context of groupproblem solving. Special Issue: The challenge of reading with understanding in the intermediate grades. *RASE: Remedial & Special Education, 9,* 53-59.

*Pany, D., & Jenkins, J.R. (1978). Learning word meanings: A comparison of instructional procedures. *Learning Disability Quarterly, 1*(2), 21-32.

*Pany, D., Jenkins, J.R., & Schreck, J. (1982). Vocabulary instruction: Effects on word knowledge and reading comprehension. *Learning Disability Quarterly, 5*(3), 202-215.

Paris, S.G., Cross, D.R., & Lipson, M.Y. (1984). Informed strategies for learning: A program to improve children's reading awareness and comprehension. *Journal of Educational Psychology, 76,* 1239-1252.

Parloff, M.B. (1984). Psychotherapy research and its incredible credibility crisis. *Clinical Psychology Review, 4,* 95-109.

*Pihl, R.O., Parkes, M., Drake, H., & Vrana, F. (1980). The intervention of a modulator with learning disabled children. *Journal of Clinical Psychology, 36*(4), 972-976.

*Porinchak, P.M. (1984). Computer-assisted instruction in secondary school reading: Interaction of cognitive and affective factors. (Doctoral dissertation, Hofstra University, 1983). *Dissertation Abstracts International, 45*(2-A), 478.

Pressley, M., & Ghatala, E.S. (1990). Self-regulated learning: Monitoring learning from text. *Educational Psychologist, 25,* 19-34.

Pressley, M., & Harris, K.R. (1994). Increasing the quality of educational intervention research. *Educational Psychology Review, 6,* 191-208.

*Prior, M., Frye, S., & Fletcher, C. (1987). Remediation for subgroups of retarded readers using a modified oral spelling procedure. *Developmental Medicine and Child Neurology, 29*(1), 64-71.

*Ratekin, N. (1979). Reading achievement of disabled learners. *Exceptional Children, 45*(6), 454-458.

*Reid, R., & Harris, K.R. (1993). Self-monitoring of attention versus self-monitoring of performance: Effects on attention and academic performance. *Exceptional Children, 60*(1), 29-40.

*Reilly, J.P. (1991). Effects of a cognitive-behavioral program designed to increase the reading comprehension skills of learning-disabled students. (Doctoral dissertation, College of William and Mary, 1991). *Dissertaton Abstracts International, 52*(3-A), 865.

Resnick, L.B. (1987). Constructing knowledge in school. In L.S. Liben (Ed.), *Development and learning: Conflict or congruence?* (pp. 19-50). Hillsdale, NJ: Lawrence Erlbaum.

*Reynolds, C.J. (1986). The effects of instruction in cognitive revision strategies on the writing skills of secondary learning disabled students. (Doctoral dissertation, The Ohio State University, 1985). *Dissertation Abstracts International, 46*(9-A), 2662.

Rosenshine, B. (1982, April). *The master teacher and the master developer.* Paper presented at the annual convention of the American Educational Research Association, New York.

Rosenshine, B. (1995). Advances in research on instruction. *Journal of Educational Research, 88*(5), 262-268.

Rosenshine, B., & Stevens, R. (1986). Teaching functions. In M.C. Wittrock (Ed.), *Handbook of research on teaching* (3rd ed.). New York: Macmillan.

Rosenthal, R. (1994). Parametric measures of effect size. In H. Cooper & L.V. Hedges (Eds.), *The handbook of research synthesis* (pp. 231-244). New York: Russell Sage Foundation.

*Ross, P.A., & Braden, J.P. (1991). The effects of token reinforcement versus cognitive behavior modification on learning-disabled students' math skills. *Psychology in the Schools, 28*(3), 247-256.

*Rudel, R.G., & Helfgott, E. (1984). Effect of piracetam on verbal memory of dyslexic boys. *American Academy of Child Psychiatry, 23*(6), 695-699.

*Ruhl, K.L., Hughes, C.A., & Gajar, A.H. (1990). Efficacy of the pause procedure for enhancing learning disabled and nondisabled college students' long-and short-term recall of facts presented through lecture. *Learning Disability Quarterly, 13*(1), 55-64.

*Sawyer, R.J., Graham, S., & Harris, K.R. (1992). Direct teaching, strategy instruction and strategy instruction with explicit self-regulation: Effects on the composition skills and self-efficacy of students with learning disabilities. *Journal of Educational Psychology, 84*(3), 340-352.

*Scanlon, D., Deshler, D.D., & Schumaker, J.B. (1996). Can a strategy be taught and learned in secondary inclusive classrooms? *Learning Disabilities Research & Practice, 11*, 41-57.

*Scheerer-Neumann, G. (1981). The utilization of intraword structure in poor readers: Experimental evidence and a training program. *Psychological Research, 43*(2), 155-178.

*Schulte, A.C., Osborne, S.S., & McKinney, J.D. (1991). Academic outcomes for students with learning disabilities in consultation and resource programs. *Exceptional Children, 57*(2), 162-172.

*Schunk, D.H. (1985). Participation in goal setting: Effects on self-efficacy and skills of learning-disabled children. *The Journal of Special Education, 19*(3), 305-317.

*Schunk, D.H., & Cox, P.D. (1986). Strategy training and attributional feedback with learning disabled students. *Journal of Educational Psychology, 78*(3), 201-209.

*Scruggs, T.E., & Mastropieri, M.A. (1989). Mnemonic instruction of LD students: A field-based evaluation. *Learning Disability Quarterly, 12*, 119-125.

*Scruggs, T.E., & Mastropieri, M.A. (1992). Classroom applications of mnemonic instruction: Acquisition, maintenance, and generalization. *Exceptional Children, 58(3)*, 219-229.

Scruggs, T.E., & Mastropieri, M.A. (1993). Issues in conduction intervention research: Secondary students. In S. Vaughn & C. Bos (Eds.), *Research issues in learning disabilities* (pp. 130-145). New York: Springer-Verlag.

*Scruggs, T.E., Mastropieri, M.A., & Tolfa-Veit, D. (1986). The effects of coaching on the standardized test performance of learning disabled and behaviorally disordered students. *Remedial and Special Education, 7*(5), 37-41.

*Scruggs, T.E., & Tolfa, D. (1985). Improving the test-taking skills of learning-disabled students. *Perceptual and Motor Skills, 60*(3), 847-850.

*Sheare, J.B. (1978). The impact of resource programs upon the self-concept and peer acceptance of learning disabled children. *Psychology in the Schools, 15*(3), 406-412.

Siegel, L.S. (1992). An evaluation of the discrepancy definition of dyslexic. *Journal of Learning Disabilities, 25*, 618-629.

Siegel, L.S. (1993). The cognitive basis of dyslexia. In M. Howe & R. Pasnak (Eds.), *Emerging themes in cognitive development* (pp. 33-52). New York: Springer-Verlag.

Siegel, L.S., & Ryan, E.B. (1989). The development of working memory in normally achieving and subtypes of learning disabled children. *Child Development, 60*, 973-980.

*Simmonds, E.P.M. (1990). The effectiveness of two methods for teaching a constraint-seeking questioning strategy to students with learning disabilities. *Journal of Learning Disabilities, 23*(4), 229-232.

*Simmonds, E.P.M. (1992). The effects of teacher training and implementation of two methods for improving the comprehension skills of students with learning disabilities. *Learning Disabilities Research & Practice, 7*(4), 194-198.

Simmons, D.C., & Kameenui, E.J. (1996). A focus on curriculum design: When children fail. *Focus on Exceptional Children, 28*(7), 1-16.

*Simpson, S.B., Swanson, J.M., & Kunkel, K. (1992). The impact of an intensive multisensory reading program on a population of learning-disabled delinquents. *Annals of Dyslexia, 42*, 54-66.

*Sinatra, R.C., Stahl-Gemake, J., & Berg, D.N. (1984). Improving reading comprehension of disabled readers through semantic mapping. *The Reading Teacher, 38(1)*, 22-29.

*Sindelar, P.T., Honsaker, M.S., & Jenkins, J.R. (1982). Response cost and reinforcement contingencies of managing the behavior of distractible children in tutorial settings. *Learning Disability Quarterly, 5*, 3-13.

Slavin, R.E. (1987). Grouping for instruction in the elementary school. *Educational Psychologist, 22*, 109-127.

Slavin, R.E., Stevens, R.J., & Madden, N.A. (1988). Accommodating student diversity in reading and writing instruction: A cooperative learning approach. Special Issue: The challenge of reading with understanding in the intermediate grades. *RASE: Remedial & Special Education, 9*(1), 60-66.

*Smith, M.A. (1989). The efficacy of mnemonics for teaching recognition of letter clusters to reading disabled students. (Doctoral dissertation, University of Oregon, 1989). *Dissertation Abstracts International, 50*(5-A), 1259-1260.

Smith, M.L., Glass, G.V., & Miller, T.L. (1980). *The benefits of psychotherapy*. Baltimore, MD: Johns Hopkins University Press.

*Smith, P.L., & Friend, M. (1986). Training learning disabled adolescents in a strategy for using text structure to aid recall of instructional prose. *Learning Disabilities Research, 2*(1), 38-44.

*Snider, V.E. (1989). Reading comprehension performance of adolescents with learning disabilities. *Learning Disability Quarterly, 12*(2), 87-96.

*Somerville, D.E., & Leach, D.J. (1988). Direct or indirect instruction?: An evaluation of three types of intervention programme for assisting students with specific reading difficulties. *Educational Research, 30*(1), 46-53.

*Sowell, V., Parker, R., Poplin, M., & Larsen, S. (1979). The effects of psycholinguistic training on improving psycholinguistic skills. *Learning Disability Quarterly, 2*(3), 69-78.

Spear-Swerling, L., & Sternberg, R.J. (1994). The road not taken: An integrative theoretical model of reading disability. *Journal of Learning Disabilities, 27*(2), 91-103, 122.

Stanovich, K.E. (1980). Toward an interactive-compensatory model of individual differences in the development of reading fluency. *Reading Research Quarterly, 16*, 32-65.

Stanovich, K.E. (1986). Matthew effects in reading: Some consequences of individual differences in the acquisition of literacy. *Reading Research Quarterly, 21*, 360-406.

Stanovich, K.E., & Siegel, L.S. (1994). Phenotypic performance profile of children with reading disabilities: A regression based test of the phonological-core difference model. *Journal of Educational Psychology, 86*, 24-53.

Stephens, T.M. (1977). *Teaching skills to children with learning and behavior disorders*. Columbus, OH: Charles E. Merrill.

*Straub, R.B., & Roberts, D.M. (1983). Effects of nonverbal-oriented social awareness training program on social interaction ability of learning disabled children. *Journal of Nonverbal Behavior, 7*(4), 195-201.

Strauss, A.A., & Kephart, N.C. (1955). *Psychopathology and education of the brain-injured child: Progress in theory and clinic* (Vol. 2). New York: Grune and Stratton.

*Sullivan, J. (1972). The effects of Kephart's perceptual motor-training on a reading clinic sample. *Journal of Learning Disabilities, 5*(10), 545-551.

Swanson, H.L. (1991). Operational definitions of learning disabilities. *Learning Disability Quarterly, 14*, 242-254.

Swanson, H.L. (1992). Generality and modifiability of working memory among skilled and less skilled readers. *Journal of Educational Psychology, 64*(4), 473-488.

Swanson, H.L. (1993). Working memory in learning disability subgroups. *Journal of Experimental Child Psychology, 56*, 87-114.

Swanson, H.L., & Alexander, J.E. (1997). Cognitive processes as predictors of word recognition and reading comprehension in learning-disabled and skilled readers: Revisiting the specificity hypothesis. *Journal of Educational Psychology, 89*(1), 128-158.

Swanson, H.L., Carson, C., & Sachse-Lee, C.M. (1996). A selective synthesis of intervention research for students with learning disabilities. *School Psychology Review, 25*(3), 370-391.

Swanson, H.L., & Hoskyn, M. (1998). Experimental intervention research for students with learning disabilities: A meta-analysis of treatment outcomes. *Review of Educational Research, 68*, 277-321.

*Swanson, H.L., & Trahan, M.F. (1992). Learning disabled readers' comprehension of computer mediated text: The influence of working memory, metacognition and attribution. *Learning Disabilities Research & Practice, 7*(2), 74-86.

Swanson, H.L., Hoskyn, M., & Lee, C. (1999). *Interventions for students with learning disabilities.* New York: Guilford.

*Tollefson, N., Tracy, D.B., Johnsen, E.P., Farmer, A.W., & Buenning, M. (1984). Goal setting and personal responsibility training for LD adolescents. *Psychology in the Schools, 21*(2), 224-233.

*Torgesen, J.K., Wagner, R.K., Rashotte, C.A., Alexander, A.W., & Conway, T. (1997). Preventive and remedial interventions for children with severe reading disabilities. *Learning Disabilities: A Multi-Disciplinary Journal, 8*(1), 51-61.

*Trapani, C., & Gettinger, M. (1989). Effects of social skills training and cross-age tutoring on academic achievement and social behaviors of boys with learning disabilities. *Journal of Research and Development in Education, 23*(1), 1-9.

*VanDaal, V.H.P., & Reitsma, P. (1990). Effects of independent word practice with segmented and whole-word sound feedback in disabled readers. *Journal of Research in Reading, 13*(2), 133-148.

*VanDaal, V.H.P., & Reitsma, P. (1993). The use of speech feedback by normal and disabled readers in computer-based reading practice. *Reading and Writing: An Interdisciplinary Journal, 5*(3), 243-259.

*VanDaal, V.H.P., & Van Der Leij, D. (1992). Computer-based reading and spelling practice for children with learning disabilities. *Journal of Learning Disabilities, 25*(3), 186-195.

*VanReusen, A.K., Bos, C.S. (1994). Facilitating student participation in individualized education programs through motivation strategy instruction. *Exceptional Children, 60*(5) 466-475.

*VanStrien, J.W., Stolk, B.D., & Zuiker, S. (1995). Hemisphere-specific treatment of dyslexia subtypes: Better reading with anxiety-laden words? *Journal of Learning Disabilities, 28*(1), 30-34.

*Vaughn, S., Schumm, J.S., & Gordon, J. (1993). Which motoric condition is most effective for teaching spelling to students with and without learning disabilities? *Journal of Learning Disabilities, 26*(3), 193-198.

Vellutino, F., & Scanlon, D.M. (1991). The effects of instructional bias on word identification. In I.L. Rieben & C.A. Perfetti (Eds.), *Learning to read: Basic research and its implications* (pp. 189-204). Hillsdale, NJ: Lawrence Erlbaum Associates.

Vellutino, F., Scanlon, D.M., Sipay, E., Small, S., Pratt, A., Chen, R., & Denckla, M. (1996). Cognitive profiles of difficult-to-remediate and readily remediated poor readers: Early intervention as a vehicle for distinguishing between cognitive and experiential deficits as basic causes of specific reading disability. *Journal of Educational Psychology, 88*, 601-638.

*Wade, J.F. (1979). The effects of component deficit remediation and academic deficit remediation on improving reading achievement of learning disabled children. (Doctoral dissertation, The University of Arizona, 1979). *Dissertation Abstracts International, 40*(3-A), 1412.

*Wade, J., & Kass, C.E. (1987). Component deficit and academic remediation of learning disabilities. *Journal of Learning Disabilities, 20*(7), 441-447.

Walczyk, J.J. (1993). Are general resource notions still viable in reading research. *Journal of Educational Psychology, 85,* 127-135.

*Wanat, P.E. (1983). Social skills: An awareness program with learning disabled adolescents. *Journal of Learning Disabilities, 16*(1), 35-38.

*Warner, J.M.R. (1973). The effects of two treatment modes upon children diagnosed as having learning disabilities. (Doctoral dissertation, University of Illinois, 1973). *Dissertation Abstracts International, 34*(3-A), 1142-1143.

Waterman, B., & Lewandowski, L. (1993). Phonological and semantic processing in reading disabled and nondisabled males at two age-levels. *Journal of Experimental Child Psychology, 55,* 87-103.

*Waterman, D.E. (1974). Remediation of word attack skills in slow readers by total body movement learning games. (Doctoral dissertation, University of Tulsa, 1973). *Dissertation Abstracts International, 34*(7-A), 4049.

Weisz, J.R., Weiss, B., Han, S.S., Granger, D.A., & Morton, T. (1995). Effects of psychotherapy with children and adolescents revisited: A meta-analysis of treatment outcome studies. *Psychological Bulletin, 117*(3), 450-468.

*Welch, M. (1992). The PLEASE strategy: A meta-cognitive learning strategy for improving the paragraph writing of students with learning disabilities. *Learning Disability Quarterly, 15*(2), 119-128.

*White, C.V., Pascarella, E.T., & Pflaum, S.W. (1981). Effects of training in sentence construction on the comprehension of learning disabled children. *Journal of Educational Psychology, 71*(5), 697-704.

*Whitman, D.M. (1986). The effects of computer-assisted instruction on mathematics achievement of mildly handicapped students. (Doctoral dissertation, University of South Carolina, 1985). *Dissertation Abstracts International, 46*(10A), 3000-3001.

Wiederholt, J.L. (1974). Historical perspectives on the education of the learning disabled. In L. Mann & D.A. Sabatino (Eds.), *The second review of special education* (pp. 103-152). Austin, TX: Pro-Ed.

Wiederholt, J.L., & Hammill, D.D. (1971). Use of the Frostig-Horne Visual Perceptual Program in the urban school. *Psychology in Schools, 8,* 268-274.

Wiederholt, J.L., Hammill, D.D., & Brown, V. (1978). *The resource teacher: A guide to effective practices.* Boston: Allyn & Bacon.

*Williams, J.P., Brown, L.G., Silverstein, A.K., & deCani, J.S. (1994). An instructional program in comprehension of narrative themes for adolescents with learning disabilities. *Learning Disability Quarterly, 17,* 205-221.

*Wilsher, C., Atkins, G., & Manfield, P. (1985). Effect of piracetam on dyslexic's reading ability. *Journal of Learning Disabilities, 18,* 19-25.

*Wilson, C.L. (1989). An analysis of a direct instruction procedure in teaching word problem-solving to learning disabled students. (Doctoral dissertation, Florida State University, 1988). *Dissertation Abstracts International, 50*(2-A), 416.

*Wilson, C., & Sindelar, P.T. (1991). Direct instruction in math word problems: Students with learning disabilities. *Exceptional Children, 57*(6), 512-519.

*Wise, B.W., Ring, J., Sessions, L., & Olson, R.K. (in press). Phonological awareness with and without articulation: A preliminary study. *Learning Disability Quarterly.*

Wong, B.Y.L. (1986). Metacognition and special education: A review of a view. *Journal of Special Education, 20*(1), 9-29.

Wong, B.Y.L. (1987). How do the results of metacognitive research impact on the learning disabled individual? *Learning Disability Quarterly, 10,* 189-195.

Wong, B.Y.L. (1991). Assessment of metacognitive research in learning disabilities: Theory, research, and practice. In H.L. Swanson (Ed.), *Handbook on the assessment of learning disabilities* (pp. 265-284). Austin, TX: PRO-ED.

*Wong, B.Y.L., Butler, D.L., Ficzere, S.A., & Kuperis, S. (1996). Teaching low achievers and students with learning disabilities to plan, write, and revise opinion essays. *Journal of Learning Disabilities, 29,* 197-212.

*Wong, B.Y.L., Butler, D.L., Ficzere, S.A., Kuperis, S., Corden, M., & Zelmer, J. (1994). Teaching problem learners revision skills and sensitivity to audience through two instructional modes: Student-teacher versus student-student interactive dialogues. *Learning Disabilities Research & Practice, 9*(2), 78-90.

*Wong, B.Y.L., & Jones, W. (1982). Increasing metacomprehension in learning disabled and normally achieving students through self-questioning training. *Learning Disability Quarterly, 5*(3), 228-240.

Zecker, S.G., & Zinner, T.E. (1987). Semantic code deficit for reading disabled children on an auditory lexical decision task. *Journal of Reading Behavior, 19,* 177-189.

*Zieffle, T.H., & Romney, D.M. (1985). Comparison of self-instruction and relaxation training in reducing impulsive and inattentive behavior of learning disabled children on cognitive tasks. *Psychological Reports, 57*(1), 271-274.

WORKING MEMORY AND COGNITIVE ABILITIES IN CHILDREN WITH SPECIFIC DIFFICULTIES IN ARITHMETIC WORD PROBLEM SOLVING

Maria Chiara Passolunghi and Cesare Cornoldi

ABSTRACT

Children with adequate general intelligence, but specific difficulties in mathematics problem solving, are common in schools, but they have not been extensively studied. This chapter reviews specific evidence concerning disabilities in word arithmetic problem solving and offers an overview of a series of studies developed in a joint project between the Universities of Padua and Trieste (Italy). In the last part of the paper, two original studies complete the view of the area, examining the particular issue of memory abilities of a selected group of children with problem solving difficulties. In the first study, using the fragment completion paradigm, it is shown that poor problem solvers meet difficulty in suppressing irrelevant information in working memory tasks, and that this information remains available in their memory

Advances in Learning and Behavioral Disabilities, Volume 14, pages 155-178.
ISBN: 0-7623-0561-4

systems more at the implicit than at the explicit level. In the second study, it is shown that the problem solving difficulty is related to a difficulty in understanding and holding a representation of the problem in working memory.

INTRODUCTION

In this chapter, we focus on children who present specific difficulties in solving arithmetic word problems commonly found in primary schools, based on the written presentation of a series of data and of a question whose solution requires the use of the four basic operations (addition, subtraction, multiplication and division) with the given data. This particular group of mathematical learning disabled children will be defined as a group of poor arithmetic word problem solvers.

A variety of theoretical frameworks have been proposed to describe the cognitive processes necessary for solving arithmetic word problems. A lot of them were focused on the role of the comprehension and construction of a representation of the problem (e.g., Nathan, Kintsch, & Young, 1992; Passolunghi, Lonciari, & Cornoldi, 1996) and on the role of control processes (e.g., Lucangeli & Cornoldi, 1997; Pressley, 1990).

Research on problem solving has widely dealt with those factors related to both the participant's characteristics and the nature of the task that can improve problem solving skills. However, less attention has been focused on the cognitive features of children with problem solving difficulties. Mayer and coauthors (Mayer, 1983, 1987, 1998; Mayer, Larkin, & Kadane, 1984), with reference to arithmetical word problems, identified three main process categories necessary for the solution: encoding, planning and algorithms execution. In the first stage, that of encoding, the problem solver, after analyzing the text, builds an inner representation of the task. Encoding therefore consists of two different processes: a translation process, in which each sentence of the text is transformed into a semantic representation in memory; and an integration process, in which the various sentences are placed together according to a coherent representation. Other studies have pointed out the role of the selection of problem schemata, in order to connect the relevant information and select it to eventually achieve the solution (e.g., Hinsley, Hayes, & Simon, 1977). The recognition of a familiar pattern in the text helps the application of problem-solving procedures. It seems, in fact, that skilled participants easily handle the whole structure of the task, enabling them to perform the task more efficiently (Berger & Wilde, 1987; Larkin, McDermott, Simon, & Simon, 1980). With respect to children, however, this hypothesis has been called into question by Swanson, Cooney, and Brock (1993).

Researchers in metacognition suggested the presence of underlying metacognitive skills that can affect the final performance (see Lucangeli & Passolunghi, 1995). It has been found that good problem solvers show a higher level of metacognitive skills than poor problem solvers (see Swanson, 1990, 1993), which enables them to better analyze the task structure, to easily choose the most appropriate strategies, and to make more profitable use of cognitive skills. In particular, Brown (1982) suggested that some metacognitive control processes involved in problem solving consist of the ability of: (a) predicting whether solvers will succeed in their task (prevision), (b) devising a plan for problem solution (planning), (c) controlling the problem solving process (monitoring), and (d) assessing the result obtained (evaluation).

In the first phase of a joint project between the Universities of Trieste and Padova (Passolunghi et al., 1995, 1996) we examined the two distinct, but interrelated, levels related respectively to the cognitive and metacognitive components involved in arithmetic word problem solving. Important theoretical bases for this study were offered by the cognitive components obtained from the model of Mayer et al. (1984), and the metacognitive components, taken from Brown's (1978) hypothesis. We assumed that metacognitive skills affect cognitive behavior at any stage of the total process in question (see Schoenfeld, 1982; Silver, 1979).

In order to examine the relationship between metacognitive skills and cognitive behavior we developed two questionnaires, and included also some tests on planning. Planning tests were added to investigate whether the relationship between general planning skills and problem solving skills could be also found in the "standard" arithmetical word problems (i.e., problem solving tasks more frequently considered with primary school participants). In these cases, children are very likely to have already encountered similar tasks, therefore word text comprehension (as measured through a standard reading comprehension test), memory of the task structure (as measured through a categorization test) and, eventually, metacognitve control skills could all prove more relevant than planning skills.

Therefore, by focusing on typical school problems, we wished to study not so much general problem solving skills, but specific school skills associated with those factors affecting in particular learning disabled children's performances. Our preliminary research investigated the effects of variables such as encoding-comprehension, planning, and metacognitive skills on successful arithmetical word problem solving. These variables might directly correlate to problem solving skills or affect them at different stages. For instance, comprehension and metacognitive skills (in the case of monitoring and evaluation) might very likely affect not only the initial stage of the interpretation of the task, but also all the other stages. On the contrary, if we consider that solving algorithms of standard problems have been widely used, planning skills might prove relevant only initially and could only affect categorization and (initial) comprehension of the task.

We tested children of different school ages (varying from 8 to 13 years), comparing the abilities of poor problem solvers to children good in problem solving.

In order to test text-comprehension, we administered the MT objective tests of Cornoldi and Colpo (1981). Tests varied according to school level, but the total number of questions and scores was the same for all school levels. To examine categorization skills, and therefore the ability of grasping the structure of the problem, we developed a categorization task on the basis of those proposed by Chi, Feltovich, and Glaser (1981) and Swanson et al. (1993). The classification task varied according to the age of the participants who were asked to classify the items applying the necessary mathematical operations. Instructions were orally given by the experimenter who clarified the request. The participant's tasks consisted in forming groups of problems to be solved with the same operations and no limitation was given to the number of groups they could place together. Within each set, each problem was presented on a different paper in order to enhance the grouping of the other problems of the same kind. Participants were said that in the various sets they could have different numbers of groupings and that some problems could also be left out of any group. The dependent measure was given by the total of correctly classified problems.

To examine planning skills, the Tower of London test of Shallice (1982) and the Porteus' (1955) maze test were used. In the Tower of London test, the dependent measures were given by the total number of attempts made by the participant for each problem solving task and by the initial planning time. Another variable was given by the total number of problems solved with the first move.

In Porteus' (1955) test, the participants were required to draw a path in a maze trying to foresee the blocked paths. According to the number of successful tests, weighed scores were given. The total execution time was also measured.

Metacognitive skills were tested through two questionnaires: one on Metamathematics and the other on Metamemory. The first questionnaire, presented in a reduced version adapted from a longer one (see Lucangeli, Cornoldi, & Tellarini, 1998), is composed of 15 items and is intended to assess prevision, planning, monitoring and evaluation skills in simple mathematical tasks.

The Metamemory Questionnaire was an Italian version of a questionnaire taken from the interview of Kreutzer, Leonard, and Flavell (1975). The questionnaire is composed of 15 items and its aim is to investigate the metacognition of some memory strategies that can help memory.

The results of this study showed that the best predictor of successful problem solving was the ability of categorization (the knowledge of the problem schemata), followed by that of text-comprehension (MT tests). This finding partially contrasts with the results obtained by Swanson et al. (1993), according to which categorization skill did not prove to be a particularly effective predictor of problem solving. The texts of our word problems were deliberately clear and explicit, and avoided the use of ambiguous terms. The study of Swanson et al. (1993) did not report examples of the word problems used. This fact does not allow us to rule out the possibility that their texts presented higher comprehension difficulties than ours. This would possibly explain why text comprehension was, in Swanson et al. (1993) a more reliable predictor of problem solving success than categorization skills. Another explanation of the difference with respect to the results of Swanson et al. (1993) might lie in the fact that they proposed another test (to identify the operations necessary for problem solving) which in fact, being strictly linked to categorization and problem solving skills, could be a more reliable predictor of problem solving skills.

After preliminary encoding the text, it seems that children with good problem solving abilities, while searching for the solution, recognized the problem's underlying structure and retrieved the solving strategies used on previous occasions and then applied them to the problem proposed. Obviously, the knowledge of problem schemata can be more easily applied to routine problem solving, such as word school problems. Experimental data on the application of a schemata approach to nonroutine problem solving are, on the other hand, very scarce.

It appears that the specific difficulties found by poor solvers concerned the comprehension of the text as well as the identification of the structure underlying the problem itself. Our results corroborate the hypothesis that skillful participants, differently from unskillful ones, are able to classify types of problems according to their underlying structure (see Chi et al., 1981; Schoenfeld & Herrmann, 1982; Silver, 1979).

We also found an important link between metacognitive and problem solving skills. Metacognition skills affected problem solving both as a control of the ability of categorizing and applying a "schema" approach to the problem (as assessed through categorization tests), and as a metacognitive knowledge, as assessed through the Metamathematics Questionnaire. In agreement with the findings of Swanson (1990), obtained through the administration of "think aloud" protocols, our results suggested that a high metacognitive knowledge is positively correlated with performance in problem solving. The influence of metacognitive knowledge occurs at various levels, including when participants use problem-space-operators leading them to the solution. In this case, more strategically able participants could monitor the solving process more carefully than less able participants.

Our study evidentiated that planning variables, which are not directly related to problem solving, are instead directly related to metacognitive ability. It is possible that in our tasks planning skills were required to a minor extent, differently from what happens with hypothetical-deductive problems (such as those used by Piaget & Inhelder, 1958). In fact, in a further investigation we examined the influence of planning variables in types of problems involving a higher use of hypothetical deductive thinking (Passolunghi, 1999). The results suggested that planning ability had a more relevant role in the hypothetical deductive problems than in the routine problems.

It should be noted that, between good and poor problem solvers, besides differences in metacognition and mathematics skills, we (Passolunghi et al., 1995, 1996) also found significant differences in more general metacognitive and memory skills. Skilled participants apparently showed higher metacognitive awareness of the importance of using proper memory strategies to enhance recall. This kind of knowledge can also positively affect problem solving. Good problem solvers might be more aware of the difficulty of recalling the information provided by the task and, consequently, employ more appropriate memory strategies. It is possible, however, that our results were due to more general abilities, either to a general metacognitive ability or to a working memory ability. A general metacognitive ability would induce children to reconsider the nature of the problem process and to develop more deep reflections in front of all the cases where it was necessary. Our results supported the hypothesis that the subject with learning difficulties had deficits in metacognitive knowledge also in areas other than those where the specific problem was present (Cornoldi, 1987, 1995). On the other hand, a more efficient working memory system should make available more cognitive resources in order to do a variety of different cognitive activities.

The second phase of the joint project between the Universities of Trieste and Padua was devoted to specifically examine the relationship between working memory and learning disabilities in arithmetic word problem solving.

WORKING MEMORY AND PROBLEM SOLVING

A well-established working memory model has been proposed by Baddeley and his coauthors in an impressive series of papers and books (e.g., Baddeley, 1986). The model makes a distinction between different components of working memory and, in particular, between a central executive system, not modality specific, involved in the control of cognitive activity, and modality specific servosystems. Baddeley focused on two servosystems, that is, the articulatory loop and visuospatial sketchpad, respectively involved in the storage and maintenance of auditory-linguistic and of visuospatial information. In arithmetic word problem solving, the most important components seem to be the central executive, in the control of the operations required to solve the problem, and the articulatory loop, in the maintenance of relevant information necessary for its solution.

Research on arithmetic abilities has been, until now, more focused on the role of the articulatory loop. For example, Siegel and Ryan (1988) studied the short term memory of children, aged between 7 and 14, with low arithmetic achievement and found that they were less influenced than controls by the phonetic similarity of stimuli. These data suggest that children poor in arithmetic make less effective use of the articulatory loop, which has been shown to be sensitive to the phonetic similarity of stimuli. With a different age group, that is, normal young adults, Logie, Gilhooly, and Wynn (1994) found that mental addition was related to vocal rehearsal, a typical function of the articulatory loop. Finally, Leather and Henry (1994) found a more general relationship between a variety of working memory tests (complex and simple memory span, phonological awareness) and success in reading and arithmetic. Data obtained by Hitch and McAuley (1991) revealed a domain specific relationship between articulatory loop and success in arithmetic: young children, poor in arithmetic, tended to count more slowly than controls and had a lower auditory digit span, but that they were not lower than controls in speech rate and other types of span.

A stricter focus on word arithmetic problem solving, rather than on more general and heterogeneous arithmetic abilities, suggests that working memory can be critically involved even when the written text must not be held in memory, but remains available all thru the solving process. Indeed, comprehension of a text requires that incoming information is integrated with previous information maintained in the working memory system (Oakhill & Yuill, 1996). Furthermore the complete comprehension of the problem requires that the solvers build up a mental representation which involves the capacity of working memory system. From the point of view of Baddeley's (1986) three component model, the central executive component could be more specifically and strongly involved than the articulatory loop. In fact, problem solving does not simply involve the maintenance of given information, but it requires its control, that is, that this information is examined for relevance, selected or inhibited—according to its relevance—integrated, used and so on. Baddeley (1990) also suggested that reading comprehension involves the central executive more than the articulatory loop. This suggestion seems to apply even more to written word arithmetic problem solving which requires not only text comprehension, but also additional operations on it (see also Turner & Engle, 1989).

After the pioneering work done by Daneman and Carpenter (1980) a relevant body of evidence has been accumulated confirming the relationship between listening span and reading comprehension. However, the exact meaning of this relationship has been widely discussed and a simple storage-processing capacity view has been questioned. A simple storage-processing capacity view assumes that human working memory is of variable capacity, definable as the number of independent chunks or pieces of information it can hold in mind in order to operate on them. Daneman and Carpenter (1980) developed a working memory test, the Reading Span Test, which requires the child to read and semantically process an increasing set of sentences (e.g., the subject has to say if the sentence is true or false) and to memorize the last word of each sentence. A parallel form of the test, the Listening Span test, required to listen rather than to read the sentences and to complete the same series of operations which are requested in the Reading Span test. Typical measures considered for both the Reading and the Listening Span tests are accuracy in answering the verification questions, the number of last sentence words correctly recalled and the span level (i.e., the number of the sets of sentences correctly recalled).

Daneman and Carpenter (1980, 1983) hypothesized that the lower span scores of students with poorer comprehension ability could be due to the fact that these students had to devote more resources than high ability students to the processing of sentences. In consequence, despite the fact they could have an initial pool of working memory resources equal to the pool of resources of the high ability participants, low ability participants would have fewer resources for the span test.

However, there is evidence that a difference between these groups is maintained also when sentences are substituted by other material (Daneman & Tardif, 1987; Yuill, Oakhill, & Parkin, 1989). This evidence suggests that a poor listening span score in low comprehension ability participants was not only due to a difficulty in the processing of sentences. Furthermore, the fact that a difference in the listening span tests between good and poor comprehenders can also be found when the two groups are matched for a measure of general intelligence (Cornoldi, De Beni, & Pazzaglia, 1996) suggests that this difference is not due to a general intelligence factor.

Swanson et al. (1993) verified the hypothesis of the relationship between working memory and children's word problem solution. Swanson and coauthors used a modification of the Daneman and Carpenter's (1980) Reading Span Test and they found that the working memory ability was significantly correlated with problem solving accuracy: however, the relationship between the two measures was far from relevant, especially when the influence of comprehension ability was partialed out. In a further research, Swanson (1994) made a distinction between a series of short-term memory tests related to the functions assigned by Baddeley (1986) to the working memory peripheral components (i.e. the digit span test, short-term memory tests for sentences or list of words) and a series of working memory tests related to the functions assigned by Baddeley (1986) to the Central Executive (i.e., story recall and the listening span). Swanson (1994) tested the children with the Listening Span Test which has the same procedure of the Reading Span Test proposed by Daneman and Carpenter (1980) with the only difference that the subject listens to the sentences instead of reading them. By comparing participants of different ages with a variety of learning disabilities (including disabilities in mathematics) and control groups, Swanson (1994) observed that short-term memory tasks and working memory tasks reflect different processes, both of which seem to separate the learning disabled and the control group.

Taken altogether, the data of Swanson and coauthors suggested that a distinction between tasks testing the central executive and tasks testing the articulatory loop can be useful in examining participants of different mathematical ability and that, in particular, the Reading and Listening span tests devised by Daneman and Carpenter (1980) can be of some utility in this field. In addition, indirect evidence of a relationship between the ability to solve word arithmetic problems and the ability to control irrelevant information was found by Low, Over, Doolan, and Mitchell (1994). They showed that training devoted to detecting necessary and sufficient information and to dropping other information can improve the ability to solve algebraic word problems. However, further evidence is needed to examine the relationship between word arithmetic problem solving accuracy and the efficiency of the Central Executive component of working memory, based on the success in Daneman and Carpenter's span tasks or in other tasks.

In a longitudinal study on a selected group of poor problem solvers, with low expertise in problem solving, but of average IQ, we (Passolunghi, Cornoldi, & De Liberto, 1999) verified that working memory is related to the arithmetic problem solving ability. In a series of experimental phases we compared two groups, longitudinally followed for a period of two school years: an experimental group of fourth-graders poor in word arithmetic problem solving ability and a control group, matched for grade, age and a measure of intelligence, but with a high word arithmetic problem solving ability. Our results supported the hypothesis that poor problem solvers have lower scores than good problem solvers in working memory tests requiring the inhibition of irrelevant information.

As we included in our selection procedure the children matched by equal general characteristics, our results supported the hypothesis that the difference we found in the working memory of math disabled children is specifically related to their problem solving ability and not to more general intellectual ability. In this way our results offered some insight about a group of poor learners largely neglected by literature (i.e., group of children who, despite having average intelligence scores, have difficulties in learning mathematics and specifically in word arithmetic problem solving). Teachers report that this case is rather frequent. They have difficulty in understanding the reasons for these difficuties and in developing adequate teaching strategies. There is evidence that the sources of difficulty in problem solving are represented by comprehension and control abilities which also involve the working memory Central Executive component (Baddeley, 1986). Our results supported with experimental data the hypothesis of a working memory deficit in poor problem solvers, furthermore they suggested that a critical problem of poor problem solvers may be due to their difficulty to inhibit irrelevant information. The role of inhibition processes in working memory had been recently proposed by a series of authors and in particular by De Beni's group (1998) who demonstrated that higher performance in working memory tests is related to a lower number of intrusion errors, that is, of memories of to-be-inhibited information.

In a first experimental phase, we demonstrated that working memory is related to arithmetic word problem solving ability (Passolunghi et al., 1999). The poor problem solvers group had a poorer performance than control group in a Italian version of the Listening Span test developed by Daneman and Carpenter (1980). As we hypothesized, this difference was due to a difficulty of poor problem solvers to avoid memory intrusions due to irrelevant information. We found that intrusions were higher in the experimental group than in the control one.

Moreover, following a procedure designed by De Beni et al. (1998) we replicated and extended this effect. We tested the two groups with a Categorization Listening Span task which required them to listen to series of strings of words (rather than series of sentences) and to do a simple categorization task, that is, to tap the table when the name of an animal is presented. This task had the advantage of eliminating the influence of text comprehension ability, and eliminating the cues which made it easier to decide which item could be the last one in the sentence (in Italian, as in many other languages, a typical subject-verb-object sentence is concluded by the object). In addition this task increased the degree of elaboration of some non-target items. All the words must be processed in order to decide whether they are animal names; but the animal names also involve a focusing process which directs the subject's response. Craik and Tulving (1975) found that items with a deeper semantic encoding (based on a semantic judgement) were better recalled if the semantic judgement was affirmative. Therefore, better remembered items might create difficulty in an inhibitory mechanism and increase the number of intrusions. The results showed that poor problem solvers had a lower listening span than good problem solvers, even when the role of sentence comprehension was eliminated. Poor problem solvers had difficulty in remembering the last words contained in the series, reporting less than half of the correct stimuli, and reporting a large number of non-target items.

In a further experimental phase we verified children's short memory ability. Learning disabled children and children with specific mathematical problems can have short-term memory and working memory problems (e.g., Siegel & Linder, 1984; Siegel & Ryan, 1988; Swanson, 1994). Nevertheless, our group of poor problem solvers had high vocabulary skills. Therefore, their verbal abilities and verbal auditory components of the working memory could be as good as those of good problem solvers. We examined our children's memory by using two versions of a word span test. One version was with the classical standard procedure (simple auditory presentation and immediate repetition of the words). The other version was with a dual-task version mirroring the procedure adopted in the Categorization Listening Span: during the presentation of the stimuli, the child had to tap the table when the name of an animal was presented. This task was devoted to rule out the hypothesis that poor problem solvers have difficulty in paying attention to two simultaneous requests.

The results showed that in the word span task poor problem solvers had good memory ability as good problem solvers. In addition the data of the dual span task clarified that the dual request did not impaired the performance of the mathematical disabled children. In a further Experiment we were able to show the direct relationship between the inhibition failure in the working memory tests and the hypothesized inhibition failure during the problem-solving process. In fact, we found that poor problem solvers, required to remember word arithmetic problems, remembered a lower number of relevant information and a higher number of irrelevant information. This result was not due to an inability to discriminate between relevant and irrelevant information, as poor problem solvers when required to underline the relevant information made the task correctly. The fact that poor problem solvers recalled a higher number of irrelevant information also in memory problem contributes to reduce the possibility that the parallel result in the working memory tests was simply due to the substitution of lost target information (final words which were no more recalled) with other information. In fact in the problem memory task children were not required to recall a specified number of informations but they could recall as much as they wanted.

In the follow up phases, one year later, we re-tested the children's working memory ability by similar versions of the listening span tests previously tested. We found that children with severe difficulties in the solution of word problems had a persistence of working memory deficit. They had a lower performance (than control group) in the listening span tests and made significantly more intrusion errors. Moreover, we verified the permanence of the mathematical disability of the poor problem solver group. The children diagnosed as poor problem solver at the beginning of the fourth grade, were still included in the mathematical disability group.

Finally we verified the incidental recall of irrelevant information presented in a working memory test. The children were tested by a listening span test; at the end of this listening span test a recognition test was given. The children were required to mark in the recognition list the names that they thought were presented in the listening span task, indipendently if the names were target items or not. The results of the recognition task clearly indicated that the irrelevant information contained in the listening span test was not completely lost either by the poor or the good problem solvers. Despite the fact that good problem solvers recalled a lower quantity of irrelevant information during the listening span, they had a higher mean number of correct recall than poor problem solver in the recogntion test. We supposed that memory of irrelevant information was equally good in both groups, and that the difference in performance in the working memory test was related to the better ability of good problem solvers to prevent the retrieval of irrelevant information.

Study 1: The Memory Status of Information which must Be Inhibited in Working Memory Tasks

The data obtained in our longitudinal study (Passolunghi et al., 1999) showed that poor problem solvers meet specific difficulties in the working memory tasks requiring a central control and the inhibition of irrelevant information. They also offered suggestions about the nature of the inhibition process. In fact, the inhibition process can be considered as a permanent elimination from memory, or as a change of memory status. The data on the long term recognition task suggested that the long term memory system of good problem solvers maintains irrelevant information as much and even better than the long term memory system of poor problem solvers. A possible interpretation of this result could be that, during the working memory tasks, good problem solvers have still in mind the irrelevant information but they are able to exclude them from the aware retrieval process and then from the elaboration process during problem solving. Another possibility could be that irrelevant information, when processed, is immediately passed to long memory systems and excluded from short term memory systems. However, the result is puzzling because seems to suggest that poor problem sovers are not poorer, but even better, at least at certain memory levels, in excluding irrelevant information from memory.

Further experimental investigation is still necessary in order to clarify the memory status of information which must be inhibited in working memory tasks. This investigation could offer a better insight both on the nature of the inhibition process and on the characteristics of the difficulty found by poor problem solvers in the solution process. Other types of memory tasks, representing a series of different memory statuses, may be proposed and could help to clarify this issue. In a further new experimental phase we verifyed the recall of irrelevant and non-target information, with a specific focus on the implicit memory status. Implicit memory (Schacter, 1987) is referred to the memory permanence of information which is not directly accessed by standard memory tests. In fact, it has been shown that, even when an individual does not explicitly recalls a certain series of information, this information can be still available in memory and affect the performance in other tasks. If applied to the case of problem solving and/or of working memory tasks, an implicit task can help to understand whether information which is not explicitly recalled is still present in an implicit status and can in some way influence the performance. As we had found that poor problem solvers have a higher working memory recall of irrelevant information, but they have a poorer explicit long term memory of irrelevant information, we wanted to the level of the implicit memory condition of irrelevant information in poor problem solvers, presumably influencing their performance in other activities. In this specific study, which was part of the follow up examination of the poor problem solving group tested by Passolunghi et al. (1999) we used, as a measure of implicit memory, a fragment completion test. A fragment completion test requires to find as quickly as possible a word which can complete a series of given letters (e.g., find the word which can complet the fragment "- R - I -," which could be TRAIN, but also other words). In the test, no mention is given to a memory requests and to the fact that already presented information could help in finding a word, but the subject is affected by this fact, often in an unaware way, reflecting the implicit status of information held in memory.

Method

Partecipants

The partecipants were the same fifth-grade children (aged 10 years and 8 months), 12 poor problem solvers and 13 good problem solvers, that we tested in the follow up phases (for the partecipants selection see Passolunghi et al., 1999).

Material and procedure. The categorization listening test span already described derived from De Beni et al. (1998), which used strings of animal and nonanimal nouns. An example of a string was: braccio (arm), squadra (team),

Table 1.

	Poor Problem Solvers		Good Problem Solvers	
Correct answers	11.25	2.45	13.00	1.00
Implicit recall of Animal nouns	2.31	1.11	2.5	1.24
Implicit recall of Nonanimal nouns	.75	.62	.54	.66

Note: Mean numbers (and standard deviations) of items correctly completed in the fragment completion task by the poor and good problem solvers group.

corvo (raven), grano (wheat). The words were auditorily presented, and, when a noun of animal was given, the child had to tap on the table. He/she had to recall only the last names of the presented strings, in this case the word "grano." At the end of the listening span task an unexpected word fragment completion test was given. The children had to complete 14 bisyllabic incomplete words which contained only few letters. The incomplete ("fragmented") words were written one per card and were presented one at a time for a limited quantity of time. Each fragmented word could be completed in many different ways, but never with the target items of the listening span test. However, these incomplete words can activate the recall of the previously presented irrelevant (i.e., nonfinal words) of the listening span test. Half of the incomplete words could activate an animal noun of the listening span test, and the other half could activate a nonanimal noun. For example the fragment word "C _ _ V O" could activate the animal noun "CORVO" (raven), and the fragment "L _ _ T A" could activate the nonanimal noun "LOTTA" (fight). Both CORVO and LOTTA were words included, in a nonfinal position, in the preceding Categorization listening span, with the difference that, in correspondence with the animal noun CORVO, the child had to tap on the table. It must be noticed that the same fragments could be completed using may other words with a similar familiarity value, but not present in the Categorization listening span test. For example the fragments "C_ _VO" could be completed with the words CERVO (deer), COEVO (of the same age), CURVO (curve), etc. and the fragments "L_ _TA" could be completed with the words LISTA (list), LENTA (slow), LIETA (happy), etc.

Results

The results of the Categorization listening span task showed that poor problem solvers had less recall of target nouns and more intrusion errors. Moreover intrusion errors for animal nouns were more frequent in the poor problem group compared to the good problem solver group (see Passolunghi et al., 1999). In this further analysis we will focus only on the fragment completion task data.

The two groups mean performance in the fragment completion task is presented in Table 1. The good problem solvers had a higher mean number of correct answers (e.g., the fragment words that were completed) than poor problem solvers; the difference was significant ($t(23) = 2.37$, $p = .026$). On the contrary there was not significant difference ($p > .49$) between the two groups in the number of implicit recall (e.g., the fragment words completed with a noun already presented in the listening span test). The two groups did not differ either in the implicit recall of animal nouns or nonanimal nouns (see Table 1).

A 2 (groups) × 2 (type of implicit recall: animal vs nonanimal nouns) ANOVA for a mixed design revealed a main effect of type of implicit recall $F(1,23) = 51,43$, $p < .0001$. This effect was due to the fact that the overall implicit recall of animal nouns was higher than that of nonanimal nouns ($t(24) = 7.33$, $p < .0001$).

DISCUSSION

The presence of words already proposed in the Categorization listening span offered a memory measure, which presumably reflected the influence of both implicit and explicit memory traces. The overall pattern of results offer two lateral but important elements. First, good problem solvers were in general better in completing the words, maybe thanks to a better working memory system. Second, the proportion of completed words which were part of the material earlier presented was relatively low, less than one third, suggesting that the representation of those words was very low. Actually, in an unpublished study we have found that, despite the fact that recognition of non-target information of a categorization listening span test can be conspicuous, its free recall tends to be very low. These observations confirm the expectation that the completion of words made by using words presented in the preceding test can be considered, at least to a large extent, a measure of implicit memory (Schacter, 1987).

The consideration of the latter aspect of performance, that is, completions using already presented words, shows a clear effect of the degree of processing (Craik & Tulving, 1975) as the animal nouns included in the Categorization listening span test were used three or more times more often than the nonanimal nouns. The animal nouns had to be identified and stressed by a tapping movement, and this fact influenced the level of activation of the trace.

No difference was found between the groups in the implicit memory measure. This result must be cautiously interpreted as the overall performance of the two groups in the fragment completion task was not identical: a lower ability of poor problem solvers in finding words appropriate for the fragment completion could increase their probability of using already presented words. However, if we consider from another point of view our results, we can see that the proportion of implicit recalls was higher in the poor problem solvers group (a mean of 3.06 implicit recalls out of 11.25 completions) than in the good problem solvers group (a mean of 3.04 implicit recalls out of 13.00 completions). This result suggests that long-intermediate term explicit memory of irrelevant information may be poorer in poor problem solvers, but not long-intermediate term implicit memory. This information, as present in a less aware way, can be identified discriminated in a less easy way and then affect to a greater extent performance in subsequent tasks. For example, during problem solving, a child reads and memorizes the problem. Some part of the information must be stored and immediately processed in a working memory system and the poor problem solver meets difficulty in excluding from consideration the irrelevant information. Another part of information is moved to more permanent memory systems but can be used or can be influential from time to time. A good problem solver can have in general better explicit memory of this information, but s/he is not affected to a greater extent by the implicit influence of it.

Study 2: The Relationship Between Good Memory and Good Problem Solution

Our line of research illustrated in the two preceding paragraphs was devoted to show a relationship between an efficient use of memory and a good problem solving ability. We assumed that, if a child can use well his/her memory systems s/he will be more successful in meeting the memory requests present during problem solving. This hypothesis was confirmed by the fact that poor problem solvers were shown to have a poorer performance both in a series of memory tasks and in the recall of relevant information included in the problems. However, the issues concerning the memory for problems and the relationship between good memory and good solution of a problem were not considered by us until now.

Memory for problems has not been extensively studied. However, the literature showed some evidence that supports the relationship of memory and problem solving. For example Mayer (1982) found that problem recall is largely schematic and when the problem is easily associable with a preexisting schema this facilitates the text problem recall. Furthermore, Hegarty, Mayer, and Monk (1995) found that the successful problem solvers were more likely to remember the situation described in the problems since they used a problem-model strategy oriented toward the development of a mental model of the problem. On the contrary, the unsuccessful problem solvers used a direct-translation strategy for encoding the problems, which lead them to recall the problem verbatim.

Swanson et al. (1993), tested the hypothesis of a relationship between immediate problem recall and problem solving accuracy. Third and fourth-graders were invited to study five, four-sentence problems for 2 minutes. Each problem contained two assignment propositions and one relation, one question, and one extraneous proposition related to the solution. After studying each problem, the children were invited to remember it. Swanson et al. (1993) found modest correlations between immediate memory of the problem and problem solving ability (the only significant correlation of .24 concerned memory for questions), whereas correlations were slightly higher for a parallel delayed memory test. Furthermore, the proportion of extraneous information recalled was high, especially for immediate recall (76%), and positively correlated with the other measures of problem recall. All problem recall measures similarly correlated with working memory and problem solving ability.

These data are against the hypothesis that problem solving ability is related to the ability of keeping irrelevant propositions out of the working memory. However, it is possible that the specific request to study the text of the problem and the large quantity of available time orientated also the children with a high problem solving ability towards studying of the whole text, including irrelevant information. On the contrary, the request of studying the text of a problem is not typically involved during the solution process, where the subject is implicitly orientated towards selecting of the main points. In this case, it is evident that some memory selection is required and useful, therefore, a different capacity of controlling the memory's accessibility to information of different relevance might affect solution ability.

As we already mentioned in the preceding paragraph, in the longitudinal study with fourth-fifth grade poor problem solvers (Passolunghi et al., 1999), we asked the participants to listen to series of problems. We used word arithmetic problems, taken directly from school material. Immediately after the presentation of each problem, the children had to recall the relevant information included in the text problem. Our results showed that poor problem solvers had difficulty in recalling the relevant information included in word arithmetic problems, despite the fact that they were able to individuate the relevant and irrelevant information in the written word problem. However, the poor problem solvers group had a complementary greater recall of irrelevant information.

In a further analysis, which unfortunately could interest only a limited number of poor problem solvers, we investigated more deeply the relationship between memory and problem solution ability. We attempted to verify if there is a tendency to better solve those problems which are better recalled. In order to explore this hypothesis we analysed the think-aloud protocols of a small group of children recalling and solving a series of problems.

Method

Partecipants

Partecipants were 10 fourth-graders (aged 9 years and 6 months), 5 poor problem solvers and 5 good problem solvers. These children, matched for age, behavior, sociocultural level, and verbal IQ, were randomly selected from the larger group of poor and good problem solvers tested in the preceding study.

Material

Twelve arithmetic word problems, taken from standard arithmetic word problems proposed in fourth grade classes. The problems varied in length and in number of arithmetic operations required for the solution. An example of a problem was the following:

> Laura goes with her mother to the supermarket. Laura and her mother buy a cake which costs 12,500 Lira and other groceries which cost 9,800 Lira. How much money does Laura's mother spend for the cake and the groceries? The mother pays with a 50,000 Lira banknote; how much money does she receive as change?

Procedure

The children were individually tested in two separate sessions. In each session they were presented with six of the 12 problems. The experimenter informed the child that s/he had to listen carefully to each problem in order to remember the problem, focusing on the relevant information included in the problem. The instructions included a short example and questions in order to check that the child had understood the task. The problems were read to the child once at the standard rate using a normal intonation (for example, the problem presented above took about 40 sec.). At the end of each problem's presentation the child was invited to recall its relevant information.

We classified the problem recall as "Good Recall" if the child's recalled the main information within a general schema (no penality was given if the child did not refer the exact amount of money, weight or of other numeric information). The problem recall was cassified as "Poor Recall" if the child' recall was vague and distorted, without the main points.

At the end of this memory task, the child was given a booklet with the six problems presented in that session and was invited to solve them. He/She had as much time as he/she liked in order to solve the problems.

Results

The results are presented in Table 2. Results are referred to the overall number of problems which were solved or were not solved by the children of the two groups considered altogether or separately. Table 2 shows that the problems that were better recalled were also better solved. In fact, the correctly solved problems corresponded to the problems more adeguately remembered. On a total of 54 correctly solved problems, the problems correctly remembered are double compared to the problem not correctly recalled (38 vs 16). We observed the opposite trend with the unsolved problems. On a total of 66 unsolved problems, 44 had a poor recall, while only 22 problems had a good recall.

Table 2.

	Solved Problems		Unsolved Problems	
	Good Recall	Poor Recall	Good Recall	Poor Recall
Poor problem solvers	4	2	14	40
Good problem solvers	34	14	8	4
Total	38	16	22	44

Notes: Relationship between problems correctly and uncorrectly solved and good or poor problem recall for the groups of poor and good problem solvers considered separately and all together.

Obviously poor problem solvers solved a lower number of word problems. Actually the five poor problem solvers, taken altogether, solved only six of the 60 problems which were proposed. In addition they had deficient memory of the problems, showing a sufficient recall of the problems only in 18 out of 60 cases. It must be noticed that, the separate analysis of the two groups does not give the possibility of examining the relationship between memory and solution of the problem, as the good problem solvers were particularly successful and the poor problem solvers were particularly weak. However data seem to suggest that the general relationship between memory of the problem and solution of the problem is stronger in the good problem solvers than in the poor problem solvers. When poor problem solvers did not solve the problem, the corresponding problems recall is poor (40 "Poor Recall" vs 14 "Good Recall"), but a good recall did not absolutely guarantee the solution of the problem.

Discussion

Our results supported the hypothesis that problem memory is related to problem solving ability. In agreement with Hegarty et al. (1995) we found that successful problem solvers are more able to recall the main point of a word problem. Our data showed that a good recall of the problem is related to the success in the problem solution. On the contrary an impoverished and deficient memory problem may generate a failure in the solution.

The oral presentation of the text problem, as in the present case, and the request to immediate recall the problem does not allow a child to memorize verbatim the whole text of a problem. The children are forced to do a selection of the information, to create a representation of the problem and to discharge the information not relevant. On some respects, this task involves cognitive components we tested in the preceding studies we have presented here, for example, the ability of developing a schematic representation of the problem, and the working memory efficiency also tested in the working memory tasks that we proposed to the groups of poor and good problem solvers (Passolunghi et al., 1999). In the listening span tasks the children have to select the target (relevant) information and to inhibit the irrelevant information that they had earlier processed. Both in listening span tasks and memory problem task poor problem solvers had poor performance. Their difficulty concerns an aspect involved in working memory: the ability to control and inhibit irrelevant information. This deficit may influence higher cognitive processes as problem solving ability.

CONCLUSIONS AND FURTHER DIRECTIONS

In the present paper we have tried to show that mathematical disabilities, with specific reference to arithmetic word problem solving, may be associated with a series of deficits in cognitive components, included a general working memory deficit. Literature has also shown that mathematical disabled children may be deficient in a specific subtype of working memory linked to arithmetic. The information performance of the children with a mathematical learning disability may be similar to that of normal achievers in a working memory task involving sentence processing, but learning disabled children may present a specific working memory deficit in the processing of numerical information (Siegel & Ryan, 1989). Cognitive impairments of matematical disabled children, not only in a working memory task thay implies a concurrent counting task, but also in counting and in auditory digit span task were found by Hitch and McAuley (1991).

One aim of another recent investigation carried out by the first author of this chapter was to ascertain whether poor problem solvers' memory deficit may be extended to different kinds of working memory tasks (Passolunghi & Siegel, 1999). More specifically the goal was to verify if poor problem solvers' deficit in memory may be generalized to the elaboration of both verbal and numerical information. In addition, we attempted to determine whether in less demanding tasks that imply mainly a passive storage of information, such as short-term memory measures, poor problem solvers may be selectively impaired only in the recall of numerical material, but not in the retention of verbal items. The results showed that poor problem solvers had an impairment in working memory involving both verbal and numerical processing (Passolunghi & Siegel, 1999). It is possible that specific deficits of learning disabled children can be found in the active component, but not in the passive component of working memory (see also Brainerd & Kingma, 1985; Cantor, Engle, & Hamilton, 1991; Swanson, 1994). In the case of our study the poor problem solvers storage component appears not to be influenced when the material involves words (as in the case of word span), however their memory passive components seem generally compromised when the material concerns numerical information (i.e., digit span). The impairment shown by poor problem solvers in the Digit Span Task may reflect a more severe deficit in arithmetic working memory system (see Hitch & McAuley, 1991; Siegel & Ryan, 1989). These findings may be a result of slower access to number representation in long-term memory, which in turn may led to slow counting and lower digit span (see also Geary, 1990, 1993).

So far several studies have investigated the relationship among working memory, reading comprehension and problem solving. The same mechanism of inhibiting irrelevant information was found important both in reading comprehension and problem solving. Converging evidence comes from the study of the role of updating ability in problem solving which seems also partially related to inhibition (Passolunghi & Pazzaglia, 1999). Many researches on reading comprehension in normal adults (Garnham & Oakhill, 1992; Glenberg, Meyer, & Lindem, 1987; Green, McKoon & Ratcliff, 1992; Mckoon & Ratcliff, 1992) demonstrated that readers construct a mental model of the text and update it (Glenberg & Langston, 1992; Morrow, Bower, & Greenspan, 1989; de Vega, 1995). Updating may refer to spatial references, but also to other framework-elements supplied by the text. The updating process imply the change of the representations active in working memory on the basis of the elimination of the information which has become irrelevant and the inclusion of new relevant information.

We can assume that updating process is involved in the problem resolution. Indeed problem solvers have to elicit a mental model of each step of the problem, and progressively to modify it passing to the next step. In the case of problem solving a particular difficulty of this task consists in the updating of the literal content of the problem (i.e., its surface cover story) by creating the conceptual model related to the arithmetical operation required for the solution (Blessing & Ross, 1996).

Palladino, Cornoldi, De Beni, and Pazzaglia (in press) used an updating test, inspired by that of Morris and Jones (1990). During this task the subjects listening several lists, each composed by words. Half of the lists contained animal words and the other objects words. At the end of each list the subjects had to recall the 3 or 5 words denoting the smallest animals (or objects). The request implied an updating of relevant information as an animal that at a certain time could be included between the pool of the smallest ones, after the presentation of another animal smaller in size, should be discarded from the selected pool maintained active in working memory. This task used a semantic criterion for updating the relevant words and it was different by Morris and Jones' task since their criterion was not semantic, but related to items ordinal position.

We administered this new updating task to good and poor problem solvers. Good and poor problem solvers differed in the total number of target words recalled (with a higher number recalled by the good problem solvers) and in the overall number of intrusions (with a higher number of intrusions made by the poor problem solvers). Our results strongly supported the hypothesis that mathematical disabled children have a difficulty in updating the mental model of the problem, and that their difficulty in the updating process is mainly due to inhibitory deficit (Passolunghi & Pazzaglia, 1999).

REFERENCES

Baddeley, A.D. (1986). *Working memory*. Oxford: Clarendon Press.

Baddeley, A.D. (1990). *Human memory: Theory and practice*. Boston: Allyn & Bacon.

Berger, D.E., & Wilde J.M. (1987). A task analysis of algebra word problems. In D.E. Berger, K. Pezdek, & W.P. Banks (Eds.) *Applications of cognitive psychology: Problem solving, education, and computing*. Hillsdale, NJ: Lawrence Erlbaum Associates.

Blessing; S.B., Ross, B.H. (1996). Content effects in problem categorization and problem solving. *Journal of Experimental Psychology: Learning, Memory, and Cognition, 22*(3), 792-810.

Brainerd, C.J., & Kingma, J. (1985). On the independence of short-term memory and working memory in cognitive development. *Cognitive Psychology, 17*, 210-247.

Brown, A.L. (1982). Metacognitive Development and Reading. In R.Y. Spiro, B.C. Bruce, & W.F. Brewer (Eds.), *Theoretical uses in reading comprehension*. Mahwah, NJ: Erlbaum.

Brown, A.L., (1978). Knowing where, and how to remember: A problem of Metacognition. In R. Glaser (Ed.), *Advances in instructional psychology* (Vol. 1). Mahwah, NJ: Erlbaum.

Cantor, J. Engle, R.W., & Hamilton, G. (1991). Short term memory, working memory and verbal abilities: How do they relate? *Intelligence, 15*, 229-246.

Chi, M.T.H., Feltovich, P.J., & Glaser, R. (1981). Categorization and representation of physics problems by experts and novices. *Cognitive Science, 5*, 121-152.

Cornoldi, C. (1987). Origins of intentional strategic memory in the child. In B. Inhelder, D. De Caprona, & A. Cornu-Wells (Eds.), *Piaget today* (pp. 183-201). Hillsdale, NJ: Erlbaum.

Cornoldi, C. (1995). *Metacognizione e apprendimento*. Bologna: Il Mulino.

Cornoldi, C., & Colpo, G. (1981). *La verifica dell'apprendimento della lettura*. Firenze: Organizzazioni speciali.

Cornoldi, C., De Beni, R., & Pazzaglia, F. (1996). Profiles of reading comprehension difficulties: An analysis of single cases. In C. Cornoldi & J. Oakhill (Eds.), *Reading Comprehension Difficulties. Processes and Intervention* (pp. 113-136). Mahwah, NJ: Erlbaum.

Craik, F.I.M., & Tulving, E. (1975). Depth of processing and the retention of words in episodic memory. *Journal of Experimental Psychology: General, 14*, 268-294.

Daneman, M., & Carpenter P.A. (1980). Individual differences in working memory and reading. *Journal of verbal Learning and Verbal Behaviour, 19*, 450-466.

Daneman, M., & Carpenter P.A. (1983). Individual differences in integrating information between and within sentences. *Journal of Experimental Psychology: Learning, Memory and Cognition, 9*, 561-583.

Daneman, M., & Tardif, T. (1987). Working memory and reading skill re-examined. In M. Coltheart (Ed.), *Attention and performance, XII: The Psychology of reading*. Hillsdale, NJ: Erlbaum.

De Beni, R., Palladino, P., Pazzaglia, F., & Cornoldi, C. (1998). Increases in intrusion errors and working memory deficit of poor comprehenders. *The Quarterly Journal of Experimental Psychology, 51A*, 305-320.

de Vega, M. (1995). Backward updating of mental models during continous reading of narratives. *Journal of Experimental Psychology: Learning, Memory & Cognition, 21*, 373-385.

Garnham, A., & Oakhill, J.V. (1992). Discourse representation and text processing from a "mental models" perspective. *Language & Cognitive Processes, 7*, 193-204.

Geary, D.C. (1990). A componential analysis of an early learning deficit in mathematics. *Journal of Experimental Child Psychology, 49*, 363-383.

Geary, D.C. (1993). Mathematical disabilities: Cognitive, neuropsychological, and genetic components. *Psychological Bulletin, 114*, 345-362.

Glenberg, A.M., Meyer, M., & Lindem, K. (1987). Mental models contribute to foregrounding during text comprehension. *Journal of Memory & Language, 26*, 69-83.

Green, S.B., McKoon, G., & Ratcliff R. (1992). Pronoun resolution and discourse model. *Journal of Experimental Psychology: Learning, Memory & Cognition, 18*, 266-283.

Hegarty, M., Mayer, R.E., & Monk, C.A.(1995). Comprehension of arithmetic word problems: A comparison of successful and unsuccessful Problem solvers. *Journal of Educational Psychology, 87*(1), 18-32.

Hinsley, D., Hayes, J.R., & Simon, H. (1977). From words to equations: meaning and representation in algebra word problems. In P.A. Carpenter & M.A. Just (Eds.), *Cognitive processes in comprehension*. Hillsdale, NJ: Lawrence Erlbaum Associates.

Hitch, G.J., & McAuley, E. (1991). Working memory in children with specific arithmetical learning difficulties. *British Journal of Psychology, 82*, 375-386.

Kreutzer, M.A., Leonard, C., & Flavell, J.H. (1975). An interview study of children's knowledge about memory. *Monographs of the Society for Research in Child Development, 40*, 1, Series No. 159.

Larkin, J., Mc Dermott, J., Simon, D.P., & Simon H.A. (1980). Expert and novice peformance in solving physic problems. *Science, 208*, 1335-1342.

Leather, C.V., & Henry, L.A. (1994). Working memory span and phonological awareness tasks as predictors of early reading ability. *Journal of Experimental Child Psychology, 58*(1), 88-111.

Logie, R.H., Gilhooly, K.J., & Wynn, V. (1994). Counting on working memory in arithmetic problem solving. *Memory and Cognition, 22*(4), 395-410.

Low, R., Over, R. Doolan, L. & Mitchell, S. (1994). Solution of algebraic word problems following training in identifying necessary and sufficient information within problems. *American Journal of Psychology, 107*(3), 423-439.

Lucangeli, D., & Cornoldi, C. (1997). Mathematics and metacognition:What is the nature of the relationship? *Mathematical Cognition, 2*, 121-139.

Lucangeli, D., Cornoldi, C. & Tellarini, M. (1998). Metacognition and learning disabilities in mathematics. In T. Scruggs & M. Mastropieri (Eds.), *Advances in learning and behavioral disabilities* (Vol. 12, pp. 219-244). Greenwich, CT: JAI Press.

Lucangeli, D., & Passolunghi, M.C. (1995). *Psicologia dell' apprendimento matematico (Pychology of learning mathematics)*. Torino: Utet.

Mayer, R.E. (1982). Memory for algebra story problems. *Journal of Educational Psychology, 74*, 199-216.

Mayer, R.E. (1983).*Thinking, problem solving, cognition.* New York: V.H. Freeman and Company.

Mayer, R.E. (1987). Learnable aspects of problem solving: Some examples. In D.E. Berger, K. Pezdek, & W.P. Banks (Eds.), *Applications of cognitive psychology: Problem solving, education and computing*. Hillsdale, NJ: Lawrence Erlbaum Associates.

Mayer, R.E. (1998). Cognitive, metacognitive, and motivational aspects of problem solving. *Instructional Science, 26*, 49-63.

Mayer, R.E., Larkin, J.H., & Kadane, J. (1984). A cognitive analysis of mathematical problem solving ability. In R. Sternberg (Ed.), *Advances in the psychology of human intelligence*. Hillsdale, NJ: Lawrence Erlbaum Associates.

McKoon, G., & Ratcliff, R. (1992). Inferences during reading. *Psychological Review, 99*, 440-466.

Morris, N., & Jones, D.M. (1990). Memory updating in working memory: The role of central executive. *British Journal of Psychology, 81*, 111-121.

Morrow, D.G., Bower, G.H., & Greenspan, S.L. (1989). Updating situation models during comprehension. *Journal of Memory & Language, 28*, 292-312.

Nathan, M.J., Kintsch, W., & Young, E. (1992). A theory of algebra word problem comprehension and its implications for the design of learning environments. *Cognition and Instructions, 4*, 329-390.

Oakhill, K., & Yuill, N. (1996). Higher order factors in comprehension disability: Processes and remediation. In C. Cornoldi & J. Oakhill (Eds.), *Reading comprehension difficulties. Processes and intervention* (pp. 69-92). Mahwah, NJ: Erlbaum.

Palladino, P., Cornoldi, C., De Beni, R., & Pazzaglia F. (in press). Working memory and updating processes in reading comprehension. *Memory & Cognition.*

Passolunghi, M.C. (1999). Influenza dell'abilità di pianificazione nella risoluzione dei problemi. *Età Evolutiva, 62,* 81-87.

Passolunghi, M.C., & Pazzaglia, F. (1999). *Differences between good and poor problem solvers in working memory and updating processes.* Trieste: University of Trieste, Department of General Psychology.

Passolunghi, M.C., Cornoldi, C., & De Liberto, S. (1999). Working memory and inhibition of irrelevant information in poor problem solvers. *Memory and Cognition,* 779-790.

Passolunghi, M.C., Lonciari, I., & Cornoldi, C. (1995). *The effects of metacognition categorization and planning ability on learning problem solving.* Presented at the 6th EARLI Conference, Nijmegen, The Netherlands.

Passolunghi, M.C., Lonciari, I., & Cornoldi, C. (1996). Abilità di pianificazione, comprensione, metacognizione e risoluzione di problemi aritmetici i tipo verbale. *Età Evolutiva,* 36-48.

Passolunghi, M.C., & Siegel, L. (1999). *Short term memory, working memory, and inhibitory control in children with specific arithmetic learning disabilities.* Trieste: University of Trieste, Department of General Psychology.

Piaget, J., & Inhelder, B. (1958). *The growth of logical thinking from childhood to adolescente.* New York: Basic Books.

Porteus, S.D. (1950). *The porteus maze test and intelligence.* Palo Alto, CA: Pacific Books. (trad. it. *Il test dei labirinti,* Organizzazioni speciali, Firenze, 1955.)

Pressley, M. (1990). *Cognitive strategy instruction that really improves children's academic performance.* Cambridge, MA: Brookline Books.

Schacter, D.L. (1987). Implicit memory: History and current status. *Journal of Experimental Psychology: Learning, Memory and Cognition, 13,* 501-518.

Schoenfeld, A.H.(1982). Some thoughts on problem solving research and mathematics education. In F.K. Lester & J. Garofalo (Eds.), *Mathematical problem solving: Issues in research.* Philadelphia: The Franklin Institute Press.

Schoenfeld, A.H., & Herrmann, D.J. (1982). Problem perception and knowledge structure in expert and novice mathematical problem solvers. *Journal of Experimental Psychology: Learning, Memory, and Cognition, 8*(5), 484-494.

Shallice, T. (1982). Specific impairments of planning. In D.E. Broadbent & L. Weiskrantz (Eds.), *The neuropsychology of cognitive function.* London: The Royal Society.

Siegel, L.S., & Linder, B.A. (1984). Short-term memory processes in children with reading and arithmetic learning disabilities. *Developmental Psycology, 20*(2), 200-207.

Siegel, L.S., & Ryan, E.B. (1988). Development of grammatical-sensitivity, phonological, and short-term memory skills in normally achieving and learning disabled children. *Developmental Psycology, 24*(1), 28-37.

Siegel, L.S., & Ryan, E. B. (1989). The development of working memory in normally achieving and subtypes of learning disabled children. *Child Development, 60,* 973-980.

Silver, E.A. (1979). Student perceptions of relatedness among mathematicl verbal problems. *Journal for Research in Mathematical Education, 12,* 54-64.

Swanson, H.L. (1994). Short-term memory and working memory: Do both contribute to our understanding of academic achievement in children and adults with learning disabilities? *Journal of Learning disabilities, 27*(1), 34-50.

Swanson, H.L. (1993). An information processing analysis of learning disabled children's problem solving. *American Educational Research Journal, 30,* 861-893.

Swanson, H.L. (1990). Influence of metacognitive knowledge and aptitude on problem solving. *Journal of Educational Psychology, 82,* 306-314.

Swanson, H.L., Cooney, J.B., & Brock, S. (1993). The influence of working memory and classification ability on children's word problem solution. *Journal of Experimental Child Psychology, 55,* 374-395.

Turner, M.L., & Engle, R.W. (1989). Is working memory capacity task dependent? *Journal of Memory and Language, 28,* 127-154.

Yuill, N., Oakhill, J., & Parkin, A. (1989). Working memory, comprehension ability and the resolution of text anomaly. *British Journal of Psychology, 80,* 351-361.

THE GREAT DIVIDE IN SPECIAL EDUCATION:
INCLUSION, IDEOLOGY, AND RESEARCH

Kenneth A. Kavale and
Steven R. Forness

ABSTRACT

Issues surrounding the integration of students with disabilities into general education are explored. The history is examined first by tracing the movement from mainstreaming and the least restrictive environment in 1975, to the call for a more integrated system during the 1980s in the Regular Education Initiative, and, finally, full inclusion with its call for all students to be completely integrated into age-appropriate general education with no separate special education. Next, the research investigating perceptions and attitudes about inclusion, the tenor of the general education classroom, and the preparation and ability of general education teachers to deal effectively with special education students is summarized. Finally, the dissonance between rhetoric and reality is explored. The inclusion debate, by ignoring research evidence, has elevated discussion to the ideological level where competing

Advances in Learning and Behavioral Disabilities, Volume 14, pages 179-215.
Copyright © 2000 by JAI Press Inc.
All rights of reproduction in any form reserved.
ISBN: 0-7623-0561-4

conflicts of vision are more difficult to resolve. It is concluded that a rational solution requires the consideration of all forms of evidence if the best possible education
for all students with disabilities is to be achieved.

INTRODUCTION

In the realm of special education, the word "inclusion" is likely to engender fer-
vent debate. Inclusion represents a movement seeking to create schools that meet
the needs of all students by establishing learning communities for students with
and without disabilities educated together in age-appropriate, general education
classrooms in neighborhood schools (Ferguson, 1996). Although questions about
the integration of students with disabilities should no longer be controversial, passionate discussion about inclusion continues to escalate because its philosophy
focuses not solely on students with disabilities of any type and severity level but
seeks to alter the education of *all* students and hence general education. For some
25 years, integration has been the norm as indicated by the U.S. Department of
Education (1997) reporting that about 95% of students with disabilities are served
in general education settings and about 75% of those students are provided
instruction in either general education classrooms or resource room settings. The
movement toward greater integration has thus resulted in a significant change in
the structure of special education, but questions remain about the success of special education. Empirical evidence about the efficacy of special education continues to be equivocal which has resulted in discussion being increasingly fueled by
political and ideological concerns. These differences have resulted in often contentious discussion about how and for whom the inclusion of students with disabilities should be accomplished (see O'Neil, 1994-1995).

Ideology and the Conflict of Visions

Inclusion appears to have created an ideological divide in special education. In
analyzing social policy, Sowell (1995) discussed such a divide as a conflict of
visions by reference to the "vision of the anointed" versus the "vision of the
benighted." The vision of the anointed involves the perceptions, beliefs, and
assumptions of an elite intelligentsia whose revelations prevail over others in
determining policy. On the other side, there is the vision of the beinghted whose
perceptions, beliefs, and assumptions "are depicted as being at best 'perceptions,'
more often 'stereotypes,' and more bluntly 'false consciousness'" (p. 187). In special education, those who advocate most forcefully for full inclusion appear to
hold the vision of the anointed. Such a vision, however, possesses a fundamental
difficulty: "Empirical evidence is neither sought beforehand nor consulted after a
policy has been instituted.... Momentous questions are dealt with essentially as
conflicts of vision" (p. 2). Consequently, the anointed do not require clear defini-

tions, logical arguments, or empirical verifications because their vision substitutes for all these things. Consequently, calls for more research to resolve fundamental problems are viewed solely as part of the vision of the benighted. Research evidence does not appear to be a major factor in the vision of the anointed.

What does appear to be a major factor in the vision of the anointed are assumptions about compassion and caring. Although these elements are seen as the special province of those with an anointed vision, in reality, compassion and caring are also integral to the vision of the benighted. The reason for the emphasis on compassion and caring among the anointed is based on the assumption that their vision possesses:

> a special state of grace for those who believe it. Those who accept this vision are deemed to be not merely factually correct but morally on a higher plane. Put differently, those who disagree with the prevailing vision are seen as being not merely in error, but in sin. For those who have this vision of the world, the anointed and the benighted do not argue on the same moral plane or play by the same cold rules of logic and evidence. The benighted are to be made "aware," to have their "consciousness raised," and the wistful hope is held out that they will "grow." Should the benighted prove recalcitrant, however, then their "mean-spiritedness" must be fought and the "real reasons" behind their arguments and actions exposed. (Sowell, 1995, pp. 2-3)

For the anointed, not only is a higher moral plane involved, but also significant ego involvement that preserves and insulates their vision. As Sowell (1995) suggested:

> Despite Hamlet's warning against self-flattery, the vision of the anointed is not simply a vision of the world and its functioning in a causal sense, but is also a vision of themselves and of their moral role in the world. *It is a vision of differential rectitude.* It is not a vision of the tragedy of the human condition: Problems exist because others are not as wise or as virtuous as the anointed. (p. 5, italics in original)

When applied to the case of inclusion, special education possesses problems, not as a result of limits on knowledge or resources but because others lack the wisdom and virtue of the "anointed." Additionally, the anointed believe that special education is primarily a social construction and not a reflection of an underlying reality. Consequently, problems can be solved only by applying the articulated visions of the anointed. Any opposition to their vision is the result of an intellectual or moral bankruptcy (or both) and not to a different reading of complex and often inconclusive research evidence. Because the vision of the anointed is independent of empirical evidence, Sowell (1995) suggested that:

> [This] is what makes it dangerous, not because a particular set of policies may be flawed or counterproductive, but because insulation from evidence virtually guarantees a never-ending supply of policies and practices fatally independent of reality. This self-contained and self-justifying vision has become a badge of honor and a proclamation of identity: To affirm it is to be one of *us* and to oppose it is to be one of *them.* (p. 241)

Special education appears to have drawn such a line between "us" and "them" over the question of inclusion. As Shanker (1994) pointed out, "Some full inclusionists talk as though they are in a battle pitting the forces of morality against the forces of immorality" (p. 7). In a later analysis, Sowell (1999) discussed the requirement to truly grasp basic ideas and concepts. Sowell, in analyzing issues of justice, argued about real need to untangle the confusions surrounding many problems by returning to square one. It is the purpose of this paper to return to square one by analyzing the inclusion issue and to demonstrate that the truth is far simpler than the many elaborate attempts to evade the truth.

HISTORICAL PERSPECTIVES: SPECIAL EDUCATION

Mainstreaming

Historically, special education developed as a specialized program within the public school system separate from general education that was embodied in the categorical special class (e.g., MacMillan & Hendrick, 1993; Safford & Safford, 1998). The special class was seen as the best means for avoiding conflicts in meeting provisions for universal education (Gerber, 1996). The special class was viewed as possessing the following advantages: (a) low teacher-pupil ratios, (b) specially trained teacher, (c) greater individualization of instruction in a homogeneous classroom, (d) an increased curricular emphasis on social and vocational goals, and (e) greater expenditure per pupil (Johnson, 1962). Although some discussion about alternative placement could be found prior to the 1960s (e.g., Shattuck, 1946), it was Dunn's (1968) famous article questioning whether separate special classes were justifiable that brought the legitimacy of special class placement to the fore.

In analyzing the Dunn (1968) article, however, MacMillan (1971) noted that it lacked scholarly rigor. Dunn argued in favor of a position (i.e., less restrictive placement) based on the lack of support for the efficacy of a contrasting condition (i.e., separate special class). Nevertheless, the Dunn article was the impetus for a number of pieces calling for the abandonment of the special class (e.g., Christopolos & Renz, 1969; Deno, 1970; Lilly, 1970), even though summaries of empirical evidence offered no unequivocal conclusion about its efficacy (Goldstein, 1967; Guskin & Spicker, 1968; Kirk, 1964).

Within the social context of the time, the Dunn article initiated an attitude in special education that eschewed empirical evidence in favor of ideology to produce change (MacMillan, Semmell, & Gerber, 1994). This attitude was manifested in a shift in focus from evaluating "best practice" to an emphasis on students in special education gaining access to general education. Advocacy thus shifted from the "child" to the "program," but left unanswered were questions about what "works" in optimally serving students with disabilities in any setting (MacMillan & Semmel, 1977). The Dunn article must also be placed in the context of strong antisegregation sentiments of the 1960s. The segregated (i.e., separate) nature of special education was targeted for change rather than the particular practices used to teach students with disabilities (Semmel, Gerber, & MacMillan, 1994).

The culmination of the debate about integration was the passage of the Education for All Handicapped Children Act (1975) (now Individuals with Disabilities Education Act [IDEA], 1990, 1992, 1997) that mandated students with disabilities be provided an appropriate education designed to meet their unique needs in the least restrictive environment (LRE) (Heller, Holtzman, & Messick, 1982; Weintraub, Abeson, Ballard, & LaVor, 1976; Zettel & Ballard, 1986). The LRE required that students with disabilities be educated to the maximum extent appropriate with peers without disabilities (i.e., mainstreamed). Mainstreaming, however, was difficult to define operationally (Kaufman, Agard, & Semmel, 1986). The legal definition focused more on what mainstreaming was not by stipulating that students can only be removed and placed in separate classes or schools when the nature or severity of their disability was such that they could not receive an appropriate education in a general education classroom with supplementary aids and services (Bateman & Chard, 1995; Osborne & DiMattia, 1994). To ensure the presence of an LRE, school districts were required to make a complete continuum of alternative placement options available as described by Reynolds (1962) and exemplified in Deno's (1970) "Cascade model." The continuum meant that the LRE was not a particular setting (i.e., general education classroom) and, although the LRE for some students with disabilities may be the general education classroom, it was neither required nor desirable in all cases (Abeson, Burgdorf, Casey, Kunz, & McNeil, 1975). This conclusion has been endorsed in a number of court cases that have also clarified the LRE concept by developing tests for determining how compliance might be achieved (Thomas & Rapport, 1998; Yell, 1995). In no instance do the tests imply that the general education classroom was anything more than an option in an LRE framework (Zirkel, 1996).

Regular Education Initiative

The LRE mandate brought structural change to special education by making the resource model the primary placement option. This option was defined by the resource room and special education teacher who provided academic instruction for specified time periods to a special education student whose primary placement was the general education classroom (Hammill & Wiederholt, 1972). By spending at least half the school day in the general education setting, the student was considered to be in the "mainstream." Nevertheless, answers to questions about the efficacy of special education remained equivocal (Madden & Slavin, 1983; Wang & Baker, 1985-86; Wiederholt & Chamberlain, 1989).

Mainstreaming was primarily concerned with access, but questions about how students should be best taught still remained unanswered (Gottlieb, 1981; Kauffman, 1995). With increased calls for school reform during the 1980s, the needs of special education were often not considered--especially how advocating for higher standards and enhanced excellence might impact students with high-incidence disabilities (Pugach & Sapon-Shevin, 1987; Shepard, 1987; Yell, 1992). In an effort to contribute to school reform, special education attempted to introduce more powerful instructional methodologies and professional practice (Biklen, 1985; Lipsky & Gartner, 1989; Wang, Reynolds, & Walberg, 1986). Along with a continued call for more inclusive instructional placements, these efforts were termed the Regular Education Initiative (REI) (Reynolds, Wang, & Walberg, 1987). Essentially, the goal was to essentially merge general and special education to create a more unified system of education (Gartner & Lipsky, 1987; Will, 1986). The REI was based on the following assumptions: (a) students were more alike than different, so truly special instruction was not required, (b) good teachers can teach all students, (c) all students can be provided with a quality education without being classified according to traditional special education categories, (d) general education classrooms can manage all students without any segregation, and (e) physically separate education was inherently discriminatory and inequitable.

The REI did not receive uniformly positive responses (Davis, 1989; Heller & Schilit, 1987; Lieberman, 1985). For example, Kauffman, Gerber, and Semmel (1988) argued against the REI by indicating that: (a) students were not overidentified for special education; (b) student failure should not be attributed solely to perceived shortcomings of teachers; (c) more competent teachers did not necessarily possess more positive attitudes toward students with disabilities; (d) variability in student performance will increase rather than decrease, when effective instruction was provided to all students; and (e) teachers will be faced with the dilemma of maximizing mean performance versus minimizing group variance. Reynolds (1988) countered with the suggestion that perceived problems resulted primarily from traditional special education: "Present practices have themselves become problematic--causing disjointedness, proceduralism, and inefficiencies in school operations" (p. 355). The rhetoric continued and can be summarized in the question posed by Jenkins, Pious, and Jewell (1990): "How ready for the REI is this country's educational system?" (p. 489).

Integration Policy: Research and Evidence

In marshaling empirical evidence for the REI, supporters used the earlier "efficacy studies," the body of research that compared students with disabilities in special class versus general education placements. Dunn (1968) used this same research evidence, but the validity of the findings have long been open to serious question. For example, most efficacy studies did not use random selection and assignment of students and thus failed to meet standards associated with true experimental designs. In fact, the few studies that did use randomization provided some support for the efficacy of the special class (Goldstein, Moss, & Jordan, 1965). Thus, it was imprudent to cite the efficacy studies as having provided evidence that special classes were not effective (Gartner & Lipsky, 1989; Lilly, 1988; Wang & Walberg, 1988).

Carlberg and Kavale (1980) conducted a meta-analysis that synthesized the findings from 50 of the best efficacy studies. The mean effect size was −.12, which indicated that the relative standing of the average special class student was reduced by about 5 percentile ranks after an average two-year stay in a special class. Thus, a small negative effect was associated with special class placement. Larger effect sizes, however, were found for student classification. For students with mild mental retardation (MMR), a mean effect size of −.14 was found, but an effect size of +.29 for students with learning (LD) or emotional and behavioral (E/BD) disabilities. Special class placement was thus disadvantageous for students with below average IQ who lost 7 percentile ranks, but advantageous for students with learning or behavior problems who improved by an average 11 percentile ranks and were better off than 61% of their counterparts placed in a general education classroom. These findings raise questions about whether *all* students with disabilities benefitted from integration. Given the magnitude of associated effects, it was evident that placement per se had only a modest influence on outcomes. The place where students with disabilities resided was not a critical factor suggesting that an examination of what goes on, instructionally and socially, in those placements should be evaluated (Leinhardt & Pallay, 1982).

Empirical evaluations of models for educating students with disabilities in a general education setting have also been used to support the REI. A prime example is the Adaptive Learning Environments Model (ALEM) that was designed to deliver effective instruction to students with disabilities without removing them from the general education classroom (Wang, Gennari, & Waxman, 1985). Evaluations of the ALEM model (Wang & Birch, 1984a,b; Wang, Peverly, & Randolph, 1984; Wang & Walberg, 1983) have been analyzed critically and found deficient and inconsistent with respect to design, analysis, and interpretation (Bryan & Bryan, 1988; Fuchs & Fuchs, 1988; Hallahan, Keller, McKinney, Lloyd, & Bryan, 1988). The equivocal research evidence suggested that the ALEM model cannot be endorsed as a prototypical model for integrating general and special education.

Given its limited empirical support, the REI was buttressed primarily with ideological arguments. Rhetoric cast opponents of the REI as segregationists (Wang & Walberg, 1988), and the current system of special education as slavery (Stainback & Stainback, 1987) and apartheid (Lipsky & Gartner, 1987). Conversely, proponents of the REI were viewed as naive liberals (Kauffman, 1989). The essential issue was framed as a debate about the future of special education between "abolitionists and conservationists" (Fuchs & Fuchs, 1991). The REI proponents appeared divided over the question of who should be integrated, however. On one side, some REI proponents suggested that the REI was aimed primarily at students with high-incidence disabilities like MMR, LD, and E/BD, with the option of separate settings remaining appropriate for students with severe and profound disabilities (Pugach & Lilly, 1984; Reynolds & Wang, 1983). For these students, there should be more progressive inclusion that was "describable in terms of a gradual shift, within a cascade model, from distal to proximal administrative arrangements and from segregated to integrated arrangements" (Reynolds, 1991, p. 14). On the other side, there was the suggestion that *all* students with disabilities be integrated regardless of disability type or severity level (Gartner & Lipsky, 1987; Stainback & Stainback, 1984b). If all students were not integrated, then two separate systems of education were maintained that represented merely "blending of the margins" (Gartner & Lipsky, 1989, p. 271) and "does not address the need to include in regular classrooms and regular education those students labeled severely and profoundly handicapped" (Stainback & Stainback, 1989, p. 43).

Inclusion

Special education was thus experiencing great tensions (Meredith & Underwood, 1995). Some called for radical change that would alter the fundamental nature of special education, while others called for a more cautious approach to change based on empirical analyses and historical considerations (Dorn, Fuchs, & Fuchs, 1996). Kauffman (1993) suggested that change in special education should be predicated on three assumptions. First, the necessity of keeping *place* in perspective, because setting per se has limited impact on outcomes for students with disabilities. Second, choosing ideas over image. For example, equating special education with segregation and apartheid were gross oversimplifications that distorted debate because image may become the measure of truth. Third, avoiding fanaticism, a passion that has become dangerous because it often leads to moral certainty with predetermined answers. Finally, Kauffman called for the strengthening of special education's empirical base through experimentation with new programs, strategies, and policies.

Fuchs and Fuchs (1994) traced the origins of the inclusive schools movement and contrasted it with the REI. A major distinction between movements was focused on the distinction between "high versus low" incidence special education populations. Many advocates for the low-incidence group (i.e., severe intellectual deficits) continued to view the REI as policy directed primarily at students with high-incidence disabilities (i.e., MMR, LD, E/BD), but nonetheless retained the goal of moving all students into the mainstream. Consequently, the strategies used by special education were not successful in convincing general education about the merits of the REI (Pugach & Sapon-Shevin, 1987). In reality, the REI was primarily a special education initiative for high-incidence disabilities that had modest success in changing special, but not general, education.

The inclusive schools movement, however, possessed the larger goal of reducing special education, as defined in the continuum of placements (Gartner & Lipsky, 1989). Later, Lipsky and Gartner (1991) suggested that, "The concept of Least Restrictive Environment--a continuum of placements, and a cascade of services--were progressive when developed but do not today promote the *full* inclusion of *all* persons with disabilities in *all* aspects of societal life" (p. 52, italics in original). The "inclusive school" was thus viewed as a setting essentially devoid of special education because the emphasis was on *all* students being included in age-appropriate general education: "No students, including those with disabilities, are relegated to the fringes of the school by placement in segregated wings, trailers, or special classes" (Stainback & Stainback, 1992, p. 34). Although it was possible to identify different models for inclusion, they all aimed at providing a restructured and unified system of special and general education (Skrtic, 1991). In the course of advocacy for inclusion, many proponents of the REI became disillusioned because of their limited influence on general education. But soon, a group associated with The Association of Persons with Severe Handicaps (TASH), "took the field by storm; they rushed into a vacuum created by others' inaction, no doubt intimidating by their vigor alone many who disagreed with their radical message" (Fuchs & Fuchs, 1994, p. 299). TASH had a significant effect on policy because of the rhetoric calling for the elimination of special education in the form of a continuum of placements (Stainback & Stainback, 1991) and a curricular focus emphasizing socialization in order to foster social competence over academic achievement (Snell, 1991).

The proponents of full inclusion predicated their position on the assumption that special education was the basic cause of many of the problems experienced by general education (Skrtic, Sailor, & Gee, 1996). Consequently, there was no need for an LRE defined by a continuum of placements because the LRE was, in fact, the general education classroom (Lipsky & Gartner, 1997; Taylor, 1988). This view of the LRE as solely a single place ignored important interactions between student needs and instructional processes (Korinek, McLaughlin, & Walther-Thomas, 1995; Morsink & Lenk, 1992). With all students in the same classroom (and no special education), TASH hoped that general education would be forced to deal with students previously avoided and thus transform itself into a more responsive and resourceful system. The essence of the message offered by TASH thus differed markedly from other advocacy and professional groups in special education (see Kauffman & Hallahan, 1995, pp. 307-348). For example, how could TASH speak for *all* students when supporting a diminished academic emphasis that represented the primary educational focus for almost all students with high-incidence disabilities. Although rejecting alternative views because of the perception that theirs was the only pure and honorable position, the TASH full inclusion position really reflected "an exclusionary, not inclusionary, mindset" that radicalized reform in special education (Fuchs & Fuchs, 1994, p. 304). For example, in contrasting the REI and full inclusion, Fuchs and Fuchs suggested that, "Full inclusionists' romanticism, insularity, and a willingness to speak for all is markedly different from REI supporters' pragmatism, big-tent philosophy and reluctance to speak for all" (p. 304). The radical proposal offered by full inclusion proponents was questioned by REI supporters who focused their attention on repairing the "disjointedness" experienced by students and programs of the "second system" at the "school margins" (Reynolds, 1989, 1992; Wang, Reynolds, & Walberg, 1988). Additionally, special education renewed interest in demonstrating its real benefits (Fuchs & Fuchs, 1995a, 1995b; Kavale & Forness, 1999; Wang, Rubenstein, & Reynolds, 1985). Special education appeared, however, to reach a status quo. Although general agreement about the possibilities of inclusive environments for students with disabilities could be found (Putnam, Spiegel, & Bruininks, 1995), special education was marked by many different approaches to inclusion that differed markedly from setting to setting. Martin (1995) suggested that "as a matter of public policy, a federal or state government, even a local school system, cannot responsibly adopt 'inclusion' without defining its proposed program" (p. 193).

PRACTICAL PERSPECTIVES:
SPECIAL EDUCATION

The emphasis on special education as a place (i.e., a setting where students with disabilities are educated) deflected attention away from the fact that special education was a more comprehensive process whose actual dynamics were major contributors to its success or failure (Kavale & Glass, 1984). A significant part of the special education process was represented in the beliefs and actions of general education. An integrated system means that special education cannot act independently as a separate system, but must formulate policy in response to the attitudes, perceptions, and behaviors of general education (Gallagher, 1994).

Attitudes

It has long been recognized (Sarason, 1982) that a major factor in the success or failure of a major policy like mainstreaming were the attitudes of the general education teacher (Hannah & Pliner, 1983; Horne, 1985; Linton & Juul, 1980). Early on, general education teachers expressed some negative attitudes, especially feelings of inadequacy in dealing with students with disabilities, although remaining generally positive about the concept of integration (Harasymiw & Horne, 1976; Ringlaben & Price, 1981; Stephens & Braun, 1980). Nevertheless, positive attitudes about students with disabilities could also be identified among teachers (Alexander & Strain, 1978; Nader, 1984; Yuker, 1988) but these positive attitudes were often accompanied by concern about the integration of students with severe disabilities, particularly those with significant intellectual deficits (Diebold & Von Eschenbach, 1991; Hirshoren & Burton, 1979; Shotel, Iano, & McGettigan, 1972). Teachers were also found to be more willing to integrate students whose disabilities did not require additional responsibilities on their part (Center & Ward, 1987; Gans, 1987; Houck & Rogers, 1994). Otherwise, they revealed a resistance to greater integration (Margolis & McGettigan, 1988). Although attempts to foster more positive attitudes about integration have been attempted (Naor & Milgram, 1980), any positive attitudinal changes achieved were found to be short-lived (Donaldson, 1980; Stainback, Stainback, Strathe, & Dedrick, 1983).

The attitudes of peers toward students with disabilities have also been investigated. Although not uniformly positive, findings generally revealed a tendency toward more tolerance with increased contact (Esposito & Reed, 1986; Towfighy-Hooshyar & Zingle, 1984; Voeltz, 1980). Generally, though, general education peers paid no particular attention to students with disabilities (Lovitt, Plavins, & Cushing, 1999). Any positive reactions to inclusion among students without disabilities (Hendrickson, Shokoohi-Yekta, Hamre-Nietupski, & Gable, 1996) also tended to be accompanied by feelings of discomfort, especially about students with moderate and severe disabilities who may possess significant communication difficulties and often lack positive social skills (Helmstetter, Peck, & Giangreco, 1994; Peck, Donaldson, & Pezzoli, 1990). Although there has been the suggestion that students with severe disabilities were in fact accepted by non-disabled peers (Evans, Salisbury, Palombaro, Berryman, & Hollowood, 1992; Hall, 1994; Janney, Snell, Beers, & Raynes, 1995), Cook and Semmel (1999) found this not to be the case particularly when atypical behavior occurs. In the case of students with mild disabilities, Cook and Semmel also found that they "do not typically appear to engender peer acceptance" (p. 57).

For parents, generally positive attitudes about inclusion appeared to be the norm, although anxiety about the actual mechanics was also seen (Bennett, DeLuca, & Bruns, 1997; Gibb et al., 1997; Green & Shinn, 1994). This anxiety was clearly seen among parents who support inclusion but have reservations about it for *their* child (Lovitt & Cushing, 1999). As a result, diverse opinion among parents was possible (Borthwick-Duffy, Palmer, & Lane, 1996). For example, Carr (1993) doubted whether inclusion would be appropriate for her child with LD because of the loss of special education services. The question and answer posed: "What has changed in education since the time my son was in elementary school that would ensure successful inclusion? The answer is, unfortunately, nothing really" (p. 59). Taylor (1994) disagreed and, in response, suggested that "regular education is not only where the responsibility lies, but also where those with learning disabilities *deserve* to be educated" (p. 579). In discussing her sons with special needs, Brucker (1994) stressed the need for change: "We have been generally unsuccessful in our current mode of service delivery, although we have had some individual successes. The operation may have been a success, but the patient died! Inclusion's time has come!" (p. 582). Grove and Fisher (1999) discussed this as a tension between the culture of educational reform (opportunities offered by inclusive education) and the culture of the school site (day-to-day demands of schooling). The attitude of the general public has also been investigated and found positive about integration but less positive if the students in question were likely to encounter difficulty in the general education classroom (Berryman, 1989; Gottlieb & Corman, 1975).

Administrators, because of their leadership positions, were viewed as playing a significant role in the success or failure of mainstreaming (Alexander & Strain, 1978; Lazar, Stodden, & Sullivan, 1976; Payne & Murray, 1974). Principals, however, often demonstrated a lack of knowledge about students with disabilities (Cline, 1981), and perceived little chance of success in general education particularly for students with the label "mentally retarded" (Bain & Dolbel, 1991; Davis, 1980). Additionally, principals indicated that pull out programs were the most effective placements, that full-time general class placements were probably more associated with social rather than academic benefits, and that support services were not likely to be provided (Barnett & Monde-Amaya, 1998; Center, Ward, Parmenter, & Nash, 1985; Wade & Garguilo, 1989-90). When the attitudes of teachers and administrators about mainstreaming were compared, the most positive attitudes about students with disabilities and their integration into general education were held by administrators, the individuals most removed from the reality of the classroom (Davis & Maheady, 1991; Glicking & Theobald, 1975; Junkala & Mooney, 1986). Garver-Pinhas and Schmelkin (1989) suggested that "principals appear to respond in a more socially appropriate manner than may actually be the case in reality" (p. 42). Additionally, Cook, Semmel, and Gerber (1999) found critical differences between principals' and teachers' opinions about inclusion including differing perceptions about enhanced academic achievement, about what really works best, and about the level of resources being committed for inclusive arrangements. The optimistic views of principals were in sharp contrast to the more pessimistic views of teachers, and were assumed to be "at least in part, based on negative experiences regarding the outcomes of inclusion or the conviction that inclusion will not produce appropriate outcomes" (p. 25).

Factors Influencing Beliefs

Attitudes about integration were thus multidimensional and reflected a variety of underlying factors. Larrivee and Cook (1979) attempted to identify these factors and found that they included: (a) academic concerns, the possible negative effects of integration on general academic progress; (b) socioemotional concerns, the negative aspects of segregating students with disabilities; (c) administrative concerns; and (d) teacher concerns, issues about support, experience, and training necessary to work with students with disabilities. These concerns appeared to be maintained even after 20 years of inclusion experience as was found to be the case in Italy (Cornoldi, Terreni, Scruggs, & Mastropieri, 1998).

The research evidence about attitudes surrounding integration tended to be inconclusive because of the very disparate opinions held. Within the context of the REI and full inclusion, studies have shown general education teachers to hold negative views about integration (Coates, 1989; Gersten, Walker, & Darch, 1988; Semmel, Abernathy, Butera, & Lesar, 1991), while, at the same time, others revealed more positive attitudes (Villa, Thousand, Meyers, & Nevin, 1996; York, Vandercock, MacDonald, Heise-Neff, & Caughey, 1992). For example, Semmel et al. (1991) found that general education teachers did not oppose pull out models of special education, while Villa et al. (1996) found that teachers favored educating all students with disabilities in the general education classroom. These differences may be related to findings suggesting more experience with inclusion being associated with more positive attitudes (Minke, Bear, Deemer, & Griffin, 1996). Nevertheless, experience with inclusion may also create sampling differences that bias findings in one direction and make any generalizations suspect.

Soodak, Podell, and Lehman (1998) examined the relationship among teacher, student, and school factors in predicting teachers' response to inclusion. Two responses were found: (a) a hostility/receptivity response reflecting teachers' feelings about their willingness to include students with disabilities and their expectations about the success of such an arrangement, and (b) an anxiety/calmness dimension that reflected teachers' emotional tension when faced with serving students with disabilities. Both responses were found related to individual teacher attributes and school conditions. Teachers who possessed low efficacy (i.e., beliefs about the impact of their teaching), who had limited teaching experience, or who demonstrated limited use of differentiated teaching practices were generally less receptive to inclusion. A major influence on the two dimensions was type of disability: Teachers held more positive attitudes toward the inclusion of students with physical disabilities rather than solely academic or behavior disorders (Mandell & Strain, 1978). The greatest hostility and anxiety was found for students with MR, and this pattern was duplicated for students with LD as teachers gained more experience in special education (Wilczenski, 1993).

In an effort to harness the complexity surrounding attitudes about integration, Scruggs and Mastropieri (1996) conducted a quantitative research synthesis of 28 investigations that surveyed the perceptions of almost 10,000 general education teachers regarding the inclusion of students with disabilities. About two-thirds of general education teachers supported the concept of integration, but a smaller majority expressed a willingness to include students with disabilities in their own classrooms. Although there was support for the concept of integration, fewer than one-third of general education teachers expressed the belief that the general education classroom was either the optimal placement or would produce greater benefits than other placements. The factors influencing these perceptions appeared to be severity level of student disability and the amount of additional teacher responsibility required. In turn, these two factors appeared to be associated with the belief, among about one-third of the sample, that including students with disabilities would have a negative impact on the general education classroom. Finally, only about one-quarter of the teachers believed that they had sufficient classroom time for inclusion efforts, that they were currently prepared, or that they would receive sufficient training for inclusion efforts. These findings were interpreted as support for the assumption that teachers viewed students with disabilities in the context of the reality of the general education classroom rather than the prevailing attitudes about integration. General education teachers thus demonstrated a certain reluctance about inclusion that must be addressed if such a policy change is to be successful (Welch, 1989).

PRACTICAL PERSPECTIVES:
GENERAL EDUCATION

General Education: Beliefs and Actions

Besides attitudes toward integration, there are also contextual realities associated with the general education classroom that might affect the success or failure of integration (Shanker, 1995). Baker and Zigmond (1990) asked the question, "Are regular education classes equipped to accommodate students with learning disabilities?" Their analysis indicated that the general education classroom was a place where undifferentiated, large-group instruction dominated, and teachers were more concerned with maintaining routine rather than meeting individual differences: "Teachers cared about children and were conscientious about their jobs--but their mind-set was conformity, not accommodation. In these regular education classes, any student who could not conform would likely be unsuccessful" (p. 319). By definition, students in special education did not conform and was the reason why they were referred to special education. If placed in general education, they might again not conform and consequently experience increased probability of failure.

McIntosh, Vaughn, Schumm, Haager, and Lee (1993) found a similar scenario for students with disabilities in the general education classroom. Although treated much like other students, albeit with lower rates of interaction with teachers and peers, their instruction was not differentiated, and few adaptations were provided. Even effective teachers were found to make few adaptations because of the belief that many adaptations were either not feasible (Schumm & Vaughn, 1991; Whinnery, Fuchs, & Fuchs, 1991; Ysseldyke, Thurlow, Wotruba, & Nania, 1990) or because students themselves did not view many adaptations favorably (Vaughn, Schumm, & Kouzekanani, 1993; Vaughn, Schumm, Niharos, & Daugherty, 1993). In fact, many students with disabilities preferred special education pull out programs (i.e., resource room) over programs delivered exclusively in the general education setting (Guterman, 1995; Jenkins & Heinen, 1989; Klingner, Vaughn, Schumm, Cohen, & Forgan, 1998). Even though many students with disabilities experienced feelings of anger, embarrassment, and frustration in a special education setting and generally viewed it as undesirable (Albinger, 1995; Lovitt et al., 1999; Reid & Button, 1995), Padeliadu and Zigmond (1996) found that most students with also felt the special education setting to be a supportive, enjoyable, and quiet environment where they could receive the extra academic assistance required for success. In a synthesis of eight studies examining the perceptions of students about their educational placements, Vaughn and Klingner (1998) concluded that, "Whether at the elementary or secondary level, many students with LD prefer to receive specialized instruction outside of the general education classroom for part of the school day" (p. 85).

In a later analysis of full-time mainstreaming with Project MELD (Mainstream Experiences for Learning Disabled), Zigmond and Baker (1994) investigated whether, "the regular education class can provide an environment in which students with LDs have more opportunities to learn, to make greater educational progress in academic skills, and to avoid the stigma associated with being less capable in academic achievement" (p. 108). After examining outcomes, they concluded that special education students, "did not get a *special* education" (p. 116). Lieberman (1996) attributed the situation to the increased demands on the general education teacher while Roberts and Mather (1995) suggested that "regular educators are not trained to provide diversified instructional methods or to cope with the needs of diverse learners" (p. 50). In fact, general education teachers were most comfortable when using generic and nonspecific teaching strategies not likely to meet the individual needs of students with disabilities (Ellet, 1993; Johnson & Pugach, 1990).

In a more comprehensive evaluation of special education students in inclusive settings, Baker and Zigmond (1995) found similar circumstances, and concluded "We saw very little 'specially designed instruction' delivered uniquely to a student with learning disabilities. We saw almost no specific, directed, individualized, intensive, remedial instruction for students who were clearly deficient academically and struggling with the schoolwork they were being given" (p. 178). Thus, a basic tenet of special education, individualization, was not being achieved (Deno, Foegen, Robinson, & Espin, 1996). Further confirmation was found in analyses of Individualized Education Programs (IEP). Generally, findings suggested that the less restrictive the setting, the less individualized the IEP (Espin, Deno, & Albayrak-Kaymak, 1998; Smith, 1990). For example, Espin et al. (1998) found special education resource teachers using information to individually tailor programs while general education teachers in inclusive programs focused primarily on information useful for teaching large groups of students. They concluded that, "the 'specialness' of special education, with its emphasis on individualized programming, seems to decrease in inclusive settings" (p. 173).

After analyzing three large-scale projects designed to restructure schools to better accommodate students with disabilities in general education classrooms, Zigmond et al. (1995) concluded that, "general education settings produce achievement outcomes for students with LD that are neither desirable nor acceptable" (p. 538). In a review assessing the academic outcomes associated with eight different models for educating students with mild disabilities in general education classrooms, Manset and Semmel (1997) concluded that, "the evidence clearly indicates that a model of wholesale inclusive programming that is superior to more traditional special education service delivery models does not exist at present" (p. 178). Although findings assessing academic outcomes associated with inclusion were mixed, they generally were not encouraging given the significant investment of resources necessary to provide these enhanced educational opportunities (Marston, 1996; SRI International, 1993; Waldron & McLeskey, 1998). A similar scenario was found in studies investigating the academic performance of students with disabilities who had been reintegrated into general education classrooms (Carlson & Parshall, 1996; Fuchs, Fuchs, & Fernstrom, 1993; Shinn, Powell-Smith, Good, & Baker, 1997).

General Education: Social Factors

In addition to academic effects, social outcomes associated with general education placement have also been investigated. Although some positive social outcomes have been found, primarily in the form of increased tolerance and more social support from students without disabilities (Banerji & Dailey, 1995; Fryxell & Kennedy, 1995; Kennedy, Shukla, & Fryxell, 1997), there appears to be continuing negative findings concerning limited confidence, poor self-perceptions, and inadequate social skills among students with disabilities (Tapasak & Walther-Thomas, 1999). Mixed findings also surrounded teacher-child interactions in inclusive settings. Although students with disabilities have been shown to engage in more positive interactions with teachers (Evans et al., 1992; Thompson, Vitale, & Jewett, 1984), studies have also shown far fewer of such positive interactions (Alves & Gottlieb, 1986; Richey & McKinney, 1978). In a study of teacher-child interactions in inclusive classrooms over the course of a school year, Chow and Kasari (1999), unlike findings showing more interaction at the beginning of the school year (Jordan, Lindsay, & Stanovich, 1997), found that the number of teacher and student interactions did not differ over the course of the school year. The problem, however, was that students with disabilities may require continuing higher levels of interaction (Wigle & Wilcox, 1996) and, "By receiving the same amount of interactions at the end of the year, the needs of children with disabilities and at-risk children may not have been sufficiently met" (Chow & Kasari, 1999, p. 231).

In a large-scale study, Vaughn, Elbaum, and Schumm (1996) assessed the effects of inclusive placements on social functioning, and found that students with disabilities were less accepted by peers, and the degree to which they were accepted and liked declined over time. In sum, students with disabilities were less often accepted and more often rejected (Roberts & Zubrick, 1992; Sale & Carey, 1995).

With respect to the self-perceptions among students with disabilities, Bear, Clever, and Proctor (1991) found low levels in the domains of global self-worth, academic competence, and behavioral conduct. One problem, noted by Mac-Millan, Gresham, and Forness (1996) was that, for students without disabilities, contact with students with disabilities in itself does not result in more favorable attitudes and improved acceptance. The nature and quality of interactions were a significant influence on the way attitudes toward students with disabilities developed. Any objectionable behavior on the part of students with disabilities quickly resulted in less favorable perceptions among their peers in general education. Additionally, if there was a strong academic focus in the classroom, then perceptions about students with disabilities "not keeping up" may result in less teacher tolerance and less peer acceptance (Cook, Gerber, & Semmel, 1997).

Teacher Skill and Ability

At a fundamental skill level, general education teachers were not well prepared for the inclusion of students with disabilities (Kearny & Durand, 1992; Myles & Simpson, 1989; Rojewski & Pollard, 1993), and consequently expressed a variety of concerns over the implementation of inclusive activities (Fox & Ysseldyke, 1997; Giangreco, Dennis, Cloninger, Edelman, & Schattman, 1993). For example, although Downing, Eichinger, and Williams (1997) found generally positive views about inclusion, residual negative attitudes on the part of teachers became significant barriers to the optimal implementation of inclusion. General education teachers expressed concern that the time and effort required to meet the needs of students with disabilities might limit their ability to provide an optimal education for students without disabilities. Special education teachers were most concerned about their perceived loss of control over the classroom and their modified job functions. Another barrier to implementation was the perception that needed resources and supports exceeded their availability (Werts, Wolery, Snyder, Caldwell, & Salisbury, 1996).

As a result of these perceived barriers and expressed concerns, the requisite individual planning for students with disabilities may not occur in general education contexts (Schumm & Vaughn, 1992; Schumm, Vaughn, Haager, McDowell, Rothlein, & Saumell, 1995; Vaughn & Schumm, 1994). Similar findings were found among rural as well as urban general education teachers (Boyer & Bandy, 1997; de Bettencourt, 1999). Although instructional adaptations for students with disabilities were viewed as desirable (Bender, Vail, & Scott, 1995; Blanton, Blanton, & Cross, 1994; Schumm, Vaughn, Gordon, & Rothlein,

1994), they may not be used unless perceived as easy to implement as well as requiring little extra time, little change in routine, or little additional assistance (Bacon & Schulz, 1991; Fuchs, Fuchs, Hamlett, Phillips, & Karns, 1995; Munson, 1986-87). The experiences of general and special education teachers working collaboratively in inclusive settings revealed some success but also remaining concerns over differences in perceived roles, teaching styles, and philosophical orientation (Salend & Garrick-Duhaney, 1999). Wather-Thomas (1997) noted pragmatic problems in collaborative arrangements related to scheduling planning time, coordinating teacher and student schedules, and obtaining administrative support. The failure of collaborative teaching teams was found to result primarily from an inability to communicate, a failure to resolve teaching-style differences, and an inability to adequately integrate special education students and teachers into the classroom (Phillips, Sapona, & Lubic, 1995).

Schumm and Vaughn (1995) summarized findings from a 5-year research project whose goal was to determine whether or not general education was prepared for inclusive education (see also Vaughn, Schumm, Jallad, Slusher, & Saumell, 1996). Using both quantitative and qualitative research methods, 18 individual research studies were conducted to gain insight into the probable success a student with a high-incidence mild disability might experience in the general education classroom. The findings affirmed many earlier conclusions suggesting that general education teachers believed they did not possess the necessary preparation to teach students with disabilities, lacked opportunities to collaborate with special education teachers, and made infrequent and unsystematic use of adaptations even though students with disabilities preferred teachers who did make such instructional adaptations. In answering the question about whether the educational stage was set for inclusion, Schumm and Vaughn provided a generally negative response. The importance of having the stage properly set was demonstrated by Mamlin (1999) in an analysis of an inclusion effort that failed. The failure was attributed to a continuing culture of segregation in the school and a leadership style that demanded too much control. In conclusion, Mamlin suggested that "not all schools are ready to make decisions on restructuring for inclusion" (p. 47).

Summary

Special education is in a state of flux. Integration has been a prominent theme for some 25 years, but its final form remains unclear (Danielson & Bellamy, 1989; Katsiyannis, Conderman, & Franks, 1995; Verstegen, 1996). The lack of agreement is evidenced in the differing position statements offered by organizations promoting full inclusion (Association for Persons with Severe Handicaps, 1992; Council of Chief State School Officers, 1992; National Association of State Boards of Education, 1992) and those advocating inclusion being only one among a number of possible placement options (Council for Exceptional Children, 1993;

Learning Disabilities Association, 1993; National Joint Committee on Learning Disabilities, 1993). Although the trend has been for greater integration for a greater number of students with disabilities, whether or not this means *all* students *all* the time has been subject to passionate debate (see Roberts & Mather, 1995, and response by McLesky & Pugach, 1995). A more cautious policy is thus warranted. Inclusion appears to be not simply something that happens but rather something that requires careful thought and preparation. The focus must not simply be on access to general education but rather the assurance that when inclusion is deemed appropriate, it is implemented with proper attitudes, accommodations, and adaptations in place (Deno, 1994; King-Sears, 1997; Scott, Vitale, & Masten, 1998).

The research evidence investigating inclusion clearly suggests caution (MacMillan et al., 1996; Salend & Garrick-Duhaney, 1999). There is much that is still not known, but what is known about the beliefs and operations of general education were not uniformly supportive and suggest the need for careful and reasoned implementation (Downing et al., 1997; Idol, 1997). Analysis of the evidence also suggests that the effectiveness of practices associated with inclusion are mixed at best (Fisher, Schumaker, & Deshler, 1995; Hunt & Goetz, 1997; Sobsey & Dreimanis, 1993). Generalizations about inclusion thus remain tentative, and it appears unwise to advocate for inclusion without insuring that it is carried out effectively. Too much time has been spent talking about inclusion and not enough time evaluating it in relation to alternative service delivery arrangements and practices (King-Sears & Cummings, 1996). Consequently, outcomes for special education are not predictable, and students with disabilities may be at risk for potentially adverse consequences with the indiscriminate implementation of a full inclusion policy.

Inclusion: Postmodern Perspectives

The realities of the general and special education nexus suggest that general education is neither ready nor willing to endorse a radical policy like full inclusion. A segment of special education, however, appears to ignore this reality. The influence of postmodern thought among this segment is significant. Postmodernism rejects the modern view of science as a system that focuses on problem solving by constructing, evaluating, and testing different conjectures about optimal solutions (Gross & Levitt, 1994). The postmodern model questions the superiority of the modern over the premodern, eschews rigid disciplinary boundaries, and challenges the possibility of creating global, all-encompassing world views (Bauman, 1987; Griffin, 1988; Turner, 1990).

The postmodern perspective has been challenged, however (Koertge, 1998; Sokal & Bricmont, 1998). The differences between modern and postmodern were described by Rosenau (1992):

Those of a modern conviction seek to isolate elements, specify relationships, and formulate a synthesis; post-modernists do the opposite. They offer indeterminary rather than determinism, diversity rather than unity, difference rather than synthesis, complexity rather than simplification. They look to the unique rather than to the general, to intertextual relations rather than causality, and to the unrepeatable rather than the re-occurring, the habitual, or the routine. With a post-modern perspective, social science becomes a more subjective and humble enterprise as truth gives way to tentativeness. (p. 8)

Within the postmodern perspective, the most questionable assumption is the rejection of all science because it is not believed to be trustworthy. Consequently, alternative ways of knowing special education possess equal merit, especially that based on an individual's own experience because it is the only one really knowable (Danforth, 1997; Sailor & Skrtic, 1996; Skrtic et al., 1996). Instead of discussing the possibilities surrounding inclusion in a real-world context buttressed by empirical research, some special educators have chosen to construct arguments within a postmodern framework that often becomes even more unreal and extreme when also based on the view that special education is a fundamentally evil enterprise (Danforth & Rhodes, 1997; Lipsky & Gartner, 1996). For example, Brantlinger (1997) suggested that the current special education system is harming students because it is driven by a privileged ideology that has made it impossible to achieve equity. Consequently, the situation can only be ameliorated by placing all students in the general education setting. In reality, such a postmodern solution is neither practical nor reliable. Although postmodernism views radical transformation as the sole remedy, a more incremental approach to positive change based on a substantive real-world empirical research foundation offers the possibility for more rational and credible solutions (Carnine, 1997; Kauffman, 1993; Zigmond, 1997).

The role and validity of research, however, has become a contentious issue, particularly with respect to preferred research methodology. The division is seen in the quantitative-qualitative research debate (Simpson & Eaves, 1985; Stainback & Stainback, 1984a). Opposing sides in the inclusion debate tend to sort themselves into quantitative or qualitative camps. Much of the support for inclusion has been based on qualitative research findings (Kozleski & Jackson, 1993; Salisbury, Palombaro, & Hollowood, 1993). Such findings are often presented in the form of discourse that emulates styles associated with literary criticism or cultural studies: "Post-modern delivery is more literary in character while modern discourse aims to be exact, precise, pragmatic, and rigorous in style" (Rosenau, 1992, p. 7). Although post-modernists may prefer "audacious and provocative forms of delivery" (p. 7), it must be emphasized that such characteristics offer no insight into the worth of the arguments presented. Contas (1998) also questioned the motivation behind postmodern form of delivery: "Is this disciplinary shift part of a rhetorical strategy being used to give the impression of erudition?" (p. 29). Contas goes on to suggest that definitive conclusions are often lacking because of "the spurious belief that ordered thinking and rational inquiry stifle the human spirit and oppress the political rights of the people we study" (p. 28). The consequences are seen in what has been termed the "cult of ambiguity and indeterminary" (Eagleton, 1996).

The proper role of research may also be at issue. For example, in discussing the famous *Brown v. Board of Education* (1954) Supreme Court decision, Gerard (1983) argued that the supporting Social Science Statement was based on well-meaning rhetoric rather than solid research evidence: "All that it said, in effect, was that because the minority child was now in a classroom with whites, he or she would no longer have the status of an outcast or a pariah. This knowledge would somehow impart to the child the self-image necessary to do well in school and later enter the mainstream of American society" (p. 869). Substitute child with disabilities for minority child and parallels to the present inclusion debate are stark.

Ideology and Inclusion

With an emphasis on ideology without reference to accompanying research evidence in making policy decisions, an objective rendering of the real-world situation may not be achieved (Kauffman, 1999). Ideology can cause arguments to be perceived in a selective manner (Cohen, 1993). A prime prior example is found in the contentious nature-nurture debate surrounding the role of heredity and environment in producing intelligence. In an early review, Pastore (1949) suggested that those taking the nature (heredity) side tended to be politically right of center, while those taking the nurture (environment) side tended to be left of center. Later, Harwood (1976, 1977) found a similar political dichotomy among those who either supported or objected to the position proposed by Jensen (1969) which suggested that the 15 IQ point advantage for whites over blacks was explained by a heritability estimate of about 80% for IQ with only about 20% of IQ differences the result of environment. Harwood also suggested that different modes of thought entered the choice of position about Jensen. Consequently, conceptual frameworks were formed by both political beliefs and styles of thinking.

Although these differences surrounding the nature-nurture debate have been recognized, there has not been significant progress in achieving closure about the question. The reason is found in the fact that not much new data have been brought to bear on the question (Cartwright & Burtis, 1968). Consequently, the different sides tended to form conclusions using the same finite body of information where differences became primarily the result of ideology, not scientific interpretation. Under such circumstances, the nature-nurture debate soon became testy. The nature side was accused of distortion, misrepresentation, and faulty logic (Deutsch, 1969; Hirsch, 1975; Lewontin, 1970), but the same charges were also leveled against those on the nurture side (Eysenck, 1971; Hernstein, 1973; Loehlin, Lindzey, & Spuhler, 1975). Thus, ideology was a significant factor in the positions taken.

Ideology, by itself, however, does not promote scientific advancement. Kuhn's (1970) well-known account of scientific development emphasized the importance of paradigms in defining concepts and methodology. While Kuhn featured the paradigm, Lakatos (1978) stressed the "research program" and its description as either "progressive" or "degenerative." When there is a lack of validating empirical research evidence, theories experience experimental failure and must be modified to accommodate the earlier theory's successes as well as the anomalies that brought the earlier theory into question. When this process is achieved successfully, the research program is termed progressive. If not progressive, the research program is termed degenerative. With no empirical successes, anomalies are met with ad hoc explanations that become increasingly inadequate. A new research program may then be necessary. The earlier cited nature vs nurture debate about IQ represents a case where the rival viewpoints can be viewed as competing research programs: Are the rival programs progressing or degenerating? Using Lakatos' critical methodology, Urbach (1974a, 1974b) concluded that the hereditarian (i.e., nature) position was stronger: "environmentalists have revised their theories in an ad hoc fashion. This patching-up process has left the environmentalist programme as little more than a collection of untestable theories which provide a 'passe partout' which explains everything because it explains nothing" (p. 253). Urbach also pointed out that such an analysis does not mean the nurture (i.e., environmental) position was wrong: "The fact that the environmentalist programme has been degenerating does not mean that no progressive programme will ever be based on its hard core" (p. 253).

Research is thus necessary to strengthen the paradigm (i.e., the common set of assumptions) in a progressive manner. Special education initially possessed a research program emphasizing the special class. The earlier-cited "efficacy studies" created an anomaly that was remedied by the continuum of placements embodied in the "Cascade model." By 1980, the special education research program was manifested in the LRE concept, but anomalies were still present (e.g., students in special education not making the progress expected). Research dealing with resource models, collaborative models, adaptive education, peer tutoring, individualized education strategies, and innovative teaching strategies demonstrated the response of the progressive special education research program.

In contrast, advocates for full inclusion have failed to provide such a progressive research program. In fact, a quantitative inclusion research program is difficult to identify. In examining the same anomalies, the full inclusion research program simply "upped the ante" by calling for all students with disabilities to be fully integrated (Biklen, 1985; Lipsky & Gartner, 1997; Stainback, Stainback, & Forest, 1989; Villa, Thousand, Stainback, & Stainback, 1992). The supportive arguments were primarily based on ideology with anecdotal case studies and testimonials but not quantitative research evidence. Thus, a solution simply calling for full inclusion without accompanying empirical support is neither logical nor rational, and results in a degenerative research program with too many ad hoc explanations. More empirical research on inclusion is thus necessary as suggested by MacMillan et al. (1996), "We need more research on inclusion, not less.... Simplification will only mislead us into adopting untried treatments with the possibility of disserving children" (p. 156).

Ideology may be useful in discussions attempting to establish goals and objectives, but actual practice is best derived from scientific inquiry. Special education had a previous example where ideology played a primary role in determining policy. The issue was deinstitutionalization where Landesman and Butterfield (1987) pointed out that, "As goals, normalization and deinstitutionalization are not terribly controversial; as *means* to achieving these goals many of the current practices related to deinstitutionalization and normalization are" (p. 809). They suggested that more data relevant to the care and treatment of individuals with MR was required. In the absence of such information, there was no basis for judging the merits of deinstitutionalization policy. Shadish (1984), in discussing deinstitutionalization policy, pointed out the tendency to view negative consequences (e.g., increase in homelessness) as merely unfortunate happenstance not connected to the ideology that initiated the policy. More positive outcomes were then sought not using new research evidence to guide practice, but rather the same ideological foundation that was reshaped with more noble intentions but the same pragmatic difficulties. The parallels with the inclusion debate are again stark, and efforts should be directed at avoiding a similar scenario.

CONCLUSION

In closing, questions about the integration of students with disabilities are not new. There has been, over the past 25 years, a steady press toward greater integration for students with disabilities. The law demands placement in the least restrictive environment but difficulties have resulted from this provision coming to be interpreted as the general education classroom especially as the optimal placement for all students regardless of type and level of disability. Although there is ideological and political support for inclusion, the empirical evidence is less convincing. The reality of general education suggests that the requisite attitudes, accommodations, and adaptations for students with disabilities are not yet in place. Consequently, a more tempered approach is necessary which formulates and implements policy on the basis of research and evaluation findings as well as ideological and political considerations. In this way, real solutions may be forthcoming that reflect neither Sowell's (1995) visions of the anointed nor benighted but rather a "vision of the rational." It is possible to draw parallels to the inclusion debate from previous contentious issues in special education, and it would be prudent to learn from these past experiences. With a rational solution, special education may then be in a better position to pursue its real mission: providing the best possible education for all students with disabilities.

REFERENCES

Abeson, A., Burgdorf, R.L., Casey, P.J., Kunz, J.W., & McNeil, W. (1975). Access to opportunity. In N. Hobbs (Ed.), *Issues in the classification of children* (Vol. 2, pp. 270-292). San Francisco: Jossey-Bass.

Albinger, P. (1995). Stories from the resource room: Piano lessons, imaginary illness, and broken-down cars. *Journal of Learning Disabilities, 28,* 615-621.

Alexander, C., & Strain, P.S. (1978). A review of educators' attitudes toward handicapped children and the concept of mainstreaming. *Psychology in the Schools, 15,* 390-396.

Alves, A.J., & Gottlieb, J. (1986). Teacher interactions with mainstreamed handicapped students and their nonhandicapped peers. *Learning Disability Quarterly, 9,* 77-83.

Association for Persons with Severe Handicaps. (1992, July). CEC slips back; ASCD steps forward. *TASH Newsletter, 18,* 1.

Bacon, E.H., & Schulz, J.B. (1991). A survey of mainstreaming practices. *Teacher Education and Special Education, 14,* 144-149.

Bain, A., & Dolbel, S. (1991). Regular and special education principals' perceptions of an integration program for students who are intellectually handicapped. *Education and Training in Mental Retardation, 26,* 33-42.

Baker, J.M., & Zigmond, N. (1990). Are regular education classes equipped to accommodate students with learning disabilities? *Exceptional Children, 56,* 515-526.

Baker, J.M., & Zigmond, N. (1995). The meaning and practices of inclusion for students with learning disabilities: Implications from the five cases. *Journal of Special Education, 29,* 163-180.

Banerji, M., & Dailey, R.A. (1995). A study of the effects of an inclusion model on students with specific learning disabilities. *Journal of Learning Disabilities, 28,* 511-522.

Barnett, C., & Monda-Amaya, L.E. (1998). Principals' knowledge of and attitudes toward inclusion. *Remedial and Special Education, 19,* 181-192.

Bateman, B., & Chard, D.J. (1995). Legal demands and constraints on placement decisions. In J.M. Kauffman, J.W. Lloyd, P. Hallahan, & T.A. Astuto (Eds.), *Issues in educational placement: Students with emotional and behavioral disorders* (pp. 285-316). Hillsdale, NJ: Erlbaum.

Bauman, Z. (1987). *Legislators and interpreters: Modernity, post-modernity, and intellectuals.* Ithaca, NY: Cornell University Press.

Bear, G.G., Clever, A., & Proctor, W.A. (1991). Self-perceptions of nonhandicapped children and children with learning disabilities in integrated classes. *The Journal of Special Education, 24,* 409-429.

Bender, W.N., Vail, C.O., & Scott, K. (1995). Teachers' attitudes toward increased mainstreaming: Implementing effective instruction for students with learning disabilities. *Journal of Learning Disabilities, 28,* 87-94.

Bennett, T., DeLuca, D., & Bruns, D. (1997). Putting inclusion into practice: Perspectives of teachers and parents. *Exceptional Children, 64,* 115-131.

Berryman, J.D. (1989). Attitudes of the public toward educational mainstreaming. *Remedial and Special Education, 10,* 44-49.

Biklen, D. (Ed.). (1985). *Achieving the complete school: Strategies for effective mainstreaming.* New York: Teachers College Press.

Blanton, L.P., Blanton, W.E., & Cross, L.S. (1994). An exploratory study of how general and special education teachers think and make instructional decisions about students with special needs. *Teacher Education and Special Education, 17,* 62-73.

Borthwick-Duffy, S.A., Palmer, D.S., & Lane, K.L. (1996). One size doesn't fit all: Full inclusion and individual differences. *Journal of Behavioral Education, 6,* 311-329.

Boyer, W.A.R., & Bandy, H. (1997). Rural teachers' perceptions of the current state of inclusion: Knowledge, training, teaching practices, and adequacy of support systems. *Exceptionality, 7,* 1-18.

Brantlinger, E. (1997). Using ideology: Cases of nonrecognition of the politics of research and practice in special education. *Review of Educational Research, 67,* 425-459.

Brown v. Board of Education. (1954). 347 U.S. 483, 74 Sup. Ct. 686.

Brucker, P.O. (1994). The advantages of inclusion for students with learning disabilities. *Journal of Learning Disabilities, 27,* 581-582.

Bryan, J.H., & Bryan, T.H. (1988). Where's the beef? A review of published research on the Adaptive Learning Environments Model. *Learning Disabilities Focus, 4,* 9-14.

Carlberg, C., & Kavale, K.A. (1980). The efficacy of special versus regular class placement for exceptional children: A meta-analysis. *Journal of Special Education, 14,* 295-309.

Carlson, E., & Parshall, L. (1996). Academic, social, and behavioral adjustment for students declassified from special education. *Exceptional Children, 63,* 89-100.

Carnine, D. (1997). Bridging the research-to-practice gap. In J. Lloyd, E. Kameenui, & D. Chard (Eds.), *Issues in educating students with disabilities* (pp. 363-373). Mahwah, NJ: Erlbaum.

Carr, M.N. (1993). A mother's thoughts on inclusion. *Journal of Learning Disabilities, 26,* 590-592.

Cartwright, W.J., & Burtis, T.R. (1968). Race and intelligence: Changing opinions in social science. *Social Science Quarterly, 49,* 603-618.

Center, Y., & Ward, J. (1987). Teachers' attitudes towards the integration of disabled children in regular schools. *The Exceptional Child, 34,* 41-56.

Center, Y., Ward, J., Parmenter, T., & Nash, R. (1985). Principals' attitudes towards the integration of disabled children into regular schools. *The Exceptional Child, 32,* 149-160.

Chow, V.T., & Kasari, C. (1999). Task-related interactions among teachers and exceptional, at-risk and typical learners in inclusive classrooms. *Remedial and Special Education, 20,* 226-232.

Christopolos, F., & Renz, P. (1969). A critical examination of special education programs. *Journal of Special Education, 3,* 371-379.

Cline, R. (1981). Principals' attitudes and knowledge about handicapped children. *Exceptional Children, 48,* 172-174.

Coates, R.D. (1989). The Regular Education Initiative and opinions of regular classroom teachers. *Journal of Learning Disabilities, 22,* 532-536.

Cohen, M. (1993). The politics of special ed. *The Special Educator, 8,* 266.

Contas, M.A. (1998). The changing nature of educational research and a critique of postmodernism. *Educational Researcher, 27,* 26-33.

Cook, B.G., Gerber, M.M., & Semmel, M.I. (1997). Are effective schools reforms effective for all students: The implications of joint outcome production for school reform. *Exceptionality, 7,* 77-95.

Cook, B.G., & Semmel, M.I. (1999). Peer acceptance of included students with disabilities as a function of severity of disability and classroom composition. *Journal of Special Education, 33,* 50-61.

Cook, B.G., Semmel, M.I., & Gerber, M.M. (1999). Attitudes of principals and special education teachers toward the inclusion of students with mild disabilities: Critical differences of opinion. *Remedial and Special Education, 20,* 199-207, 243.

Cornoldi, C., Terreni, A., Scruggs, T.E., & Mastropieri, M.A. (1998). Teacher attitudes in Italy after twenty years of inclusion. *Remedial and Special Education, 19,* 350-356.

Council for Exceptional Children. (1993, April). *Statement on inclusive schools and communities.* Reston, VA: Author.

Council of Chief State School Officers. (1992, March). Special education and school restructuring. *Concerns, 35,* 1-7.

Danforth, S. (1997). On what basis hope? Modern progress and postmodern possibilities. *Mental Retardation, 35,* 93-106.

Danforth, S., & Rhodes, W.C. (1997). Deconstructing disability: A philosophy for inclusion. *Remedial and Special Education, 18,* 357-366.

Danielson, L.C., & Bellamy, G.T. (1989). State variation in placement of children with handicaps in segregated environments. *Exceptional Children, 55,* 448-455.

Davis, J.C., & Maheady, L. (1991). The Regular Education Initiative: What do three groups of education professionals think? *Teacher Education and Special Education, 14,* 211-220.

Davis, W.E. (1980). Public schools principals' attitudes toward mainstreaming retarded pupils. *Education and Training of the Mentally Retarded, 15,* 174-178.

Davis, W.E. (1989). The Regular Education Initiative debate: Its promises and problems. *Exceptional Children, 55,* 440-446.

de Bettencourt, L.V. (1999). General educators' attitudes toward students with mild disabilities and their use of instructional strategies. *Remedial and Special Education, 20,* 27-35.

Deno, E. (1970). Special education as developmental capital. *Exceptional Children, 37,* 229-237.

Deno, E. (1994). Special education as developmental capital revisited: A quarter-century appraisal of means versus ends. *Journal of Special Education, 27,* 375-392.

Deno, S.L., Foegen, A.M., Robinson, S., & Espin, C.A. (1996). Commentary: Facing the realities of inclusion: Students with mild disabilities. *Journal of Special Education, 62,* 497-514.

Deutsch, M. (1969). Happenings on the way back from the forum: Social science, IQ, and race revisited. *Harvard Educational Review, 39,* 523-554.

Diebold, M.H., & Von Eschenbach, J.F. (1991). Teacher educator predictions of regular class teacher perceptions of mainstreaming. *Teacher Education and Special Education, 14,* 221-227.

Donaldson, J. (1980). Changing attitudes toward handicapped persons: A review and analysis of research. *Exceptional Children, 46,* 504-514.

Dorn, S., Fuchs, D., & Fuchs, L.S. (1996). A historical perspective on special education reform. *Theory Into Practice, 35,* 12-19.

Downing, J.E., Eichinger, J., & Williams, L.J. (1997). Inclusive education for students with severe disabilities: Comparative views of principals and educators at different levels of implementation. *Remedial and Special Education, 18,* 133-142, 165.

Dunn, L.M. (1968). Special education for the mildly retarded--Is much of it justifiable? *Exceptional Children, 35,* 5-22.

Eagleton, T. (1996). *Illusion of postmodernism.* London: Blackwell.

Education for All Handicapped Children Act (P.L. No. 94-142), 20 U.S.C. 1401 *et seq.* (1975).

Ellet, L. (1993). Instructional practices in mainstreamed secondary classrooms. *Journal of Learning Disabilities, 26,* 57-64.

Espin, C.A., Deno, S.L., & Albayrak-Kaymak, D. (1998). Individualized Education Programs in resource and inclusive settings: How "individualized" are they? *Journal of Special Education, 32,* 164-174.

Esposito, B.G., & Reed, T.M. (1986). The effects of contact with handicapped persons on young children's attitudes. *Exceptional Children, 53,* 224-229.

Evans, I.M., Salisbury, C.L., Palombaro, M.M., Berryman, J., & Hollowood, T.M. (1992). Peer interactions and social competence of elementary-age children with severe disabilities in an inclusive school. *Journal of the Association for Persons with Severe Handicaps, 17,* 205-217.

Eysenck, H.J. (1971). *The IQ argument: Race, intelligence, and education.* New York: Library Press.

Ferguson, D.L. (1996). Is it inclusion yet? Bursting the bubbles. In M.S. Berres, D.L. Ferguson, P. Knoblock, & C. Woods (Eds.), *Creating tomorrow's schools today: Stories of inclusion, change, and renewal* (pp. 16-37). New York: Teachers College Press.

Fisher, J.B., Schumaker, J.B., & Deshler, D.D. (1995). Searching for validated inclusive practices: A review of the literature. *Focus on Exceptional Children, 28,* 1-20.

Fox, N.E., & Ysseldyke, J.E. (1997). Implementing inclusion at the middle school level: Lessons from a negative example. *Exceptional Children, 64,* 81-98.

Fryxell, D., & Kennedy, C. (1995). Placement along the continuum of services and its impact on students' social relationships. *Journal of the Association for Persons with Severe Handicaps, 20,* 259-269.

Fuchs, D., & Fuchs, L.S. (1988). An evaluation of the Adaptive Learning Environments Model. *Exceptional Children, 55,* 115-127.

Fuchs, D., & Fuchs, L.S. (1991). Framing the REI debate: Abolitionists versus conservationists. In J.W. Lloyd, A.C. Repp, & N.N. Singh (Eds.), *The Regular Education Initiative: Alternative perspectives on concepts, issues, and models* (pp. 241-255). Sycamore, IL: Sycamore.

Fuchs, D., & Fuchs, L.S. (1994). Inclusive schools movement and the radicalization of special education reform. *Exceptional Children, 60,* 294-309.

Fuchs, D., & Fuchs, L.S. (1995a). Special education can work. In J.M. Kauffman, J.W. Lloyd, D.P. Hallahan, & T.A. Astuto (Eds.), *Issues in educational placement: Students with emotional and behavior disorders* (pp. 363-377). Hillsdale, NJ: Erlbaum.

Fuchs, D., & Fuchs, L.S. (1995b). What's 'special' about special education? *Phi Delta Kappan, 76,* 22-30.

Fuchs, D., Fuchs, L.S., & Fernstrom, P. (1993). A conservative approach to special education reform: Mainstreaming through transenvironmental programming and curriculum-based measurement. *American Educational Research Journal, 30,* 149-177.

Fuchs, L.S., Fuchs, D., Hamlett, C.L., Phillips, N.B., & Karns, K. (1995). General educators' specialized adaptation for students with learning disabilities. *Exceptional Children, 61,* 440-459.

Gallagher, J.J. (1994). The pull of societal forces on special education. *Journal of Special Education, 27,* 521-530.

Gans, K.D. (1987). Willingness of regular and special educators to teach students with handicaps. *Exceptional Children, 54,* 41-45.

Gartner, A., & Lipsky, D.K. (1987). Beyond special education: Toward a quality system for all students. *Harvard Educational Review, 57,* 367-390.

Gartner, A., & Lipsky, D.K. (1989). *The yoke of special education: How to break it.* Rochester, NY: National Center on Education and the Economy.

Garvar-Pinhas, A., & Schmelkin, L.P. (1989). Administrators' and teachers' attitudes toward mainstreaming. *Remedial and Special Education, 10,* 38-43.

Gerard, H.B. (1983). School desegregation: The social science role. *American Psychologist, 38,* 869-877.

Gerber, M.M. (1996). Reforming special education: "Beyond inclusion." In C. Christensen & F. Rizvi (Eds.), *Disability and the dilemmas of education and justice* (pp. 156-174). Philadelphia: Open University Press.

Gersten, R., Walker, H., & Darch, C. (1988). Relationships between teachers' effectiveness and their tolerance for handicapped students. *Exceptional Children, 54,* 433-438.

Giangreco, M.F., Dennis, R., Cloninger, C., Edelman, S., & Schattman, R. (1993). "I've counted Jon": Transformational experiences of teachers educating students with disabilities. *Exceptional Children, 59,* 359-372.

Gibb, G.S., Young, J.R., Allred, K.W., Dyches, T.T., Egan, M.W., & Ingram, C.F. (1997). A team-based junior high inclusion program: Parent perceptions and feedback. *Remedial and Special Education, 18,* 243-249, 256.

Glicking, E.E., & Theobald, J.T. (1975). Mainstreaming: Affect or effect? *Journal of Special Education, 9,* 317-328.

Goldstein, H. (1967). The efficacy of special classes and regular classes in the education of educable mentally retarded children. In J. Zubin & G.A. Jervis (Eds.), *Psychopathology of mental development* (pp. 580-602). New York: Grune & Stratton.

Goldstein, H., Moss, J.W., & Jordan, L.J. (1965). *The efficacy of special class training on the development of mentally retarded children.* U.S. Office of Education, Cooperative Research Project No. 619. Urbana, IL: University of Illinois, Institute for Research on Exceptional Children. (ERIC Document Reproduction Service No. ED 002 907)

Gottlieb, J. (1981). Mainstreaming: Fulfilling the promise? *American Journal of Mental Deficiency, 86,* 115-126.

Gottlieb, J., & Corman, L. (1975). Public attitudes toward menatlly retarded children. *American Journal of Mental Deficiency, 80,* 72-80.

Green, S.K., & Shinn, M.R. (1994). Parent attitudes about special education and reintegration: What is the role of student outcomes? *Exceptional Children, 61,* 269-281.

Griffin, D.R. (Ed.). (1988). *The reenchantment of science: Postmodern proposals.* Albany: State University of New York Press.

Gross, P.R., & Levitt, N. (1994). *Higher superstition: The academic left and its quarrels with science.* Baltimore, MD: Johns Hopkins University Press.

Grove, K.A., & Fisher, D. (1999). Entrepreneurs of meaning: Parents and the process of inclusive education. *Remedial and Special Education, 20,* 208-215, 256.

Guskin, S.L., & Spicker, H.H. (1968). Educational research in mental retardation. In N.R. Ellis (Ed.), *International review of research in mental retardation* (Vol. 3, pp. 217-278). New York: Academic Press.

Guterman, B.R. (1995). The validity of categorical learning disabilities services: The consumer's view. *Exceptional Children, 62,* 111-124

Hall, L.J. (1994). A descriptive assessment of social relationships in integrated classrooms. *Journal of the Association for Persons with Severe Handicaps, 12,* 280-286.

Hallahan, D.P., Keller, C.E., McKinney, J.D., Lloyd, J.W., & Bryan, T. (1988). Examining the research base of the Regular Education Initiative: Efficacy studies and the Adaptive Learning Enviornments Model. *Journal of Learning Disabilities, 21,* 29-35, 55.

Hammill, D.D., & Wiederholt, J.L. (1972). *The resource room: Rationale and implementation.* Philadelphia: JSE Press.

Hannah, M.E., & Pliner, S. (1983). Teacher attitudes toward handicapped children. A review and syntheses. *School Psychology Review, 12,* 12-25.

Harasymiw, S.J., & Horne, M.D. (1976). Teacher attitudes toward handicapped children and regular class integration. *Journal of Special Education, 10,* 393-400.

Harwood, J. (1976). The race-intelligence controversy: A sociological approach I--External factors. *Social Studies of Science, 6,* 369-394.

Harwood, J. (1977). The race-intelligence controversy: A sociological approach II--External factors. *Social Studies of Science, 7,* 1-30.

Heller, K., Holtzman, W., & Messick, S. (1982). *Placing children in special education: A strategy for equity.* Washington, DC: National Academy of Science Press.

Heller, W.H., & Schilit, J. (1987). The Regular Education Initiative: A concerned response. *Focus on Exceptional Children, 20,* 1-6.

Helmstetter, E., Peck, C.A., & Giangreco, M.F. (1994). Outcomes of interactions with peers with moderate or severe disabilities: A state-wide survey of high school students. *Journal of the Association of Persons with Severe Handicaps, 19,* 263-276.

Hendrickson, J.M., Shokoohi-Yekta, M., Hamre-Nietupski, S., & Gable, R.A. (1996). Middle and high school students' perceptions on being friends with peers with severe disabilities. *Exceptional Children, 63,* 19-28.

Hernstein, R.J. (1973). *IQ in the meritocracy.* Boston: Little, Brown.

Hirsch, J. (1975). Jensenism: The bankruptcy of "science" without scholarship. *Educational Theory, 25,* 3-28.

Hirshoren, A., & Burton, T.E. (1979). Willingness of regular teachers to participate in mainstreaming handicapped children. *Journal of Research and Development in Education, 12,* 93-100.

Horne, M.D. (1985). *Attitudes toward handicapped students: Professional, peer, and parent reactions.* Hillsdale, NJ: Erlbaum.

Houck, C.K., & Rogers, C.J. (1994). The special/general education integration initiative for students with specific learning disabilities: A "snapshot" of program change. *Journal of Learning Disabilities, 27,* 58-62.

Hunt, P., & Goetz, L. (1997). Research on inclusive educational programs, practices, and outcomes for students with severe disabilities. *The Journal of Special Education, 31,* 3-29.

Idol, L. (1997). Key questions related to building collaborative and inclusive schools. *Journal of Learning Disabilities, 30,* 384-394.

Individuals with Disabilities Education Act, 20 U.S.C. 1400 *et seq.* (1990).

Individuals with Disabilities Education Act Regulations, 34 C.F.R., 300.533 (1992).

Individuals with Disabilities Education Act, 20 U.S.C. 1401 *et seq.,* Amendments. (1997).

Janney, R.E., Snell, M.E., Beers, M.K., & Raynes, M. (1995). Integrating students with moderate and severe disabilities into general education classes. *Exceptional Children, 61,* 425-439.

Jenkins, J.R., & Heinen, A. (1989). Students' preferences for service delivery: Pull-out, in-class, or integrated models. *Exceptional Children, 60,* 6-16.

Jenkins, J.R., Pious, C.G., & Jewell, M. (1990). Special education and the Regular Education Initiative: Basic assumptions. *Exceptional Children, 56,* 479-491.

Jensen, A.R. (1969). How much can we boost IQ and scholastic achievement. *Harvard Educational Review, 39,* 1-123.

Johnson, G.O. (1962). Special education for the mentally handicapped: A paradox. *Exceptional Children, 19,* 62-69.

Johnson, L.J., & Pugach, M.C. (1990). Classroom teachers' views of intervention strategies for learning and behavior problems: Which are reasonable and how frequently are they used? *Journal of Special Education, 24,* 69-84.

Jordan, A., Lindsay, L., & Stanovich, P.J. (1997). Classroom teachers' instructional interactions with students who are exceptional, at risk, and typically achieving. *Remedial and Special Education, 18,* 82-93.

Junkala, J., & Mooney, J.F. (1986). Special education students in regular classes: What happened to the pyramid? *Journal of Learning Disabilities, 19,* 218-221.

Katsiyannis, A., Conderman, G., & Franks, D.J. (1995). State practices on inclusion: A national review. *Remedial and Special Education, 16,* 279-287.

Kauffman, J.M. (1989). The Regular Education Initiative as Reagan-Bush educational policy: A trickle-down theory of education of the hard-to-teach. *Journal of Special Education, 23,* 256-278.

Kauffman, J.M. (1993). How we might achieve the radical reform of special education. *Exceptional Children, 60,* 6-16.

Kauffman, J.M. (1995). Why we must celebrate a diversity of restrictive environments. *Learning Disabilities Research and Practice, 10,* 225-232.

Kauffman, J.M. (1999). Commentary: Today's special education and its messages for tomorrow. *Journal of Special Education, 32,* 244-254.

Kauffman, J.M., Gerber, M.M., & Semmel, M.I. (1988). Arguable assumptions underlying the Regular Education Initiative. *Journal of learning Disabilities, 21,* 6-11.

Kauffman, J.M., & Hallahan, D.P. (Eds.). (1995). *The illusion of full inclusion: A comprehensive critique of a current special education bandwagon.* Austin, TX: PRO-ED.

Kaufman, M.J., Agard, J.A., & Semmel, M.I. (1986). *Mainstreaming: Learners and their environment.* Cambridge, MA: Brookline.

Kavale, K.A., & Forness, S.R. (1999). *Efficacy of special education and related services.* Washington, DC: American Association on Mental Retardation.

Kavale, K.A., & Glass, G.V. (1984). Meta-analysis and policy decisions in special education. In B.K. Keogh (Ed.), *Advances in special education* (Vol. 4, pp. 195-248). Greenwich, CT: JAI Press.

Kearny, C.A., & Durand, V.M. (1992). How prepared are our teachers for mainstreamed classroom settings? A survey of postsecondary schools of education in New York State. *Exceptional Children, 58*, 8-11.

Kennedy, C.H., Shukla, S., & Fryxell, D. (1997). Comparing the effects of educational placement on the social relationships of intermediate school students with severe disabilities. *Exceptional Children, 64*, 31-47.

King-Sears, M.E. (1997). Best academic practices for inclusive classrooms. *Focus on Exceptional Children, 29*, 1-22.

King-Sears, M.E., & Cummings, C.S. (1996). Inclusive practices of classroom teachers. *Remedial and Special Education, 17*, 217-225.

Kirk, S.A. (1964). Research in education. In H.A. Stevens & R. Heber (Eds.), *Mental retardation: A review of research* (pp. 57-99). Chicago: University of Chicago Press.

Klingner, J.K., Vaughn, S., Schumm, J.S., Cohen, P., & Forgan, J.W. (1998). Inclusion or pull-out: Which do students prefer? *Journal of Learning Disabilities, 31*, 148-158.

Koertge, N. (Ed.). (1998). *A house built on sand: Exposing postmodernist myths about science*. New York: Oxford University Press.

Korinek, L., & McLaughlin, V., & Walther-Thomas, C.S. (1995). Least restrictive environment and collaboration: A bridge over troubled waters. *Preventing School Failure, 39*, 6-12.

Kozleski, E.B., & Jackson, L. (1993). Taylor's story: Full inclusion in her neighborhood elementary school. *Exceptionality, 4*, 153-176.

Kuhn, T.S. (1970). *The structure of scientific revolutions* (2nd ed.). Chicago: University of Chicago Press.

Lakatos, I. (1978). *The methodology of scientific research programs*. Cambridge: Cambridge University Press.

Landesman, S., & Butterfield, E.C. (1987). Normalization and deinstitutionalization of mentally retarded individuals: Controversy and facts. *American Psychologist, 42*, 809-816.

Larrivee, B., & Cook, L. (1979). Mainstreaming: A study of the variables affecting teacher attitude. *Journal of Special Education, 13*, 315-324.

Lazar, A.L., Stodden, R.L., & Sullivan, N.V. (1976). A comparison of attitudes held by male and female future school administrators toward instructional goals, personal adjustment, and the handicapped. *Rehabilitation Literature, 37*, 198-222.

Learning Disabilities Association. (1993, January). Position paper on full inclusion of all students with learning disabilities in the regular education classroom. *LDA Newsbriefs, 28*, 1-2.

Leinhardt, G., & Pallay, A. (1982). Restrictive educational settings: Exile or haven? *Review of Educational Research, 52*, 557-578.

Lewontin, R.C. (1970). Race and intelligence. *Bulletin of the Atomic Scientist, 26*, 2-8.

Lieberman, L.M. (1985). Special education and regular education: A merger made in heaven? *Exceptional Children, 51*, 513-516.

Lieberman, L.M. (1996). Preserving special education...for those who need it. In W. Stainback & S. Stainback (Eds.), *Controversial issues confronting special education* (pp. 16-27). Needham Heights, MA: Allyn & Bacon.

Lilly, M.S. (1970). Special education: A teapot in a tempest. *Exceptional Children, 37*, 43-49.

Lilly, M.S. (1988). The Regular Education Initiative: A force for change in general and special education. *Education and Training in Mental Retardation, 23*, 253-260.

Linton, T.E., & Juul, K.D. (1980). Mainstreaming: Time for reassessment. *Educational Leadership, 37*, 433-437.

Lipsky, D.K., & Gartner, A. (1987). Capable of achievement and worthy of respect: Education for handicapped students as if they were full-fledged human beings. *Exceptional Children, 54*, 69-74.

Lipsky, D.K., & Gartner, A. (Eds.). (1989). *Beyond separate education: Quality education for all*. Baltimore, MD: Brookes.

Lipsky, D.K., & Gartner, A. (1991). Restructuring for quality. In J.W. Lloyd, A.C. Repp, & N.N. Singh (Eds.), *The Regular Education Initiative: Alternative perspectives on concepts, issues, and models* (pp. 43-56). Sycamore, IL: Sycamore.

Lipsky, D.K., & Gartner, A. (1996). Equity requires inclusion: The future for all students with disabilities. In C. Christensen & F. Rizvi (Eds.), *Disability and the dilemmas of education and justice* (pp. 144-155). Philadelphia: Open University Press.

Lipsky, D.K., & Gartner, A. (Eds.). (1997). *Inclusion and school reform: Transforming American classrooms.* Baltimore, MD: Brookes.

Loehlin, J.C., Lindzey, G., & Spuhler, J.N. (1975). *Race differences in intelligence.* San Francisco: Freeman.

Lovitt, T.C., & Cushing, S. (1999). Parents of youth with disabilities: Their perceptions of school programs. *Remedial and Special Education, 20,* 134-142.

Lovitt, T.C., Plavins, M., & Cushing, S. (1999). What do pupils with disabilities have to say about their experience in high school? *Remedial and Special Education, 20,* 67-76, 83.

MacMillan, D.L. (1971). Special education for the mildly retarded: Servant or savant? *Focus on Exceptional Children, 2,* 1-11.

MacMillan, D.L., Gresham, F.M., & Forness, S.R. (1996). Full inclusion: An empirical perspective. *Behavioral Disorders, 21,* 145-159.

MacMillan, D.L., & Hendrick, I.G. (1993). Evolution and legacies. In J.I. Goodlad & T.C. Lovitt (Eds.), *Integrating general and special education* (pp. 23-48). New York: Merrill.

MacMillan, D.L., & Semmel, M.I. (1977). Evaluation of mainstreaming programs. *Focus on Exceptional Children, 9,* 1-14.

MacMillan, D.L., Semmel, M.I., & Gerber, M.M. (1994). The social context of Dunn: Then and now. *Journal of Special Education, 27,* 466-480.

Madden, N.A., & Slavin, R.E. (1983). Mainstreaming students with mild handicaps: Academic and social outcomes. *Review of Educational Research, 53,* 519-569.

Mamlin, N. (1999). Despite best intentions: When inclusion fails. *Journal of Special Education, 33,* 36-49.

Mandell, C.J., & Strain, P.S. (1978). An analysis of factors related to the attitudes of regular classroom teachers toward mainstreaming mildly handicapped children. *Contemporary Educational Psychology, 3,* 154-162.

Manset, G., & Semmel, M.I. (1997). Are inclusive programs for students with mild disabilities effective? A comparative review of model programs. *The Journal of Special Education, 31,* 155-180.

Margolis, H., & McGettigan, J. (1988). Managing resistance to instructional modifications in mainstreamed environments. *Remedial and Special Education, 9,* 15-21.

Marston, D. (1996). A comparison of inclusion only, pull-out only, and combined service models for students with mild disabilities. *The Journal of Special Education, 30,* 121-132.

Martin, E.W. (1995). Case studies on inclusion: Worst fears realized. *Journal of Special Education, 29,* 192-199.

McIntosh, R., Vaughn, S., Schumm, J.S., Haager, D., & Lee, O. (1993). Observations of students with learning disabilities in general education classrooms. *Exceptional Children, 60,* 249-261.

McLesky, J., & Pugach, M.C. (1995). The real sellout: Failing to give inclusion a chance. A response to Roberts and Mather. *Learning Disabilities Research and Practice, 10,* 233-238.

Meredith, B., & Underwood, J. (1995). Irreconcilable differences? Defining the rising conflict between regular and special education. *Journal of Law and Education, 24,* 195-226.

Minke, K.M., Bear, G.G., Deemer, S.A., & Griffin, S.M. (1996). Teachers' experiences with inclusive classrooms: Implications for special education reform. *Journal of Special Education, 30,* 152-186.

Mocsink, C.V., & Lenk, L.L. (1992). The delivery of special education programs and services. *Remedial and Special Education, 13,* 33-43.

Munson, S.M. (1986-87). Regular education teacher modifications for mainstreamed mildly handicapped students. *Journal of Special Education, 20,* 490-499.

Myles, B.S., & Simpson, R.L. (1989). Regular educators' modification preferences for mainstreaming mildly handicapped children. *Journal of Special Education, 22,* 479-489.

Nader, A. (1984). Teacher attitude toward the elementary exceptional child. *International Journal of Rehabilitation Research, 7,* 37-46.

Naor, M., & Milgram, R. (1980). Two preservice strategies for preparing regular classroom teachers for mainstreaming. *Exceptional Children, 47,* 126-129.

National Association of State Boards of Education, (1992, October). *Winners all: A call for inclusive schools.* Washington, DC: Author.

National Joint Committee on Learning Disabilities. (1993). A reaction to full inclusion: A reaffirmation of the right of students with learning disabilities to a continuum of services. *Journal of Learning Disabilities, 26,* 596.

O'Neil, J. (1994-95). Can inclusion work? A conversation with Jim Kauffman and Mara Sapon-Shevin. *Educational Leadership, 52,* 7-11.

Osborne, A.G., & DiMattia, P. (1994). The IDEA's least restrictive environment mandate: Legal implications. *Exceptional Children, 61,* 6-14.

Padeliadu, S., & Zigmond, N. (1996). Perspectives of students with learning disabilities about special education placement. *Learning Disabilities Research & Practice, 11,* 15-23.

Pastore, N. (1949). *The nature-nurture controversy.* New York: King's Crown Press.

Payne, R., & Murray, C. (1974). Principals' attitudes toward integration of the handicapped. *Exceptional Children, 41,* 123-125.

Peck, C.A., Donaldson, J., & Pezzoli, M. (1990). Some benefits nonhandicapped adolescents perceive for themselves from their social relationships with peers who have severe handicaps. *Journal of the Association for Persons with Severe Handicaps, 15,* 241-249.

Phillips, L., Sapona, R.H., & Lubic, B. L. (1995). Developing partnerships in inclusive education: One school's approach. *Intervention in School and Clinic, 30,* 262-272.

Pugach, M., & Lilly, M.S. (1984). Reconceptualizing support services for classroom teachers: Implications for teacher education. *Journal of Teacher Education, 35,* 48-55.

Pugach, M., & Sapon-Shevin, M. (1987). New agendas for special education policy: What the regular education reports haven't said. *Exceptional Children, 53,* 295-299.

Putnam, J.W., Spiegel, A.N., & Bruininks, R.N. (1995). Future directions in education and inclusion of students with disabilities: A Delphi investigation. *Exceptional Children, 61,* 553-576.

Reid, D.K., & Button, L.J. (1995). Anna's story: Narratives of personal experience about being labeled learning disabled. *Journal of Learning Disabilities, 28,* 602-614.

Reynolds, M.C. (1962). A framework for considering some issues in special education. *Exceptional Children, 28,* 367-370.

Reynolds, M.C. (1988). A reaction to the JLD Special Series on the Regular Education Initiative. *Journal of Learning Disabilities, 21,* 352-356.

Reynolds, M.C. (1989). An historical perspective: The delivery of special education to mildly disabled and at-risk students. *Remedial and Special Education, 10,* 7-11.

Reynolds, M.C. (1991, December). Progressive inclusion. *Quality Outcomes Driven Education,* 11-14.

Reynolds, M.C. (1992). Students and programs at the school margins: Disorder and needed repairs. *School Psychology Quarterly, 7,* 233-244.

Reynolds, M.C., & Wang, M.C. (1983). Restructuring "special" school programs: A position paper. *Policy Studies Review, 2,* 189-212.

Reynolds, M.C., Wang, M.C., & Walberg, H.J. (1987). The necessary restructuring of special and general education. *Exceptional Children, 53,* 391-398.

Richey, D., & McKinney, J.D. (1978). Classroom behavioral styles of learning disabled children. *Journal of Learning Disabilities, 11,* 297-302.

Ringlaben, R.P., & Price, J.R. (1981). Regular classroom teachers' perceptions of mainstreaming effects. *Exceptional Children, 47,* 302-304.

Roberts, C., & Zubrick, S. (1992). Factors influencing the social status of children with mild academic disabilities in regular classrooms. *Exceptional Children, 59,* 192-202.

Roberts, R., & Mather, N. (1995). The return of students with learning disabilities to regular classrooms: A sellout? *Learning Disabilities Research and Practice, 10,* 46-58.

Rojewski, J.W., & Pollard, R.R. (1993). A multivariate analysis of perceptions held by secondary academic teachers toward students with special needs. *Teacher Education and Special Education, 16,* 330-341.

Rosenau, P.M. (1992). *Post-modernism and the social sciences: Insights, inroads, and intrusions.* Princeton, NJ: Princeton University Press.

Safford, P.L., & Safford, E.J. (1998). Visions of the special class. *Remedial and Special Education, 19,* 229-238.

Sailor, W., & Skrtic, T.M. (1996). School-linked services integration: Crisis and opportunity in the transition to a postmodern society. *Remedial and Special Education, 17,* 271-283.

Sale, P., & Carey, D.M. (1995). The sociometric status of students with disabilities in a full-inclusion school. *Exceptional Children, 62,* 6-19.

Salend, S.J., & Garrick Duhaney, L.M. (1999). The impact of inclusion on students with and without disabilities and their educators. *Remedial and Special Education, 20,* 114-126.

Salend, S.J., Johansen, M., Mumper, J., Chase, A., Pike, K.M., & Dorney, J.A. (1997). Cooperative teaching: The voices of two teachers. *Remedial and Special Education, 18,* 3-11.

Salisbury, C.L., Palombaro, M.M., & Hollowood, T.M. (1993). On the nature and change of an inclusive elementary school. *Journal of the Association for Persons with Severe Handicaps, 18,* 75-84.

Sarason, S.B. (1982). *The culture of the school and the problem of change.* Boston: Allyn & Bacon.

Schumm, J.S., & Vaughn, S. (1991). Making adaptations for mainstreamed students: General classroom teachers' perspectives. *Remedial and Special Education, 12,* 18-25.

Schumm, J.S., & Vaughn, S. (1992). Planning for mainstreamed special education students: Perceptions of general classroom teachers. *Exceptionality, 3,* 81-90.

Schumm, J.S., & Vaughn, S. (1995). Getting ready for inclusion. Is the stage set? *Learning Disabilities Research and Practice, 10,* 169-179.

Schumm, J.S., Vaughn, S., Gordon, J., & Rothlein, L. (1994). General education teachers' beliefs, skills, and practices in planning for mainstreamed students with learning disabilities. *Teacher Education and Special Education, 17,* 22-37.

Schumm, J.S., Vaughn, S., Haager, D., McDowell, J., Rothlein, L., & Saumell, L. (1995). General education teacher planning: What can students with learning disabilities expect? *Exceptional Children, 61,* 335-352.

Scott, B.J., Vitale, M.R., & Masten, W.G. (1998). Implementing instructional adaptations for students with disabilities in inclusive classrooms: A literature review. *Remedial and Special Education, 19,* 106-119.

Scruggs, T.E., & Mastropieri, M.A. (1996). Teacher perceptions of mainstreaming/inclusion, 1958-1995: A research synthesis. *Exceptional Children, 63,* 59-74.

Semmel, M.I., Abernathy, T.V., Butera, G., & Lesar, S. (1991). Teacher perceptions of the Regular Education Initiative. *Exceptional Children, 58,* 9-24.

Semmel, M.I., Gerber, M.M., & MacMillan, D.L. (1994). Twenty-five years after Dunn's article: A legacy of policy analysis research in special education. *Journal of Special Education, 27,* 481-495.

Shadish, W.R. (1984). Policy research: Lessons from the implementation of deinstitutionalization. *American Psychologist, 39,* 725-738.

Shanker, A. (1994, February 6). Inclusion and ideology. *The New York Times,* p. E7.

Shanker, A. (1995). Full inclusion is neither free nor appropriate. *Educational Leadership, 52,* 18-21.

Shattuck, M. (1946). Segregation versus non-segregation of exceptional children. *Journal of Exceptional Children, 12,* 235-240.

Shepard, L.A. (1987). The new push for excellence: Widening the schism between regular and special education. *Exceptional Children, 53,* 327-329.

Shinn, M.R., Powell-Smith, K.A., Good, R.H., & Baker, S. (1997). The effects of reintegration into general education reading instruction for students with mild disabilities. *Exceptional Children, 64,* 59-79.

Shotel, J.R., Iano, R.P., & McGettigan, J.F. (1972). Teacher attitudes associated with the integration of handicapped children. *Exceptional Children, 38,* 677-683.

Simpson, R.G., & Eaves, R.C. (1985). Do we need more qualitative research or more good research? A reaction to Stainback and Stainback. *Exceptional Children, 51,* 325-329.

Skrtic, T.M. (1991). The special education paradox: Equity as the way to excellence. *Harvard Educational Review, 61,* 148-162.

Skrtic, T.M., Sailor, W., & Gee, K. (1996). Voice, collaboration, and inclusion: Democratic themes in educational and social reform initiatives. *Remedial and Special Education, 17,* 142-157.

Smith, S.W. (1990). Comparison of Individualized Education Programs (IEPs) of students with behavioral disorders and learning disabilities. *Journal of Special Education, 24,* 85-100.

Snell, M.E. (1991). Schools are for all kids: The importance of integration for students with severe disabilities and their peers. In J.W. Lloyd, A.C. Repp, & N.N. Singh (Eds.), *The Regular Education Initiative: Alternative perspectives on concepts, issues, and models* (pp. 133-138). Sycamore, IL: Sycamore.

Sobsey, D., & Dreimanis, M. (1993). Integration outcomes: Theoretical models and empirical investigations. *Developmental Disabilities Bulletin, 21,* 1-14.

Sokal, A., & Bricmont, A. (1998). *Fashionable nonsense: Postmodern intellectuals' abuse of science.* New York: St. Martin's Press.

Soodak, L.C., Podell, D.M., & Lehman, L.R. (1998). Teacher, student, and school attributes as predictors of teachers' responses to inclusion. *Journal of Special Education, 31,* 480-497.

Sowell, T. (1995). *The vision of the anointed: Self-congratulation as a basis for social policy.* New York: Basic Books.

Sowell, T. (1999). *The quest for cosmic justice.* New York: Free Press.

SRI International. (1993). *Transversing the mainstream: Regular education and students with disabilities in secondary school.* Menlo Park, CA: Author.

Stainback, S., & Stainback, W. (1984a). Broadening the research perspective in special education. *Exceptional Children, 51,* 400-408.

Stainback, S., & Stainback, W. (1984b). A rationale for the merger of special and regular education. *Exceptional Children, 51,* 102-111.

Stainback, S., & Stainback, W. (1987). Integration versus cooperation: A commentary on "Educating children with learning problems: A shared responsibility." *Exceptional Children, 54,* 66-68.

Stainback, S., & Stainback, W. (1989). Integration of students with mild and moderate handicaps. In D.K. Lipsky & A. Gartner (Eds.), *Beyond separate education: Quality education for all* (pp. 41-52). Baltimore: Brookes.

Stainback, S., & Stainback, W. (1992). *Curriculum considerations in inclusive classrooms: Facilitating learning for all students.* Baltimore, MD: Brookes.

Stainback, S., Stainback, W., & Forest, M. (1989). *Educating all students in the mainstream of regular education.* Baltimore, MD: Brookes.

Stainback, S., Stainback, W., Strathe, M., & Dedrick, C. (1983). Preparing regular classroom teachers for the integration of severely handicapped students: An experimental study. *Education and Training of the Mentally Retarded, 18,* 205-209.

Stainback, W., & Stainback, S. (1991). Rationale for integration and restructuring: A synopsis. In J.W. Lloyd, A.C. Repp, & N.N. Singh (Eds.), *The Regular Education Initiative: Alternative perspectives on concepts, issues, and models* (pp. 225-239). Sycamore, IL: Sycamore.

Stephens, T.M., & Braun, B.L. (1980). Measures of regular classroom teachers' attitudes toward handicapped children. *Exceptional Children, 46,* 292-294.

Tapasak, R.C., & Walther-Thomas, C.S. (1999). Evaluation of a first-year inclusion program: Student perceptions and classroom performance. *Remedial and Special Education, 20,* 216-225.

Taylor, B.R. (1994). Inclusion: Time for a change--A response to Margaret N. Carr. *Journal for Learning Disabilities, 27,* 579-580.

Taylor, S. (1988). Caught in the continuum: A critical analysis of the principle of the least restrictive environment. *Journal of the Association for Persons with Severe Handicaps, 13,* 41-53.

Thomas, S.B., & Rapport, M.J.K. (1998). Least restrictive environment: Understanding the direction of the courts. *Journal of Special Education, 32,* 66-78.

Thompson, R.H., Vitale, P.A., & Jewett, J.P. (1984). Teacher-student interaction patterns in full-inclusion classrooms. *Remedial and Special Education, 5,* 51-61.

Towfighy-Hooshyar, N., & Zingle, H.W. (1984). Regular class students: Attitudes toward integrated multiply handicapped peers. *American Journal of Mental Deficiency, 88,* 630-637.

Turner, B.S. (Ed.). (1990). *Theories of modernity and postmodernity.* Newbury Park, CA: Sage.

U.S. Department of Education. (1997). *Nineteenth annual report to Congress on the implementation of the Individuals with Disabilities Education Act.* Washington, DC: U. S. Government Printing Office.

Urbach, P. (1974a). Progress and degeneration in the "IQ debate"--Part I. *British Journal for the Philosophy of Science, 25,* 99-135.

Urbach, P. (1974b). Progress and degeneration in the "IQ debate"--Part II. *British Journal for the Philosophy of Science, 25,* 235-259.

Vaughn, S., Elbaum, B.E., & Schumm, J.S. (1996). The effects of inclusion on the social functioning of students with learning disabilities. *Journal of Learning Disabilities, 29,* 598-608.

Vaughn, S., & Klingner, J.K. (1998). Students' perceptions of inclusion and resource room settings. *Journal of Special Education, 32,* 79-88.

Vaughn, S., & Schumm, J.S. (1994). Middle school teachers' planning for students with learning disabilities. *Remedial and Special Education, 15,* 152-161.

Vaughn, S., Schumm, J.S., Jallad, B., Slusher, J., & Saumell, L. (1996). Teachers' views of inclusion. *Learning Disabilities Research and Practice, 11,* 96-106.

Vaughn, S., Schumm, J.S., & Kouzekanani, K. (1993). What do students with learning disabilities think when their general education teachers make adaptations? *Journal of Learning Disabilities, 26,* 545-555.

Vaughn, S., Schumm, J.S., Niharos, F., & Daugherty, T. (1993). What do students think when teachers make adaptations? *Teaching and Teacher Education, 9,* 107-118.

Verstegen, D.A. (1996). Integrating services and resources for children under the Individuals with Disabilities Education Act (IDEA): Federal perspectives and issues. *Journal of Education Finance, 21,* 477-505.

Villa, R., Thousand, J., Stainback, W., & Stainback, S. (Eds.). (1992). *Restructuring for caring and effective education.* Baltimore, MD: Brookes.

Villa, R.A., Thousand, J.S., Meyers, H., & Nevin, A. (1996). Teacher and administrator perceptions of heterogeneous education. *Exceptional Children, 63,* 29-45.

Voeltz, L. (1980). Children's attitudes toward handicapped peers. *American Journal of Mental Deficiency, 84,* 455-464.

Wade, P., & Garguilo, R.M. (1989-90). Public school administrators concerns with implementing the least restrictive environment provision of Public Law 94-142. *National Forum of Special Education Journal, 1,* 59-66.

Waldron, N.L., & McLeskey, J. (1998). The effects of an inclusive school program on students with mild and severe learning disabilities. *Exceptional Children, 64,* 395-405.

Walther-Thomas, C.S. (1997). Co-teaching experiences: The benefits and problems that teachers and principals report over time. *Journal of Learning Disabilities, 30,* 395-407.

Wang, M.C., & Baker, E.T. (1985-86). Mainstreaming programs: Design features and effects. *Journal of Special Education, 19,* 504-521.

Wang, M.C., & Birch, J.W. (1984a). Comparison of a full-time mainstreaming program and a resource room approach. *Exceptional Children, 51,* 33-40.

Wang, M.C., & Birch, J.W. (1984b). Effective special education in regular classes. *Exceptional Children, 50,* 391-398.

Wang, M.C., Gennari, P., & Waxman, H.C. (1985). The Adaptive Learning Environments Model: Design, implementation, and effects. In M C. Wang & H.J. Walberg (Eds.), *Adapting instruction to individual differences* (pp. 191-235). Berkeley, CA: McCutchan.

Wang, M.C., Peverly, S., & Randolph, R. (1984). An investigation of the implementation and effects of a full-time mainstreaming program. *Remedial and Special Education, 5,* 21-32.

Wang, M.C., Reynolds, M.C., & Walberg, H.J. (1986). Rethinking special education. *Educational Leadership, 44,* 26-31.

Wang, M.C., Reynolds, M.C., & Walberg, H.J. (1988). Integrating children of the second system. *Phi Delta Kappan, 70,* 248-251.

Wang, M.C., Rubenstein, J.L., & Reynolds, M.C. (1985). Clearing the road to success for students with special needs. *Educational Leadership, 43,* 62-67.

Wang, M.C., & Walberg, H.J. (1983). Adaptive instruction and classroom time. *American Educational Research Journal, 20,* 601-626.

Wang, M.C., & Walberg, H.J. (1988). Four fallacies of segregationism. *Exceptional Children, 55,* 128-137.

Weigel, R.H., Wiser, P.L., & Cook, S.W. (1975). The impact of cooperative learning experiences on cross-ethnic relations and attitudes. *Journal of Social Issues, 31,* 219-244.

Weintraub, F.J., Abeson, A., Ballard, J., & LaVor, M. (Eds.). (1976). *Public policy and the education of exceptional children.* Reston, VA: Council for Exceptional Children.

Welch, M. (1989). A cultural perspective and the second wave of educational reform. *Journal of Learning Disabilities, 22,* 537-540, 560.

Werts, M.G., Wolery, M., Snyder, E.D., Caldwell, N.K., & Salisbury, C.L. (1996). Supports and resources associated with inclusive schooling: Perceptions of elementary school teachers about need and availability. *The Journal of Special Education, 30,* 187-203.

Wiederholt, J.L., & Chamberlain, S.P. (1989). A critical analysis of resource programs. *Remedial and Special Education, 10,* 15-37.

Wigle, S.E., & Wilcox, D.J. (1996). Inclusion: Criteria for the preparation of education personnel. *Remedial and Special Education, 17,* 323-328.

Whinnery, K.W., Fuchs, L.S., & Fuchs, D. (1991). General, special, and remedial teachers' acceptance of behavioral and instructional strategies for mainstreaming students with mild handicaps. *Remedial and Special Education, 12,* 6-17.

Wilczenski, F. (1993). Changes in attitudes toward mainstreaming among undergraduate education students. *Educational Research Quarterly, 17,* 5-17.

Will, M.C. (1986). Educating children with learning problems: A shared responsibility. *Exceptional Children, 52,* 411-416.

Wolfensberger, W. (1994). A personal interpretation of the mental retardation scene in light of the "signs of the times." *Mental Retardation, 32,* 19-33.

Yell, M.L. (1992). School reform and special education: A legal analysis. *Preventing School Failure, 36,* 25-28.

Yell, M.L. (1995). Least restrictive environment, inclusion, and students with disabilities: A legal analysis. *Journal of Special Education, 28,* 389-404.

York, J., Vandercook, T., MacDonald, C., Hiese-Neff, C., & Caughey, E. (1992). Feedback about integrating middle-school students with severe disabilities in general education classes. *Exceptional Children, 58,* 244-258.

Ysseldyke, J.E., Thurlow, M.L., Wotruba, J.W., & Nania, P.A. (1990). Instructional arrangements: Perceptions from general education. *Teaching Exceptional Children, 22,* 4-7.

Yuker, H.E. (Ed.). (1988). *Attitudes toward persons with disabilities.* New York: Springer-Verlag.

Zettel, J.J., & Ballard, J. (1986). The education for all handicapped children act of 1975 (P.L. 94-142): Its history, origins, and concepts. In J. Ballard, B.A. Ramirez, & F.J. Weintraub (Eds.), *Special education in America: Its legal and governmental foundations* (pp. 11-22). Reston, VA: Council for Exceptional Children.

Zigmond, N. (1997). Educating students with disabilities: The future of special education. In J. Lloyd, E. Kameenui, & D. Chard (Eds.), *Issues in educating students with disabilities* (pp. 377-390). Mahwah, NJ: Erlbaum.

Zigmond, N., & Baker, J.M. (1994). Is the mainstream a more appropriate educational setting for Randy? A case study of one student with learning disabilities. *Learning Disabilities Research and Practice, 9,* 108-117.

Zigmond, N., Jenkins, J.R., Fuchs, L.S., Deno, S., Fuchs, D., Baker, J.M., Jenkins, L., & Couthino, M. (1995). Special education in restructured schools: Findings from three multi-year studies. *Phi Delta Kappan, 76,* 531-541.

Zirkel, P. (1996). Inclusion: Return of the pendulum? *The Special Educator, 12,* 1, 5.

CO-TEACHING AND THE MODEL OF SHARED RESPONSIBILITY: WHAT DOES THE RESEARCH SUPPORT?

Margaret P. Weiss and Frederick J. Brigham

ABSTRACT

Co-teaching is a frequently employed option for special education service delivery that involves special education and general education teachers working together in various ways. In this paper, we summarize the empirical literature regarding several features related to co-teaching. From an original pool of over seven hundred documents related to co-teaching, we were able to identify only 23 that actually provided some sort of evaluative or interpretative data. The findings suggest that co-teaching is an option that is highly variable in the way it is implemented and is used more often than it is evaluated. Reports of satisfaction with the model are most often based on teacher-satisfaction data not related to student outcome measures, and successful implementation of co-teaching appears to be related to variables that are often beyond the control of the school (e.g., preexisting friendships among teachers). We conclude that co-teaching is a potentially useful strategy for service delivery that may be appropriate for some students with certain teachers in some schools. The data available to date does not, how-

Advances in Learning and Behavioral Disabilities, Volume 14, pages 217-245.
Copyright © 2000 by JAI Press Inc.
All rights of reproduction in any form reserved.
ISBN: 0-7623-0561-4

ever, justify large-scale restructuring of special education programs in favor of co-teaching over other service delivery options.

INTRODUCTION

Across the United States, educational reform has become a topic of intense political and popular press interest. According to the U.S. Department of Education (1994), only 13% of high school graduates earned the recommended number of units in English, science, social studies, and math; 33% of students were enrolled in remedial math courses; and 11% of sophomores in 1980 left high school by 1982 without a degree. Many broad-based attempts to reform education followed: Goals 2000, outcome-based education, and high stakes testing. Each reform attempted to increase the accountability of schools to produce well-prepared students. Thus, current educational reforms related to achievement seek to increase the homogeneity of school outcomes.

In 1995, the total percentage of minority students in schools was 35%, up from 24% in 1976 (U.S. Department of Education, 1998). In 1993-1994, 46% of all public schools had students of limited English proficiency. Forty-four percent of all schools provided bilingual or English-as-a-second-language instruction, up from 40% in 1987-88 (U.S. Department of Education, 1997). In 1996, the number of students receiving special education services was 5,500,000, up from 3,700,000 in 1977 (U.S. Department of Education, 1998). Schools are struggling to find effective structures and practices that will meet the demands of the public and the needs of this changing student population.

Reform efforts in special education have placed a greater number of students with disabilities in the general education classroom at both the elementary and secondary levels. Comparing data from the *Annual Reports to Congress on the Implementation of the Individuals with Disabilities Education Act* (IDEA) for 1988-89 and 1994-95, McLeskey, Henry, and Hodges (1998) concluded, "there has been a gradual increase over the past six years in the cumulative placement rate for students with disabilities who are placed in general education classrooms, from 30 of 1,000 identified students in 1988-89 to 48 of 1,000 in 1994-95, representing an increase of 60%" (p. 7). Additionally, some advocates have called for an increased sharing of responsibility between general and special educators for students with disabilities (e.g., Will, 1986). To provide support for the necessary instructional change in general education, schools have had to restructure their service delivery models so that special educators move with their students into the general education framework, redefine professional roles, drop professional labels, and establish a collaborative teaming process (Thousand & Villa, 1989). The instructional partnerships between special and regular education exist under the umbrella term of collaboration and include co-teaching.

Evolving from the interdisciplinary team teaching ideas of the 1960s and 1970s, the term co-teaching refers to cooperative teaching, collaborative teaching, collaborative instruction, or team teaching. Bauwens, Hourcade, and Friend (1989) define co-teaching as "an educational approach in which general and special educators work in a coactive and coordinated fashion to jointly teach academically and behaviorally heterogeneous groups of students in educationally integrated settings" (p. 18). Proponents argue that co-teaching is an effective use of the specific and unique skills each professional brings to the classroom. In a co-taught classroom, "teachers strive to create a classroom community in which all students are valued members, and they develop innovative teaching strategies that would not be possible if only one teacher was present (Friend, Reising, & Cook, 1993, p. 6.). According to the National Center for Educational Restructuring and Inclusion (1995), schools use co-teaching more often than other models to implement their inclusion programs.

Much has been written about the effective implementation of co-teaching in schools. The ERIC and University of Virginia (VIRGO) library databases identified 272 articles and 38 books with the keywords collaboration, co-teach, or co-teach and special education. Many of these articles and books provide definitions of co-teaching and include step-by-step guidelines for its implementation without mention of research supporting its use. As with any educational reform, there are a number of questions that must be asked about a new process or structure. Is there a consensus in definition of the structure? What components are necessary in the theoretical model? Is the structure practical for implementation in public school contexts? Proponents of co-teaching have addressed these questions in numerous descriptions, outlines, and manuals for co-teaching. Also, researchers must address questions of actions and outcomes. What do teachers actually do in this structure? Is this structure effective for students with disabilities in general or for students with specific disabilities? What impact does the structure have on schools, teachers, students, and parents? Is this structure an appropriate use of resources? Research to date indicates that the impact of co-teaching on teachers and their relationships has been studied extensively but few other questions have been addressed. In this review, we summarize the current database on co-teaching by research question, discuss the limitations of this research, and present questions for further study.

STUDY IDENTIFICATION AND SELECTION

We completed a systematic search for original research studies on co-teaching, using ERIC, PsycLit, and Dissertation Abstracts International databases from 1966 to 1998. For keywords, we used co-teach, co-teaching, collaborative instruction, collaboration, and cooperative teaching with the wildcard feature for all forms of each term. Also, we combined collaboration and cooperative teaching with special education. Reference lists from studies and position papers were then used to identify additional sources. Finally, we searched the following journals by hand for the years 1998 and 1999: *Teacher Education and Special Education, Remedial and Special Education, Journal of Learning Disabilities, Remedial and Special Education, Learning Disabilities Research and Practice, Exceptional Children, Teaching Exceptional Children, Journal of Special Education, Intervention in School and Clinic,* and *Preventing School Failure.* This search yielded approximately 350 journal articles about co-teaching and collaboration and an equal number of dissertations.

Inclusion Criteria

We included articles or dissertations in this review if they were reports of original research evaluating co-teaching or collaborative teaching relationships between in-service special education teachers and in-service general education teachers. This review excludes studies of co-teaching between teachers and speech language or other related service personnel as well as co-teaching in pre-service programs. Also, this review excludes opinion or "how-to" papers. Although opinion and descriptive papers made up the bulk of the articles we found, they did not match the criteria we established for inclusion in this review. Specifically, the criteria for including a paper in this review included: (a) inclusion of some form of evaluation or interpretation of data collected, not just program description; (b) co-teaching as the subject of evaluation, not as a part of a larger inclusion project described in the article; and (c) the study took place in the United States. All included studies defined co-teaching or collaboration as special educators working within the general education classroom in a teaching capacity. We excluded studies that defined co-teaching or collaboration as consultation between special and general education teachers only. Finally, we excluded ERIC documents and books because the studies in these sources are not subjected to peer review. After applying these criteria, we had a corpus of 23 studies, 3% of all titles found.

Coded Variables

We coded each study according to the variables that most clearly described the nature of the classroom, the participants in the study, the activities engaged in by the teachers and the students, and the outcomes measured. The variables coded for each study are displayed in Table 1.

Characteristics of Included Studies

The 23 studies that met the criteria included eight quantitative studies and 15 qualitative studies. Nineteen of the studies were published in professional jour-

Table 1. Coded Variables

- Author
- Type of study
- Research design
- Research question
- Grade level
- Students
- Special educator
- General educator
- Content area
- Dependent variable or data source
- Training
- Impetus for program
- Planning time
- Results

---

nals and four were dissertations. We identified three other dissertations as potentially relevant but we were unable to obtain copies of them. The studies were published from 1987 to 1999, with eight studies published from 1997 to 1999. Three studies included a single teaching pair, 17 included more than one teaching pair, and three did not indicate pairs but rather general and special educators who participated in co-teaching. Nine studies were conducted at the elementary level, five at middle school, three at high school, two combined elementary and middle, and three combined middle and high school. One study did not state grade levels (see Table 2).

RESULTS

The studies included in this review addressed five general categories of research questions about co-teaching: (a) how are programs evaluated by participants; (b) what are the teacher perceptions of roles; (c) what are teacher perceptions of the process and impact of co-teaching; (d) is co-teaching special education; and (e) what do teachers do during instruction in co-taught classrooms? The results related to each of these questions are summarized in the following sections.

Program Evaluations

Five papers that described program evaluations met the criteria for inclusion in this review. The program evaluation reports were published in education journals between 1987 and 1996. No dissertations were included in the program evaluation section.

Table 2. Studies Included

Authors	Year Published	Research Question	Grade Level
Adams & Cessna	1993	What are the metaphors of a co-taught classroom?	none stated
Baker	1995(a)	What are the special education services received by students in co-taught classrooms in Minnesota?	2, 6
Baker	1995(b)	What are the special education services received by students in co-taught classrooms in Virginia?	3, 5
Boudah, Schumacher, & Deshler	1997	Whether the CI model influenced teacher performance, student engagement, and academic outcomes?	6, 7, 8, 10
Flicek, Olsen, Chivers, Kaufman, & Anderson	1996	Whether CCM influenced parent satisfaction and student performance?	4, 5
Harris, Harvey, Garcia, Innes, Lynn, Munoz, Sexton, & Stoica	1987	How does co-teaching meet the needs of high school students with disabilities?	high
Hines	1995	What are the instructional and noninstructional time expenditures of general educators in co-taught, mainstream, and regular classrooms?	6-8
Johnston	1994	Whether the co-teaching program in this middle school was successful?	4, 5, 6
Karge, McClure, & Patton,	1995	Whether middle and junior high schools are using collaborative models and how?	6-8, 7-8
Newman	1997	How do high school teachers implement a collaborative team teaching model?	high
Norris	1997	What are teachers' perceptions of co-teaching in an inclusive classroom in middle school?	middle
Nowacek	1992	How do teachers implement co-teaching?	middle high
Phillips, Sapona, & Lubic	1995	How do teachers implement co-teaching and how does it evolve?	elementary
Salend, Johansen, Mumper, Chase, Pike, & Dorney	1997	What is the impact of co-teaching on teachers?	kindergarten

(continued)

Table 2. (Continued)

Authors	Year Published	Research Question	Grade Level
Trent	1998	What are the difficulties and complexities faced by a general education secondary social studies teacher who agrees to collaborate with special educators?	11
Voltz, Elliott, & Cobb	1994	What are the similarities and differences in special education and general education teachers' perceptions of roles in collaboration?	elementary
Walther-Thomas	1997	What are the benefits and problems over time of implementing co-teaching?	elementary middle
Walther-Thomas & Carter	1993	Whether the co-teaching program in this middle school was successful?	8
Weiss	1999	What are the actions of secondary special educators in co-taught and special education classrooms?	Middle High school
Wiedmeyer, & Lehman	1991	Whether the co-teaching program in this middle school was successful?	8
Wood	1998	What are the teachers' feelings of obligation, responsibility, and commitment to educational goals for inclusion and what are the barriers?	elementary
Zigmond	1995(a)	What are the special education services received by students in co-taught classrooms in Kansas?	2, 5
Zigmond	1995(b)	What are the special education services received by students in co-taught classrooms in Pennsylvania?	2, 5

Walther-Thomas and Carter (1993) and Wiedmeyer and Lehman (1991) conducted surveys to evaluate the implementation of a co-teaching model in middle schools. Walther-Thomas and Carter (1993) surveyed all students and teachers and interviewed special education teachers and students in the co-teaching program at the end of the year. The co-teaching program was implemented in a civics class of ten students without disabilities and nine students with learning disabilities (LD), a science class with 14 students without disabilities and seven students with LD, and an exploratory foreign language class with nine students without disabilities and six students with LD. The special educator co-taught in civics for the entire school year, foreign language for nine weeks at the end of the school year, and in science for the entire second semester. Participation in co-teaching was voluntary for all teachers and the special educator had individual and team planning time with her co-teachers.

The authors reported that "daily assignments and unit test scores in the co-taught class were comparable to those in the other civics classes" and "daily assignment and test score averages for the year ranged from 70-89% for students with disabilities" in the civics class (Walther-Thomas & Carter, 1993, p. 36). In science, "special education students' grade averages ranged from C to A on daily work and quizzes" (p. 36) and in foreign language, the daily assignment and weekly quiz averages for students with learning disabilities ranged from 77-96%. Students receiving special education stated that they liked having the special educator in the classroom and that it helped them enough so that other students in the class did not even know they had disabilities. All students reported that the two teachers were equals in the classroom and that the special educator primarily taught strategies for learning. Of the civics students, 84% said they received more help and their grades were better. Ninety-three percent of the foreign language students and 71% of the science students said that the special education teacher's presence improved the instruction in their classes. Approximately 62% of science students said they received higher grades because of the special educator's presence. General education teachers reported improved class averages, improved instruction, and improved student behavior with the special educator's help. They developed new skills in strategy instruction and content presentation. Special educators stated that students with disabilities improved in their behavior and written work and that they were able to develop rapport with general education students. There was no indication of how many general education students were involved in this survey nor was there documentation of actual student grade or work changes.

Wiedmeyer and Lehman (1991) conducted a survey of parents, teachers, and students after the first year of implementation of a co-teaching program at the eighth grade level, with three general educators and one special educator. Teachers had common team planning times but the authors gave no information about who began program implementation or whether the teachers received any training. All four teachers indicated "100% agreement that the collaborative teaching program was a viable alternative to the pull-out program" (p. 9). The teachers stated that the students with learning disabilities had a chance to try the mainstream and could be part of the eighth grade. Ninety-five percent of the parents of the students with LD indicated they were happy with the changes in student grades, attitude toward school, and self-concept. Ninety-two percent of students had positive comments, including feeling better about themselves and school. Finally, eight of the 15 students with LD made the B honor roll all four quarters, and none received a failing grade in co-taught classes. The authors stated that these grades were higher than their grades in similar content courses the previous year without co-teaching, though no specifics about those programs or grades were given.

Flicek, Olsen, Chivers, Kaufman, and Anderson (1996) implemented a model of co-teaching for nine students with LD and emotional or behavioral disorders (EBD) in a general education classroom of 19 students without disabilities. This model included co-teaching of academic and social skills by a general educator and a special education resource teacher, university support for teachers, and a school-based teacher assistance team. The students were in fourth and fifth grade and the classes included all content areas and social skills instruction. Parents and students completed surveys using a Likert scale to rank their satisfaction with the program. The parent scale had a reliability coefficient of .72 and the student .80. The authors also compared the year-end scores of students with disabilities on the Stanford Achievement Test with their scores from the previous year and they examined the students' behavior report cards.

For parents, the answers to six items were combined into a Parent Satisfaction Score, ranging from a low of one to a high of five. Parents of students without disabilities gave an average rating of 3.96 (SD = 1.0), parents of students with LD gave a rating of 3.63 (SD = 1.16), and parents with students with EBD gave a rating of 4.89 (SD = 0.06). All of these scores were in the high to very high range of satisfaction, according to the authors. The scale for students included seven items and the average was the Student Satisfaction Score, ranging from a low of three to a high of one. Students without disabilities gave an average rating of 1.54 (SD = 0.45), students with LD gave a rating of 1.71 (SD = 0.44), and students with EBD gave a rating of 1.81 (SD = 0.33). The average for students without disabilities was in the high range but the scores for students with disabilities were in the neutral range. For standardized test outcomes, the authors used matched pairs *t* tests to compare year-end scores. There was a statistically significant increase in the math NCE on the Stanford Achievement Test but no other significant differences, and no significant differences in grade point averages were reported. Flicek et al. (1996) reported that students with EBD improved significantly in their behavior reports and were functioning well above average on overall behavior scores in the classroom though no evidence was given to support this conclusion.

Johnston (1994) briefly described a program of co-teaching at the 4th to 6th grade levels and its evaluation. This study involved two special educators and six general educators who worked with students with LD. Two special educators taught within six general education classrooms for a total of 110 minutes per day. Each special educator was split between three general education teachers and classrooms. The teachers all had common planning time and the administration provided substitutes for the teams once a grading period for planning activities. The administration asked teachers to volunteer for the program and the teachers participated in conferences and direct training in co-teaching. The author reported scores from the Virginia Literacy Passport test, Iowa Test of Basic Skills (ITBS), Self-esteem Index, and multi-dimensional self-concept scale, along with peer ratings, number of discipline referrals, student reports, and teacher questionnaires as dependent measures. Student participation in collaborative or non-collaborative classrooms was the independent variable.

Johnston reported that students with LD in collaborative classrooms outscored those in noncollaborative classrooms on all tests. In addition, non-disabled students in collaborative classrooms outscored nondisabled students in noncollaborative classrooms in seven of eight areas on the ITBS. Students with LD and students without disabilities scored higher on both self-esteem instruments than peers in noncollaborative classrooms. Students in collaborative classrooms showed a broader level of acceptance by peers than those in noncollaborative classrooms. The number of students with LD sent to the office for behavior dropped by 59% from the previous year. Teacher questionnaires indicated that there was an increased concern for effective communication between special education and regular education teachers and there was an increased sense of shared responsibility for students. Finally, Johnston (1994) stated that there were an unprecedented number of nondisabled student and parent requests for placement in a collaborative classroom. However, the author gave no evidence for how these conclusions were reached or whether they were statistically significant.

Harris et al. (1987) described and evaluated a co-teaching and consultation program in a high school. Eighteen regular educators worked with special educators in a co-teaching arrangement in Basic Math and Freshman Studies (English). The special educators viewed their roles as support to the regular educator. They were responsible for team and small group instruction, behavior management, and curriculum modification. Administrators chose regular educators to participate.

Harris et al. (1987) administered questionnaires to evaluate this program from both teachers' and students' perspectives. Sixty-four percent of the special education students and 73% of the general education teachers completed the survey. The Likert scale items had a One (negative response) to Seven (positive response) range. When asked whether students liked having the special educator in the regular class, the mean response was 4.06. When asked if their grades and behavior were better than last year, mean student responses were 4.61 and 5.57, respectively. The authors asked general educators how they felt about having special educators in their classrooms. Their average response was 5.46. When asked if having the special educator in the classroom affected achievement and behavior of students, the general education teachers' mean responses were 4.13 and 4.43, respectively.

In addition, Harris et al. (1987) compared mean report card grades of regular education students to special education students in the co-taught English and math courses. On a 4.0 scale, report card grade averages were 1.73 for regular education students in English and 2.02 for special education students. In math, regular education students averaged 1.34 and special education students averaged 1.72. In all cases, citizenship grades were in the "needs improvement" range. Although few differences were found between students with and without disabilities in this report, the educational outcomes noted would hardly be considered acceptable under current reform initiatives calling for increased achievement and higher standards for behavior. It is unclear whether or not the similarities between the student achievement scores would be obtained when the general education students demonstrated greater academic proficiency.

Summary of Program Evaluation Reports

Five reports of program evaluations published between 1987 and 1996 were located for this review. All of the reports were conducted with students in grades four through nine. One study included students with EBD; the remaining studies focused on students with LD. Most of the data reported was in the form of parent, teacher, or student satisfaction with co-teaching as measured by a variety of survey instruments. These reports were uniform in reporting satisfaction on the part of the participants. Further, students with disabilities reported that they felt better accepted when they attended co-taught classes than when they were receiving more traditional models of service delivery.

Achievement data were present in only three of the program evaluation reports. Comparisons of students in co-taught and more traditional models was provided in only one study. Co-taught students out-performed their more traditionally instructed peers on seven of eight academic measures included in the study. However, questions regarding the assignment of students to the experimental condition make it impossible to interpret this finding in favor of the co-teaching model. Two other studies included achievement data. In one, the scores of students in co-taught classes were compared to their own scores from the previous year's administration of the Stanford Achievement Test. Only math scores improved from one year to the next. In the other study reporting achievement data, the grades of students with disabilities in a co-taught class were not significantly different from their classmates without disabilities; however, the achievement of the students without disabilities was mediocre at best.

Although the participants in these studies were generally satisfied with co-teaching, they represent a very small number of teachers, parents, and students.

The findings presented here suggest that most participants will be pleased with the interpersonal aspects of co-teaching but that the academic outcomes are likely to be mixed. Whether or not the personal satisfaction will continue in the absence of stronger academic outcomes remains an open question. In the next section, we turn to the perception of roles and responsibilities held by teachers participating in co-teaching programs.

Teacher Perceptions of Roles

Only two reports that provided data regarding the perception of the roles of participants in co-teaching were located in the literature reviewed in this study. The studies by Karge, McClure, and Patton (1995) and Voltz, Elliott, and Cobb (1994) both used surveys to identify the perceptions teachers, general and special, had of their roles in schools that used collaborative models.

Karge et al. (1995) asked special education resource teachers at the middle school level to give descriptions of their collaborative models and demographics of their school, using a survey of specific demographic questions and ten Likert-style questions about collaboration. The authors stated that they had piloted the survey before using it but no other information was given. Of the 200 teachers contacted, 93 teachers (46% response rate) returned usable surveys. Most teachers responded that they used their preparation periods during the school day to plan for collaborative teaching, but that much of it was done on a "catch as you can" basis (p. 83). Eighty-six percent of the teachers indicated that they spent 40% of their week collaborating and that the administration pushed them into it. Fifty-three percent ($n = 48$) of teachers participated in co-teaching, 62% ($n = 53$) did modifications for the classroom, and 54% ($n = 49$) tutored students in the general education classroom. Seventy-one percent ($n = 64$) liked the combination of consultation, collaboration, and pullout but 22% ($n = 20$) preferred consultation and 4% ($n = 4$) preferred pullout. Teachers indicated that the general educator's attitude was the most important factor to success or failure of a collaborative partnership. When ranking statements of roles, special educators ranked the statements "general educators know they must do this" and "full inclusion can work" highest and "training is provided" and "adequate amount of time to prepare" as lowest.

Voltz et al. (1994) compared the role perceptions of elementary teachers of students with LD and regular elementary teachers in collaboration. Eighty-three of 100 resource teachers and 64 of 100 general educators with between four and 17 years of experience responded to the Special Education Teacher-General Education Teacher Interaction Scale. The questionnaire included statements of 22 roles for special educators and seven roles for general educators. Authors asked teachers to rate each statement as "often or always done" (always = 1) to "never or seldom done" (never = 5) in both real situations and in ideal situations. The reliability coefficient for the scale was .87 for actual and .92 for ideal.

Over 60% of resource teachers responded that they always exchanged student progress information, shared testing information, provided input for grades, conducted joint parent conferences, and provided instruction in special education settings. The majority of general education teachers "failed to indicate that resource teachers performed any of the 22 roles often or always" (p. 529). Fifty-six percent of general educators indicated that special educators never met with them to develop instructional plans, 51% said they never coordinated instructional material, 81% said they never observed special education students in the general education classroom, 56% said they never suggested effective material and strategies, 70% said they never supplied special learning materials, 92% said they never team taught, 68% said they never directed small group instruction in general education, and 67% said they never planned for the transfer of skills from special education to general education. Special educators agreed that they never directed small group instruction in general education and that they did not team-teach. Fifty-nine percent of special educators even responded that in the ideal situation, they would never direct small group instruction in the general education classroom or team-teach! Moreover, 57% of general educators agreed that, even in an ideal situation, special educators should not team-teach. According to both groups, general educators were responsible for observing special education students in special education classrooms and special educators thought they should coordinate their material with resource material. Both groups said that lack of scheduling provisions and lack of time due to instructional responsibilities were major constraints to collaboration in any form (Voltz et al., 1994).

Summary of Teacher Perception of Roles Reports

The studies described in this section provide information from 241 general and special education teachers engaged in co-teaching. Both groups report responsibilities for modification of classroom materials and observation of student progress in general education classrooms were clearly roles to be fulfilled by special education teachers. Additionally, both groups of teachers reported that lack of common planning time and resources were the major impediments to successful co-teaching. Special education teachers were, however, divided in their evaluation of the appropriateness of their teaching individuals or small groups in the general education setting. Some teachers stated that they already did such teaching and were satisfied with the practice. Others reported that they did little teaching in general education classrooms. A substantial number of the special education teachers responding to the surveys reported here indicated that they believed that they should have no direct instructional responsibility in the general education classroom. Special education teachers cited the attitude of the general educator as the most crucial factor for success of co-teaching models. Although general education teachers indicated perceptions of role responsibility that were similar to their colleagues in special education, they reported that special education teachers almost never fulfilled these roles.

Clearly, the data presented here are too limited to generalize to the population of co-teachers as a whole. However, the data suggests at least one serious potential problem in implementation of co-teaching. Special education teachers view the attitude of general educators as most important in co-teaching while general educators view the efforts of special educators as insufficient to the tasks presented in co-teaching. Both perceptions are probably partially correct. General educators are charged with a different mission than special educators. Special educators often do not have the time and resources to carry out their roles as they desire. Failure to acknowledge the legitimate constraints faced by each party in the co-teaching setting will certainly limit the attractiveness and viability of this service-delivery model.

Teacher Perceptions of the Co-teaching Process

Eight of the nine studies reviewed in this section employed qualitative research designs to investigate the perceptions of teachers involved in co-teaching situations regarding the various processes involved in co-teaching. They addressed the metaphors teachers use, the difficulties and complexities of implementing co-teaching, the feelings about and barriers for inclusion, and the benefits and problems of co-teaching over time.

Metaphors

Adams and Cessna (1993) gathered co-teachers in Colorado who were recommended by their supervisors for focus group discussions. The authors evaluated taped sessions using "grounded theory research and a qualitative process" (p. 28). They found teachers used three metaphors in talking about co-teaching. The first, Yin and Yang, describes how co-teaching "appreciates the uniqueness and honors the unity of two teachers" (p. 29). It combines the strengths of two competent and confident individuals in unique ways to enrich the instructional environment. According to the authors, in this metaphor, teachers have distinct roles within the classroom that are influenced by the content of the lesson, the instructional process, the group of students in the class, and the individual students.

The second metaphor, the dance, illustrates how teachers are equally responsible for what happens in the classroom. These teachers share the "gentle and tough roles" (p. 30), make important decisions together, and carry their part of the workload. The third metaphor, the particle and the stream, relates to the responsibility of the general educator to move the instruction forward at an appropriate pace (the stream) and the responsibility of the special education teacher to keep the individual students (the particles) from being pushed out of the stream or left behind and to support them in ways that will allow them to re-enter the stream as quickly as possible. The idea is that one teacher moves the class along so that students who experience difficulty do not stop or slow down the pace of instruction received by the other students in the class. No information about the experience of the teachers, the content areas or grade levels in which they taught, nor the amount and kind of instructional and administrative support that the teachers received was provided in the Adams and Cessna (1993) report.

Difficulties and Complexities of Co-teaching

Nowacek (1992), Phillips, Sapona, and Lubic (1995), Trent (1998), and Salend et al. (1997) all used naturalistic inquiry to explore the experiences of teaching pairs in implementing co-teaching at their schools. Nowacek (1992) interviewed a middle school pair of experienced teachers, a special educator and an English teacher who had co-taught together for two years. Nowacek's teachers reported that they had some inservice training and administrative support but that *they* asked the administration to begin the program. The teachers in this study reported that they had no common planning time. These teachers stated that they began the year by hand-scheduling students into the classroom, keeping the number of special education students in the class below 50%. They selected each other as collaborators because they knew that they were each strong teachers. The teachers in this study consistently reported that they did not want to partner with a marginal teacher. These teachers reported that their roles evolved, changing from class to class and day to day, as they grew more comfortable with each other. They planned how to meet problems together and they worked together to develop lessons, compromising and modifying their individual ideas. The teachers constantly monitored their program by talking to each other and making changes for students' needs. Pre- and post-tests of special education students in spelling showed that "all but one of Carol and Susan's special education students gained at least one year" (p. 270).

Nowacek (1992) also interviewed a special educator who had worked as a world history co-teacher and as a U.S. history co-teacher. The administration encouraged teachers to participate in collaboration and teachers were sent to observe co-taught classrooms before they began. The special educator had common planning time with the co-teacher the second year of the program but not the first. This teacher stated that her roles evolved throughout the year and that she did play a part in the learning process but not in delivering instruction. She helped plan lessons and modify them to meet student needs. However, in the second year, the teacher did not want to take on the role of the disciplinarian. Although the special educator indicated that she gained quite a bit of knowledge about the curriculum and the general education classroom, the special education teachers at the high school decided to use a consulting model the next year in order to be involved in a greater number of classrooms than was possible under the co-teaching model.

Phillips et al. (1995) interviewed ten of 12 teachers who worked together in collaboration, six general educators and four special educators, at the end of the first year of co-teaching in all content areas at the elementary level. The classes included students with LD, mild mental disabilities, and EBD. The administration strongly encouraged teachers to collaborate with one another. One special educator had had a workshop in co-teaching before the school year started and the other teachers participated in a workshop later in the year. The results of the interviews indicated that the teams went through seven stages in a cycle of development: (a) experiencing anxiety, (b) working out logistics, (c) determining classroom roles, (d) sharing planning and curriculum development, (e) recognizing and articulating the benefits of collaboration, (f) learning to recognize when a more restrictive setting may be appropriate, and (g) evaluating the overall effort (p. 265). These teachers expressed a great deal of anxiety because they lacked a definition of collaboration and they had a strong sense of being judged by the other teacher during daily instruction. Partners that worked together well developed a definition of collaboration that was for the benefit of students and they developed mutual trust throughout the year. All teachers felt they had the support of the principal although he was learning about co-teaching at the same time. There were problems with the special educator collaborating with more than one general educator and with trying not to overload classes with special education students. The teachers felt challenged by negotiating roles in the class and trying to figure out their partner's style of instruction. During the initial stages of co-teaching, much of the teachers' time was spent in planning, but as the teachers gained experience in co-teaching, they developed more efficient ways of organizing their time and making plans. The teachers developed a sense of trust to talk about things that were not working and how to make changes. They said they shared a sense of support and common experiences that helped them learn from one another and that they could see benefits for students. Finally, the teachers said they could develop an "eye for what is working and what is not" (p. 271). One group, a special educator and two regular educators, did not develop through these stages. These teachers said different teaching styles, communication techniques, and anxiety were the major causes for problems. Also, the special educator noted she did not know what was to take place in the classroom and a general educator reported "her partner's students didn't really become part of the classroom learning community" (p. 271).

Trent (1998) employed a different approach in his study of co-teachers. He explored the co-teaching experiences of a general educator who had two different special education co-teachers in two years. Trent used observations, interviews, and archival data to develop a picture of what happened with this teacher in a two-year time span. In the first year, the co-teachers were interviewed together but in the second year, the co-teachers were interviewed both together and separately to get more information. The first year, this 11th grade U.S. History teacher co-taught with a teacher of students with LD. Originally, the general educator was to co-teach with a friend but circumstances changed right before school started. In any event, the teachers had common planning time and reportedly "they hit it off right away" (p. 505). They shared compatible goals in trying to help students with LD succeed in the general education classroom. The general educator presented content and the special educator monitored students, made curricular adaptations, and taught organizational skills. The teachers stated that the benefits of the program were that the special educator learned how to handle large classes and became familiar with the general education curriculum and the general educator learned how to modify the content. The benefits for students included a smaller student-teacher ratio, helpful study guides, and organizational skill activities. The special educator stated that she was concerned about the students' perception of her role, about not using her education training, and about wanting to be an active participant. The general educator felt the worst problem was the lack of planning time.

In the second year, the history teacher worked with a second-year teacher of students with LD and emotional and behavioral disorders. They had a common planning period and both had attended school-sponsored inservice training sessions for co-teaching. In this situation, the teachers did not choose to work together. The roles evolved so that the general educator delivered content and the special educator monitored behavior and performance. In this partnership, the teachers encountered more problems. They both admitted to having incompatible operational and communicative styles. The special educator did not see changing anyone's teaching as her job. The general educator said that the special educator began to not show up for class, did not follow through on responsibilities, and administered discipline in ways that contradicted her. The general educator also stated that she compared this teacher with her earlier partner, that there were structural constraints such as class schedule and lack of planning time, that the special educator did not think it was important to plan together, and that the administration did not listen to teacher suggestions. The only benefit these teachers saw in co-teaching was a second pair of hands in the classroom (Trent, 1998).

Finally, Salend et al. (1997) investigated the impact that co-teaching had on teachers. These authors evaluated the journals kept by a special educator and general educator co-teaching at the kindergarten level. They also conducted interviews with these teachers. The program included seven students with various disabilities in a class of 17 students without disabilities. Both teachers had 20 years or more of teaching experience. They collaborated through a half-day session in all content areas. These teachers asked the administration to collaborate although they had no training in it. They reported that they had noticed and appreciated each other's skills, as well as their different perspectives and areas of expertise before the co-teaching experience began. This pair of teachers stated that they enjoyed teaching again because they developed an environment in which they were comfortable taking risks in instruction. The two teachers confronted differences they had directly once they had spent time adjusting to roles, teaching styles, and philosophical differences. The teachers developed a sense of community that helped their students collaborate, be sensitive to peers, and improve in social, developmental, and preacademic skills. Finally, the teachers reported that the support of their principal was instrumental in making their program work (Salend et al., 1997).

Feelings and Barriers to Inclusion

Wood (1998) studied three pairs of teachers who shared their feelings of obligation, responsibility, and commitment to the goals of inclusion. The teachers all worked at the elementary level and included students with severe disabilities in their co-taught classes. The author conducted semi-structured interviews throughout the first year of the program. The teachers did not have any training in co-teaching and the administration forced the teachers to participate in the program. The special educators took on the roles of providing individual instruction for students with disabilities in math, reading, and language; they modeled effective methods of instruction; they developed behavior plans; and they oversaw the responsibilities of the paraprofessionals. The general educators were relinquished "of duties towards the goals and objectives set forth by the parents and special educators in IEP meetings" (p. 187). They did not make any program decisions and may have been aware of the goals but were not responsible for the their implementation. They were mainly responsible for the social behavior agenda.

When asked if they worked together, the general educators responded that they were only to provide a setting of acceptance, maintain class standards, structure classroom routines, and promote interactions between the students with disabilities and the non-disabled students. As time went on, the general educator did assume more of an academic role, if the special education student's ability allowed. Assistance from the special educator was appreciated but could be disruptive and the teachers reported being territorial about special education techniques in the general education classroom. Altogether, the general education teachers felt the role of the special educator was a waste of a capable teacher. Most groups had ownership struggles, and there was a general lack of understanding of special educator's and general educator's responsibilities (Wood, 1998).

Problems and Benefits over Time

Walther-Thomas (1997) examined a co-teaching program with 18 elementary and seven middle school teams over a period of three years. The study included a total of 119 teachers and 24 administrators, who varied from year to year due to staff turnover. The author conducted yearly classroom observations, an annual spring interview, document reviews, and informal contacts.

Many of the informal contacts came in graduate classes taught by the author at a local university.

Walther-Thomas (1997) concluded that there were four basic benefits for students with disabilities who received instruction through co-teaching: (a) positive feelings about themselves as capable learners, (b) enhanced academic performance, (c) improved social skills, and (d) stronger peer relationships. The researcher also stated that there were five basic benefits for students without disabilities: (a) improved academic performance, (b) more time with and attention from teachers, (c) an increased emphasis on cognitive strategies and study skills, (d) increased emphasis on social skills, and (e) improved classroom communities. The teachers stated that they felt increased professional satisfaction, more opportunities for professional growth and personal support, and increased opportunities for collaboration. There were, however, persistent problems. These included planning time, student schedules, caseload concerns, administrative support, and staff development opportunities.

Process

Two dissertation studies evaluated the process of implementation of co-teaching from teachers' perspectives. Newman (1997) used an ethnographic research design to investigate how high school teachers implemented co-teaching in five classrooms. Following observations, interviews, and document analysis, Newman concluded: (a) co-teachers have divergent perceptions of roles taken; (b) administrators' difficulties putting together and scheduling co-teacher teams, divergent backgrounds and personalities and a paucity of planning time together impact the co-teachers' ability to cooperate; (c) teacher personalities and levels of tolerance affect the level of cooperation established; and (d) team teachers are not sufficiently prepared to take over their new duties (p. 345).

Norris (1997) found similar results in perceptions, roles, and skills in a middle school setting. These teachers developed through three identifiable stages in their co-teaching: (a) forming stage, (b) storming stage, and (c) norming stage. The forming stage was very positive for participants and each was aware of the roles and expectations of the others. When time wore on, however, most groups entered the storming stage in which there was disagreement about what should happen in the classroom and conflict between teachers. Finally, some groups made it to the norming stage where they were back in agreement, albeit through compromise, about what was to happen in the classroom. Not all groups made it through all stages and, within groups, some teachers arrived at stages at different times than their partners. This created some conflict and discontentment (Norris, 1997).

Summary of Teacher Perceptions of the Co-teaching Process

Nine studies were located that provided data regarding the perceptions of teachers involved with co-teaching regarding the potentials and pitfalls of providing instruction in this model. Two studies (Trent, 1998; Newman, 1997) examined the perceptions of high school teachers, three studies (Phillips, et al, 1995; Salend et al., 1997; Walther-Thomas, 1997) examined teachers at the middle school level, three studies (Newman, 1997; Norris, 1997; Nowacek, 1992) focused on teachers at the elementary school level. The remaining study (Adams & Cessna, 1993) solicited information from teachers across a wide variety of grade levels. The most clear observation that can be drawn from this literature is that co-teaching means different things to different teachers in different schools. No particular vision or metaphor describing co-teaching appears to be associated with stronger teacher-perceptions of effectiveness than are the others. However, teachers who report positive perceptions of co-teaching are most often voluntary participants in the model. Further, teachers with positive perceptions of co-teaching report mutual respect for one another, higher levels of administrative support for co-teaching and collaboration, more planning time, and greater commonality in their beliefs about classroom instruction and behavior management. Teachers who are dissatisfied with co-teaching are often involuntary participants with limited planning time and lower levels of administrative support for teacher collaboration. When teachers are able to resolve conflicts in roles and responsibilities in the classroom in a satisfactory manner, they usually report satisfaction with co-teaching. However, some special educators report that co-teaching limits the number of general education teachers that they are able to work with. Special educators often assume responsibilities for student behavior or the instructional component of the IEPs of students with severe disabilities in the general education classroom. The extent to which co-teaching is able to deliver instruction that can be described as "special education" is examined in the next section.

How is Co-teaching Special Education?

"Special education means specially designed instruction that meets the unusual needs of an exceptional student" (Hallahan & Kauffman, 2000, p. 12). Four studies provided data on the extent to which specially designed instruction was provided in classrooms using the co-teaching model. Zigmond (1995a,b) and Baker (1995a,b) reported case studies of students with LD in inclusion programs that used co-teaching models. Their purpose was to observe and report the educational programs that specific students received in these settings in order to determine what special education these students received. The authors defined special education as "specially designed instruction" (Zigmond, 1995a, p. 110).

Zigmond (1995a) described a co-teaching model, developed in an elementary school in Kansas as a part of a school district initiative. Under this program, the general educator was responsible for content presentation and the special educator was responsible for student monitoring, curriculum delivery, and learning strategies. The special educator spent two hours in the general education classroom four days a week. The general educator collaborated with more than one special educator. The annual IEP language arts and reading goals for Andrew, a second grader in this program, were to use correct grammar and mechanics in writing, and to increase from Level 1 to Level 2 in the reading series. From observation, the author concluded that special education in language arts and reading for Andrew consisted of instruction by two teachers, additional monitoring within the classroom, differentiated spelling lists, and a partner to work with in the class. Gladys, a fifth grader, had an annual goal of "meeting requirements of mainstream courses" (p. 151). Her special education took the form of two teachers in one classroom for 4 hours per day, extensive use of partnering and group instruction in strategies for content and behavior. However, the special education teacher said, "Fifth grade is a struggle for her.... Sometimes I have pulled...Gladys away from the group and we've worked in either skill groups or out in the hall" (p. 152).

Zigmond (1995b) observed an elementary school in Pennsylvania that implemented co-teaching with the help of the University of Pittsburgh. In this situation, the special educator was responsible for accommodations and modifications to the curriculum. The two special educators co-taught 30 minutes per day, 4 days a week, in the 10 classrooms where 19 students with disabilities were integrated. General educators co-taught and co-planned with both special educators. Jason, a second grader, received in-class accommodations, in-class Chapter I services, parallel teaching, drill with an aide, reduced math assignments, and peer tutoring as special education services in the mainstream. His IEP goals were to increase reading skills, general academic skills, and self-esteem. Norman, a fifth grade student, received special education in the form of additional help in the mainstream. His parents set up weekly tutoring sessions with a first grade teacher to help him in reading. The tutor and Norman's teacher did not coordinate activities. Norman's IEP goals were "to maintain above-average grades with accommodations and learning support interventions" (p. 131).

Baker (1995a) described a co-teaching model in an intermediate school program in Minnesota. The special educator's role was to monitor student performance, teach small skills lessons, and to provide remedial instruction to small groups of students. The special educator worked with the language arts teacher for 90 minutes a day and the math teacher for 50 minutes a day. This special educator also provided pull out services for students. Chris, a sixth grader, received special education in the form of remediation in math and modification of tests in both classes. Chris's IEP goals included improving reading comprehension, written language, task completion, and peer interactions.

Finally, Baker (1995b) completed a case study of an elementary school in Virginia. Twenty-three of the 40 students with LD were included in collaborative classrooms with two of seven special education teachers. Each teacher spent 90 minutes per day in one of the third, fourth, or fifth grade collaborative classrooms. The special educator monitored students, taught strategies, retaught in one-to-one situations, carried out accommodations, and helped plan in the regular classroom. Rose, a third grader, received special education in the form of group strategy instruction and one-to-one related services after school. Rose's IEP goals were to demonstrate measurable progress in language arts and improve efficiency in functional independence. Leslie, a fifth grader, received group strategy instruction and optional one-to-one services during extended day. Leslie's IEP goals included showing measurable progress in language arts and mathematics.

Summary of Studies Examining the Extent to
Which Co-teaching Provides Special Education

The four case studies described in this section provide uniformly disappointing results. The instruction provided in the co-taught classrooms most often reflected the instruction provided to the other students with the addition of an extra teacher, smaller groups, or peer tutoring. All of these supports are justified in the special education literature. However, the authors of the reports considered in this section concluded that the efforts of the teachers on behalf of students with disabilities lacked the intensity and distinctiveness to be considered "specially designed instruction to meet the unusual needs of an exceptional student." It is premature to conclude that special education cannot be provided in co-taught settings. However, the documentation that appropriate and specially designed instruction can be carried out in a general education classroom along with the instruction provided for most other students has yet to appear in the empirical literature regarding services for students with disabilities. In the next section, we describe the studies reporting the behavior of teachers working in co-taught classrooms.

Teacher Behavior

Hines (1995) examined the percentage of class time spent in instruction by 16 regular educators at the middle school level under co-taught, mainstreamed, and regular education conditions. In co-teaching, a special educator taught with the general educator and students labeled Educable Mentally Handicapped (EMH) and LD were integrated into the classroom. In mainstream situations, students with EMH and LD were integrated into the regular education classroom without a special educator present. In regular classrooms, no students with disabilities were present. There was no significant difference in percentage of time spent on instruction in the three types of classrooms ($F = [1,32]$, $p = 0.276$). There was a significant difference between groups on the percentage of time spent managing students ($F = [4,6]$, $p = 0.015$). Univariate F-tests indicated that the difference occurred between co-taught and mainstream settings with a smaller percentage of time spent in managing students in the co-taught classroom. In addition, a significant difference existed between all conditions on the percentage of time spent correcting student behavior ($F = [5,9]$, $p = 0.01$). Teachers engaged in interactions to correct student behavior more often in the mainstream classroom. In a survey of teacher attitudes, regular education teachers felt the most success in their regular education classrooms but did prefer to co-teach than to have students in a mainstream setting (Hines, 1995).

Weiss (1999) examined the actions of six secondary special educators in co-taught and special education settings in a middle school and high school. Using direct observations, interviews, and document analysis, the author identified four roles that the special educator took on in co-taught settings during teacher-directed instruction. The first was that of providing support in which the special educator explained information or examples to individual students while the general educator instructed the whole group. In this role, the special educator had no instructional responsibilities but functioned much as an instructional aide. The second role involved teaching the same content in a separate classroom. In this role, the special educator removed half of the students from the co-taught classroom (mainly special education students) and was responsible for providing all instruction on the same subject in a different classroom from the general educator. The third role was that of teaching a different part of the content in the same classroom. For example, in English, the general educator was responsible for whole group instruction of literature and writing. Once that was completed, the special educator was responsible for whole group instruction in grammar and vocabulary. The final role identified was that of team teacher, in which the special educator and general educator both provided whole group instruction interchangeably. While one teacher instructed, the other provided support to individual students. In all cases, the special educators defined these models of teaching as co-teaching.

There were a number of similarities in the explaining, questioning, giving help, and giving feedback actions of the special educators between the co-taught and special education settings. However, the teachers emphasized very different aspects of instruction in the different settings. Special educators in co-taught classrooms focused on moving students with disabilities through the material provided by the general educator during whole group instruction. In the special education classroom, however, special educators provided more strategy and individualized instruction for students with disabilities (Weiss, 1999).

Boudah, Schumaker, and Deshler (1997) provided the only study in the review that evaluated the behaviors of both special and regular education teachers within the classroom and student outcomes following those behaviors. The research question was whether the collaborative instruction model developed by the authors influenced teacher performance, student engagement, and academic outcomes. Students at the sixth, seventh, eighth, and tenth grade levels participated, 32 in the experimental group and 32 in the control group. Sixteen students in each group were classified as having mild disabilities (MD) and 16 were students who

were characterized as low achieving (LA). Four teams of teachers (special educator and general educator) participated in each condition. The teachers co-taught in
science, history, and English. The dependent measures included: (a) percentage of
time engaged in presenting content, mediating student learning (teacher cues student strategy use or prior knowledge), circulating (teacher provides individual
instruction), and noninstructional behaviors; (b) number of role exchanges (teachers switch between presenter and mediator); (c) student engagement; (d) mastery
of strategic skills; and (e) content test performance. The teachers in the experimental group had two training sessions in the collaborative instruction model and
support from the researchers.

Before training, experimental teacher teams spent an average 8% (SD = 5.25)
of a class period mediating instruction. Following training, they averaged 22%
(SD = 9.44). Before training, teams averaged five (SD = 7.02) role exchanges in
one class period. After training, the average was 17 (SD = 13.44). Presenting content averaged 8% (SD = 5.23) of class time before training and 6% (SD = 3.28)
after training. Before training, teachers spent 19% (SD = 13.45) of a class period
circulating to help individual students and, following training, they spent an average of 16% (SD = 13.21). Teachers were involved in noninstructional behaviors
for an average of 61% (SD = 10.99) of a class period before training and 54%
(SD = 12.51) after training.

Boudah et al. (1997) examined classroom engagement of the students with a
series of one-way ANOVAs and determined that the only significant differences
between students with MD across conditions was in their use of strategic skills,
favoring the experimental condition. For students with LA, there was a significant
difference in use of strategic skills and engagement by the special education
teacher, also favoring the intervention condition. In the intervention classrooms,
there were significant differences favoring the LA students over the MD students
at baseline and intervention in engagement by the general education teacher, voluntary responses, responses requiring knowledge recall, and correct responses.
The authors reported that, on average, the MD and LA students were engaged by
teachers only two or three times during whole-group instruction (Boudah et al.,
1997).

Boudah et al. (1997) also reported changes in student test and quiz scores. For
the MD group in the experimental condition, baseline test and quiz scores averaged 64% and the average grade point average was 1.75 on a 4.0 scale. Following
intervention, the MD group averaged 58% on tests and quizzes and .75 GPA. For
the LA group, test scores averaged 67% and GPAs were 2.07 before intervention.
The average test scores increased to 72% after teacher training but GPAs fell to
1.83. At baseline, one third of the MD students and one third of the LA students
had failing grades. After implementation, one half of the MD students and one
fourth of the LA students had failing grades. The authors summarized the results
in this way:

Even when two teachers increased the amount of instructional time spent mediating student learning and also were satisfied with their performance, rates of student engagement were low, and only some strategic skills increased for MD and LA students.... Moreover, test and quiz scores decreased slightly for the MD students in the intervention conditions, whereas those of LA students improved only slightly. (p. 312)

Summary of Studies Examining Teacher Behavior in Co-teaching Settings

Three studies examined the actual behavior of teachers in co-taught classrooms. Consistent with the variability of definition and attitudes toward co-teaching reported in earlier sections of this paper, the behavior of teachers in co-taught classrooms varies widely. One study (Boudah et al., 1997) examined the effects of training in collaboration on the behavior of teachers in co-teaching. The results of this study suggested that with the proper support, teachers could dramatically increase the amount of instructional time and support provided to students with low achievement and students with disabilities in co-taught classes. However, the impact of this increased teacher performance on student outcomes was disappointing. In fact, students with disabilities actually attained lower scores on classroom tests and quizzes under the enhanced instructional conditions in co-taught classes. The remaining studies suggest that special education teachers engaged in co-teaching models focus on student behavior and the content and methods employed by the general educator.

DISCUSSION

The present review demonstrates that even though the model has spread rapidly in the public schools, the research on co-teaching is still in its infancy. Over 300 published articles describe or give guidelines for collaboration and co-teaching but only 23 or 3% of those articles report research. The studies that have been done on co-teaching, though attempting to fill a void, present six basic problems in interpretation.

First, in studies that used surveys and test scores, authors leave out many vital pieces of information about measures. For example, Karge et al. (1995) surveyed participants using a questionnaire that "was piloted with a small group of resource teachers to assess user friendliness" (p. 82) but no other information was given. The same problem characterizes the reports by Walther-Thomas and Carter (1993) as well as Wiedmeyer and Lehman (1991). Johnston (1994) compared the number of behavioral referrals of students with LD to the office in the year of co-teaching versus the year before co-teaching. No information was given about how many students were involved in co-teaching and how many were in other special education programs, whether these are the same students as last year, or whether there are other changes that could account for the change in numbers. In the same study, the author indicated that "learning disabled students in collaborative classrooms outscored those in non-collaborative rooms on all sections of both tests" (p. 13). However, Johnston (1994) gave no information about whether the students in both classes were similar in test scores at the outset or whether the differences were statistically significant. More information about how authors came to their conclusions about co-teaching is necessary for interpretation and replication of the currently existing research.

Second, in all but four reports of teaching pairs, authors interviewed teachers in which co-teaching was deemed successful by the participants. The participants were happy with the situation and they wanted to tell about their successes. There is a strong probability that these reports are biased in favor of co-teaching by their participant selection process. Only the dissertations provided any detail about why the participants were selected for the study. For example, Adams and Cessna (1993), used teachers "recommended by their supervisors as good co-teachers" (p. 1) but the reader has no indication of what that meant. Nowacek (1992), Phillips et al. (1995), Salend et al. (1997), and Wood (1998) described the sample but not why these teachers were selected for the studies. Many of the studies took place at the elementary level but none of the authors gave a reason for their choice in grade level. The ways that the teachers in these studies are representative of those doing co-teaching in most schools remains unclear.

Third, many of the teachers involved in these studies indicated that the major variable in success or failure of a co-teaching situation was a teacher's personality or style. This was evident in the results of Karge et al. (1995), Phillips et al. (1995), Salend et al. (1997), and Trent (1998). Across the studies, neither choice in participation, training, experience, grade level, nor content area were consistently related to success in co-teaching. This poses a number of problems for research and implementation; such as, is personality truly a major factor as teachers say, who has the personality to co-teach, why is personality such a big factor, and how can some standard definition for co-teaching be set when a variable like personality is such a large influence?

Fourth, it appeared evident in many studies, most clearly in Voltz et al. (1994), that general and special educators did not have a clear definition for collaboration and co-teaching. In most of the qualitative studies, teachers talked about their roles evolving and changing. Special educators worried about wasting their education training and about their appearance as disciplinarians (Nowacek, 1992). General educators commented on ownership and territorialism (Wood, 1998). Authors in most studies considered in this review asserted definitions in introductory statements but did not include the definition as one of their variables in interviews. Yet, the studies seemed to indicate a continuum of partnerships from successful to not successful. Thus, it remains unclear how professional, administrative, and personal definitions affect co-teaching situations.

Fifth, due to the design of the research, the behavioral and grade changes given in Adams and Cessna (1993), Nowacek (1992), Phillips et al. (1995), Salend et al. (1997), and Wood (1998) are stated in qualitative terms such as "improved" or "more accepted." There are statements from teachers about effectiveness and ineffectiveness of the co-teaching model for students with no data to illustrate how the conclusions were made. When data such as pre- and post-test scores or GPAs are used, as in Boudah et al. (1997) or Harris et al. (1997), the results for students with disabilities are not positive. The studies in this review indicate that the effectiveness of co-teaching is supported by the personal impressions of participants but refuted by more stringent analysis of student outcome data. Thus the answer to the question "Is co-teaching effective for students with disabilities?" depends on what is meant by effective. In regard to achievement, the answer is no. In regard to consumer satisfaction, the answer is sometimes. Hardly a ringing endorsement.

Finally, and perhaps most importantly, only the reports by Boudah et al. (1997), Zigmond (1995a, 1995b), Baker (1995a, 1995b), and Weiss (1999), gave evidence of what the special educator actually did in the co-taught classroom. In fact, in some studies (e.g, Karge et al., 1995), special educators and general educators clearly disagreed about what they *should* do in co-teaching and collaboration. The dissertation studies of Newman (1997) and Norris (1997) give some description of the classrooms they observed but no specifics about teacher actions. Boudah et al. (1997) identified a number of behaviors they determined to be important to their model: mediating instruction, circulating, delivering content, and noninstructional behaviors. They evaluated the amount of time that either of the teachers spent in these behaviors. This gives an indication of what was going on in that classroom as a whole but not specifically what the special educator was doing. In the Zigmond and Baker case studies, we see that there is little special education happening. The same is true in Weiss (1999) when comparisons are made between actions in special education and co-taught classrooms. More information is necessary about what the special educator is doing in those classrooms. Does the special educator have the opportunity to explain content and question students to assess understanding within the co-taught classroom? Does the special educator get an opportunity to teach strategies or provide instructional support? Can the special education teacher deliver instruction or help to deliver instruction that meets the needs of special education students? Are there different ways that teachers participate in the classroom structure? What determines how special educators act in the co-taught class?

Literature on co-teaching has addressed the relationships of teachers, the changing roles of the teachers, and the perceived student outcomes or benefits in subjective terms. Boudah et al. (1997) began the data-based evaluation of co-taught classrooms, measuring teacher behaviors, student grades, and skill mastery. We still do not know, however, what teachers do in the co-taught class on a daily basis nor do we know how special education teachers' actions are different in co-taught and special education classrooms. In a time of dramatic shortages in special education personnel (Brownell & Smith, 1992), it is prudent to identify the actions of the special education teacher in both the co-taught and special education classrooms, compare them, and evaluate the possible links those actions have to student achievement in order to provide the most effective services to students with disabilities. Teaching models that are unlinked to substantive improvements for the students who receive them can hardly be endorsed as best practices. The evidence on co-teaching gathered to date suggests that although co-teaching is a viable option for some students with particular teachers in certain schools, a wide-spread endorsement of this option for service delivery for most students, with most teachers, in most schools is premature and ill-considered.

REFERENCES

Adams, L., & Cessna, K. (1993). Metaphors of the co-taught classroom. *Preventing School Failure, 37*, 28-31.

Baker, J.M. (1995a) Inclusion in Minnesota: Educational experiences of students with learning disabilities in two elementary schools. *Journal of Special Education, 29*, 133-143.

Baker, J.M. (1995b) Inclusion in Virginia: Educational experiences of students with learning disabilities in one elementary school. *Journal of Special Education, 29*, 116-123.

Bauwens, J., Hourcade, J.J., & Friend, M. (1989). Cooperative teaching: A model for general and special education integration. *Remedial and Special Education, 10*, 17-22.

Boudah, D.J., Schumaker, J.B., & Deshler, D.D. (1997). Collaborative instruction: Is it an effective option for inclusion in secondary classrooms? *Learning Disability Quarterly, 20*, 293-316.

Brownell, M., & Smith, S. (1992). Attrition/retention of special education teachers: Critique of current research and recommedations for retention efforts. *Teacher Education and Special Education, 15*, 229-248.

Flicek, M., Olsen, C., Chivers, R., Kaufman, C.J., & Anderson, J.A. (1996). The combined classroom model for serving elementary students with and without behavioral disorders. *Behavioral Disorders, 21*, 241-248.

Friend, M., Reising, M., & Cook, L. (1993). Coteaching: An overview of the past, a glimpse at the present, and considerations for the future. *Preventing School Failure, 37*, 6-10.

Hallahan, D.P., & Kauffman, J.M. (2000). *Exceptional learners: Introduction to special education* (8th ed.). Boston: Allyn and Bacon.

Harris, K.C., Harvey, P., Garcia, L., Innes, D., Lynn, P., Munoz, D., Sexton, K., & Stoica, R. (1987). Meeting the needs of special high school students in regular education classrooms. *Teacher Education and Special Education, 10*, 143-152.

Hines, R.A. (1995). *Instructional and non-instructional time expenditures by teachers in inclusion and non-inclusion classrooms.* Unpublished dissertation, University of Virginia.

Johnston, W.F. (1994). How to educate all the students...together. *Schools in the Middle, 3*, 3-12.

Karge, B.D., McClure, M., & Patton, P.L. (1995). The success of collaboration resource programs for students with disabilities in grades 6 through 8. *Remedial and Special Education, 16*, 79-89.

McLeskey, J., Henry, D., & Hodges, D. (1998). Inclusion: Where is it happening? *Teaching Exceptional Children, 31* (1), 4-10.

National Center for Educational Restructuring and Inclusion. (1995). *National study on inclusion: Overview and summary report.* New York: Author.

Newman, F. (1997). *Ethnographic observation of five high school co-teacher teams implementing a cooperative/collaborative team teaching model: The nature of regular and special educator role interaction.* Unpublished dissertation, Georgia State University.

Norris, D.M. (1997). *Teachers' perceptions of co-teaching in an inclusive classroom in a middle school: A look at general education and special education teachers working together with students with learning disabilities*. Unpublished dissertation, George Mason University.

Nowacek, E.J. (1992). Professionals talk about teaching together: Interviews with five collaborating teachers. *Intervention in School and Clinic, 27*, 262-276.

Phillips, L., Sapona, R.H., & Lubic, B.L. (1995). Developing partnerships in inclusive education: One school's approach. *Intervention in School and Clinic, 30,* 262-272.

Salend, S.J., Johansen, M., Mumper, J., Chase, A.S., Pike, K.M., & Dorney, J.A. (1997). Cooperative teaching: The voices of two teachers. *Remedial and Special Education, 18*, 3-11.

Thousand, J.S., & Villa, R.A. (1989). Enhancing success in heterogeneous schools. In S. Stainback, W. Stainback, & M. Forest (Eds.), *Educating all students in the mainstream of regular education* (pp. 89-103). Baltimore, MD: Paul H. Brookes.

Trent, S.C. (1998). False starts and other dilemmas of a secondary general education collaborative teacher: A case study. *Journal of Learning Disabilities, 31*, 503-513.

U.S. Department of Education. (1994). *Conditions of Education 1994: High school students ten years after A Nation at Risk*. Washington, DC: Author.

U.S. Department of Education. (1997). *Condition of Education* (NCES 97-388). Washington, DC: Author.

U.S. Department of Education (1998*). Condition of Education*. Washington, DC: Author.

Voltz, D.L., Elliott, R.N., & Cobb, H.B. (1994). Collaborative teacher roles: Special and general educators. *Journal of Learning Disabilities, 27*, 527-535.

Walther-Thomas, C.S. (1997). Co-teaching experiences: The benefits and problems that teachers and principals report over time. *Journal of Learning Disabilities, 30*, 395-407.

Walther-Thomas, C.S., & Carter, K.L. (1993). Cooperative teaching: Helping students with disabilities succeed in mainstream classrooms. *Middle School Journal, 25*, 33-38.

Weiss, M.P. (1999). *The actions of secondary special educators in co-taught and special education settings*. Unpublished dissertation: University of Virginia.

Wiedmeyer, D., & Lehman, J. (1991). The House Plan approach to collaborative teaching and consultation. *Teaching Exceptional Children, 23*, 6-10.

Will, M.C. (1986). Educating children with learning problems: A shared responsibility. *Exceptional Children. 52*, 411-415.

Wood, M. (1998). Whose job is it anyway? Educational roles in inclusion. *Exceptional Children, 64*, 181-195.

Zigmond, N. (1995a). Inclusion in Kansas: Educational experiences of students with learning disabilities in one elementary school. *Journal of Special Education, 29*, 144-154.

Zigmond, N. (1995b). Inclusion in Pennsylvania: Educational experiences of students with learning disabilities in one elementary school. *Journal of Special Education, 29*, 124-132.

STUDENTS WITH DISABILITIES AS TUTORS:
AN UPDATED RESEARCH SYNTHESIS

Margo A. Mastropieri, Vicky Spencer,
Thomas E. Scruggs, and Elizabeth Talbott

ABSTRACT

This chapter presents an updated research synthesis on the use of students with disabilities as tutors. Thirty-five studies from 1980 to 2000 were identified in which students with disabilities were tutors. Specific categories of exceptionality represented in the studies included students with learning disabilities, students with emotional disabilities, students with mental retardation, and students with attention deficit hyperactivity disorder. The specific tutoring arrangements across studies varied. For example, in some studies cross-age tutoring or reciprocal situations were implemented in which students exchanged roles during tutoring sessions and acted as both tutors and tutees while in other studies students with disabilities only assumed the roles of tutors. In some cases, tutors were either older than their tutees. In some studies, both tutors and tutees were students with disabilities; while in other studies, tutoring partners were average-achieving students. Findings generally supported the efficacy of tutoring, with more positive findings reported for tutees than

Advances in Learning and Behavioral Disabilities, Volume 14, pages 247-279.
Copyright © 2000 by JAI Press Inc.
All rights of reproduction in any form reserved.
ISBN: 0-7623-0561-4

for tutors, for criterion referenced over norm referenced measures, and for academic over social-behavioral, self-concept, and attitudinal measures. More interestingly, however, the focus and content used during tutoring has shifted over the years. Tutoring, as an instructional delivery system, has tended to parallel what is known in instructional research. For example, earlier tutoring research focused on basic sight word recognition, spelling, and math facts, while more recent tutoring research has included cognitive strategy instruction, such as use of reading comprehension strategies and peer planning, editing, and revising in written composition instruction. Moreover, more recent tutoring configurations have involved a reciprocity of roles during which students assume the role of equal partners in their learning experiences. Implications for future research and practice are discussed.

INTRODUCTION

Tutoring is one type of peer mediation that has become increasingly popular in both inclusive and special education settings (see Topping & Ehly, 1998, for extensive reviews). Reasons for this increased popularity are attributable to a variety of sources. One reported advantage of tutoring includes increased practice opportunities for learners. During tutoring sessions, for example, students have access to one to one instruction, more opportunities to respond, more corrective feedback, increased academic engagement, and more relevant on task behaviors (Greenwood, Delaquadri, & Hall, 1984). Moreover, reported results indicate that both tutors and tutees not only increase in academic performance, but also improve in their social functioning, demonstrate increased social responsibility, and enjoy participating in tutoring (e.g., Utley, Mortweet, & Greenwood, 1997). Given such positive findings, it is not surprising that tutoring has become even more attractive to both regular and special educators with recent emphases on standards of learning, state-wide competency testing (e.g., Virginia Standards of Learning, 1999), and simultaneous demands for meeting the needs of diverse learners within a single classroom setting (Fuchs, Fuchs, Hamlett, Phillips, & Bentz, 1994).

A variety of peer tutoring models and configurations also exist. Tutors and tutees may be the same age or grade level. Cross-age tutoring typically involves older students tutoring younger students, although in some cases, younger students may be the tutors. Reciprocal tutoring refers to the exchanging of the tutoring roles during tutoring sessions, in which students serve as both tutor and tutee. In addition, several classwide peer tutoring models, in which all students within a single class participate in tutoring, have received more research attention (e.g., Greenwood, Delaquadri, & Hall, 1984; Fuchs, Fuchs, Phillips, Hamlett, & Karns, 1995; Maheady, Harper, & Mallette, 1991). Greenwood et al. (1984) have specifically referred to their model as classwide peer tutoring (CWPT), while Fuchs et al. (1995) have coined the term Peer Assisted Learning Strategies or PALS to refer to their model in which tutors are referred to as "coaches," and tutees are referred to as "players." Both models share similar components, including: (a) all students within a class are participants during the tutoring; (b) explicit training procedures and rules exist for tutors and tutees; (c) increased opportunities for responding are created for all students; (d) careful recording of responses is completed during tutoring; (e) points are awarded for correct responding and appropriate behavior; and (f) the class is divided into two teams of dyads that compete for a total number of points. Both models have commonly been implemented in general education classrooms to accommodate diverse learning needs including those of students with disabilities. Finally, both models typically employ reciprocity of roles, such that students switch tutor and tutees roles during the sessions. Findings from both models have yielded positive results. All students, but especially the tutees or the lower functioning student from the dyad, appear to benefit in some way from participating in the tutoring experiences, especially with respect to the acquisition of the specific content being instructed during tutoring sessions.

These models diverge slightly with respect to the particular content and formats employed within tutoring sessions. CWPT, the earliest model, has implemented peer tutoring studies in basic skill areas including reading, word recognition, arithmetic, and spelling predominantly at the elementary level using rehearsal or repetition as a dominant learning strategy (e.g., Utley et al., 1997). Extensive teacher training manuals provide detailed descriptions for the design and implementation of the tutoring for teachers (Greenwood, Delquadri, & Carta, 1996). For example, sample directions for the tutors in spelling include presenting the spelling words from the list one at a time, watching as tutees spell and write the word, modeling the correct spelling, and awarding points. PALs research studies replicated components of CWPT and extended the model. For example, PALS investigated the teaching of reading and math primarily at the upper elementary levels, but also implemented more strategic teaching, rather than rote rehearsal, within the tutoring sessions (e.g., Fuchs, Fuchs, Phillips, Hamlett, & Karns, 1995). The PALS math training materials include, for example, tutor instructions for coaching students through math problems (e.g., "Look at the sign. What kind of problem is it? Where do you start?" Fuchs, Fuchs, Karns, & Phillips, 1995, p. 4). The reading materials include partner reading, a strategy for summarizing main ideas, a prediction strategy, and a story mapping strategy for identifying the main characters, the settings, the problems, story outcomes, and major events (Fuchs, Mathes, & Fuchs, 1995). Both these models typically pair a lower functioning student or one with disabilities with an average-achieving student. Taken together, these models provide positive evidence toward the use of tutoring as a supplemental model of delivery of instruction to enhance the performance of students.

More pertinent to the present review, however, are two previously conducted research syntheses that specifically targeted students with disabilities as tutors as their primary focus (Cook, Scruggs, Mastropieri, & Casto, 1985-1986;

Osguthorpe & Scruggs, 1986). Both reviews examined previously conducted investigations involving students with disabilities as tutors and reported some promising preliminary findings across those studies. The Cook et al. meta-analysis reported positive effect sizes for tutors, although effect sizes for tutors were somewhat smaller than those found for tutees in the same studies. In addition, more positive findings were found in academic areas than on self-concept measures. Osguthorpe and Scruggs (1986) provided findings that highlighted increased social interactions among tutors and tutees outside of the tutoring situations. In particular, positive interactions were obtained when students with mental retardation tutored general education students in sign language, and increased interactions among tutors and tutees were observed on playground activities. The majority of the tutoring interventions described in both of those syntheses involved more rote-like tutoring behaviors using academic areas such as word recognition, spelling, math facts, or basic sign language that relied mostly on rehearsal and repetition as the learning or instructional strategy.

Although students with disabilities were seen to be effective at participating in tutoring configurations through 1986, their primary role appeared to be delegated to facilitating a factual learning type scenario in which tutors asked simple questions and provided simple feedback based upon accuracy of responses. The teaching strategies that tutors used paralleled the dominant teaching strategies of rehearsal and repetition. These findings were encouraging, and provided initial evidence about the circumstances under which students with disabilities could potentially function as tutors. However, over the past fifteen years, we have seen an increase in cognitive strategy research that has demonstrated even more impressive effects on student learning. We wanted to examine the extent to which findings from cognitive strategy research and peer tutoring research have been combined and to examine whether the tutoring delivery and practice systems have also yielded similar positive findings when increased in complexity and systematically implemented by students with disabilities.

PURPOSE

Previous reviews of students with disabilities as tutors have provided the field with important information pertaining to the academic and social benefits of tutoring (Cook et al., 1985-1986; Osguthorpe & Scruggs, 1986). However, in the past fifteen years, we have seen an increased number of tutoring studies and a shift in the type of tutoring activities undertaken during tutoring. This review is intended to provide an updated synthesis on peer tutoring research when students with disabilities were tutors. Specifically, we were interested in examining the situations under which students with disabilities have served as tutors, whether they have been involved in more strategic tutoring, and the outcomes of those investigations.

Table 1. Descrptive Information on Studies Included in the Synthesis

Study	Design	Subject	Tutors/Tutees	Duration of Intervention	Dependent Measures	Author Reported Findings
Campbell, Brady, & Linehan (1991)	Mult. Baseline	Written capitalization skills	Same age tutors-tutees Tutors N=4 LD (mean age=9.5)` Tutees N=2 LD, N=1 MR (mean age=11.1) elementary students	Intervention lasted 17-28 continuous days; daily 15 to 20 minutes; maintenance probes were conducted for 3 weeks following completion	Percentage of words capitalized correctly	Positive gains on capitalization accuracy Mixed results on generalization in sentence writing
Carlton, Litton, & Zinkgraf (1985)	Exp. vs. Control	Vocabulary	Same age tutor-tutee N=74, MMR (mid-point age = 12 yrs) Control group N=62	Intervention lasted 6 weeks; students tutored 5 times a week for 20 minutes	Gates-MacGinitie Reading Test	Positive gains in reading for both tutors and tutees
Cochran, Feng, Carledge, & Hamilton (1993)	Exp. vs. Control	Sight words	Older tutors & younger tutees Tutors N=4, BD, 5th graders Tutees N=4, BD 2nd graders Control group N=8	Intervention lasted 8 weeks; students tutored thirty-two 25 minute sessions	Sight word lists Social Skills Rating System Direct observations Social validity	Positive gains in reading sight words for both tutors and tutees Mixed findings on measures of social behavior
Du Paul & Hennington (1993)	ABAB	Math	Same age reciprocal tutoring Tutor—Target Student N=1, ADHD (7 years) Tutee—Regular education peerss	CWPT intervention with role switching after 10 minutes	Math computation Correct digits written on curriculum based measures On-task behaviors	Positive findings for attention to instruction and acquisition of math skills

251

(continued)

Table 1. (Continued)

Study	Design	Subject	Tutors/Tutees	Duration of Intervention	Dependent Measures	Author Reported Findings
Franca, Kerr, Reitz, & Lambert (1990)	Multi. Baseline	Math	Same age tutor-tutee Middle school, ED/BD (midpoint age—15.1) Tutors N=4 Tutees N=4	Intervention lasted a mean of 14.3 weeks; students tutored daily for 15 minutes	Math Worksheets Estes Attitude Toward Math Subscale Piers-Harris Children's Self-Concept Scale	Positive gains in math for tutors and tutees Mixed findings on socio-metric and self-concept measures
Fuchs, Fuchs, & Kazdan (1999)	Exp. vs. Control	Reading	Same age reciprocal tutoring N=52, LD, MMR, Remedial, Other High school students in special ed. and remedial classes Control group N=50	Intervention lasted 5 times every 2 weeks for 16 weeks	Comprehensive Reading Assessment Battery	Mixed findings between reading comprehension and fluency
Fuchs, Fuchs, Mathes & Simmons (1997)	Exp. vs. Control	Reading	Same age reciprocal tutoring N=20 LD, N=20 LP, N= 20 AA, 2nd-6th graders Control group N=60	Intervention lasted 15 weeks; students tutored 3 times a week for 35 minutes	Comprehensive Reading Assessment Battery	Positive gains in reading
Higgins (1982)	Single subject	Spelling	Same age reciprocal tutoring N=8, LD, 7th-8th graders (mean age=14.4)	Intervention lasted 5 weeks; students tutored 3 times a week for 20 minutes	Spelling words taken from Dale's List of 769 Easy Words	Positive gains in spelling performance

(continued)

Table 1. (Continued)

Study	Design	Subject	Tutors/Tutees	Duration of Intervention	Dependent Intervention Measures	Author Reported Findings
Hogan & Prater (1993)	Multi. Baseline	Spelling,Self-management: On-task, academic and disruptive behaviors	Older tutor and younger tutee Tutor—N=1 BD high school (15 year old) Tutee—N=1 LD high school (14 year old)	Three phases of intervention across resource and general eduction classes: 1. Peer tutoring in spelling and vocabulary (15 sessions 15 mminute each) 2. Self-instruction (5 sessions) 3. Self-instruction with self monitoring (16 sessions)	Spelling and vocabulary test scores On task behavior Disruptive behavioral outbursts	Tutee's spelling increased with tutoring On task behavior increased with package of intervention Tutor's disruptive behavior reduced only after all 3 intervention phases
Koury & Browder 1986	Multi. Baseline	Sight words	Older tutors & younger tutees Tutors N = 5, moderately MR, intermediate class (midpoint age=10 yrs.) Tutees N = 6, moderately MR, primary class (midpoint age=7.5 yrs)	Intervention lasted approximately 10-20 minute sessions with one session per day and four to five sessions per week.	Sight words chosen from primary students' reading series.	Positive gains on identifying sight words

(continued)

253

Table 1. (Continued)

Study	Design	Subject	Tutors/Tutees	Duration of Intervention	Dependent Measures	Author Reported Findings
Lamport (1982)	Exp. vs. Control	Reading	Older tutors & younger tutees Tutors $N=12$, reading disabled, 6th graders Tutees $N=12$, reading disabled, 2nd – 4th graders Control group $N=24$	Intervention lasted 8 weeks; students tutored 3 times a week for 30 minutes	Stanford Diagnostic Reading Test Quality of School Life Scale Devereaux Elementary School Behavior Rating Scale	Mixed findings in reading and behavioral measures for both tutors and tutees
Lazerson (1980)	Exp. vs. Control	Not given	Older tutors & younger tutees Tutors $N=20$, withdrawn or aggressive, 5th – 8th graders Tutees $N=20$, withdrawn or aggressive, 2nd-4th graders Control group $N=20$	Intervention lasted 5 weeks; students tutored 5 times a week for 20 to 30 minutes	Self-concept Scale Devereaux Elementary School Behavior Rating Scale	Positive gains in self-concept and behavior for both tutors and tutees
Lazerson, Foster, Brown, & Hummel (1988)	Pre-post	Not given	Older tutors & younger tutees Tutors $N=16$ junior high, LD (mean age=12.5) Tutees $N=16$ elementary, LD (midpoint age = 8 yrs.)	Intervention lasted 6 weeks; students tutored at least 3 times a week for 20 minutes	Bailer Locus of Control Scale	Positive gains in locus of control for tutors

(continued)

Table 1. (Continued)

Study	Design	Subject	Tutors/Tutees	Duration of Intervention	Dependent Measures	Author Reported Findings
Locke & Fuchs (1995)	ABAB	Reading	Same age reciprocal tutoring N=13, BD, 5th- 6th graders	Intervention lasted 9 sessions	On task & Social interaction behavior	Positive findings on the on-task behavior and social interactions
MacArthur, Schwartz, & Graham (1991)	Exp. vs. Control	Written lang. Skills	Same age reciprocal tutoring 4th- 6th graders, LD N=13 (mean age=11.5) Control group N=16	Intervention lasted a mean of 7.5 weeks; students tutored 4 times a week for 45 minutes	Quality of final drafts	Positive gains in revising and quality of writing
Maheady, Harper, & Sacca (1988)	Single subject	Social studies	Same age reciprocal tutoring N=20, LD, BD, EMR 9th–12th graders (mean age=16.2)	Intervention lasted 20 weeks; number of sessions varied weekly; sessions were 30 minutes	Weekly Social studies quizzes	Positive gains on social studies quizzes
Maheady, Sacca, & Harper (1988)	Mult. Baseline	Social Studies	Same age reciprocal tutoring N=14, mildly handicapped N=36 non-disabled, 10th graders	Intervention lasted 20 weeks; 2 times a week for 30 minutes and 3 days a week for 20 minutes	Social studies Weekly tests	Positive gains on weekly social studies tests

(continued)

255

Table 1. (Continued)

Study	Design	Subject	Tutors/Tutees	Duration of Intervention	Dependent Measures	Author Reported Findings
Maher (1982)	Pre-post	Reading, Writing, Math	Older tutors & younger tutees Tutors N= 6 ED, high school (mean age=16.2) Tutees N= 6 EMR, elementary (midpoint age=9) (N= 6 tutored by general ed. students; N= 6 received group counseling—not included in coding)	Intervention lasted 10 weeks; students tutored 2 times a week for 30 minutes	Student's Grades Number of Disciplinary referrals Percentage of school Attendance	Positive gains in social science and language arts for tutors Reduced rates of absenteeism and disciplinary referrals for tutors
Maher (1984)	Multi. Baseline	Reading, Language Arts, Math	Older tutors & younger tutees Tutors N= 8, ED, high school (midpoint age =15.5) Tutees N=8, EMR, elementary (midpoint age-11yrs.)	Intervention lasted 10 weeks; students tutored 2 times a week for 30 minutes	Percentage completion of assignments Percentage items correct on tests & quizzes Disciplinary Referrals	Increase for tutors and tutees in percentage of completion of assignments and items correct on tests & quizzes Decrease in disciplinary referrals for both tutors and tutees

(continued)

Table 1. (Continued)

Study	Design	Subject	Tutors/Tutees	Duration of Intervention	Dependent Measures	Author Reported Findings
Mallette, Harper, Maheady, & Dempsey (1991)	Pre-post	Spelling	Same age reciprocal tutoring N=9 MMR, N=1 non-disabled (mean age=100.13 months, SD 12.53)	Intervention lasted 12 weeks;	Weekly Spelling tests Student satisfaction survey	Positive gains on weekly spelling tests Positive attitudes towards CWPT
Mastropieri, Scruggs, Mohler, Beranek, Spencer, & Talbott (2000)	Exp. vs. Control	Reading,	Same age reciprocal tutoring N=16, LD, MMR, 7th–8th graders Control group N=12	Intervention lasted 5 weeks; students tutored daily for 55 minutes	Reading comprehension test Attitudes toward tutoring	Positive gains in reading Positive attitudes toward tutoring
Mathes & Fuchs (1993)	Exp. vs. Control	Reading	Same age reciprocal tutoring N=45, LD, 4th-6th graders Control group N=22	Intervention lasted 10 weeks; students tutored 3 times a week for 25 minutes on sustained- reading and 40 minutes on repeated-reading	Comprehensive Reading Assessment Battery	Mixed findings in reading dependent on experimental condition
Osguthorpe, Eiserman, & Shisler (1985)	Exp. vs. Control	Sign language	Same age tutor-tutee 4th–6th graders Tutors N= 17, EMR Tutees N= 17, average-achieving Control group N= 16	Intervention lasted 10 weeks; students tutored 3 times a week for 15 minutes	Free Play Interaction Form Sign Language tests	Positive findings in social interactions between tutors and tutees and sign language

257

(continued)

Table 1. (Continued)

Study	Design	Subject	Tutors/Tutees	Duration of Intervention	Dependent Measures	Author Reported Findings
Schloss & Kobza (1997)	Multi. Baseline across subjects	Functiona l math skills (money cards)	Same age reciprocal tutoring N=6 moderately MR junior high, high school (mean age=15.7)	Intervention lasted approximately 15 minute sessions Follow-up probes one week after completion	Teacher-made money cards	Positive gains in teaching functional math skills
Scruggs, Mastropieri, Veit, & Osguthorpe, (1986)	Exp. vs. Control	Language, Social behaviors	Same age tutor-tutee 3rd – 5th graders Tutors N= 24, BD Tutees N=3, SMH Control group N= 12 (3 new tutors rotated every 5 weeks, so tutors were also control group)	Intervention lasted for 20 weeks (4 - five week tutoring sessions); students tutored 4 times a week for 20 minutes	Stanford Achievement Test Absence Discipline Attitude Toward School Devereaux Behavior Rating Scale	No behavior changes were noted
Scruggs & Osguthorpe (1986) Experiment #1	Exp. vs. Control	Reading	Older tutors & younger tutees Tutors N= 13 older elementary LD, BD Tutees N= 14 younger elementary LD, BD Control group n=20	Intervention lasted 10 weeks; six students tutored 5 times a week, two students tutored 4 times a week, 19 students tutored 2 or three times a week for 30 minutes	Harrison Beginning Reading I & II Woodcock-Johnson Attitude Toward School Measure	Positive gains in reading for both tutors and tutees Attitude gains for the tutees

(continued)

258

Table 1. (Continued)

Study	Design	Subject	Tutors/Tutees	Duration of Intervention	Dependent Measures	Author Reported Findings
Scruggs & Osguthorpe 1986) Experiment #2	Exp. vs. Control	Reading	Same age reciprocal tutoring 2nd- 5th graders, LD, BD $N=12$ LD $N=4$ BD Control group $N=15$	Intervention lasted 8 weeks; six students tutored 5 times a week, four students tutored 4 days a week, and six students tutored 2 times a week for 30 minutes;	Harrison Beginning Reading I or II Woodcock-Johnson Attitude Toward School Measure	Positive gains in reading for both tutors and tutees No attitudinal gains observed
Shisler, Top, & Osguthorpe (1986) Experiment #1	Exp. vs. Control	Reading	Older tutors & younger tutees Tutors $N=10$, BD, upper elementary Tutees $N=12$, average, 1st graders Control group $N=28$	Intervention lasted 12 weeks; tutoring sessions lasted 15 minutes	Woodock-Johnson Students' Perception of Ability Scale Inferred Self-Concept Scale Harrison Beginning Reading I	Positive gains in reading for both tutors and tutees No gains on self-esteem
Shisler, Top, & Osguthorpe (1986) Experiment #2	Exp. vs. Control	Sign language	Same age tutors-tutees Tutors $N=10$, BD 4th graders Tutees $N=30$, gifted students Control group $N=48$	Intervention lasted 8 weeks; students tutored one time a week for 15 minutes	Attitude questionnaire	Positive effects on gifted tutees' attitudes toward their BD tutors

259

(continued)

Table 1. (Continued)

Study	Design	Subject	Tutors/Tutees	Duration of Intervention	Dependent Measures	Author Reported Findings
Simmons, Fuchs, Fuchs, Hodge, & Mathes (1994)	Exp. vs. Control	Reading	Same age reciprocal tutoring $N=58$ LD, $N=27$ LP, $N=33$ AA, $2^{nd}-5^{th}$ graders Control group $N=14$ LD, $N=6$ LP, $N=6$ AA	Intervention lasted 14 weeks; students tutored 3 times a week for 35 – 40 minutes	Comprehensive Reading Assessment Battery	Mixed findings in reading dependent on experimental condition
Top & Osguthorpe (1987)	Exp. vs. Control	Reading	Older tutors & younger tutees $N=39$ BD, LD $N=82$ average Tutors BD, LD, $4^{th}-6^{th}$ graders Tutees average 1st graders Control group $N=39$	Intervention lasted 14 weeks; students tutored 4 times a week for 15-20 minutes	Piers-Harris Children's Self-Concept Scale Students' Perception of Ability Scale Inferred Self-Concept Scale Woodcock-Johnson Harrison Beginning Reading I	Positive gains in reading for both tutors and tutees Mixed findings on measures of self-concept and perception

(continued)

260

Table 1. (Continued)

Study	Design	Subject	Tutors/Tutees	Duration of Intervention	Dependent Measures	Author Reported Findings
Trapani & Gettinger (1989)	Exp. vs. Control	Social Skills and Spelling	Older tutors and younger tutees $N=20$ LD Experiment $N=14$ Tutors LD, 4th-6th graders Tutees average 2nd graders Control group $N=6$	Phase 1: All students with LD trained for 7 sessions, 30 minutes per session on social skills. Phase 2: Half the students with LD tutored younger average ability students in spelling for 20 minutes a week over 4 weeks.	Walker Problem Behavior Identification Checklist Direct observations of behavior Spelling on Test of Written Spelling	Positive gains on spelling, no difference on WPBIC more positive greeting and question responding for tutors
Utay & Utay 1997	Exp. vs. Control	Written language	Older tutors & younger tutees $N=38$, LD Tutors 2nd-4th graders Tutees 4th-5th graders Control group $N=34$	Intervention lasted 12 weeks; students tutored 2 times a week for unspecified time	Test of Written Language –2 Woodcock-Johnson	No gains were found in the improvement of writing skills for tutors and tutees
Wong, Butler, Ficzere, & Kuperis (1997)	Pre-post	Written language	Same age reciprocal tutoring $N=14$ LD, $N=7$ LA, 9th-10th graders (mean age = 15.5)	Intervention duration unclear	Quality of essay Self-efficacy questionnaire	Positive gains in the quality of written language No increase in self-efficacy of writing

(continued)

261

Table 1. (Continued)

Study	Design	Subject	Tutors/Tutees	Duration of Intervention	Dependent Measures	Author Reported Findings
Wong, Butler, Ficzere, & Kuperis (1996)	Exp. vs. Control	Written language	Same age reciprocal tutoring N=18, LD, LA, 8th-9th graders (mean age=14.5) Control N=20	Intervention duration unclear	Quality of essay Self-efficacy questionnaire Meta-cognition	Positive gains in the quality of written language Small effects for self-efficacy and meta-cognition
Wong, Butler, Ficzere, Kuperis, Corden, & Zelmer (1994)	Exp. vs. Control	Written language	Same age reciprocal tutoring N=8 dyadic condition LD and ESL 8th-9th graders Teacher directed instruction comparison N=9 Control group N=13	Intervention duration unclear	Quality of essays Self-efficacy Attitude questionnaire	
Yasutake, Bryan, & Dohrn (1996)	Pre-post	Math, Reading, following directions	Older tutors & younger tutees Tutors N=54 older elementary, LD, At-risk Tutees N=39 younger elementary, average-achieving	Intervention lasted 5 weeks at one school and 8-10 weeks at a second school; mean 37.5 minute sessions, students tutored 2 times a week for a mean of 37.5 minute sessions	Perceived Competence Scale for Children Pictorial Scale of Perceived Competence Acceptance for Young Children Attribution Circle Scale Forced Choice Attribution Scale Smiley Faces	Positive gains in attribution training combined with peer tutoring for both tutors and tutees

LITERATURE SEARCH PROCEDURES

Major data bases in education were searched using peer tutoring and students with disabilities as descriptors as well as the specific categories of exceptionality including learning disabilities, behavioral disabilities, and mental retardation from the years 1980 until the present. Previous peer tutoring reviews were acquired and examined, along with the reference lists of all obtained articles. In addition, recent issues of all major special education journals such as *Exceptional Children, Journal of Special Education, Learning Disabilities Research & Practice, Learning Disability Quarterly, Behavioral Disorders,* and *Remedial and Special Education* were examined for relevant articles. These procedures resulted in a pool of 35 research studies that employed students with disabilities as tutors and in which we could examine the results of the tutoring for those individuals. A listing of all obtained and reviewed articles is appended following the reference list.

OVERALL CHARACTERISTICS OF THE DATA SET

Studies and Sources

Thirty-five studies were identified during the period from 1982 to 2000. Journals included were *Psychology in the Schools, Remedial and Special Education, Behavioral Disorders, Education and Treatment of Children, Exceptional Children, Education and Training of the Mentally Retarded, Learning Disabilities Research & Practice, Journal of Computing in Childhood Education, Journal of Research and Development in Education, B. C. Journal of Special Education, Elementary School Journal, American Educational Research Journal, Journal of Emotional and Behavioral Disorders,* unpublished dissertations, and a paper presented at a national conference. Table 1 contains a summary of each study's individual characteristics.

Sample

A total of 1208 students with varying disabilities served as tutors and/or tutees. Fourteen studies employed students with learning disabilities (LD) as tutors; nine studies used students with behavior disorders (BD) or emotional disturbance (ED) as tutors; five used students who were classified as mentally retarded; one study used a student with attention deficit hyperactivity disorder as a tutor, and six studies used students representing mixed disability areas such as students with learning disabilities and students with mental retardation or students with learning disabilities and students with emotional disabilities. The tutees represented all of those disability areas as well as average achieving students.

Table 2.   Means and Standard Deviations of Selected Study Characteristics

Characteristic	Mean (SD)	Range	Total N	Number of Studies Reporting (out of 35)
N of Students	36.6 (31.4)	1-122	1208	33
Age of Tutors	12.88 ((2.8)	7-16.2	—	18
IQ of Tutors	86.9 (22.1)	45-123	—	10
N of Males	25.4 (4.6)	3-70	484	19
N weeks of Tutoring	10.7 (5.0)	4-20	—	25

The total sample included 16 studies using elementary age students as tutors, seven studies with middle school students, six studies with high school students, and one with junior-senior high school aged students as tutors (several studies used students of varying age/grade levels). Nineteen of the studies had elementary aged tutees, five studies middle school, and four studies high school aged tutees. Table 2 presents additional demographic data from the studies. Unfortunately, many studies presented incomplete information on the participants which is why the totals are inconsistent.

Research Designs

The majority of the studies employed group research designs ($N = 24$), of which 19 were experimental-control group designs and five were pre-post designs, while 11 studies employed single subject methodology.

Intervention Description

Tutoring Configurations

Seventeen studies (46%) implemented a role reciprocity feature during peer tutoring in which students with disabilities assumed roles of both tutor and tutee during the sessions. Fourteen studies (37%) implemented cross age tutoring in which older students with disabilities tutored younger students and five studies (14%) implemented a same age tutor-tutee configuration but students did not switch roles during tutoring. (Note: These figures are based on 36 studies, as one study had two experiments employing different tutoring configurations in each experiment.)

Content of Tutoring Sessions

A wide variety of content areas was used during the tutoring interventions. The majority of the studies implemented reading interventions ($N = 12$). Other content areas implemented included written language ($N = 6$), spelling ($N = 4$),

Table 3.   Percentage of Cases and Mean Tutor and Tutee Effect
Sizes for Selected Academic and Social Dependent Measures

Variable	Reciprocal Tutoring		Same Age Tutors-Tutees		Older Tutors Younger Tutees	
	Effect Size (SD)	Nes	Effect Size (SD)	Nes	Effect Size (SD)	Nes
Reading	.40 (.29)	11	.35 (7.13)	6	.69 (.65)	35
Written Language	1.77 (.60)	4	—		−.01 (.44)	4
Math	—		.36 (8.48)	2	.45 —	1
Attitudes	.13 (1.4)	2	.12	1	.49 (.39)	3
Self-concept	.16 (.45)	3	—		.17 (.51)	4
Behavior rating scales	—		.20 (.42)	5	.19 (.49)	9

math ($N = 2$), social studies ($N = 2$), or combinations of reading, math, language or social skills ($N = 4$), and the content was not provided in 2 studies.

Length, Duration, and Intensity of Tutoring

Tutoring sessions ranged in length from 15 to 45 minutes, from three times a week to daily sessions, or a varied number of sessions per week. Total length of number of weeks of tutoring ranged from 4 to 20 weeks.

Outcomes of Tutoring

Across all studies the outcomes reported by authors were generally positive for the benefits of tutoring. Table 1 presents descriptive findings as reported by authors. Table 3 presents effect size data for the various outcome measures by type of tutoring configuration when effect sizes could be computed. Outcomes of the single subject research designs and those group research designs for which effect sizes could not be calculated generally yielded similar findings. The overall effect size was .49 ($SD = .60$) with a range of −.51 to 2.94 across the 94 computed effect sizes. This means that overall, the effect size for tutoring approached one half standard deviation, which is generally considered educationally significant. The overall mean effect size for tutoring interventions in which role reciprocity occurred was somewhat higher ($M = .63$; $SD = .68$; $Nes = 21$), while the mean effect size for tutors versus control group was .36 ($SD = .52$, $Nes = 36$), and the mean effect size for tutees versus control groups was .55 ($SD = .67$, $Nes = 28$). These findings parallel those reported by Cook et al. (1985-1986), in that effect sizes were greater for tutees than tutors.

Outcomes by specific measure were highest for written language ($M = .89, SD = 1.07$, $Nes = 8$), followed by those in reading ($M = .59, SD = .56, Nes = 52$). Other academic outcomes were smaller in math and spelling. Mean effect sizes for self concept, attitude, and social behavior measures were substantially lower, with a mean of .16 ($SD = .45$,

Nes = 7) for self-concept, .30 (*SD* = .32, *Nes* = 6) for attitudinal measures, and a mean of .20 (*SD* = 45, *Nes* = 14) for social behavior measures. Again, these findings parallel those reported in previous syntheses. Table 3 presents additional effect size breakdowns.

COGNITIVE STRATEGY TRAINING TUTORING STUDIES

As can be seen with the increase in number of tutoring studies over the past 20 years, there has also been an increase in the sophistication of the training procedures used during the tutoring sessions. As the field of special education has benefited from the positive findings associated with cognitive strategy training research, so too has the tutoring research. Several studies addressing different content areas with various cognitive strategies are described in detail as exemplars to demonstrate the complexities associated with the particular cognitive strategies and the way in which this cognitive strategy instruction has been combined successfully in tutoring scenarios in which students with disabilities have been tutors. Moreover, several studies have begun extending the research from primary and elementary aged students to middle and secondary level students with disabilities. Following is a discussion of selected tutoring investigations that appear to represent a significant departure from earlier work in tutoring.

Elementary Level Reading

Simmons, Fuchs, Fuchs, Hodge, and Mathes (1994) examined a number of variables relevant to the implementation of classwide peer tutoring in reading. Of particular interest to this investigation were the value of role reciprocity in tutoring, and the effectiveness of two instructional procedures intended to increase, respectively, fluency and reading comprehension. By reciprocity was meant that tutoring pairs would alternate tutor and tutee roles. According to some thinking (e.g., Bierman & Furman, 1981), social benefits accruing to the tutor in the form of increased perceptions of competence may be sufficient to enhance academic learning without role reciprocity. However, it could also be argued that tutors themselves could benefit from the increased engagement with text provided by an alternating tutor-tutee role.

Repeated readings is a strategy considered to be beneficial in building fluency (Samuels, 1979) through repeated exposure and familiarity with text. This strategy has previously received some qualified support with students with learning disabilities (Rashotte & Torgesen, 1985), and it is a strategy that could be implemented easily in a tutoring program. Paragraph summarization is another instructional strategy that has previous research support (Jenkins, Heliotis, Stein, & Hayes, 1987; Malone & Mastropieri, 1992), and is seemingly relatively easy to implement within a peer tutoring program. Whether all of these strategies could be successfully implemented during a classwide peer tutoring program, and the relative effectiveness of these strategies, however, was unknown.

Simmons et al. (1994) assigned 23 teachers and their second to fifth grade level classrooms at random to one of four different variations of classwide peer tutoring (CWPT). In all conditions, general education teachers implemented CWPT three times a week, for 35-40 minute sessions, over a period of 14 weeks. Lower-functioning students were paired with higher-functioning students, and pairs remained together for four-week periods. In one condition (CWPT), students met in pairs, and tutees ("readers") read to tutors. After 10 minutes of reading, tutees responded to 5 minutes of "who," "what," "where," "why," and "when" questions posed by the tutor. Following this, tutees read another segment of text for 10 minutes, followed by 5 more minutes of comprehension questions. A second condition (CWPT-Reciprocity) was the same as the first condition, with the exception that after the first 15 minutes, roles were reversed and the "first tutor" read and answered questions for the "first reader." In a third condition (Modified CWPT), three instructional components were added: repeated reading, paragraph summary, and story retell. Tutees read for one minute, received feedback, and repeated the passage twice more. After the three readings, the tutee identified who the paragraph was about and the main event described. In the fourth condition (Modified CWPT-Reciprocity), tutors and tutees implemented Modified CWPT but alternated roles. In addition to these four conditions, eight teachers served as control condition teachers, and did not implement any peer tutoring procedures. Data were collected on students with learning disabilities, low achieving students, and average achieving students in each classroom.

After 14 weeks of tutoring, students were posttested on a standardized measure of reading fluency, accuracy, and comprehension. Students in all four tutoring conditions outperformed control condition students on words read correct and questions answered correctly. However, none of the tutoring configurations differed from another on any of the measures. Differences among learner types were observed on words correct and mazes correct.

It is possible that the most efficacious feature of CWPT is the increased engaged time-on-task and opportunities to respond it provides for students (Greenwood et al., 1984). And, in fact, engaged time-on-task has been seen to be one of the most consistently powerful instructional variables, in general and special education (Mastropieri & Scruggs, 2000). However, it was interesting to note that no other tutoring feature appeared to exert any additional influence on student learning—neither reciprocity, nor paragraph summary, nor repeated readings. Since Scheffé tests were employed to evaluate pairwise differences among 5 separate experimental conditions, it is possible that statistical power was limited (Mastropieri & Scruggs, 1994) to the extent that some "real" treatment differences may have been obscured. It may be of interest to examine CWPT configurations in further research that considers fewer treatment variations simultaneously and to examine whether students with disabilities who were all experiencing reading difficulties could function effectively as partners during tutoring.

Secondary Level Reading Comprehension

Mastropieri et al. (2000) speculated that peer tutoring procedures would increase the amount of strategic teaching and practice using cognitive learning strategies for students with serious reading difficulties at the middle school level. These authors formed a collaborative working relationship among teachers, students enrolled in the local university, and researchers in order to devise the study. This collaborative relationship resulted in the development of a study designed to assess the effects of teaching cognitive strategies with junior high school aged students with disabilities.

They implemented a tutoring program at the middle school level designed to examine the effects on reading comprehension for students with learning disabilities and students with mild mental handicaps with serious deficits in reading. IQ scores ranged from 67 to 107, and reading achievement grade equivalent scores ranged from 1.5 to 4.7. Students were randomly assigned to peer tutoring or traditional instruction conditions that took place for the entire period (approximately 55 minutes daily) that was assigned as the reading/English class period. Traditional instruction consisted of the same procedures that had been used throughout the school year during that reading class. In the traditional condition the class was directed by the teacher, students read materials aloud and silently, practiced vocabulary activities, and answered comprehension questions aloud as well as by completing accompanying worksheet activities that asked comprehension questions about the stories. Procedures for the tutoring condition were modeled after the CWPT and PALS by the researchers, the special education teacher, and an undergraduate who worked collaboratively to design the tutoring rules, procedures, and materials. Students were matched based upon social behaviors as well as reading levels such that the readers were ranked from highest to lowest and then the highest performer was matched with the middle level reader, the second highest with the next lowest and so on. Students of different genders expressed a desire not to be partners; however, in one case this was unavoidable and remained slightly problematic throughout the study.

Procedures were implemented following the guidelines provided by Fuchs et al. (1995). Tutors were "coaches" and tutees "players" as in the Fuchs et al. investigation, and "coach" was the assigned name to the "first reader" and higher performing reader in the dyad. Folders for each dyad were made that included copies of all necessary materials for tutoring, including copies of the mystery stories to be read and record keeping materials, which the students were to pick up as they entered the classroom for tutoring. Tutoring passages included stories from trade books written on an appropriate grade level, including *Zoo Clues: Making the Most of Your Visit to the Zoo* (Gerstenfeld, 1991), and *The Story of the Three*

Whales (Johnson, 1991). Rules for tutoring behaviors were established and reviewed with the students on the first day of tutoring. Teachers modeled and demonstrated appropriate use of voice, correct use of tone, and how to keep conversations limited to the tutoring project at hand, followed by student practice. Next, teachers provided the same type of practice and instruction for correcting reading errors that included identifying an incorrectly pronounced word, prompting correctness, supplying the correct word, and rereading the sentence in which the word appeared. Examples were demonstrated and modeled and students were provided with time for guided practice in correcting their partners using the newly introduced procedures.

The cognitive strategy instruction for reading comprehension was derived from the research literature on cognitive strategies for facilitating reading comprehension and from the PALS literature (Fuchs et al., 1995; Mastropieri & Scruggs, 1997; Talbott, Lloyd, & Tankersley, 1994). This research has indicated that when paragraph restatement and summarization strategies have been taught to students with disabilities, their reading comprehension levels have increased (Bakken, Mastropieri, & Scruggs, 1997: Malone & Mastropieri, 1992). For story restatement, students asked their partners, "What was the first thing you learned?" followed by, "What was the next thing you learned?" as often as needed to restate the story. The first (more fluent) reader read first for 5 minutes, and answered restatement questions, followed by the second reader, who also read for 5 minutes and answered restatement questions.

For the summarization strategies, students asked their partners after reading, "What is the most important what or who in the text?", followed by "What is the most important thing about the what or who in the text?", and "What is the main idea?" For the latter question, students were asked to answer in 10 words or less. A similar schedule was followed in which the first reader read for 5 minutes and answered questions, followed by the second reader reading for 5 minutes and answering questions.

While students were tutoring, teachers completed for each tutor dyad a "peer tutoring checklist" to monitor whether all aspects of the peer tutoring program were being implemented successfully, and provided immediate corrective feedback whenever necessary. Results indicated that students who participated in the peer tutoring performed significantly better on a measure of reading comprehension that involved reading a new story and answering comprehension questions. Moreover, all students indicated that they enjoyed the tutoring, that they felt they benefited from the tutoring experience and that they would like to tutor in many more of their academic subject classes such as science and social studies. These students also appeared to use the reading comprehension strategies practiced during tutoring sessions independently. The teachers who participated also indicated that, although there was more work initially in designing and setting up the training procedures and materials for peer tutoring, they also thoroughly enjoyed the tutoring and would like to continue the procedures. The major obstacle was the matching of some partners during the tutoring sessions, as some partners were not good matches and it was challenging to find good matches for some students. These findings also provide some important information, in that they replicate the Simmons et al. (1994) and extend the MacArthur, Schwartz, and Graham (1991) written language findings to the area of reading comprehension, and to older and somewhat lower functioning students with disabilities than employed in the Simmons et al. (1994) and the Fuchs, Fuchs, and Kazdan (1999) investigations.

Elementary Level Writing

MacArthur et al. (1991) examined the effects of a reciprocal peer editing strategy on students with learning disabilities written compositions. Twenty-nine students from grades four, five, and six participated in the peer editing experimental condition or the control condition. All students were already familiar with the process approach to writing, the use of word processors and spell checkers and they received writing workshops four times per week. During writing activities, students selected their own topics, met individually with their teachers, and met in groups with peers and their teachers to discuss their work. In the experimental condition students were introduced to the peer editing strategy. The peer editing strategy took place between two peer partners (or tutors) and consisted of the following strategic steps that were reciprocal in nature: (a) listening and reading along with your partner; (b) telling your partner what you liked best about the paper and the topic of the paper; (c) re-reading the paper and making revision notes, such as noting whether anything was unclear and whether additional details should be included; and (d) discussing suggestions with each other (MacArthur, Schwartz, & Graham, 1991).

Teachers presented these strategic steps to the students with learning disabilities in a very systematic fashion. Teachers described the importance of the peer editing strategy, described the steps and the rationale for each step, and emphasized the importance of providing positive feedback to their partners. Students then viewed a video of students using think alouds when trying out the peer editing strategy followed by more discussion of all of the strategic steps involved. Students were then required to write out and memorize the steps. Teachers then modeled and demonstrated the steps followed by student practice and another viewing of the video. Finally, students practiced using the strategy. Findings indicated that students in the experimental condition used most of the strategy steps with their partners and their revisions and revised papers were significantly better than control condition students on all measures, including quality, mechanical, and metacognitive interviews. Students with learning disabilities were able to help each other using these strategic steps to improve the quality of their written papers. These findings are important in several ways. First, the writing strategy was complex and included many steps. Second, elementary aged students with learning disabilities successfully learned and implemented this strategy in a reciprocal peer-tutoring configuration. Finally, the strategy has important implications for generalized use for individuals.

Secondary Level Writing

Wong and her colleagues (Wong, Butler, Ficzere, & Kuperis, 1996; Wong, Butler, Ficzere, & Kuperis, 1997; Wong, Butler, Ficzere, Kuperis, Cordern, & Zelmar, 1994; Wong, Wong, Darlington, & Jones, 1991) replicated and extended the findings of MacArthur et al. (1991) to adolescents with learning disabilities. In a series of investigations, they demonstrated that an interactive teaching approach among students with disabilities has proven successful for assisting adolescents with learning disabilities with planning, writing, and revising written compositions. In the first study, Wong et al. (1991) identified an interactive teaching sequence that appeared to enhance the quality of written compositions that included planning, sentence generation, and revising based upon a sequence devised by Flowers and Hayes (1980). This study tested the effects of the model between a teacher and adolescents with learning disabilities. Phase 1 of their instruction including keyboard training. Phase 2 involved teaching students about the planning process for writing "reporting essays" and included using think alouds and writing plans on the computers. The third instructional phase involved writing and revising the essays during which students interacted continually with the teacher. In a follow-up study, Wong et al. (1994) compared the interactive teaching with teachers with student-student interactions and found that both conditions were equally successful compared to a control condition. The student-student interactions appear remarkably similar to the reciprocity of roles undertaken during peer tutoring or peer mediated instruction. Further studies applied the model to teaching opinion essays (Wong, Butler, Ficzere, & Kuperis, 1996) and compare-contrast essays (Wong, Butler, Ficzere, & Kuperis, 1997) with junior high school students with learning disabilities. In both investigations, students were taught to collaborate with peer-partners to plan, write and revise their essays using the sequence of steps describe earlier. In both studies, students were also provided with planning sheets to help generate ideas for their respective essays. Opinion essays planning sheets depicted a scale and balance on top and had two columns under the headings: "What I know, think, or believe," or "What my partner knows, thinks, or believes." The compare-contrast essay planning sheet contained a line for writing the general topic, places for specifying both categories of the topic to be compared and contrasted, a space for brainstorming ideas, and three columns in which the features or major themes could be written. Also included were a column for the major ideas or details of those features, and a final column to identify whether those ideas were similar or different. Students were provided with prompt cards that contained signal words that could be used for opening important sentences in their papers, such as statements for the introductory phrases including "In my opinion, ... From my point of view" (Wong et al.,

1996, p. 204); Countering phrases such as, "On the other hand," "On the contrary" (p. 204), and concluding phrases such as "After considering both sides," "To sum up," or "In conclusion" (p. 204). In the compare contrast essay students were also provided with "helpers in writing" sheets that contained cues and prompts such as introductory statement such as "In this essay I am going to compare and contrast _____ and ____. I have chosen to write on three features: (1), (2), and (3)." (Wong et al., 1997, p. 6).

Students were taught the planning phase by teachers, after which they wrote independently using computers. This was followed by dyadic interaction with their partners during the revision phase. Students were to provide one another with feedback regarding ambiguities and clarifications and then were to write their final versions. Findings indicated that these procedures successfully enhanced the quality of students' writing, moreover self-efficacy and metacognitive measures indicated that students attributed their success to learning better planning, writing, and revising strategies. Although these findings are positive in that they add to the growing literature base on peers helping peers with more complex cognitive tasks, additional information on the peer tutoring interaction training and component would be beneficial for future replication efforts.

Secondary Level School Social Studies

An interesting extension of the CWPT model from elementary to secondary classes and to the social studies content area was undertaken by Maheady and his colleagues (e.g., Maheady, Sacca, & Harper, 1988; Maheady, Harper, & Sacca, 1988). Maheady, Sacca, and Harper (1988) designed and implemented a variation of CWPT in tenth grade inclusive social studies classes that included 14 students with mild disabilities, and Maheady, Harper, and Sacca (1988) implemented a similar tutoring program in high school resource programs for 20 students with mild disabilities (learning disabilities and mental retardation).

In the inclusive classroom study, teachers identified critical social studies content for students. General and special educators worked collaboratively to develop weekly 30-item study guides and 20-item quizzes taken from the content area textbook (Mazour & Peoples, 1975). Topics covered included the Egyptians, Greek and Roman civilization, the Middle Ages, the American and French Revolutions, and World War I. The study guides consisted of comprehension questions and answers covering the objectives considered important by teachers. Six weeks of study guides and quizzes were developed prior to the initiation of the study.

Using a multiple baseline across classrooms students tutored one another using the pre-designed study guides. Training procedures for tutoring paralleled those used in the CWPT models implemented by Greenwood and colleagues (Greenwood et al., 1996) and were modified to meet the needs of secondary level students. Most items on the study guides required learning of factual information

Findings indicated that student performance levels in social studies increased with the implementation of the peer tutoring.

In the resource room study, teachers also developed 30-item study guides from the class social studies materials (Maheady, Harper, & Sacca, 1988). Teachers identified relevant instructional objectives, and wrote questions and answers based upon those for the study guides. Items on the study guides consisted of facts and details from the content (e.g., "What is the major export of Brazil?" p. 78). Procedures developed in the CWPT model were followed in that students were matched with tutoring partners, the class was divided into two teams of dyads, and points were awarded based upon behavior and performance. During the tutoring, students asked each other the study guide questions, required one another to write responses, provided corrective feedback, and exchanged roles as tutor and tutee after fifteen minutes. Performance was assessed by weekly quizzes covering the same content. Performance increased after tutoring and students and teachers reported enjoying the tutoring activities. These findings extend the CWPT model to high school age students with disabilities and provide some initial positive results with social studies content using rehearsal as the dominant strategy for learning factual information.

SUMMARY AND CONCLUSIONS

This synthesis has yielded some very interesting extensions of the peer tutoring research. First, positive findings parallel those reported in earlier syntheses by Cook et al., (1985-1986) and Osguthorpe and Scruggs (1986). Positive academic gains were uniformly reported by authors who conducted peer tutoring research. These gains were found across the academic domains of reading, spelling, and writing, although these findings were more pronounced on criterion reference measures than norm reference tests. These positive findings were seen across the various disability areas including, students with learning disabilities, students with emotional disabilities, students with mental retardation, and students with attention deficit hyperactivity disorder. As in previously reported syntheses, higher academic gains were found for tutees than for tutors.

The present review also uncovered an increase in studies with students with disabilities as tutors and increasing trend toward the use of more role reciprocity in tutoring research. Thirty-five studies were located in which students with disabilities were tutors. Although some studies were cross-age, in that older students with disabilities tutored younger less proficient tutees, many studies employed reciprocity of roles during the tutoring interventions. In other words, students with disabilities functioned as tutors and tutees or peer partners or, more often, were involved in both roles during the peer mediation activities. This means that students with disabilities were able to assume both roles effectively during this research. This is an encouraging finding because of the implications for having students with disabilities assume more responsible positions with their own instruction.

As in previous research, social and attitudinal or self-concept effects were not as evident across studies. This finding is not surprising given the global nature of self-concept and the fact that few researchers have impacted changes in self-concept. However, the few studies that assessed attitudinal measures did report positive findings on the part of the students as well as teachers. In fact, most self-reports from participating teachers indicated that tutoring was an enjoyable classroom activity for them and for their students. Further many students with disabilities indicated they would like to do more tutoring in school as they felt more involved in that academic content area and they enjoyed the interactive nature of the instruction. Future research could examine additional social-emotional measures in attempts to uncover other aspects of social-emotional functioning.

There also appears to be an increase in applications to middle and secondary level students in this tutoring research. This is especially true when examining the tutoring research employing role reciprocity. For example, Wong and her colleagues (Wong, Butler, Ficzere, & Kuperis, 1997; Wong, Butler, Ficzere, & Kuperis, 1996) have extended the peer editing mediation tutoring to junior high school students learning of writing opinion and compare contrast essays. Maheady and his colleagues (Maheady, Harper, & Sacca, 1988; Maheady, Harper, & Sacca, 1988) extended the CWPT model to high school students with learning disabilities and mental retardation in inclusive and special education settings. Mastropieri et al. (2000) successfully extended a variation of the PALS model to middle school students with learning disabilities and mental retardation, and Fuchs, Fuchs, and Kazdan, (1999) most recently reported extending PALS to high school students with learning disabilities with mixed findings. Taken together, these extensions offer promising findings for possible alternative delivery strategies for a middle and secondary level students with disabilities who often present more challenging behaviors and more serious learning needs than elementary aged students.

Finally, and yet most importantly, there has been a significant increase in cognitive strategy research applied to peer mediation strategies. Peer tutoring as a delivery system has tended to parallel the instructional delivery systems of the times. Previous research highlighted the rote rehearsal strategies during tutoring (e.g. Cook et al, 1985-1986; Osguthorpe & Scruggs, 1986). However, this synthesis has revealed that as research in strategic instruction has accumulated in the areas of reading, reading comprehension, and written composition, the model of peer tutoring has expanded to include findings from that research into its practices. Researchers have taken what has been learned about effective teaching and learning in a teacher delivery model based on more sophisticated cognitive learning strategies and applied those findings to a "peer" delivered model in peer tutoring. As a result we have seen an increase in the complexity of tasks taught by peer tutors. For example, previous reading research focused on repeated readings for fluency development, while the PALS model has convincingly demonstrated that reading comprehension strategy instruction can be successfully practiced during peer tutoring (Fuchs, et al., 1997; Mastropieri, et al. 2000). Variations of peer mediation have also been seen to enhance the quality of written products such as essays of compare-contrast and opinion papers (e.g., Wong et al., 1996; Wong et al., 1997). Perhaps even more importantly, this research provides some initial evidence that students with disabilities have been able to successfully assume the role of partner in their own instruction with learning and becoming proficient at using cognitive strategies that are known to facilitate learning.

Taken together, findings from all these studies indicated a resurgence of interest in peer tutoring, especially scenarios in which students with disabilities are serving as tutors. More importantly, there is an increasing trend to incorporate cognitive strategy instruction with the peer mediation structure. Cognitive strategy instruction in reading, reading comprehension, planning, writing, and revising are among the several important advances that have been positively implemented and practices when students with disabilities serve as tutors. Most often there is a reciprocity of roles during these interventions, in which students with disabilities assume the role of tutor and tutee (or coach and player). More interestingly, perhaps, is the finding that often both partners may be students with disabilities.

There are, however, several important unanswered questions from the tutoring research. For example, special education researchers have lamented the fact that research findings are rarely translated into classroom practices. Since teachers and students alike seem to enjoy peer tutoring, can the instructional delivery system of peer tutoring be a vehicle through which researchers can help translate more cognitive strategy research into practice? Second, can the preliminary positive findings from tutoring be replicated and extended with more students with disabilities at the middle and secondary school levels? These students and their content area classes present additional challenges that sometimes leave teachers overwhelmed with what to do and where to begin. Perhaps tutoring can be a vehicle to help improve instruction for students with disabilities at the secondary levels. Do we know exactly what happens during peer mediation between two students with disabilities, for example, so we can be assured that learning and social behaviors improve? Finally, do we the know the limits or the extent to which students with disabilities are able to function as peer partners during their learning? These and other questions await future research efforts.

REFERENCES

Bakken, J.P., Mastropieri, M.A., & Scruggs, T.E. (1997). Reading comprehension of expository science material and students with learning disabilities: A comparison of strategies. *Journal of Special Education, 31,* 300-324.

Bierman, K., & Furman, W. (1981). Effects of role and assignment rationale on attitudes formed during peer tutoring. *Journal of Educational Psychology, 73,* 33-40.

Cook, S., Scruggs, T.E., Mastropieri, M.A., & Casto, G. (1985-1986) Handicapped students as tutors. *Journal of Special Education, 19,* 483-492.

Delquadri, J., Greenwood, C.R., Whorton, D., Carta, J.J., & Hall, R.V. (1986). Classwide peer tutoring. *Exceptional Children, 52,* 535-542.

Flowers, L.S., & Hayes, J.R. (1980). The dynamics of composing: Making plans and juggling constraints. In L.W. Greg and E.R. Steinberg (Eds.), *Cognitive processes in writing* (pp. 31-50). Hillsdale, NJ: Erlbaum.

Fuchs, L.S., Fuchs, D., Karns, K., & Phillips, N. (1995). *Peabody peer-assisted learning strategies (PALS): Math methods.* Nashville, TN: Peabody College, Vanderbilt University.

Fuchs, L.S., Fuchs, D., & Kazdan, S. (1999). Effects of peer-assisted learning strategies on high school students with serious reading difficulties. *Remedial and Special Education, 20,* 309-318.

Fuchs, D., Mathes, P.G., & Fuchs, L.S. (1995). *Peabody peer-assisted learning strategies (PALS): Reading methods.* Nashville, TN: Peabody College, Vanderbilt University.

Fuchs, L.S., Fuchs, D., Phillips, N.B., Hamlett, C.L., & Karns, K. (1995). Acquisition and transfer effects of classwide peer-assisted learning strategies in mathematics for students with varying learning histories. *School Psychology Review, 24,* 604-620.

Fuchs, L.S., Fuchs, D., Hamlett, C.L., Phillips, N., & Bentz, J. (1994). Class-wide curriculum-based measurement: Helping general educators meet the challenge of student diversity. *Exceptional Children, 60,* 518-537.

Gerstenfeld, S. (1991). *Zoo clues: Making the most of your visit to the zoo.* New York: Puffin Books.

Greenwood, C.R., Delquadri, J.C., & Carta, J.J. (1996). *Classwide Peer Tutoring (CWPT): Teachers Manual: Programs for spelling, math, and reading.* Juniper Gardens Children's project, Kansas City: University of Kansas.

Greenwood, C.R., Delaquadri, J.C., & Hall, R.V. (1984). Opportunity to respond and student academic performance. In W.L. Heward, T.E. Heron, J. Trap-Porter, & S.D. Hill (Eds.), *Focus on behavior analysis in education* (pp. 58-88). Columbus, OH: Merrill.

Jenkins, J.R., Heliotis, J.D., Stein, M., & Hayes, M. (1987). Improving reading comprehension by using paragraph restatements. *Exceptional Children, 54,* 54-59.

Johnson, J. (1991). "The story of the three whales." In *Highlights animal books: Whales.* Columbus, OH: Highlights for Children.

MacArthur, C.A., Schwartz, S.S., & Graham, S. (1991). Effects of a reciprocal peer revision strategy in special education classrooms. *Learning Disabilities Research & Practice, 6,* 201-210.

Maheady, L., Harper, G.F., & Mallette, B. (1991). Peer-mediated instruction: A review of potential applications for special education. *Reading, Writing, and Learning Disabilities, 7,* 75-103.

Maheady, L., Harper, G.F., & Sacca, M.K. (1988). A classwide peer tutoring system in a secondary, resource room program for the mildly handicapped. *Journal of Research and Development in Education 21*(3), 76-83.

Maheady, L., Sacca, M.K., & Harper, G.F. (1988). Classwide peer tutoring with mildly handicapped high school students. *Exceptional Children, 55*(1), 52-59.

Malone, L.D., & Mastropieri, M.A. (1992). Reading comprehension instruction: Summarization and self-monitoring training for students with learning disabilities. *Exceptional Children, 58,* 270-279.

Mastropieri, M.A., & Scruggs, T.E. (1994). Issues in intervention research: Secondary students. In S. Vaughn & C. Bos (Eds.), *Research in learning disabilities: Theory, methodology, assessment, and ethics* (pp. 130-145). New York: Springer Verlag.

Mastropieri, M.A., & Scruggs, T.E. (1997). Best practices in promoting reading comprehension in students with learning disabilities. *Remedial and Special Education, 18,* 197-213.

Mastropieri, M.A., & Scruggs, T.E. (2000). *The inclusive classroom: Strategies for effective instruction.* Columbus, OH: Prentice-Hall.

Mastropieri, M.A., Scruggs, T.E., Mohler, L., Beranek, M., Spencer, V., & Talbott, E. (April, 2000). *Qualitative and quantitative outcomes of peer tutoring in reading comprehension for students with mild disabilities*. Paper presented at the American Educational Research Association Conference. New Orleans.

Mathes, P.G., Howard, J.K., Allen, S., & Fuchs, D. (1998). Peer-assisted learning strategies for first-grade readers: Making early reading instruction more responsive to the needs of diverse learners. *Reading Research Quarterly, 33,* 62-95.

Mazour, A.G., & Peoples, J.M. (1975). *Men and nations: A world history.* New York: Harcourt, Brace, & Jovanovich.

Osguthorpe, R.T., & Scruggs, T.E., (1986). Special education students as tutors: A review and analysis. *Remedial and Special Education, 7(4),* 15-26.

Rashotte, C., & Torgesen, J. (1985). Repeated reading and reading fluency in learning disabled children. *Reading Research Quarterly, 20,* 180-188.

Samuels, S.J. (1979). The method of repeated readings. *The Reading Teacher, 32,* 403-408.

Scruggs, T.E., & Osguthorpe, R.T. (1986). Tutoring interventions within special education settings: A comparison of cross-age and peer tutoring. *Psychology in the Schools, 23,* 187-193.

Simmons, D.C., Fuchs, D., Fuchs, L.S., Hodge, J.P., & Mathes, P.G. (1994). Importance of instructional complexity and role reciprocity to classwide peer tutoring. *Learning Disabilities Research & Practice, 9,* 203-212.

Talbott, E., Lloyd, J.W., & Tankersley, M. (1994). Effects of reading comprehension interventions for students with learning disabilities. *Learning Disability Quarterly, 17,* 223-232.

Topping, K., & Ehly, S. (1998). *Peer-assisted learning.* Mahwah, NJ: Lawrence Erlbaum Associates.

Utley, C., Mortweet, S.L., & Greenwood, C.R. (1997). Peer mediated instruction and interventions. *Focus on Exceptional Children, 29(5),* 1-23.

Virginia Standards of Learning. (1999). Virginia Department of Education: Author.

Wong, B.Y.L., Butler, D. L., Ficzere, S.A., & Kuperis, S. (1997). Teaching adolescents with learning disabilities and low achievers to plan, write, and revise compare-and-contrast essays. *Learning Disabilities Research & Practice, 12,* 2-15.

Wong, B.Y.L., Butler, D.L., Ficzere, S.A., Kuperis, S., Cordern, M., & Zelmar, J. (1994). Teaching problem learners revision skills and sensitivity to audience through two instructional modes: Teacher versus student-student interactive dialogues. *Learning Disabilities Research & Practice, 9,* 78-90.

Wong, B.Y.L., Butler, D.L., Ficzere, S.A., & Kuperis, S. (1996). Teaching adolescents with learning disabilities and low achievers to plan, write, and revise opinion essays. *Journal of Learning Disabilities, 29,* 197-212.

Wong, B.Y.L., Wong, R., Darlington, D., & Jones, W. (1991). Interactive teaching: An effective way to teach revision skills to adolescents with learning disabilities. *Learning Disabilities Research & Practice, 6,* 117-127.

ARTICLES INCLUDED IN THE RESEARCH SYNTHESIS

Campbell, B.J., Brady, M.P., & Linehan, S. (1991). Effects of peer-mediated instruction on the acquisition and generalization of written capitalization skills. *Journal of Learning Disabilities, 24,* 6-14.

Carlton, M.B., Litton, F.W., & Zinkgraf, S.A. (1985). The effects of an intraclass peer tutoring program on the sight-word recognition ability of students who are mildly mentally retarded. *Mental Retardation, 23,* 74-78.

Cochran, L., Feng, H. Cartledge, G., & Hamilton, S. (1993). The effects of cross-age tutoring on the academic achievement, social behaviors, and self-perceptions of low-achieving African-American males with behavioral disorders, *Behavioral Disorders 18,* 292-302.

DuPaul, G.J., Henningson, P.N. (1993). Peer tutoring on the classroom performance of children with attention deficit disorder. *School Psychology Review, 22(1),* 134-133.

Franca, V.M., Kerr, M.M., Reitz, A.L., & Lambert, D. (1990). Peer tutoring among behaviorally disordered students: Academic and social benefits to tutor and tutee. *Education and Treatment of Children, 13,* 109-128.

Fuchs, L.S., Fuchs, D., & Kazdan, S. (1999). Effects of peer-assisted learning strategies on high school students with serious reading problems. *Remedial and Special Education, 20,* 309-318.

Fuchs, D., Fuchs, L.S., Mathes, P.G., & Simmons, D.C. (1997). Peer-assisted learning strategies: Making classrooms more responsive to diversity. *American Educational Research Journal, 34,* 174-206.

Higgins, T.S. (1982). A comparison of two methods of practice on the spelling performance of learning disabled adolescents. *Dissertation Abstracts International, 43,* 402 1 B.

Hogan, S., & Prater, M.A. (1993). The effects of peer tutoring and self-management training on on-task, academic, and disruptive behaviors. *Behavioral Disorders, 18,* 118-128.

Koury, M., & Browder, D.M. (1986). The use of delay to teach sight words by peer tutors classified as moderately mentally retarded. *Education and Training of the Mentally Retarded, 21,* 252-258.

Lamport, K.C. (1982). The effects of inverse tutoring on reading disabled students in a public school setting. *Dissertation Abstracts International, 44,* 729A.

Lazerson, D.B. (1980). "I must be good if I can teach!"—Peer tutoring with aggressive and withdrawn children. *Journal of Learning Disabilities, 13*(3), 43-48.

Lazerson, D.B., Foster, H.L., Brown, S.I., & Hummel, J.W. (1988). The effectiveness of cross-age tutoring with truant, junior high school students with learning disabilities. *Journal of Learning Disabilities, 21,* 253-255.

Locke, W.R., & Fuchs, L.S. (1995). Effects of peer-mediated reading instruction on the on-task behavior and social interaction of children with behavior disorders. *Journal of Emotional and Behavioral Disorders, 3,* 92-99.

MacArthur, C.A., Schwartz, S.S., & Graham, S. (1991). Effects of a reciprocal peer revision strategy in special education classrooms. *Learning Disabilities Research & Practice, 6,* 201-210.

Maheady, L., Sacca, M.K., & Harper, G.F. (1988). Classwide peer tutoring with mildly handicapped high school students. *Exceptional Children, 55,* 52-59.

Maheady, L., Harper, G.F., & Sacca, M.K. (1988). A classwide peer tutoring system in a secondary, resource room program for the mildly handicapped. *Journal of Research and Development in Education 21*(3), 76-83.

Maher, C.A. (1982). Behavioral effects of using conduct problem adolescents as cross-age tutors. *Psychology in the Schools, 19,* 360-364.

Maher, C.A. (1984). Handicapped adolescents as cross-age tutors: Program description and evaluation. *Exceptional Children, 51,* 56-63.

Mallette, B., Harper, G.F., Maheady, L., Dempsey, M. (1991). Retention of spelling words acquired using a peer-mediated instructional procedure. *Education and Training in Mental Retardation, 26,* 156-164.

Mastropieri, M.A., Scruggs, T.E., Mohler, L., Beranek, M., Spencer, V., & Talbott, E. (2000, April). *Qualitative and quantitative outcomes of peer tutoring in reading comprehension for students with mild disabilities.* Paper presented at the American Educational Research Association Conference, New Orleans.

Mathes, P.G., & Fuchs, L.S. (1993). Peer-mediated reading instruction in special education resource rooms. *Learning Disabilities Research & Practice, 8,* 233-243.

Osguthorpe, R.T., Eiserman, W.D., & Shisler, L. (1985). Increasing social acceptance: Mentally retarded students tutoring regular class peers. *Education and Training of the Mentally Retarded, 20,* 235-240.

Schloss, P.J., & Kobza, S.A. (1997). The use of peer tutoring for the acquisition of functional math skills among students with moderate retardation. *Education & Treatment of Children, 20,* 189-209.

Scruggs, T.E., Mastropieri, M.A., Veit, D.T., & Osguthorpe, R.T. (1986). Behaviorally disordered students as tutors: Effects on social behavior. *Behavioral Disorders, 12,* 36-44.

Scruggs, T.E., & Osguthorpe, R.T. (1986). Tutoring interventions within special education settings: A comparison of cross-age and peer-tutoring. *Psychology in the Schools, 23,* 187-103.

Shisler, L., Top, B.L., & Osguthorpe, R.T. (1986). Behaviorally disordered students as reverse-role tutors: Increasing social acceptance and reading skills. *B. C. Journal of Special Education, 10,* 101-119.

Simmons, D.C., Fuchs, D., Fuchs, L.S., Hodge, J.P., & Mathes, P.G. (1994). Importance of instructional complexity and role reciprocity to classwide peer tutoring. *Learning Disabilities Research & Practice, 9,* 203-212.

Top, B.L., & Osguthorpe, R.T. (1987). Reverse-role tutoring: The effects of handicapped students tutoring regular class students. *The Elementary School Journal, 87,* 413-423.

Trapani, C., & Gettinger, M. (1989). Effects of social skills training and cross-age tutoring on academic achievement and social behaviors of boys with learning disabilities. *Journal of Research and Development in Education, 23,* 1-9.

Utay, C. & Utay, J. (1997). Peer-assisted learning: The effects of cooperative learning and cross-age peer tutoring with word processing on writing skills of students with learning disabilities. *Journal of Computing in Childhood Education, 8,* 165-185.

Wong, B.Y.L., Butler, D.L., Ficzere, S.A., & Kuperis, S. (1997). Teaching adolescents with learning disabilities and low achievers to plan, write, and revise compare-and-contrast essays. *Learning Disabilities Research & Practice, 12,* 2-15.

Wong, B.Y.L., Butler, D.L., Ficzere, S.A., & Kuperis, S. (1996). Teaching adolescents with learning disabilities and low achievers to plan, write, and revise opinion essays. *Journal of Learning Disabilities, 29,* 197-212.

Wong, B.Y.L., Butler, D.L., Ficzere, S.A., & Kuperis, S., Corden, M. & Zelmer, J. (1994). Teaching problem learners revision skills and sensitivity to audience through two instructional modes: Student-teacher versus student-student interactive dialogues. *Learning Disabilities Research & Practice, 9,* 78-90.

Yasutake, D., Bryan, T., & Dohrn, E. (1996). The effects of combining peer tutoring and attribution training on students' perceived self-competence. *Remedial and Special Education, 17,* 83-91.